What Have They Done to the Bible?

What Have They Done to the Bible?

A History of Modern Biblical Interpretation

John Sandys-Wunsch

A Michael Glazier Book

LITURGICAL PRESS
Collegeville, Minnesota

www.litpress.org

A Michael Glazier book published by Liturgical Press.

Cover design by David Manahan, O.S.B. Illustration provided by Photos.com.

1   2   3   4   5   6   7   8   9

Library of Congress Cataloging-in-Publication Data

Sandys-Wunsch, John, 1936–
    What have they done to the Bible? : a history of modern biblical
interpretation / John Sandys-Wunsch.
        p. cm.
    Includes bibliographical references and index.
    ISBN 13: 978-0-8146-5028-8 (pbk. : alk. paper)
    ISBN 10: 0-8146-5028-7
    1. Bible—Criticism, interpretation, etc.—History—Modern period, 1500–
I. Title.

BS500.S26   2005
220.6'09—dc22
                                                                    2004017108

TO MY WIFE SHEILA

"Many women have done excellently,
but you surpass them all."

—Proverbs 30:29

Contents

Preface

This book is for those who enjoy learning, who take pleasure in learning about ideas and their developments, as well as in the varieties of behavior our species shows—saints, rogues, the balanced, the eccentrics; the rational learned with their feet on the ground and the helpless victims carried off by a predatory idea like a rabbit in an eagle's claws; the religious and the irreligious and the would-be religious—a panoply of human beings who had in common a concern with explaining the Bible, and sometimes little else.

The way the Bible has come to be seen in the Western world since the beginning of the modern period is one of the great cultural changes that have occurred in human cultural history. This work attempts to give a general overview of what took place between 1450 and 1889, for by the end of the nineteenth century the competing variety of attitudes, assumptions, and critical questions on which subsequent scholarship has been based had been defined. This development is important not just to those who still look to the Bible for religious guidance but for anyone who wishes to make sense of modern Western culture. John Spencer, one of the authors discussed in this work, gave as his first motive for research "the joy of knowing."

I have tried to make this book accessible for those who have not been initiated into the arcane language of the discipline of biblical studies without "dumbing it down" to "Dick and Jane meet Erasmus." I hope that some of what I say may also be of interest to my professional colleagues, especially to that small guild of those who study the history of biblical interpretation in a serious manner.

Apart from disinterested learning, I hope that this work may be of use also to those whose religious faith is based on the Bible or parts of it. In my experience, ignorance of this subject is rampant, and the intensity of the debates that break out in churches and synagogues might be attenuated if some of the scholarship discussed here were better known.

The author of the book

I should admit to a glaring weakness. I consider it important to be as fair as possible to everyone I discuss, especially to those whose opinions I do not share. However, on occasion my own opinions may seep through the prose, and a whiff of Gilbert and Sullivan whimsy may spoil the academic dignity so dear to the hearts of some of my more solemn colleagues. As an example, I find it hard to warm to Bossuet because of his treatment of Richard Simon, and I would like to record my sincere conviction that the fact that Bossuet has gone down in history with the title of Bishop of Condom is one of the few irrefutable proofs of the existence of a just God who combines righteous judgment with humor.

A few words about how I have tried to fulfill my task:

1. *The basis for choosing certain commentators and ignoring the rest*

i. In studying the history of scholarly biblical exegesis, one takes seriously only the work of those who have the learning and the intellectual integrity to offer interpretations open to reasonable discussion. Here the difficulty is that there is a matter of discernment involved. Some cases are easy; the Elizabethan preacher who denounced a certain type of hairdressing on the basis of the text "top knot come down" can be dismissed by consulting the actual text and seeing that it reads "let he who is on a house top not come down." In other cases our evaluation is a little more difficult, such as the example of Guilaume Postel, whose extraordinary learning was an integral part of an equally extraordinary eccentricity.

ii. There also remains an arbitrary factor; no book the size of this one can hope to discuss all the competent scholars of the past five hundred years. The best any historian can hope for is that his or her choice comes from genuine erudition and not from personal preference, and that his or her choice is a reasonable selection from the scholars who were eligible.

2. *Method in history*

All history is characterized by the interplay of great movements and unpredictable individual occurrences. Thus historians have recognized that the history of the whole Roman Empire might have been different if only Cleopatra's nose had been less symmetrical. When an inch or two of cartilage can shake great empires, it means that the history of biblical scholarship, like other types of intellectual history, is better described as the parallelogram of forces rather than as a straight line heading direct to its goal.

Biblical interpretation, then, does not take place without a context, and the context is not always directly related to the discipline. Thus the arrival of scholars and manuscripts as a result of the fall of Constantinople and the discovery of peoples hitherto unknown are partially responsible for the burst of scholarship in the sixteenth century, yet it would be far-fetched to suggest that Sultan Mohammed II and Prince Henry the Navigator should be hailed as cofounders of modern biblical studies. Without being exhaustive, here is a list of the sort of factors that will be referred to in this work.

i. The nature of society: Is a country or a coherent geographical area unified with a coherent national policy of censorship, or is it sufficiently fragmented to allow for censored authors to slip through the gaps? Is it religious or secular, and to what extent? If it has an established church, is it Roman Catholic, Lutheran, Reformed, or Anglican?

ii. Means for the dissemination of ideas: Does a country have an established printing industry, and what is the level of its competence? Are there easy means of communication, such as obliging scholars or learned journals? How are the universities supported, and from where do they draw their faculty and students? Are the universities marked by innovation and serious scholarship, or are they intellectually unexciting?

iii. The intellectual and religious life of a country: Are there interesting developments in science, philosophy, political thought, and exploration, as well as in theology and biblical studies?

iv. The scholarly study of the Bible: What is being done in the areas of textual criticism, language, translation? Are internal problems with making sense of the text, such as contradictions, parallel passages, or incoherent statements, being recognized, and how are they being addressed by scholars? Are there interesting suggestions about authorship and literary dependence of biblical books?

v. Evidence from other areas of knowledge: How is the Bible being related to new discoveries in cognate disciplines, such as world history, languages, and ethnology?

Some warnings:

1. *Objectivity and subjectivity*

There is currently a fashion for postmodernism, a movement derived in part from European thinkers such as Foucauld and in part from the American physicist Thomas Kuhn's work on scientific revolutions. What various forms of postmodernism have in common is a feeling that we cannot achieve impartial, objective statements; I have seen suggestions that even mathematics is a social construct. Now if postmodernism means that absolute objectivity or absolute truth escapes our efforts, the news is not new. But if it is taken to mean that everything is completely arbitrary and subjective, then it follows that anything can mean anything, and therefore nothing means anything. I see here the fatal self-contradiction that is at the root of all skepticism of which post-modernism is a variant, namely, if you assert that nothing is objectively true, then you have cut off the branch you are sitting on, for unless the statement "nothing is objectively true" is itself an objectively true state-ment, your position is a little hard to explain.

Perhaps one can say that a belief in objective truth is more fundamen-tal than arguments against it, or else no one would bother to translate Foucauld himself unless there was some hope of an objective rendering of his thought. A useful image to indicate the level of objectivity we can hope for at our best is that while no swimmer ever gets his or her body completely out of the water, the more successful ones nonetheless man-age to keep at least their noses in contact with the air. Even so, while our interpretations of the Bible or of our predecessors are inevitably infected with our own cultural presuppositions, we can nevertheless hope that some part of what we do in scholarship will turn out to have enduring importance. One may take some comfort in Pope's description of the human condition in the second epistle of his *Essay on Man:*

> A Being darkly wise, and rudely great:
> With too much knowledge for the Sceptic side,
> With too much weakness for the Stoic's pride,
> He hangs between; in doubt to act, or rest;
> In doubt to deem himself a God, or Beast;
> In doubt his Mind or Body to prefer;
> Born but to die, and reasoning but to err;
> Alike in ignorance, his reason such,
> Whether he thinks too little, or too much:
> Chaos of Thought and Passion, all confused;

Still by himself abused, or disabused;
Created half to rise, and half to fall;
Great lord of all things, yet a prey to all;
Sole judge of Truth, in endless Error hurled:
The glory, jest, and riddle of the world!

2. *A note about words and reality*

The history of ideas properly done has the benefit of making us aware of the dangers of the popular words we all are prone to. When we use words such as "liberal," "reactionary," "right wing," "left wing," we are lulled into thinking that they are as objective and unambiguous as words like "four," "kilometer," "hour," and so on. They are not. For example, when I declare myself to be conservative in my politics, I might mean I want a society where a citizen's rights are as clearly defined as a citizen's duties; I might also mean that I want a society where I do not have to pay taxes to provide health care and education for the less affluent.

In the history of biblical interpretation and in its larger relative ecclesiastical history, words like "orthodox" and "heretical" have been notorious shape-shifters. Immanuel Hirsch pointed out that the heresy of one century can often become the orthodoxy of the next. Guardians of orthodoxy often appear to be self-appointed; it is also true that the orthodoxy they proclaim is generally a comfortable fit with their own vision of the truth.

One word that needs special attention at the outset of this book is "criticism" and its various derivatives. The root meaning comes from the Greek word *krinein*, "to judge." Criticism of a text consists of making judgments about its origins and composition, its subject and meaning, and finally its importance for us, if any. In popular parlance "criticism" has the undertone of negativity, antagonism, and scorn, but this was not how the discipline of "critica sacra" was thought of from the time of the Renaissance on. It is sometimes said that "we do not judge the Bible; it judges us." While rhetorically this has a fine ring to it, it is of course utter nonsense. Only humans judge; books without readers are inanimate objects. If we wish to say that we should never make negative comments about anything in the Bible, this statement is based on our prior judgment about the Bible's contents, and therefore we have already begun by judging the Bible, albeit in a very positive way.

Biblical criticism is the careful examination of all aspects of the Bible; in theory this examination is based on the reasonable examination of the evidence and is open for public debate. Like all statements about human behavior, this belief requires a certain amount of qualification, for no one is innocent of prejudice, *amour propre,* or even just plain bad temper. But having admitted that much, it is interesting to see that despite the foregoing, there is often a respect among scholars that leaps across the boundaries of confession, nationality, and personal dislike.

3. *A particular class of expressions that education should teach us to be wary of is the generalization*

A generalization is the sort of expression that says, "In the Renaissance people believed X." Generalizations are inevitable, especially in a book like this one; therefore the unwary should be warned that while generalizations have their uses, they can be treacherous allies, for they have the effect of covering over the almost infinite variations of opinion among humans, even among educated authors who claim that they all believe the same things. Perhaps generalizations are best treated as road maps; when we have never visited a place, they show us where interesting sites are located; when we have actually seen the sites, the maps serve to remind us of the details we now know. Similarly, generalizations are useful both at the beginning and the end of an investigation, but those who rely on them for real knowledge are like those who feel they understand the Middle East because they know where Damascus is located.

4. *Right and wrong directions in the history of biblical criticism*

It is the charm of generalizations that has often skewed the history of biblical interpretation, for the temptation is to find a general pattern in the development of the discipline that can then be used to either praise or denounce its nature. There are two points of view that are guilty in this respect, namely, the whigs and the conspirators. I use the word "whig" as a remembrance of the Whig history of England, which sees British history as a graph recording the inevitable progress toward a more enlightened and democratic society as the obscure clouds of superstition and ancient abuse are dispelled by the dawning light of new perceptions.

In the history of biblical interpretation, the whig view is analogous to the picture drawn by F. W. Farrar, who saw biblical interpretation as the record of the gradual victory of liberal theology over religious obscurantism. The contrast to the whig view of history is that of history as the record of the conspiracy of devious and wicked men to overthrow the best a society has to offer. In other words, the line on the graph is still there, but it goes down rather than up. This is essentially the view of Alistair McGrath among others. I will argue that history is never so neat, never so much the product of a single cause, as both the whigs and the conspiracy detectors imagine.

The value of the history of biblical interpretation:

1. It saves us from absolutizing our own current situation. Seeing how a discipline has evolved helps us to see that it is neither a decline from nor a steady progress to truths of an almost absolute essence. To see how an institution has developed, how processes along the way have either helped or hindered it in the past, is to see it three-dimensionally against the background of its origins. This can help us to judge whether current fashionable movements, such as feminist or postmodern biblical criticism, are legitimate insights or wild aberrations.

2. Seeing the past in its own terms rather than in the cartoon fashion of popular thought is an important intellectual discipline comparable with the usefulness of meeting and trying to understand foreign cultures. The angular edges of a particular human identity present obstacles to a genuine understanding on our part, but without the pain involved we cannot enter into another way of thinking. No one is as dangerous as the leader of a nation who knows all that is worth knowing about people he or she has never met. True comprehension is a moral pursuit in that it puts limits to our assumptions that others should be as ourselves. When we enter the past, even the past that we fancy is our own, the attempt to understand our predecessors "from within" is a strenuous undertaking in the interest of our own moral development.

3. There is a genuine and important pleasure in the admiration and emulation of a past in which there were giants in the land. We all, especially the young, should learn to read great men on our knees, figuratively speaking—men such as Erasmus, Hugo Grotius, and Richard Simon. We need not agree, but we can admire the erudition they display and the ability with which they argue their points. Some of what they say is outmoded by more recent developments, but the quality of their minds is an example to follow, even if they do

not always give us conclusions to accept. To see a point well argued is a great aesthetic pleasure, even if we do not agree.

The format and peculiarities of this book:

It is hoped that this book will be readable by anyone with an inquiring mind, whether he or she is familiar with the Bible and the methods of interpreting it. With this in mind, the first chapter is designed as a general introduction to the subject and will set the stage for the discussions that follow. Chapters are self-contained so some material is repeated.

A question of vocabulary:

For Judaism the Bible is the Hebrew Bible; it is sometimes referred to by the acronym "Tenak," which stands for the three main divisions of the Jewish Bible, namely, Law (Torah), Prophets (Neviim), and Writings (Kethuvim). The Christian Bible is made up of two parts: the Old Testament and the New Testament. The Old Testament for Protestants is identical with the Jewish Tenak. However, for Roman Catholics the Old Testament contains books that are not found in the Tenak but which were either written or preserved in Greek and are included in the Septuagint, the third-century B.C.E. version of the sacred books of the Jews that was made in Egypt.

Sometimes it is asserted that the term "Hebrew Bible" should be used generally on the grounds that an Old Testament presupposes a New Testament, an opinion Jews do not share. There is no reason why in interfaith discussion one should not use this expression in consideration of the convictions of our Jewish cousins, and I would endorse the courtesy implied. However, for the purposes of this book, the term "Old Testament" is actually more accurate, for it includes the possibility of the canonicity of books that are accepted as biblical by a large part of the Christian Church and that are included as a matter of course in Roman Catholic versions of the first part of the Christian Bible.

Limitations of this book

After thirty years' work on this subject, I am left with a strong sense of my own ignorance. I have attempted to cover an extraordinarily wide range of material, and obviously there is a great deal I have had to omit in the interests of reasonable length, but there is also a great deal I have omitted by reason of ignorance. Winston Churchill once described another politician as "a modest man; so much to be modest about." This may apply to myself.

However, I have tried to read in the original languages at least the authors I discuss where the works are available to me. This does not mean that I have gone through their works in toto; if one has a look at the size of, say, Pererius's commentary on Genesis, I hope the reason will be self-evident. I have also tried to cover the secondary literature on the scholars I discuss, but I make no claim to have read everything. I apologize both to the authors and the scholarly community for egregious faults of omission.

Acknowledgments

After thirty years' work, a complete list of everyone who has advised me, lent or given me books, or helped me in various ways might well compare with the length of the book itself. I have enjoyed the kindness and hospitality of many major libraries: Cambridge, the British Library, Erlangen, Göttingen, Wolfenbüttel, Harvard, Yale, and Toronto, as well as those of universities where I have had the honor to be a student—Victoria, U.B.C., Oxford, Strasbourg, and Tübingen—who welcomed me back in a gracious manner. I would, however, like to thank those whose advice has improved this work in many ways. Its faults, of course, remain my own.

Mr. Ian Baird, Microform Librarian, University of Victoria

Dr. Robin A. Butlin, University of Leeds

Dr. Peter Fothergill-Payne, University of Calgary

Dr. William Harris, former Archivist, Princeton Theological Seminary Library

Professor Jean-Georges Heintz, University of Strasbourg

Professor Henk J. de Jonge, University of Leiden

Dr. Sally Katary, Thorneloe University

Ms. Susan Killoren, Librarian, Harris-Manchester College, Oxford

The Rev. Robert Morgan, Linacre College, Oxford

Professor Bertram Schwarzbach, University of Paris

Dr. Robert Sider, Dickinson College

The Rev. Dr. Norman Siefferman

Professor Rudolph Smend, University of Göttingen

Dr. Peter Smith, University of Victoria

Clergy of the diocese of British Columbia who read parts of the book in manuscript: The Revs. Dr. Michael Ayvert, Ron Corcoran, Michael Hemmings, Dr. Harold Munn, John Steele, Wynn Taylor

I have received special help from:

Dr. Xiaofei Tu, my research assistant, and his wife Wei Xie, who have done so much to send me copies of material that I otherwise would not have been able to get.

Ms. Sonia Furstenau, whose editing skills have improved the clarity of the text.

The Rev. Professor Roy Porter, my former doctoral thesis supervisor and a lifelong friend, many of whose incidental comments helped shape the project of this book.

Mr. John Schneider, my copy editor, who corrected so many of my mistakes.

Two units of the University of Victoria have given me invaluable assistance:

Special Collections: Mr. Christopher Petter and his staff have been an unending source of help far beyond the call of their duty in providing me with books and the facilities to consult them.

The Centre for Studies in Religion and Society: Both its former director, Dr. Harold Coward and its current director Dr. Conrad Brunk along with the staff have been most kind. The fellowship I hold at the Centre has been a great boon to me in the form of support, suggestions, and services from my colleagues there.

Chapter 1

Introduction to the Nature and Concerns of Biblical Exegesis

A somewhat mischievous professor of mine once caused a stir in the college library by complaining to the librarian that he could not find the Bible listed in the catalogue. The librarian asked him where he was looking, and he said under "G." The librarian, a bit puzzled, asked why "G." He replied he was making a search under "Author" and naturally looked the Bible up under its author, namely "God." There persists the feeling that somehow the Bible is not, or should not be, like other books, and that the truth or the falsity of the religion it describes depends on its special origins.

A classic example of this special status is found in Bacon's *New Atlantis* (1627), in which the people who do not have contact with the rest of the world receive the Bible in a miraculous way. A copy of the text of the Bible written personally by the Apostle Barnabas is delivered by supernatural means in a special chest that floats on the water without getting wet. The text of this Bible is itself miraculous, for it contains even books of the Bible not yet written at the time of its delivery to New Atlantis. This implies that the Bible as we have it is an exact replica of an eternal Bible existing in eternity that could conceivably be delivered anywhere at any point in time.

Whether consciously or not, this image of a miraculous book that comes directly from heaven haunts the understanding of the Bible for many people, whether they are its defenders or its antagonists. In particular, there are still those who feel that if the King James (Authorized)

1

Version of the Bible was good enough for Jesus and St. Paul, it is good enough for them. Unfortunately, the unchangeable book that fell down from heaven is only a literary device by Bacon. What is not always appreciated is that even if this story were factual, there would still be problems that remain, as will become apparent in this chapter.

Before one can appreciate the history of biblical exegesis, it is necessary to understand why there are a certain number of problems that cannot be avoided by the professional scholar and that ought to be borne in mind by the informed reader. These can be summed up as questions of text, language, translation, canon, and the wider questions of understanding and interpreting the Bible that depend upon the results of the other disciplines. As in many other human occupations, the reader should be warned that in practice matters are never as simple as they should be.

This chapter, then, is intended to be a guide to the complexities of the interpretation of the Bible. To be honest, the problems we shall discuss are not altogether different from the problems we face even when we try to understand the writings by people who are still alive, for as Socrates pointed out, poets are not necessarily the best interpreters of their own works.

I. The Text of the Bible

1. *The problem*

The term "text" refers to the physical means by which the Bible has come down to us. Since it is the only concrete evidence we actually have in biblical interpretation, it is an excellent place to begin.

The Bible is a work that has come down to us from antiquity. However, in no case in ancient documents do we have the author's own autograph[1] copy of an ancient book. Our only sources for the Bible's con-

---

[1] "Autograph" in its technical sense comes from two Greek words for "self" and "write"; it describes the author's self-written copy of his work (or more likely the one he dictated to a professional scribe). In the rare cases where we have the autograph copy it means we have information we might not otherwise have. For example, in the case of Gray's "Elegy Written in a Country Church-Yard," Gray's own autograph copy is still extant, and from it we can see it was written in stages over a period of several years and that the later part represents a change in sensibility on the part of the poet.

tents are handwritten manuscripts[2] that are copies of copies of copies, etc., passed down by a process of transmission that goes back to ancient manuscripts that have long since perished. The problem is that manuscripts, written by hand, as the name implies, are subject to the frailties of human nature. It is very hard to copy more than a page or two by hand without making some sort of mistake, such as leaving out a word or putting it in twice at the break of a line. The method of producing books may play a part in the sort of mistakes that are made. If a scribe copies from a written page, the old problem of reading somebody else's handwriting arises, especially in the case of the letters that are easily mistaken for each other when either choice would give a recognizable word.

On the other hand, if scribes are writing out what is dictated by a supervisor, there is a problem of hearing. The dangers of dictating can be illustrated from a problem in the text of Shakespeare. In earlier editions, part of the account of the death of Falstaff in *Henry V* was the phrase "a table of green fields." This was hard to understand, until an eighteenth-century critic had the brilliant idea that since typesetting was often done to dictation, suppose the reader came from the North of England, where "he" is often pronounced "ah." If the typesetter was from the South, perhaps he did not quite understand what the reader meant and simply wrote down the words phonetically. But once you assume that "he" was meant in this quotation, it is possible to emend it to "*he* babbled of green fields," which makes good sense in the case of a dying man's delirium. Now while professional scribes have always been aware of the sort of mistakes they made and developed ways of avoiding or correcting them, sooner or later errors slipped through.

Then there is always the problem of deliberate changes made by a copyist who decides that what he or she sees is not what ought to be there or who has an extra piece of information that seems to cry out for a place in a new manuscript. For example, notes in any quality version of the Bible will indicate that the story of the woman taken in adultery (John 7:53–8:11) was likely an addition to the text of John's Gospel. The reason for this statement is that in many manuscripts of John's Gospel this incident is not recorded, and the best explanation is that it was added to one particular manuscript by a scribe who thought that this

---

[2] The word "manuscript" is derived from the Latin "*manus*," meaning "hand" and "*scripto*," meaning "I write." Hence a manuscript is primarily a handwritten document, though the word can be used in extended senses to cover typewritten or computer-generated material.

was a good place to insert this little story, which, incidentally, is considered by some critics to be a genuine historical incident, albeit not a part of John's work.

After one or two thousand years of copying, a certain number of mistakes inevitably creep into the manuscript tradition. Textual criticism involves the comparison of ancient manuscripts in the hopes of getting back to the original author's own text by comparing different manuscripts and trying to decide which is the correct reading.[3] At the end of this process a scholar may put together a format that he or she considers to be a more accurate approximation of the original autograph manuscript than any one of the individual texts he or she has been working with. This is a "text" in a particular sense of the word; it is in theory better than any of the individual manuscripts that have come down to us. The most notable text in this sense of the word for the New Testament is the *Textus Receptus*, which was the reigning text for several centuries and which will be discussed in another chapter.

2. *Evidence from the versions of the biblical books*

Textual criticism of the Bible is, according to your point of view, enriched or complicated by evidence from ancient translations, or as they are usually called, versions. Both the Old and the New Testament were translated into other languages in antiquity; by looking at these ancient translations, one can make a reasonable guess about what sort of text the translator had in front of him or her. Yet the versions also present difficulties; it is possible that the translator was working from a manuscript that was itself defective, and one must also face the fact that versions, too, have their own problems arising from errors in the textual transmission.

3. *Two examples of textual criticism from antiquity*

From the point of view of the history of interpretation, the discipline of textual criticism is the most ancient form of critical study. The most famous exponent in the early period of the church is the great church father Origen (185–c. 254).[4] Among his many works was his Hexapla, an

---

[3] "Reading" is a technical term for one manuscript's evidence; for example, in Mark 1:2 the reading in some manuscripts is "in the prophet Isaiah"; in others the reading is "in the prophets."

[4] Origen is remembered not only for his extraordinary erudition but also for his having, in a moment of misguided youthful piety, "Abelarded" himself.

edition of the Old Testament arranged in six columns containing the Hebrew text, the Hebrew text transliterated into Greek letters, and four translations—the Septuagint, Aquila, Symmachus, and Theodotion.[5] He later added more versions to this work. His autograph manuscript has not survived, but copies of parts of the work give an idea of its magnitude.

The traditional text of the Hebrew Bible as preserved in the synagogues is known as the Masoretic Text (MT). This is a standardized text, that is, it appears to be the result of a process of editing various biblical manuscripts by the Masora (teachers) of the Jewish community at an early point in the common era. For reasons that can only be guessed at, the Masoretic Text crowded out the different readings of the different biblical manuscripts the Masoretes had to work with. The result is that the text of the Hebrew Bible in the Jewish synagogue tradition exhibits only relatively minor variants among the manuscripts.

Our main source of information about the sort of variants that the Masoretes had in front of them as they worked is the third-century B.C.E. translation known as the Septuagint (LXX), for although it is a translation, it does give some idea of the variety in the manuscript tradition that the Masoretes suppressed. Other ancient versions also provide some help, but it was always a hope that somehow older, pre-Masoretic texts in Hebrew might emerge. This is why sixteenth-century scholars were interested in the Hebrew Bible of the Samaritan community in Palestine (a text that included only the Pentateuch); they hoped that it might be an independent witness. When copies of the Samaritan Pentateuch were finally brought to Europe in the seventeenth century, they initially caused a stir. In the long run, the Samaritan text has failed to live up to expectations, and evidence for textual traditions prior to the Masoretic standardization would have to wait for the discovery of the Dead Sea Scrolls in the middle of the twentieth century.

4. *The Vulgate version*

Of all the versions of the Bible, it is the Latin Vulgate that is the most important, not only for its merits but also for the importance attributed

---

[5] The Septuagint (usually referred to as LXX) was a translation of the Old Testament into Greek made probably in stages sometime after 300 B.C.E. Aquila, Symmachus, and Theodotion, the names of the translators, were Greek versions of the Old Testament made probably in the second century C.E.

to it at various points in history. A brief and perhaps oversimplified explanation may help to understand the situation. Originally the church in Rome appears to have been Greek-speaking—in the Latin Mass there is a remnant of this in the words *Kyrie eleison,* which are Greek and not Latin. Eventually translations of the Bible into Latin appeared. This is the so-called Old Latin version, which was not really a single work but a collection of various translations of individual books of the Bible.

Since there was a certain lack of uniformity in the Old Latin version, a more standard version was provided by Jerome, possibly the best textual scholar among the church fathers, and undoubtedly the worst-tempered. Jerome translated the Old Testament, revised the Gospels, but did not touch the Epistles. All this went into what became the Vulgate, which continued to undergo revisions until it became in effect the official Bible of the Western church in the eighth and ninth centuries. But copyists continued to make the inevitable changes, so that by the sixteenth century there were, Erasmus complains, as many Vulgates as Bibles.[6] Since Latin remained a living language for liturgy and learned discourse, the Vulgate had a dominant place in biblical interpretation up to the rise of Humanism,[7] a position reinforced by the Council of Trent.

Now, whatever role the Vulgate played in church history and whatever faults it might have had as a translation, it is important as a textual source because Jerome consulted many manuscripts, including Origen's Hexapla, and some of his Old Testament readings may be from manuscripts that preserved readings from the pre-Masoretic tradition.

5. *Some further points*

One could be pardoned for seeing text as a welcome island of objectivity in scholarship, for textual differences are concrete and their existence beyond the refutation of anything short of applying a razor blade. In some cases the situation may indeed be so clear as to compel general agreement. For example, the longer ending of Mark 16:9-20 is so poorly

---

[6] For a good discussion see H.F.D. Sparks, " Jerome as Biblical Scholar," in *Cambridge History of the Bible,* vol. 1 (Cambridge: Cambridge University Press, 1970) 510–41.

[7] It is interesting to note two points. First, Latin was not seen as a dead language in the way Greek and Hebrew were. Second, even Protestants used Latin for academic instruction, to the point that Protestants made translations of the Bible from the original languages into Latin for the benefit of students. Even today there is a Communion service in Latin in the Oxford University church (St. Mary's) once a term.

attested in the manuscript tradition that few would argue that it is an original part of the manuscript of Mark's Gospel. But not all matters are so simple. For example, in the Lukan narrative of the institution of the Lord's Supper[8] there appear to be two cups; is this a case of homoio-teleuton—that at some point a scribe copied a passage twice—or is this a reflection of different eucharistic practices within the early church? How one deals with this issue depends eventually on one's evaluation of Luke as a writer. Rather than text giving the base for exegesis, this is one case where exegesis has to interfere in the reconstruction of a text.[9]

Furthermore, in the assessment of texts there is an inevitable element of human judgment involved. In much of textual criticism from the nineteenth century on, it has been assumed that one family of manuscripts can be considered to be "neutral" in that it has fewer additions, and therefore it is closer to the earlier form(s) of the text.[10] The reasons adduced are not imaginary, but can they be relied upon absolutely? The only sure way for making statements would be the recovery of the autograph copy of each book in the New Testament, something that is not likely to happen.

There are yet more problems, for the word "autograph" above presupposes that at one given moment St. Mark threw down his pen, announced that his Gospel was finally finished, and then gave the staff the rest of the day off to celebrate. But can we be sure that this is how things happened in the early church? We have no reliable information about the procedures followed for book production in the early church, and it is at least possible that different versions of the same text circulated from the beginning.

Nonetheless, in the modern period from 1500 on, a great deal of time and effort has gone into collecting not only manuscripts in Hebrew and Aramaic of the Old Testament or in Greek of the New, but also manuscripts of ancient translations of the Bible, which are additional evidence for the underlying original the translator used. In the sixteenth century scholarly editions of the texts began to have notes in their margins indicating important variants found in different manuscripts; eventually these marginal notes were transferred to an *apparatus criticus* at the bottom

[8] Luke 22:14-23.

[9] See the discussion in Joachim Jeremias, *The Eucharistic Words of Jesus*, trans. Norman Perrin (London: SCM, 1966) 138–59, for details about the problem.

[10] See Bruce M. Metzger, *The Text of the New Testament: Its Transmission, Corruption, and Restoration*, 3rd ed. (Oxford: Oxford University Press, 1992) 133ff.

of the page.[11] While the awareness of textual problems was scarcely novel, the systematic attempt to collate manuscripts and make intelligent choices among their readings is a feature of the new approach to biblical studies that was emerging.

II. Language and Translation

In a complex world we all rely on translations in an ever-increasing fashion. What should always be borne in mind is that there is no such thing as a perfect translation. To appreciate why this is the case, it is necessary to say something about language itself.

1. *Understanding language*

It is important to bear in mind that language is both complicated and more often ambiguous than people are tempted to think. Even in one's own language it is possible to make a mistake. In an English class many years ago, the phrase in Carlyle, "Kings wrestling naked on the green with Carmen" produced some riveting, if not altogether appropriately serious, images for myself and others about the privileges of royalty, until we noticed the footnote that the Carmen referred to were cart drivers, not the enchanting lady whom Bizet was to immortalize several years after Carlyle's work was completed.

But it is only when one tries to understand or speak a foreign language that one realizes just how many problems and nuances there are. Words usually have a range of meanings in any given language, but their nominal equivalents in other tongues seldom have the same ranges. We are all aware of the non-English speaker whose efforts at communication may be inappropriate; if, when being introduced, a nice, young, Arabic-speaking girl says, "I love you," English-speaking males would be wise to take this as nothing more than the equivalent of "I am pleased to meet you," particularly if her father and brothers are standing nearby and are armed to the teeth.

To understand what is written, one has to be aware that every language has in it the debris of its speakers' religious imagery, historical

---

[11] To be fair, the comparison and correction of manuscripts had existed long before this in both the Jewish and the Christian traditions. What was new was the extent to which even important variants which were rejected were recorded.

memory, and possibly philosophical thought. The importance of knowing at least a second language well is clear when one becomes bilingual, for one becomes aware that certain expressions in any language have an implicit resonance from that language's past. When you go from English to French, you leave behind the imprint of Mill and the Utilitarians and instead find that Descartes and Bergson live on in the intricacies of the meaning of words. In turn, going from French to English means becoming aware of the sonorities of the King James Bible and the Book of Common Prayer that lurk underneath the syntax and influence the meaning. Some bilingual people claim that they find they assume a slightly different identity when they switch from one of their languages to the other.[12]

Biblical languages are no longer spoken colloquially, at least in their ancient form. In reading texts in these languages, we are faced with the problem that we lack the context for many of the words. This is particularly true in the case of *hapax legomena,* words that occur only once in the biblical text.[13] Much of the history of biblical interpretation deals with the efforts of scholars to recover the exact range of meaning[14] of terms used in the original biblical languages, either by examining their use elsewhere in the text of the Bible itself if possible, or by seeking parallels from non-biblical ancient documents or from cognate languages such as Arabic.

But style can be as important as grammar in studying a text. Those who have a sense of good style in classical Greek find some of the Greek in the New Testament less than pleasing, not least of all St. Mark's. In seventeenth-century Holland there were debates about whether New Testament Greek was good Greek; in more recent times scholars have been more ready to admit the Semitic cast of the style of Mark in comparison with that of Luke, or the excellence of the style of the Epistle to the Hebrews in contrast to that of the genuine Pauline epistles.

---

[12] It has been observed that being bilingual is like having a wife and a mistress; one is never quite sure of either one or the other.

[13] In biblical Hebrew there are less than a thousand different words. Reasonable estimates suggest this represents about 20 percent of the actual vocabulary used in Hebrew in biblical times.

[14] Most words in most languages have not a single meaning but a range of meanings. For example, consider the possible meanings of the word "right" from political through directional to civil entitlement. As an adjective "right" has an additional meaning of "correct," something not necessarily found in its corresponding noun.

The history of modern biblical interpretation was marked from the beginning by the Renaissance Humanist concern with and love of language, especially recovering the purity of the classical tongues of Latin and Greek, but there was also a similar effort to master Hebrew and Aramaic and any other language that might help to understand the Bible. As time went on, there was a mutual interaction between the study of biblical languages and the study and theory of language itself.

2. *Translation*

One effect of the Reformation was a revival of the tradition of translating the canon of Scripture into the languages usually spoken by the general membership of the church. While the initial impulse for this effort was Protestant, eventually the Roman Catholic Church was forced by circumstances in some countries to follow suit. In English the King James Version dominated the field, to the point of discouraging many other translations, but in French and German in the seventeenth and eighteenth centuries it was not unknown for a scholar to publish his own version.

Accurate translation is not a simple task. The French saying *traduire, c'est trahire* sums up the matter and is itself appropriately only translatable as the much less effective "to translate is to betray," where the nuance carried by the pun is lost. The problems of trying to translate accurately are summed up by the somewhat timeworn story of the computer asked to translate "The spirit is willing but the flesh is weak" into Russian, which produced a sentence that meant "The vodka is good but the meat is bad." Words represent a spectrum of meanings, and it is not always clear which meaning the context requires. Thus in Genesis 1:2 the sentence translated "the spirit of God moved over the face of the waters" might actually mean "an almighty wind was blowing over the flood."

Even a common word presents problems when its range of meanings is not duplicated by any word in the language into which one is translating; the most outstanding case is the opening of John's Gospel: "In the beginning was the *logos*." How does one translate *logos* here? The usual translation into English is "word," but this does not have the resonance of *logos* in Greek, which would suggest "the word of God" to those familiar with the Hebrew Bible and "the principle behind the world" to those aware of Greek philosophy. Erasmus got into a certain amount of trouble with his use of the Latin *sermo*, and in the first act of Goethe's *Faust* the hero has so much trouble with the same problem that he winds up selling his soul to the Devil, something all translators are driven to sooner or later, but usually in a less dramatic fashion.

A further problem of translation is that there is a fundamental circularity that is the bane of logical explanation. Put honestly, one cannot translate a passage unless one already has an idea of what it means. Even in conversation in one's native language, one may not really grasp what is being said, though most of the words are familiar, as is discovered by the ordinary citizen when he or she tries to figure out what the nice man in the computer store means as he babbles on about the esoteric qualities of his wares. In written material from ancient cultures, the problem is worse.

One book in the Old Testament that is an example of this principle is the Song of Songs. If you see it as some sort of allegory of the soul with its creator, or Christ and the church, then you may not wish to give an erotic interpretation to many passages. On the other hand, if you see it as a secular love poem, you may feel less inhibited in how you render it. Even the tone of a narrative can present problems. Humor in particular is often damaged by being transported from one culture to another; what is uproariously funny in one culture may be seen as cruel or obscene in another. At least with contemporary cultures we can get corroborative information about what is supposed to be funny. With ancient documents it is not always clear. Is the climax (literally) of the story of Ruth tinged with a certain ribald humor? If you look at the meaning carefully, Naomi's advice to Ruth is to find out where Boaz is sleeping, grab him by his private parts, and he will tell you what to do. Indeed.

Inadequate knowledge of language can often lead to bad interpretation. For example, much has been made of the fact that the Hebrew *ruach,* which means "spirit" or "wind," is feminine. This is drawn into discussion about the feminine in the Godhead. While the intention is laudable, the interpretation is lamentable, for in the New Testament the word that is more or less the equivalent of *ruach* is *pneuma,* which is neuter. The fact is, gender in grammar is not inevitably correlated with sex as a physiological fact; otherwise one would have to conclude that since the German word for girl, *Mädchen,* is neuter, German girls are essentially sexless, a suggestion not supported by the empirical evidence.

One of the sources of uneasiness about the Bible by the end of the seventeenth century was the accuracy of biblical translations. Even nonacademic circles caught a whiff of the problem. In Vanbrugh's play *The Provok'd Wife* (1697), Lady Brute deals with the rebuke that the Bible requires us to return good for evil with "That may be a mistake in the translation."[15]

III. Canon

All religions depend on tradition and tend to derive their legitimacy from it. The issue of canon emerges whenever any group decides that some books are especially important for defining the tradition, but then the group runs into the problems of who decides which books are sacred and which are not; the relationship between the written word and other parts of the tradition; and the possibility of new additions to the tradition.

1. *The authority for establishing the canon in the Christian tradition*

In Christian history several possible foundations of canonicity have been suggested, sometimes in combination with each other. One basis is the argument from the tradition of the church—such books have been always and everywhere accepted as scriptural. In the case of the Roman Catholic Church, this tradition is enforced by a central authority that provides an authoritative interpretation of the tradition.

A second basis for choosing books to be included in the canon is the argument that the authors of the books of the Bible were known to be knowledgeable and reliable persons, that is, eyewitnesses of the events they report or at least close to the original sources. This position has often been put forward as an additional support for other positions, but one author who argued for it as the principal explanation was the sixteenth-century writer Faustus Socinius, whose arguments in *De authoritate* [sic] *sacrae scripturae* were taken over by Grotius in his *Truth of Christianity*.

A third justification has been an appeal to the Holy Spirit, whose internal testimony to the reader confirms the sacred nature of the text. This position was argued most forcefully by Calvin and has occasionally been adopted by other Protestants. However, it should be pointed out that the earlier Luther flirted with a fourth standard for canonicity based on whether a given book contained the essence of the doctrine of justification by faith, which was essential for Scripture. By this criterion, Luther had doubts about some of the lesser New Testament epistles, such as that of James, who argued that faith without works is of no avail.

---

[15] Act I, scene i. I owe this reference to Christopher Hill, *The English Bible and the Seventeenth-Century Revolution* (London: Allen Lane/Penguin, 1993) 429.

2. *The extent of the Christian canon*

The decision about the exact contents of the Christian Old Testament has been complicated by the fact that the Old Testament is the Bible of Judaism. Before the Christian era began, Judaism began to look on certain books as sacred (literally "books that defiled the hands"). It is alleged with some degree of probability that the first five books of the Hebrew Bible (the Law or Pentateuch) were edited and canonized after the destruction of the Jerusalem temple in 586 B.C.E. This is not to deny that at least parts of this work existed earlier, but the loss of the temple and the exile of part of the population into Babylonia meant that the most important part of the Jewish faith and worship shifted from the temple to the Law. We do not know how the decision about the early canon was made, nor is it really clear by what stages other books were added to it, but by the time of Jesus canonical Scriptures were an essential part of the Jewish faith, and Jesus' disputes with religious authorities were based on the interpretation of these works.

With the destruction of the second temple in 70 C.E., once again Judaism had to regroup around the Law alone. One result was the final choice about which books were scriptural. This selection took place around 100 C.E., when the criterion applied was possibly antiquity—no book after Ezra was to be considered canonical.[16] This Hebrew Bible was the Old Testament canon that came to be accepted by the Protestant churches at the time of the Reformation.

However, this is not the whole story of the matter in the Christian church, for in Greek-speaking Judaism a translation of the Hebrew Scriptures into Greek had been made starting possibly in the third century B.C.E. This translation, known as the Septuagint or LXX after the seventy-two elders who had traditionally produced it, included a wider selection of books than was eventually accepted into the Hebrew canon in the first century C.E. It was this larger canon that was taken over as the Old Testament by the overwhelmingly Greek-speaking Christian church. The church fathers were aware of their difference with Judaism on this point and were not always sure how to resolve the matter, though St. Jerome himself referred to these extra books as the "Apocrypha" and had his reservations about their legitimate place in the canon. At the time of the Reformation, when the Protestant churches reverted to the

---

[16] Many scholars would now say that a few of the books admitted (e.g., Ecclesiastes, Daniel) were much later than the time of Ezra.

Hebrew canon, the Roman Catholic Church at the Council of Trent accepted all but one of the extra works in the Septuagint as an integral part of the Old Testament.[17]

IV. Exegesis in the Wider Sense

Once the issues of text, language, translation, and canon are settled, logically (but not always in practice), one proceeds to exegesis proper, which in fact means making sense of a written work.

There are those who will argue—or perhaps "proclaim" is a more appropriate word—that interpretation is not appropriate for the Bible when one should simply read it as it is. This suggestion has the charm of simplicity, but like many other simple statements, it is based on a naive view of what we do as human beings. It was Socrates (or perhaps it was Plato) who got it right about written material:

> I cannot help feeling, Phaedrus, that writing is unfortunately like painting; for the creations of the painter have the attitude of life, and yet if you ask them a question they preserve a solemn silence. And the same may be said of speeches. You would imagine that they had intelligence, but if you want to know anything and put a question to one of them, the speaker always gives one unvarying answer. And when they have been once written down they are tumbled about anywhere among those who may or may not understand them, and know not to whom they should reply, to whom not: and, if they are maltreated or abused, they have no parent to protect them; and they cannot protect or defend themselves.[18]

Interpretation is what we all do when we make sense of a book. Inevitably, either the book needs a defender or we need an explainer. Yet Plato's argument can be countered to some extent by the obvious point that without his written text, we would not be made aware of his discussion of the problems of interpreting documents; therefore he himself was confident that his text at least could be understood in the manner he intended. And if his text made sense, could not the same be true of others?

---

[17] For a clear and comprehensive discussion of the Apocrypha, see the article by Bruce Metzger in *The New Oxford Annotated Bible with the Apocryphal/DeuteroCanonical Books* (Oxford: 1991) iiiAP–xvAP.

[18] Jowett translation.

Here, in an admittedly artificial format, are several concerns that inevitably raise their heads when we get on to making sense of the Bible.

1. *The dates of biblical documents*

Given that the Bible consists of documents from different times, one has to take into account the date of the composition of a biblical book. In the Old Testament the dates for the actual writing down of its various contents can swing from about 1300 B.C.E. to 150 B.C.E. Few of the books are dated exactly, and of those that are, there are good reasons to argue that the date for a book like Daniel is completely fictitious. Relative dating is the best we can hope for in many cases, such as the generally accepted dating that the Deuteronomic History (a name given to the historical books from Joshua to 2 Kings, except for Ruth) is considerably earlier than the two books of Chronicles. In the New Testament, relative dating is very important in some cases, in particular for the Synoptic Gospels (Matthew, Mark, and Luke), for it is clear that there is a direct literary relationship between them, and if only we could find it out, it would make it easier to interpret each of them.

2. *The authorship and unity of the books in the Bible*

When there is too much confusion and discontinuity within a biblical book, the question arises whether we are dealing with a work by a single author or a compilation of different documents made by various hands, or even perhaps a case of pseudonymous attribution. Here are some examples.

A relatively easy case is Ecclesiastes, most of which is marked by a consistent, gentle cynicism that is very different from the assurance of the prophets. It makes sense to treat this as the work of a single person, probably someone in the second century B.C.E., who was well-known in Jerusalem. But at the end of Ecclesiastes (12:9ff.) there is an addition that looks like an attempt to bring the work back into the charmed circle of the respectable and is patently an editorial addition. In the case of the Pentateuch opinions differ. At the outset of the modern period, most scholars would have seen it as a work by Moses himself. The difficulty is that there are too many problems to make this an easily supported theory, and as time went on, the likelihood of Moses' authorship of all the material in the Pentateuch gradually changed into the view that in fact Moses' contribution was vestigial at the best.

In the New Testament there are problems with the authorship of the Pauline epistles, that is, the books that have been attributed to Paul. In the case of Colossians and Ephesians, the problem is that while there are similarities, there are also significant differences. In the case of the Pastoral Epistles (1 and 2 Timothy and Titus), there are good scholars who still defend the Pauline authorship, but hoping that a convincing proof of Paul's authorship of the Epistle to the Hebrews will be found is looking more and more as sensible as keeping the lights on for Amelia Earhart.

3. *The type of book*

We do not read cookbooks in the same way we read novels. Some sort of prior understanding lies behind any attempt at interpretation, although sometimes the weight of evidence leads to a change of perception. In interpreting the books of the Bible, we have to make a judgment about their genre. A clear case involves the Song of Songs in the Old Testament. Is this an allegorical presentation of the relationship between the soul and God, or is it a love poem, only too firmly grounded in the realities of human nature?

In the New Testament one of the interesting questions is, what sort of work is a Gospel? This is far from a simple question, but the starting point is that the Gospels do not really give us the information we would expect from a biography. When was Jesus' birthday, what did he look like, and what did he do for the first thirty years of his life are all questions the Gospels do not give us much information about.

4. *Two sorts of vexing problems*

Sooner or later any serious attempt to read the Bible carefully runs into two types of problems that affect how one approaches exegesis.

The first sort of problem is the question of consistency or believability. In Genesis 6:2 it is stated that the sons of God saw that the daughters of men were fair, with the expected results. It does seem that here there is some reference to semidivine beings. In another case of angels being less than angelic, even St. Paul gives as a reason why women should keep their heads covered is because of angels in 1 Corinthians 11:10. Consistency in details is apparent in such a matter as why David decided to hold a census in Israel and thereby bring down on his people the punishment of God. In 2 Samuel 24:1, David does this because God provokes him to do it; in 1 Chronicles 21:1, it is Satan who moves David to do this. Obviously, some sort of explanation is required.

The second sort of problem is a perceived immorality in the Bible. When Joshua invades Canaan, he carries out the sort of ethnic cleansing that would have got him hauled up before a war crimes tribunal today. To add to the problem, he does this under God's express command (Josh 6:1-21). When Saul defeats the Amalekites, the only rebuke he gets is that he did not kill everything he could get his hands on; in particular, he spares Agag the king, an omission that is rectified by Samuel, who hews Agag in pieces before the Lord, that is, in the temple (1 Sam 15:1-33).

These difficulties with the morality of some of the stories in the Bible lead to another question, namely, does the Bible require special treatment? In the history of biblical interpretation, the debate has been about the appropriateness of applying the same criteria to the Bible that we apply to secular works, criteria such as consistency of style and content. For example, up to the early eighteenth century, in Protestant interpretation the principle of the *analogia fidei* was applied in exegesis, that is, the conviction that there was complete doctrinal agreement within the Bible, and it was simply bad exegesis to suggest otherwise. In the present day most scholars would tend to treat this unity of the Bible as a point of discussion rather than a presupposition of interpretation.

5. *Taking our own culture into account*[19]

The other side of interpretation from the text is ourselves. We do not approach a written text from within a sanitized vacuum. As part of the cost of being alive, we all have personal convictions, perceptions, and tastes that may hinder how we interpret what we read. But these are the same characteristics that render us capable of any interpretation at all. The reason why people read books and dogs do not is that people can find meaning, thanks to their accumulated personal experience, but the process of interpretation can itself interfere in understanding the texts we read (or for that matter, the words other humans say to us personally). The problems that arise when we read the Bible in the twenty-first century come from our inability to ignore what we know about the shape of the universe, the source of diseases, the laws of genetics, the

---

[19] Anthony C. Thiselton, *The Two Horizons: New Testament Hermeneutics and Philosophical Description* (Grand Rapids, Mich.: Wm. B. Eerdmans, 1980) provides an excellent, if demanding, discussion of this matter.

processes of biology, and the role of biochemistry in behavior, as well as political constructs such as human rights, the scope of law, the lessons of economics. All these considerations would have been foreign to the author(s) of the Pentateuch.

The difficulty we face is which pieces of our mental furniture fit into older mansions and to what extent we should ignore our presuppositions. We suspend our concerns about historical accuracy in reading Shakespeare, about physiological possibility in reading the tale of Snow White, and about factual truth in reading political autobiography. On the other hand, we feel justified to some extent in applying concerns of feminist sensitivity to parts of the Bible where feminism was not an overriding concern on the part of the original author.

6. *Exegesis and its relation to theology in general*

Because of the complexity of the enterprise, it is difficult to rule absolutely about where exegesis, the understanding of the biblical text, leaves off and the appropriation of the sense of Scripture to the direction of human life in the present begins. In the Dutch universities in the early seventeenth century, the attempt was made to forbid the teaching of systematic theology and to teach exegesis alone. The result was that dogmatics simply made its way into the classroom under the guise of exegesis.

However, in theory at least, it is possible to distinguish three separate activities. Exegesis proper, termed *explicatio*, is the scholarly working out of what the author(s) of the text meant to say. When one goes on to explain how this original meaning throws light on decisions we have to make in the present world, one has moved beyond pure *explicatio* to *meditatio* or dogmatic theology. All this is without effect until one then decides for oneself how the two foregoing steps apply to one's own life; this is *applicatio*. A good illustration of "application" is the actions of Albert Schweitzer, who on hearing the parable of the rich man and Lazarus in church one day, decided that he, as a prosperous European, was the rich man, and Lazarus stood for the sick in Africa, and from that moment he decided to give up a promising career and go as a medical missionary to Africa.

7. *The quest for certainty: A complicating factor in exegesis*

The neat schema for interpretation given above should not be confused with how exegesis was practiced in the past or even today. Among the complications that will emerge in the course of this history, there is one constant factor that needs to be discussed at the outset, and that is the human desire for certainty.

It is human to wish for absolute truth, though the taste is stronger in some people than in others. Between the absolute skeptic, who doubts that anything certain can be known, and the absolute dogmatist, who wants every hair in place even on his cat, there is a somewhat ill-defined and uncomfortable no-man's-land where, set in the midst of many and great dangers, most of us have to live and move and have our being.

In the history of modern exegesis two different approaches to the question of certainty were made. The Council of Trent proclaimed that all biblical interpretation should be in line with the testimony of the fathers as laid down by proper authority, that is, the Curia of the Roman Catholic Church. Protestants tended to insist on the inner testimony of the Holy Spirit. There is no doubt that as a device in controversy the Roman Catholic approach was an effective instrument in the gains made by the Counter-Reformation. The drawback was how an authoritarian system escapes from an exegetically questionable decision such as setting up the Vulgate as the final word in matters of text. The Protestant appeal to the Holy Spirit did open the way to a sense of freedom from human institutions, but it had its own drawback in that Protestants did not always agree with one another.[20] As a counterbalance to the weakness of this appeal, Protestant scholars tended to look to the development of sound exegesis as a way of deflecting the criticism that individual idiosyncrasy was given free reign in Protestant exegesis. This meant that since Protestants could not simply fall back on an established authority, there was always the spur of the necessity of searching for unassailable exegesis to goad them on.

V. External Factors Affecting Exegesis

Like any other human investigation, biblical exegesis is influenced by the environment of the place and time where biblical scholars find

---

[20] See Hobbes's remark at the end of his discussion of the Christian Commonwealth (*Leviathan*, ch. 43): "For it is not the bare words, but the scope of the writer, that giveth the true light by which any writing is to be interpreted; and they that insist upon single texts, without considering the main design, can derive no thing from them clearly; but rather, by casting atoms of Scripture as dust before men's eyes, make

themselves. This is not to say that the conclusions of exegesis are the inevitable consequences of social forces beyond the ken or control of human ingenuity, but it is vain to deny the influence of material conditions and contemporary traditions.[21] What, then, are the sort of major external factors that can influence the interpretation of the Bible? Obviously, unless scholars have the means, the opportunity, and the tranquility to get on with their studies, much scholarship is not likely to ensue. These conditions are affected by the nature of the state, its current condition, its relationship with the church and other faiths. The ability of scholars to have access to books, to communicate with other scholars, to disseminate ideas will also have to be borne in mind.

1. *Technology*

The effect of the invention of movable type will be discussed in the next chapter (pp. 38–40). However, there is one technological change that is sometimes overlooked, namely, the invention of the codex (from the Latin meaning "a block of wood"), which is the form of a book made up of pages bound together at one side. The codex made its appearance just about the same time as the Christian church, and it is possible that this format was invented by Christians. It was certainly used by them. This change was to have implications for scholarship, for the codex was much more usable than the unwieldy scroll that had been the general form for books up to that time.

The best way for seeing the difference that this new technology made is to use the modern equivalent of the scroll, namely, the microfilm copy of a book. Even when one is using a machine with a power winder, one's heart sinks when at page 801 of book 3, one realizes that one has to go back to page 2 in book 1 to check a reference. It is a medium that does not encourage comparison of passages, whereas a book format permits easier and faster comparisons between passages and between books. Handsome as the Torah scrolls of a synagogue are, one would hate to have to move between different passages with six of them.

---

everything more obscure than it is, an ordinary artifice of those that seek not the truth, but their own advantage."

[21] For a discussion of the importance of tradition in many areas of human life, not least of all in science, see Edward Shils, *Tradition* (Chicago: University of Chicago Press, 1981).

2. *Sources of knowledge external to the Bible as*
   criteria authority for biblical criticism

One necessary condition for a critical assessment of the Bible is the assumption that one has access to a source of truth separate from the Bible and from which the Bible can be viewed and judged. This separate source can be philosophically based, as in the cases of Vanini and Spinoza. In the early seventeenth century Lucilio Vanini (1585–1619), eventually burned at the stake for his views, argued from classical philosophy for a type of unbelief in religion based on a firm sense of the impossibility of miracles combined with a sense of the deceit used by those who had a vested interest in promoting religion. Somewhat later, Spinoza based his mature opinion about the Bible on his philosophical system, which, he argued, provided clear and undiluted guidance on moral matters in comparison with which the Bible was a flawed document, albeit of some use to those not gifted with philosophical acumen.

Sometimes the separate source could be generated by a comparison of the contents of the Bible with material from other sources. Thus the legends about Apollonius of Tyana provided Anthony Blount with an argument for showing that the New Testament is not very different from other documents of its time, thereby casting doubt on its divine origins. But the most notable separate source of truth in the past two centuries has been science. This issue is very complicated and will be given a fuller discussion in the later chapters of this work.

VI. The Weaknesses of Exegesis at the Beginning of the Modern Period (i.e., from 1500 C.E.)

At the beginning of the modern period, biblical interpreters, through no fault of their own, lacked certain sorts of material that have since then proved critical in biblical studies.

1. Much of the basic knowledge in linguistics that we take for granted today was present only in part. It was considered reasonable at the time to assume that Hebrew was the most ancient language of humanity, since Peleg, an obscure link in the genealogy of Genesis, was not present at the disaster of the confusion of tongues at Babel. This belief was also fostered by the fact that while some progress had been made in the revival of knowledge of the biblical languages, systematic knowledge of other languages, such as Arabic, Persian,

Armenian, and Ethiopic, was in its initial stages as scholars struggled to cope with interpreting the wealth of manuscripts that were being collected in western Europe.

2. The manuscript tradition behind biblical works was not well-known. For example, Erasmus had to work from a handful of manuscripts in his edition of the Greek New Testament, and indeed, for lack of comparison, reasonable criteria for distinguishing among varying readings would only be developed two centuries later. In the case of the Old Testament, Christian scholars were feeling their way with the help available from Jewish sources, but even at the beginning of the seventeenth century Johannes Buxtorff (Senior, 1564–1629) produced a Hebrew Bible that did not address textual problems seriously.

3. There was also a lack of good information about non-Graeco-Roman antiquity, that is, of the civilizations that surrounded and influenced biblical Israel. People were fascinated by Egypt, but there was no solid information available about it from before the time of Alexander; on the contrary, there was a great deal of misinformation, some of which lingers today. Similarly, information about Israel's other neighbors in Mesopotamia, Syria, and Asia Minor was sparse and inaccurate. In other words, there was not enough knowledge available to get a three-dimensional picture of the Old Testament against its background. Yet, if there was not much accurate information, there was a critical spirit and a zest for research that were to lead to our modern picture of the biblical world.

4. There was also a lack of scientific information about the age of the human race and the planet on which it lives. Because the Bible was seen as the most ancient document available, there was a natural tendency to see it as the record of the whole of ancient humanity and to assume that the origin of human beings coincided with the origin of the world. Collision with the emerging science of geology was already beginning to become apparent at the end of the seventeenth century, and this was to prove the curtain-raiser to the debate about evolution two centuries later.

5. Even more of a handicap was the lack of a sense of the effects of history and cultural differences. By cultural differences is meant an awareness that people separated from us by either time or space often find as natural and normal ideas and practices we might class

as repugnant. To be fair, chronology was a highly developed concern at the beginning of our period, but the extent of the difference between western Europe and the world of the Bible was not really appreciated. While it was not until the nineteenth century that reliable information about other ancient civilizations was obtained, one can see in the various eighteenth-century attempts to find the origin of language a stretching of the outlook derived from the Bible.

6. Furthermore, a lack of historical awareness meant that discordances between biblical verses tended to be explained in terms of philosophical distinctions rather than different periods of culture. It was to be one of the advances of the period of the later Enlightenment that the importance of the history of human culture and the difference among human cultures became apparent.

VII. The Role of Belief and Unbelief in the History of Biblical Interpretation

The Bible is undoubtedly a religious book, however you wish to define religion. It presupposes both belief in the sense of a view of the nature of reality and belief in the sense of a personal commitment required of human beings who adopt this view as prescriptive rather than descriptive.[22] If the Bible is seen as making authoritative claims on how we live and the choices we should make, how does this affect scholarly interpretation?

Now the complicating factor is that most if not all people have beliefs of both types, however inchoate these beliefs may happen to be. If one adopts Tillich's suggestion that everyone has some sort of "ultimate concern," then everyone has some sort of faith, for even the belief that all religious systems are mistaken remains a belief. The problem of defining religion in contrast to irreligion, then, is that it is hard to say when a particular type of concern falls over into the category of religious belief; for example, the reverence shown to national flags or even some forms of vegetarianism take on a religious coloring that is unmistakable.

It is clear, then, that there is no such thing as an impartial standpoint from which one can judge a religious document. It is sometimes asserted

---

[22] The difference between descriptive and prescriptive is illustrated by two statements: "The planet Mars has mountains" and "Eating people is wrong."

that only a person without religious commitment can discuss religion in a scientific manner; this is really no more than a tragic naiveté about philosophy that elicits the appropriate feelings of sorrow and pity.

Any religious system will have adherents who are more or less committed to the cause. Almost inevitably there will also be around them those who do not accept the tenets of the faith, whatever it may happen to be. This is not a new situation; in ancient Egypt and Mesopotamia one finds written records of unbelief, and one wonders how many others who also did not believe in the gods at that time remained unnoticed because they failed to record their disagreement for posterity.[23] Unbelief is the inevitable *Doppelgänger* of faith; even in the so-called age of faith of the medieval period, doubt is attested, but in the sixteenth century, especially in Italy, the outright rejection of Christian beliefs was more openly espoused.

How, then, does objection to Christianity and Judaism affect biblical interpretation? Obviously, each case must be dealt with on its own terms, but a certain generalization seems appropriate. Among people who know little or nothing about the criticism of the Bible, there are both those who have a high opinion of its authority and those who think the Bible is nonsense. In each case, while the volume of the discourse is high, the quality of the content is low. Then in the case of people who know a great deal about the Bible, there are those who find its contents authoritative and those who do not; members of either group can contribute to our knowledge of the Bible. For example, while Renan and Strauss, to be discussed below in chapter 7, were unbelievers but nonetheless worth reading for their observations, Voltaire was not. Similarly, while Robertson Smith, definitely a believer, is worth reading on the subject of the Bible, Pusey, also a believer, is not.

One caution should be made. There is always the tendency to adopt language that hints that our own beliefs are the true ones, and abstract words can act as our secret agents—words such as "modern," "scientific," "critical," or "rationalist." A variant of this temptation is to approach figures in the past with the intention of recruiting them as witnesses to our own ultimate concerns. Thus there are great battles over Hobbes's real convictions about religion; given that he was always very cautious

---

[23] Even within the Old Testament, the author of Ecclesiastes, who was writing probably in the second century B.C.E., essentially rejects most of the basic tenets of the Jewish faith. The sudden reversal of the book's argument in the last chapter has the appearance of a later addition.

about his own opinions on the subject, perhaps we should leave him his privacy and judge his opinions on the rational grounds of their coherence and their dependence on others.

Conclusion: An interim working hypothesis for understanding the history of modern exegesis

The emergence of modern biblical studies should not be described in a simplistic fashion either as an analogue of the Whig interpretation of history, that is, an orderly progression from the unenlightened to the enlightened, or as a variant of conspiracy theory as one contemplates a downward spiral as insidious elements within and without the churches chip away at the foundations of the faith. The sorts of questions raised by serious scholars in trying to make sense of the Bible do not always present any neat pattern, and intentions were as varied as the men who had them. What can be said is that various factors set in motion by Renaissance scholars were to have an effect on the history of the discipline, but other considerations, especially the importance of history in human culture and the emergence of science, were to have a decisive effect on what took place.

A note of warning should be sounded at this point. Even if the reconstruction of the history of biblical interpretation offered in this book is accepted, one should be careful of making sweeping judgments about the future of the discipline. It may be that the results so far may be neither complete nor even headed in the right direction. It is also conceivable that biblical studies may have gone as far as they can go, and from now on they will be a matter for erudition rather than discovery. Fairness requires one to admit that we see in part and know in part. As Lawrence P. Berra, the great twentieth-century American philosopher of the paradox remarked, "Predicting is very hard, especially about the future."

Chapter 2

The Renaissance

The basic question of the history of biblical interpretation is, Should we praise or patronize our predecessors? Do we build monuments to their memory or simply drag their dead bodies around the arena? There are, of course, other motives than these for studying the past, such as the simple joy of learning for its own sake, but in the case of the history of exegesis there is much in the subject to be learned for our guidance and our warning. This discipline acts as the ghost at the banquet who rebukes revelers who are insensitive to their crimes, for it is a bad habit of scholars to assume that the latest is the best and what is past is irrelevant. Those who ignore history of any sort easily fall into the assumption that their own opinions are self-authenticating truths, independent of accident and circumstance, and not requiring any measurement against the standards of the past. The history of biblical interpretation is rich in interesting observations that have been spurned or forgotten, to the disadvantage of those responsible and their successors. Santayana did have it right: those who ignore their own history are destined to repeat it.

I. Background

1. *A word of warning about generalizations*

Since no complex human activity occurs in isolation, it is necessary to indicate the climate of opinion in which a scholar worked. However, a word of caution is appropriate. One should always bear in mind that there are dangers in giving objectivity to cultural matters. Thus, while it may be helpful to generalize about the Renaissance idea of the soul for example, the fact remains that ideas are essentially viruses of the mind, a virus being an organism that cannot have life outside another living being.[1] Therefore, while there was a considerable overlap in the idea various people had about the soul in the time of the Renaissance, the idea itself had existence only to the extent that it was held by individual human beings, each of whom gave his or her own emphasis to the doctrine.[2] To ignore this is to commit the common fault of assuming that because you know of somebody who lived in the period of the Renaissance, you then know what he or she must have thought about any given subject.

Let me start from the cultural setting of biblical exegesis in the period I am discussing, say 1450 to 1600. In exegesis at that time, almost all the problems and all the interests of humanity were treated, for out of the Bible was derived the dominant view about humanity and the world it inhabited, including religious truth, ethical standards, political guidance, legal principles, and scientific knowledge. This meant that works about the Bible were sources not only of knowledge about the Bible itself but themselves played a part in the cultural discourse of the day in a way we no longer feel appropriate or even possible. For example, Milton's *Paradise Lost*, the last and greatest of biblical epics, was in a literary tradition which went back several hundred years and which depended as much on the learned biblical commentaries as science fiction movies today depend on our current notions of antimatter, black holes, and DNA. When Addison commented negatively on *Paradise Lost* that Milton had fabricated all sorts of incidents and details that were not to be found in the Bible, it was simply that Addison was not taking into account the long

---

[1] The analogy is borrowed from Richard Dawkins, who described religion as a virus of the mind—in his view a harmful virus. While I do not share his opinions, I think that his analogy is very fruitful for understanding intellectual history, for there is no such thing as a pure idea independent of and unaffected by all who think hold to it.

[2] This is my principal objection to the otherwise fascinating work of William J. Bowsma, *The Waning of the Renaissance* (New Haven: Yale, 2002). Dr. Bowsma tends to talk about Renaissance ideas in an abstract way that obscures the fact that no two people held exactly the same notion, and many people were able to hold essentially self-contradictory notions about the soul, as well as about any of the other major concepts that we are pleased to identify as typically Renaissance.

tradition of creative fiction and biblical commentary that informed Milton's imagination. One example is Milton's description of how Satan, in preparing to tempt Adam and Eve, wriggled his way into a snake's body with great difficulty and disgust. This picture is dependent on an exegetical suggestion by the scholar Johannes C. Drusius.

2. *The Renaissance itself*

The Renaissance, the source of many aspects of the worldwide culture that is engulfing our planet, is not easily handled in a few well-rounded sentences, but let me begin with a small incident in Dante's *Inferno*, namely, Dante's meeting with Ulysses (or Odysseus if you prefer the Greek form of the name).

In Homer, Odysseus, having spent ten years in the siege of Troy, is trying to get home but is impeded in his efforts by angry gods and alluring women. But Dante's Ulysses is in hell because he deliberately chooses to stay away from home. Having reached the Pillars of Hercules, he urges his companions to sail on with these words:

> "So little is the vigil we see remain
> Still for our sense, that you should not choose
> To deny it the experience—behind the sun
> Leading us onward—of the world which has
> No people in it. Consider well your seed:
> You were not born to live as a mere brute does,
> But for the pursuit of knowledge and the good."
> Then all of my companions grew so keen
> To journey, spurred by this little speech I made
> I would have found them difficult to restrain.[3]

In other words, it is more fun to explore than to go home to the wife. This change in Ulysses' character is a key to the Renaissance; it was a time when Europe's interest in discovery exploded in the exploration of this planet. We should not forget how unique this impulse for systematic, universal exploration is to western Europe.

Two observations about discovery are appropriate here. First, it is not enough for someone to have seen a place; this experience must be recorded in a way to make it known to the world in general. Thus, while

---

[3] Dante, *Inferno*, xxvi, ll.109–118 (Pinsky translation).

Columbus was very far from being the first man in America, he did discover it in that he made the existence of America known to more people than those who actually lived there. Second, it is true that often there is a technological component in discovery, for advances in ship design made major European exploration possible in the Renaissance, but ship technology does not of itself necessarily lead to discovery.

The most stunning example of technology that was not linked to the impulse to explore (and exploit) is the history of the Chinese fleet which visited India in the sixteenth century and which may well have gone on to South America. The result of this voyage was not an increase in Chinese curiosity about the rest of the world, but rather the opposite; in fact, the records of the voyage were eventually destroyed, and the building of oceangoing ships was prohibited. This was in spite of the fact that the Chinese junk is a superb design, arguably better even than the Portuguese caravel, and for the record, the Chinese admiral's flagship was ten times the size of Vasco da Gama's.

3. *Humanism*

Exploration was not confined to the physical world but also included the exploration of the inner world of matters such as religion, literature, philosophy, and mathematics. For Montaigne, even the personal inner world of the writer became a legitimate object of curiosity. Renaissance Humanism[4] attempted to rediscover the classical culture of the Graeco-Roman world in a form unalloyed by what it saw as the deformations of the intervening period. This meant assiduous attention to the manuscript tradition, grammar, and the niceties of word usage, as well as the correct interpretation of technical vocabulary. Resources were devoted to this effort; manuscripts were collected, libraries were built to house them, and scholars were encouraged to use the collections. Techniques for assessing the age and integrity of manuscripts were developed and improved texts made available for all of Europe through the printing press.[5] Knowledge of the proper use of language became a social perqui-

---

[4] I am using the word "Humanism" in its original sense of "the study of the Humanities," not as a synonym for atheism, as it tends to function today.

[5] For a compact introduction to the methods, the backgrounds, and the feuds of the Renaissance Humanists, see Anthony Grafton, *Joseph Scaliger: A Study in the History and Methods of Classical Scholarship*, 4 vols. (Oxford: Clarendon, 1983) 1:1–100. Grafton's argument is that it was Angelo Poliziano (1454–1494) rather than Valla who was the central figure in this development.

site. The faint echo of this view is found in the origins of our modern word "glamour," for this was as close as the Scots could get to pronouncing "grammar," a sought-after accomplishment of that time that distinguished one from the unwashed and unlettered masses. (Glamour magazines of today appear to place little emphasis on their philological roots.)

In university circles the fault line lay between the old-fashioned scholastics and the new Humanists, who endorsed the latest studies in documents and languages.[6] As is usually the case in the conflict between older and newer movements in the university, the older group saw the newer one as uninformed and badly trained. Thus it was only to be expected that those of the older persuasion tended to look down on the academic respectability of Erasmus's doctorate. While Humanism took an interest in all the documents alleged or genuine from antiquity, it was the documents of the Bible that attracted much of the interest.

From the point of view of technical biblical studies, the scholastic/ Humanist split was more significant than the slightly later split between Reformers and Roman Catholics. Humanists could be found on both sides of the Reformation divide, and while in theory those on one side disapproved of those on the other, they nonetheless read each others' works with care, attention, and sometimes grudging approval. They in fact had much in common; a curious piece of information often cited is that Erasmus, Calvin, and Ignatius Loyola were all members of the same college at the University of Paris, though not at the same time.[7]

4. *Lorenzo Valla*

Of the new type of scholar who was coming onto the scene, the most interesting from the point of view of biblical interpretation was Lorenzo Valla (1407–1457), who deserves a closer look.[8]

---

[6] See Erika Rummel, *The Humanist-Scholastic Debate in the Reformation* (Cambridge, Mass.: Harvard University Press, 1995); "The Importance of Being Doctor: The Quarrel over Competency Between Humanists and Theologians in the Renaissance," *Catholic Historical Review* (1996) 187–230.

[7] They did agree that the cooking was execrable.

[8] The literature on Valla is very large; useful introductions are: Christopher S. Celenza, "Renaissance Humanism and the New Testament: Lorenzo Valla's annotations to the Vulgate," *Journal of Medieval and Renaissance Studies* 24 (1994) 33–52; Donald R. Kelley, *Foundations of Modern Historical Scholarship* (New York: Columbia University Press, 1970); Lisa Jardine, "Lorenzo Valla: Academic Skepticism and the New Humanist Dialectic," in Myles Burnyeat, ed., *The Skeptical Tradition* (Berkeley: University of California, 1983) 253–86.

In the Middle Ages the attempt of the medieval papacy to exercise both temporal and spiritual power did not receive universal approval, particularly by kings and princes, whose authority was being challenged. One response of the papacy to its critics was to cite as evidence a document that officially sanctioned the claims of the pope to secular power by showing how Constantine, the first Christian Roman emperor, had officially made Pope Sylvester the heir to much of his empire. This document, known as the *Donation of Constantine,* was in fact a shameless forgery; this had been suspected, but it was Lorenzo Valla who provided the most elaborate and convincing proof of the document's inauthenticity. The criteria he worked out were to have application in many other areas, not least of all biblical interpretation.[9]

Valla had several criteria: historical credibility, a reliable historical record of the event, the evidence for the textual transmission of the document, and the inner coherence and historical accuracy within the document.[10] He also added a couple of other considerations that are more about law than documents, namely, that if Pope Sylvester once held title, the subsequent loss of the lands he possessed could not be remedied after such a long time and that the Pope's possession could not have been won through prescription, no matter how long he had held them.

Let us take a look at Valla's arguments and see where we come across things that will crop up in how critics came to look at the Bible.

i. Would an emperor give up his empire? It is not likely, but it was argued that Constantine had been cured of leprosy by the Pope. Valla pointed out that this story looks very much like the biblical account of Elisha and Naaman, the Syrian general, and was probably copied from it.

ii. Had Sylvester been given the empire, why was there no account of the years of his reign? While coins of other emperors abounded, there were no coins to be found of the emperor Sylvester. In fact, there was no physical evidence at all that Sylvester ever reigned as emperor.

---

[9] On the practice and prevalence of forgery in the Middle Ages, see Anthony Grafton, *Forgers and Critics: Creativity and Duplicity in Western Scholarship* (Princeton: Princeton University Press, 1990) 23–35.

[10] Clearly these are also used in the evaluation of secular historical documents as well. Many of the tools of history in general were forged by the biblical scholarship.

iii. The document of the so-called *Donation* was supposed to be included in the collection of legal documents made by Gratian, but it is not found in the oldest manuscripts.[11] Furthermore, where it is found in newer manuscripts, it interrupts the flow of the discourse so abruptly that it is clearly a separate document added later.

iv. Then there is the language of the *Donation*. Valla, the author of the *Elegantiae*, a sort of lexicon of good Latin, had an extensive knowledge of changes in Latin style. He pointed out that the way the text was dated and the anachronistic terms applied to Roman officials showed that this document was the work of an ignorant forger.

There are two points worth making at the end of this discussion. Valla's work was eventually put on the *Index Librorum Prohibitorum* in the sixteenth century for obvious reasons, but the temporal pretensions of the papacy never really came to an end until 1870, when the papal territories were reduced to the city of the Vatican. The second point is that Valla was himself not writing a work in which he discussed matters in a purely rational way; he was mounting an attack on the papacy as it was then. This raises the issue of how free from political or religious controversy we are going to find any work of biblical criticism.

For our purposes, what makes Valla supremely interesting is that he also wrote *Adnotationes* on the New Testament.[12] These were published only after Valla's lifetime by Erasmus in 1507. Valla applied to the New Testament the critical linguistic knowledge he had applied to the *Donation of Constantine*, not to discredit the New Testament as such, but to show that the original Greek did not support some possible interpretations that could be deduced from the Latin of the Vulgate, the translation of the Bible into Latin revised by Jerome in the fifth century C.E. Valla's critical annotations marked a significant departure in the study of the Bible. From that point on, the way was open to a new approach to the Bible as a historical document to be discussed by the methods appropriate to the critical examination of any historical document. Not all the implications of this departure were immediately recognized, but there was no turning back.

[11] Gratian was a twelfth-century monk who collected and arranged in systematic order a vast collection of patristic texts, conciliar decrees, and papal pronouncements. This became the standard reference work for Roman Catholic canon law.

[12] On the difference between commentaries and annotations, see Grafton, *Scaliger*, 1:15–18.

5. *Predecessors to Humanism*

Renaissance scholars had no illusions about beginning from nothing. They had two sources they were immediately aware of for their critical study of the Old Testament. The first source was the writings of the fathers of the church, especially Origen (c. 185–c. 254), Jerome (c. 347–420), and Augustine of Hippo (354–430). Origen was among the most influential, for he had learned Hebrew, and his great collection of texts, the Hexapla, was a source of reference for centuries. Jerome was perhaps the only Western father of the church who had a firsthand acquaintance with the Hebrew language and thus was able to investigate problems of text and translation. Furthermore, Jerome had a sense of Latin style that was to impress the aesthetic sense of Humanists in search of the recovery of Latin at its best. Among the Eastern fathers, influential but often misleading was Jerome's contemporary Augustine, whose voluminous writings included whole treatises on the Bible and incidental remarks on the subject of the Bible in other works. Unfortunately, Augustine's knowledge of biblical languages was poor and, as Richard Simon observed, had Augustine known Hebrew, he would not have had to take back so many of his opinions so often. However, in the Western church it was often Augustine's position that was selected as the one to beat.

For the Old Testament, even more important than the fathers was the heritage from medieval rabbinic Judaism. During the Middle Ages, in order to read the Bible in the original, Christian scholars had begun to learn Hebrew from the Jews, sometimes with curious results, such as the creation of the divine name Jehovah, but this linguistic knowledge also opened to Christians the Jewish *peschat* tradition, which consisted in a careful examination of difficult and contested texts. The influence of Abraham Ibn Ezra (c. 1092–1167), David (c. 1160–1235) and Joseph (c. 1105–1170) Kimchi, and Moses Maimonides (c. 1135–1204), and others on the whole course of the Renaissance has still not been given enough weight.[13] One should also mention the great Jewish scholar Elias Levita (1469–1549), who played such a prominent role in training Christian scholars and who was actually offered a chair in Hebrew at Paris. In the effort to comprehend the Old Testament, then, it was often the rabbis who were the dialogue partners of the new Christian Humanists.

---

[13] Abraham Ibn Ezra should be distinguished from Moses Ibn Ezra, a later scholar. The name "Kimchi" can also be spelled "Kimḥi." David Kimchi is sometimes referred to by the acronym Radak; Joseph Kimchi as Rikam; and Maimonides as Rambam.

There was in fact a third influence at work among the Humanists, though they may have been less aware of or even less generous about it. This was a different idea of knowledge that had originated in the Middle Ages. The change that had taken place was that there was a shift in emphasis from the pursuit of wisdom to the acquiring of information. It is interesting that it was only during the Middle Ages that the Bible was divided up into numbered chapters, which made finding information much easier. At the same time, indexes to books became more common, a development that also made information more available. It also became usual to include references to other texts in the margins or at the bottom of the page. During the Renaissance this process was extended, so that the Bible and other standard works were divided into smaller units such as verses for even faster reference.

There was also another factor connected with the foregoing that is easier to describe than to account for. While many of the debates in the Renaissance were the repetition or development of arguments that had taken place within the classical world of Graeco-Roman civilization, there was a new emphasis on the completeness of all knowledge. Classical cartographers had drawn maps of the world, and various classical scholars had interpretations of the order of historical events, but now there was a wish for "the complete picture" that would take into account all the facts. World globes were built to get all the geographical landmasses set out in their relation to one another; chronology tried to link the different eras of all of human history and to specify the exact duration of kings and empires and their relationships to one another. I do not think it is an accident that the professions of theologian and geographer overlapped; in particular, Gerardus Mercator, whose projection of the world map did so much for the relative size of Greenland, also wrote a harmony of the Gospels that was an analogous undertaking to get all the data into a format where its shape could easily be perceived.[14] Harmonies of the Gospels multiplied as scholars struggled to provide a coherent picture of the different accounts about Jesus, and eventually in the eighteenth century this led to the source criticism of Griesbach. The drive to unify knowledge was to have its effect on the study of the Bible.

---

[14] Tatian (d. c. 185) was the first to write such a Gospel harmony in his *Diatessaron* ("through four [Gospels]").

6. *How "critical" were the Renaissance scholars?*

It is fairly common in discussions of the history of biblical interpretation to make a distinction between the "precritical" and the "critical" eras, even to suggesting that somehow we should go back to the Edenic innocence of a precritical era. In accord with this distinction, the question then arises as to who was the "father" of biblical criticism, and to judge from the number of candidates put forward, the infant discipline never lacked for parental care. It is worth pointing out that one person named in the paternity suit, Richard Simon, discussed below in chapter four (pp. 154–60), did not see himself as the originator of something new, but rather as one more practitioner of a discipline that went back for centuries. In this he was quite correct, for both Christians and Jews had been struggling with critical problems in the Bible for a long time.

The misleading implication of the word "precritical" suggests that Jewish and Christian scholars before the Enlightenment looked at biblical texts with a bland naiveté that masked all the problems that any first-year undergraduate notices with ease. At the end of this chapter some examples of the critical acuity of the Renaissance scholars will be discussed, and whatever one may think of their conclusions, it will be abundantly clear that they were acutely aware of problems, and they were honest enough to admit when they were stumped.

All this was part of a distinct discipline among Renaissance biblical scholars known as *critica sacra*. This was the recognition, the discussion, and sometimes even the resolution of problems of translation, text, or coherence in the biblical manuscripts. They were quite aware that they had had predecessors in the church fathers, not to mention the medieval Jewish scholars, and on the whole they cannot be faulted for failure of nerve in admitting what they noticed was hard to explain in the text.

This is not to say that the Renaissance scholars saw the Bible the same way most critical scholars do today; the whole point of this book is to set out what happened and what is different. Since their time we have learned a great deal about physical science, languages, ethnology, and above all history, to name a few major areas of knowledge, but the critical faculties of our intellectual forebears were as acute as our own. If "precritical" is carefully defined in terms of the sort of authority Renaissance scholars attributed to the Bible and of a particular notion of its inspiration that made it different in kind from other books, the distinction would be appropriate. Still, as a matter of fairness and accuracy, it is reasonable to expect a present-day historian to define such terms precisely if he or she decides to use them.

There are those who suggest that somehow we should return to the precritical era, however defined. It is hard to avoid the conclusion that this approach suggests that we should pretend that we do not know about the rich discoveries and discussions that have gone on in biblical studies for the past five hundred years and assumes that we can interpret the Bible as if we were sixteenth-century Reformers or Counter-Reformers. I am not sure this is really a viable option.

7. *The political situation*

The progress of biblical interpretation was not necessarily on everyone's mind in the time of the Renaissance, but certain political factors did play a part in how the discipline developed or, more precisely, why it attracted political interference. State and religion were understood to be an organic whole, and loyalty to one's religion tended to be seen in much the same way as loyalty to the state. Thus it was considered a reasonable settlement in some of the petty states of the Holy Roman Empire that the religion of the sovereign would be the religion of the state, and those who wished to follow another type of faith could move to an area where such a faith was espoused by the local ruler.

An integral part of statecraft involved religious regulation and support. Religious toleration, to the extent that it did exist, was much more a product of circumstance than actual policy, for rare were those who advocated toleration for its own sake. This situation was to persist on into the eighteenth century, when the German philosopher Christian Wolff was given forty-eight hours to leave Halle on pain of death. This meant that biblical scholars and those tempted to comment on the Bible might well face occupational hazards not known today. Things were at their worst in territories where the Roman Catholic Inquisition held sway; but Protestants, too, could invoke the heavy hand of the law.

The Bible inevitably had a political significance both as a guide to government policy and as one of the institutions of government that had to be protected. Blasphemy against the Bible or heretical interpretations of its contents were treated as criminal acts to be punished in singularly barbarous ways. Obviously, there were variations and fluctuations in the arrangements between church and state, but aspects of their legally defined relationship continued a long time.[15] Straying from locally established norms of religious belief could get you into serious trouble, for while in the sixteenth century someone like Sebastian Castellio[16] could appeal for a more tolerant approach to dissent, only in the seventeenth century did toleration become a matter for general discussion.

On the positive side, state resources could be used to support editions or translations of the Bible. Cardinal Francisco Ximenez de Cisneros (1436–1517), as part of his secular political power, brought about the production of the Complutensian Polyglot (to be discussed below, pp. 50–51). James I of England considered it a matter of national importance to convene the Hampton Court Conference, where a generally acceptable English version of the Bible was planned. This came to be referred to in later times as the King James Version or Authorized Version, or sometimes in a less accurate variant, the Saint James Version, an emendation that gives a little too much credit to the king for the quality of his life.

At the same time the Bible could be authoritative in politics in a manner hard to imagine today. In seventeenth-century England it provided the imagery for radical political movements, such as the Fifth Monarchy Men, whose name went back to the four kingdoms in Daniel 2. The inspiration provided by the apocalyptic parts of the Bible was important even for government itself; the Commonwealth parliament paid for Joseph Mede's *Clavis Apocalypticum*[17] to be translated into English, and permission for Jews to return to England was based on an interpretation of the Bible that linked the reintegration of the Jews into Western society with the onset of the kingdom of God.

8. *Technical innovation: printing*

The place of technology in general in the reshaping of western European thought and practice is too complex to cover here, but the invention of printing with movable type in the fifteenth century demands special

---

[15] Remnants of this system still remain in some parts of Europe, where nominally even now the Vatican is a separate state. Clergy have still not disappeared as state-salaried employees in various European countries, something that existed, surprisingly enough, even in some Iron Curtain countries at the height of Communist power in Eastern Europe.

[16] See Sebastian Castellio, *Concerning Heretics*, trans. Ronald Bainton (New York: Octagon, 1965). Bainton has some very useful notes and comments. "Castellio" can also be spelled "Castalio," "Châtillon," and "Chateillon."

[17] Mede was Milton's tutor at Cambridge.

mention. The Bible was indeed one of the earliest and most profitable books published by Gutenberg, but printing enabled not only the production of learned editions of the biblical text or commentaries on its content, but it also widened the extent of debate about religious matters. In Victor Hugo's *Hunchback of Notre Dame*, Frollo, comparing a printing press with his old cathedral, says: *"Ceci tuera cela"*—"This will kill that." Frollo was perhaps too confident about the effect of the spread of information and ideas, but it is true that printing did mean that ideas that were either negative about the Bible or socially unacceptable in other respects could be easily disseminated and find their way into the general cultural debate.

There is also a nontechnical, social factor that was responsible for the format the printed book was to take. In the later medieval period[18] a shift in the idea of knowledge led to knowledge being perceived as a storehouse of information where inventory control was important. This led to texts that were easier to access and refer to, such as the insertion of chapter divisions within the Bible, attributed to Stephen Langton in the thirteenth century. The logical continuation of this process was the further subdivision of the Bible into verses in the sixteenth century by the French printer Robert Estienne (Stephanus). Indexes and concordances to books were also part of this new vision of how knowledge should be made available.

The social effect of the invention of printing has been discussed in many books, and the Renaissance scholar at work in his study with a revolving set of shelves on his desk full of the books he wishes to compare is a well-known figure. Only two points need to be added to this picture. The first is the limited number of books that were available in comparison with our own times. It is a modern cliché that knowledge doubles every ten years or so, by which is really meant that the number of books and articles published is such that no one can be expected to have read even all the basic books in his or her chosen subject of specialization.[19] By contrast, up to the early part of the seventeenth century, it would have

[18] See Paul Saenger, "Silent Reading: Its impact on late medieval script and society," *Viator* 13 (1982) 367–414.

[19] No one appears to have made any calculations about the amount of knowledge that is forgotten every ten years, although the astonishing ignorance about the great works of the past that is to be found among university graduates should be reason for concern by the calculators of knowledge, if they themselves were only to discover how important the past can be.

been feasible for an educated person to have read most of the serious books ever published; Burton's lament in the *Anatomy of Melancholy* about the number of books being published is a sign of the end of an era. Second, the importance of the Bible as a central icon of Renaissance culture meant that biblical commentaries were among the best printed and the finest works of the day, and they remain a source of aesthetic pleasure for those who have to read them.

9. *The Medieval University*

Another factor in the development of biblical interpretation was the creation of the university in the Middle Ages. There had always been schools or places for educating people at a higher level, but the medieval university developed an institutional identity which meant that it did not depend upon a single teacher or founder and which gave it the flexibility to change and adapt to new movements of thought. Furthermore, a university could hope for benefactions from both the state and charitably minded individuals who chose to endow colleges and libraries.

As centers of learning, universities could preserve and develop links to Europe's cultural past—classical, Christian, and Jewish. Much of what was achieved in biblical interpretation in the modern period was made possible by the impulse provided by scholarly traditions from these earlier sources. There was one intellectual pursuit that the medieval university passed on to Western culture, namely, discussion and argument as means of arriving at the truth. One should not assume that therefore censorship was unknown, but the cherishing of debate did distinguish the West from traditions of learning where there was no place for challenging accepted lore. Some Renaissance biblical commentaries preserved the old question-and-answer format, which has an inconvenient side: what happens when the question raised is more impressive than the answer offered?

10. *European culture—the Republic of Letters*

Renaissance Europe continued on in the medieval tradition of a common culture among the educated of Europe, and in particular the use of Latin as the language of scholarly communication, at least among the Christian majority. This was called the Republic of Letters, a transnational and later transconfessional abstraction that defined a sentiment of a common interest among the learned. While national and linguistic sentiments were far from unknown, there was a set of common cultural assumptions that made communication easier. Unlike Greek, Latin was not seen as a dead language, but rather as an unbroken, ongoing tradition that made scholarly discussion possible and pleasant. That is why translations of the Bible into Latin were made by Roman Catholics and by Protestants up to the end of the seventeenth century. Similarly, academic lectures in the university were in Latin, and this meant that students who attended foreign universities were able to do so without the attendant difficulties of becoming fluent in a different language.[20]

While one should not be too idealistic about the Republic of Letters in Renaissance times, nonetheless the loss of an ideal and the means of expressing it can be regretted. The gradual changeover to vernacular languages in universities in the eighteenth century was a factor in the emergence of nationalism at the outset of the nineteenth century, with its attendant emphasis on language as the essence of national identity. This confusion of language and national identity has on the whole had a destructive effect in many parts of the world politically; even when the learned meet, the simple choice of language of discourse is often literally a political statement.

11. *The emergence of unbelief* [21]

During the Renaissance established religious beliefs (and this includes Judaism as well as Christianity) were challenged by alternative systems such as atheism, revived pagan systems, such as that of Pyrrho,[22] or esoteric doctrines of one sort or another. Obviously, this new strain of thought created anxieties that often led to physical cruelty. The unconscionable savagery of Vanini's[23] execution is an example of how

---

[20] Even in the nineteenth century, dissertations were still written in Latin in some countries.

[21] The word "skepticism" is often used instead of "unbelief," but I consider this misleading, for skepticism may simply describe a critical approach to discussion rather than a naive one. In theory there is a form of skepticism whose adherents believe that nothing is sure, but in practice it tends to be rare.

[22] Pyrrho of Elis (365–275 B.C.E.) is credited with being the founder of the Skeptics. He wrote nothing himself, but his teachings were recorded by Sextus Empiricus (c. 190 C.E.) in his *Pyrrhonean Sketches,* an edition of which was printed in the sixteenth century.

[23] Lucilio Vanini (1585–1619) was burned at the stake after his tongue had been torn out.

anxieties produced reactions that were as out of keeping with Christian beliefs in practice as Vanini's intellectual objections were in theory.

That this combative form of unbelief was well-known in the sixteenth century is clear from the fourth session of the Council of Trent (1546):

> Besides the above, wishing to repress that temerity, by which the words and sentences of sacred Scripture are turned and twisted to all sorts of profane uses, to wit, to things scurrilous, fabulous, vain, to flatteries, detractions, superstitions, impious and diabolical incantations, sorceries, and defamatory libels; (the Synod) commands and enjoins, for the doing away with this kind of irreverence and contempt, and that no one may hence forth dare in any way to apply the words of sacred Scripture to these and such like purposes; that all men of this description, profaners and violators of the word of God, be by the bishops restrained by the penalties of law, and others of their own appointment.[24]

The question for the history of biblical interpretation is to what extent this current of unbelief contributed to the study of the Bible before the seventeenth century. What is possible, though rather hard to prove, is that by challenging the sacred status of the Bible, open unbelief in Italy and France made a reasoned defense of Scripture necessary, just as the teachings of the Manicheans forced Augustine to defend the Old Testament. Certainly it is recorded of Faustus Socinus that his main regret at the loss of his manuscripts when a mob destroyed his library was the destruction of his work against atheism. That elsewhere he worked out a defense of the reliability of the New Testament documents suggests that much of his argument would have centered around a discussion of the Bible.

12. *The Reformation and the Counter-Reformation*

It has already been mentioned above that it is possible that the Reformation and the Counter-Reformation had in the long run less effect on the development of biblical studies than is often assumed. That is to say that while undoubtedly these developments in Europe shaped the directions scholars were to take, the actual impulse to understand and clarify knowledge of the Bible as the most important foundational document of

---

[24] Session IV, as in J. Waterworth, trans., *The Canons and Decrees of the Sacred and Oecumenical Council of Trent* (London: Burns and Oates, n.d.) 20–21.

the Christian faith had already begun with the Humanist interest in the recovery of all ancient documents. It was not the Protestants as such who started scholarly investigation, nor were the Protestants necessarily the best scholars. For two centuries Roman Catholic scholars ranked among the best; in fact, Milton complained that in England many Protestants preferred them to the Protestant commentators.[25] It was not until the late seventeenth century that obscurantist, authoritarian ecclesiastical politicians such as Bossuet succeeded in discouraging serious scholarship, and Richard Simon had no worthy successors.

Nonetheless, the upheavals of the Reformation left marks on biblical interpretation.

i. PROTESTANTISM

Luther's challenge to the authority of the papacy and the practice of the church was linked to the Humanist appeal to the authority of the Bible cleansed from later corruptions. One can, however, find a certain difference of emphasis between the younger and the later Luther. The younger Luther appealed to the standard of Paul's doctrine of justification by faith, more particularly justification by faith alone. On this basis Luther experimented with judging which books belonged in the canon of Scripture. His earlier prefaces to his translation of the Bible cast doubt on the value of some of the New Testament epistles, especially James. His later prefaces show a certain amount of backtracking on his part, for he seems to accept as canonical the traditional New Testament collection. Nonetheless, his first standard of canonicity remained to haunt his successors, and in the eighteenth century those who objected to the hardened orthodoxy of the day appealed to Luther against Lutheranism.

Furthermore, the Protestant appeal to the Bible raised in an acute form the problem of how one interprets an ancient book for a contemporary situation. The temptation is to short-circuit the process and deny the gap. Thus the University of Leiden in its origins did not permit lectures on dogmatic theology, but only lectures on biblical interpretation. The theory was that the New Testament is by itself immediately relevant; what actually happened was that essentially dogmatic lectures were given under the guise of exegesis. Similarly, in England Richard

---

[25] Arnold Williams, *The Common Expositor: An Account of the Commentaries on Genesis 1527–1633* (Chapel Hill: The University of North Carolina Press, 1948) 33. Williams' work represents very fine scholarship and should be consulted by those interested in Renaissance biblical interpretation and its influence.

Hooker (1554–1600) pointed out that the Puritan appeal to the Bible alone as the standard for how the church was to be governed relied on a selective use of the Bible. The boundaries between the philological and historical meaning of Scripture and its wider implications have always been problematic for churches, and it was arguably not until the eighteenth century that the real extent of the difficulty was recognized.

While the history of dogma lies outside our concern here, it is usual in church history to see Protestantism after Luther and Calvin being drawn more and more into a mass of doctrinal statements and positions that left less and less room for the experience of active faith faced with the Bible. The emergence of Pietism and its British offshoot Methodism is then interpreted as a return to the Bible, with its emphasis on personal religious experience and its transforming effect on the lives of the faithful. If this picture is granted, it must be added that neither a hardened orthodoxy nor a personally centered sense of certainty of themselves were conducive to progress in understanding the Bible in a scholarly way.

Furthermore, the standard of *sola scriptura* was not without its inconvenient side, for more radical reformers could produce their own interpretations of Scripture, most notably the Socinians, who argued that the traditional church doctrine of the incarnation was not to be found in Scripture itself and therefore should not be required of Christians. While the Socinians were reviled for their christological views, they had a greater influence on biblical interpretation than they are sometimes given credit for.

ii. ROMAN CATHOLICISM

On the other side of the debate, the Council of Trent in its fourth session felt the need to fence itself off from the Protestant appeal to the original documents of the Bible. The text of its decision in English translation reads as follows:

DECREE CONCERNING THE EDITION,
AND THE USE, OF THE SACRED BOOKS

Moreover, the same sacred and holy Synod,—considering that no small utility may accrue to the Church of God, if it be made known which out of all the Latin editions, now in circulation, of the sacred books, is to be held as authentic,—ordains and declares, that the said old and Vulgate edition, which, by the lengthened usage of so many years, has been approved of in the Church, be, in public lectures, disputations, sermons and expositions, held as authentic; and that no one is to dare, or presume to reject it under any pretext whatever.

Furthermore, in order to restrain petulant spirits, It decrees, that no one, relying on his own skill, shall,—in matters of faith, and of morals pertaining to the edification of Christian doctrine,—wresting the sacred Scriptures to his own senses, presume to interpret the said sacred Scripture contrary to that sense which holy mother Church,— whose it is to judge of the true sense and interpretation of the holy Scriptures,—hath held and doth hold; or even contrary to the unanimous consent of the Fathers; even though such interpretations were never (intended) to be at any time published. Contraveners shall be made known by their Ordinaries, and be punished with the penalties by law established.[26]

Two consequences followed. First, since the interpretation of the Bible could only be settled by an appeal to the views of the church fathers, Roman Catholic apologists had a vested interest in showing how difficult, not to say ambiguous, biblical texts were. Second, since the texts of the Bible in the original languages were not clear, it was the text of the Vulgate where clarity was to be found; this meant that the authoritative, canonical Bible was the Vulgate translation. This left open the obvious problem that the text of the Vulgate also had its own textual problems, and this situation was not settled until the end of the sixteenth century, when the edition approved by Pope Clement VIII was adopted as the standard edition.[27]

In the interests of fairness, it should be added that in its fifth session the Council of Trent also specified that lectureships in biblical matters should be reinstated or introduced in order that "the heavenly treasure of the sacred books, which the Holy Ghost has with the greatest liberality delivered unto men, may not lie neglected. . . ."[28]

iii. ON THE DIFFERENCES BETWEEN THE PROTESTANTS AND ROMAN CATHOLICS IN THE MATTER OF EXEGESIS

It is, of course, the prerogative of historians to be wise after the fact. In this tradition one can say that each side left itself with insoluble

---

[26] Waterworth, *Canons*, 19–20.

[27] This edition was the successor to various earlier attempts. It was Pope Sixtus V who was responsible for getting this edition under way, and its first form was published in 1590. However, this edition was not satisfactory, and a corrected version was produced under the direction of Cardinal Bellarmine and published in 1592 in the pontificate of Clement VIII.

[28] Waterworth, *Canons*, 24.

problems. Protestants were pushed toward an ever-increasing emphasis on the direct and perfect divine inspiration of an infallible text. This doctrine of literal inspiration was to be a thorn in the side of responsible Protestant scholars and an unnecessary source of conflict with scientific discoveries, which continues today. Roman Catholics, for their part, were faced with the dilemma of choosing between the impossible problem of making the fathers of the church agree among themselves about biblical interpretation or with accepting an increasing emphasis on the authority of the papacy, which resulted in the disastrous decrees of the Biblical Commission set up in 1902, whose decisions about historical matters, such as the historicity of Adam and Eve, are best left to the obscurity in which they now languish. On both sides of the Reformation divide, each party locked itself into a position that rendered it less able to deal with the problems that were going to be presented as the modern world developed.

On the matter of freedom of inquiry, the differences between Protestants and Roman Catholics was one of degree rather than of kind. Michael Servetus was sent to the stake in 1553 for his interpretation of the New Testament, and when Castellio wrote a book to persuade Calvin that burning people was wrong, he too would have gotten into trouble had not he died before Calvin's agents could get the legal machinery of the city of Basel into action.

This sort of state interference in Protestant circles continued into the eighteenth century. However, the Roman Catholic emphasis on the duty of obedience to the church tended to produce heavier forms of censorship. Richard Simon, himself a Roman Catholic, commented on the effect of the Spanish Inquisition, namely, that it wished to close the mouth of everyone in the country. The heavy weight of a repressive and fairly efficient inquisitorial machinery was a severe hindrance to many excellent Roman Catholic scholars, and ultimately it was to vitiate a great tradition. Furthermore, censorship provides far too much leeway for human frailty, for it opens the way to actions motivated by concerns other than the defense of the truth. In this respect, Richard Simon records the bon mot of Bernardin Ochin on the subject of Ambrose Catherin's furious criticism of Cardinal Cajetan's orthodoxy. Ochin felt that the real reason for Catherin's attack was simply his ambition to be made a bishop, a conviction he summed up in the biting *"Di Doctore ti facesite Cortigiano,"* "You have gone from doctor to courtier." Simon, despite his reservations about Ochin as a person, certainly took this comment as something that might have been true.

II. What Was Done in Biblical Interpretation?

1. *Text and languages*

I once had, very briefly, a potential graduate student who felt that the knowledge of the biblical languages was no longer necessary for research because modern translations of the Bible are more accurate than the originals. His outlook was not very different from that of the traditional scholastic theologians, who felt that the Humanists' interest in the original text and languages of the Bible was unnecessary because the Latin Vulgate was much clearer and even divinely inspired.

Valla's successors nonetheless persisted. What made their task easier was the increased flow of manuscripts from the East, beginning with the Council of Florence in the fifteenth century and added to by scholars escaping from Constantinople after the Turkish conquest, who brought their manuscript collections with them. These manuscripts stimulated an interest not only in biblical languages properly speaking but also in other Eastern languages, such as Coptic, Syriac, Armenian, and Arabic.[29]

In the sixteenth century various European nations, in particular the English, the French, and the Dutch, were granted trading privileges by the Ottoman Empire. They were able to set up trading sites, called factories, in which the employees enjoyed a considerable independence from local control. From these vantage points antiquarians or their agents were able to purchase biblical and other ancient manuscripts. Furthermore, some truly adventurous spirits, such as Guillaume Postel (1510?–1581), managed to travel widely and even to reside for considerable periods in the Ottoman domains, picking up a colloquial knowledge of the languages, along with interesting manuscripts.

It was Postel who got wind of a Pentateuch tradition preserved in the Samaritan community. The possibility of a Hebrew textual tradition that might go behind the standardized Masoretic Text aroused the interest of scholars.[30] Postel was able to acquire a couple of Samaritan manuscripts, but not the Pentateuch he had hoped for. However, the manuscripts were written in the archaic Hebrew script in use before the adoption of

---

[29] Alistair Hamilton has a useful, illustrated article on the subject "Eastern Churches and Western Scholarship," in Anthony Grafton, ed., *Rome Reborn: The Vatican Library and Renaissance Culture* (Washington: Library of Congress; New Haven: Yale University Press in association with the Biblioteca Apostolica Vaticana, Vatican City, 1993) 225–49.

[30] See p. 5 in chapter 1 on "text" for details.

the Aramaic square script sometime after the Babylonian Exile, and the awareness of this script was to give rise to various speculations for the next hundred years. It was not until roughly forty years after Postel's death that copies of the Samaritan Pentateuch reached Europe.

2. *Hebrew*

Among Christians, the knowledge of Hebrew had never been extraordinary; of the church fathers, only Origen and Jerome had any competence in the area, and it was only from the twelfth century on that Christians tried to learn Hebrew from Jewish rabbis. In their enthusiasm they inadvertently created a new name for God, namely, "Jehovah." This hitherto nonexistent name emerged when Christian beginners in Hebrew failed to take account of the fact that Jews were forbidden to pronounce the proper name of God, which is written in four consonants in the Hebrew Bible, JHWH—the Tetragrammaton. Instead, when they came across the name JHWH in reading the Bible aloud, Jews said "Adonai," which means "my Lord"; as a result, when vowel pointing was added to the Hebrew text at a later date, the points for "Adonai" were put under the name JHWH. The result is unpronounceable if one tries to read it literally, but that did not discourage well-meaning if misguided students who produced the name "Jehovah" in their efforts. It was to take the Christian scholars a couple of centuries before they were willing to admit their mistake, during which time their new construct established itself in English usage as well as in other European languages.[31]

The care with which Renaissance scholars at their best could devote to questions of philology is shown by two extended treatments of the divine names *elohim* and JHWH by Drusius, which take up over ninety folio pages.[32] He worked carefully through different problems and included notes to back up his assertions in an essay that is still worth reading today as a model of scholarship, if not as an up-to-date treatment.

---

[31] For example, the work with a preface by (H)Adrian Reland, *Decas exercitationum philologicarum de vera pronunciatione nominis JEHOVA* (Utrecht: 1707), reviewed in the *Supplement du Journal des Savans*, du dernier Juin 1709, 241–53. The reviewer lists five scholars who argued against the historicity of the pronunciation "Jehovah: "Drusius, Amana, Cappel, Buxtorf, and Alting, and three who took the other side: Fuller, Gataker, and Leuschen.

[32] These were reprinted in the *Critici Sacri*, a work discussed below, p. 134.

In the Middle Ages, Nicholas de Lyra (c. 1270–1349), in his *Postilla litteralis,* a commentary on both Testaments, had shown a knowledge of Hebrew. However, Christian knowledge of Hebrew was destined to improve considerably when Elias Levita (1469–1549) taught various Christian scholars, among whom were a Roman Catholic cardinal (Egidio de Viterbo) and a Protestant Reformer (Paul Fagius). Elias Levita also published a Hebrew grammar and dictionary, which were used as textbooks throughout Europe. From this point on, many Christian Humanists became reasonably competent in the language and were able to access not only the biblical texts but also rabbinical commentaries in the original. Within a hundred years Johann Buxtorff (Senior) was sufficiently fluent in the language that members of the Jewish community in Basel consulted him on matters of interpretation.

The other biblical language in the Old Testament is Aramaic, but once one knows Hebrew well, one can almost read one's way into Aramaic. This meant that Renaissance biblical commentators were able not only to read the Aramaic sections of the Old Testament, but they could also take into account the Targums (more properly "Targumim"), which were early translations of the Hebrew Bible into Aramaic. While these translations were not, strictly speaking, literal, they could be of use in dealing with a Hebrew text that had become corrupt.

Printing in Hebrew characters developed very early, and in fact the first Hebrew Bible in the original languages was printed at Soncino in 1488, before the New Testament in Greek. Other traditional Jewish literature was also printed, and of these works Bomberg's edition of the Talmud was an extraordinary achievement, comparable to Gutenberg's Latin Bible.[33]

3. *Other languages*

It is not just the biblical languages properly speaking that are needed for textual criticism. At various times in antiquity, both Old and New Testament books were translated into other languages. These translations or versions were made from ancient manuscripts which no longer

---

[33] Daniel Bomberg (1483–1553) created layouts for the rabbinic Bible, the Babylonian Talmud, and Maimonides' *Mishneh Torah* ("Code of the Torah"), which are basic for later editions up to the present day. For a useful bibliography see "Bomberg, Daniel" in *Dictionary of Biblical Interpretation,* 2 vols., ed. John H. Hayes (Nashville: Abingdon, 1999) 1:134.

exist but which might have contained important readings of texts, or the versions might be witnesses to the extent of the textual tradition in a given area. By translating back the text of these versions into the original language, one can make a reasonable guess of what might have been written in the manuscripts from which they were derived. That is why a modern edition of a biblical text will note the readings of the versions as well as of the manuscripts in the biblical languages. During the sixteenth century, knowledge of Armenian, Coptic, Syriac, and Arabic was either recovered or improved.

4. Greek

Knowledge of Greek had never really disappeared completely in western Europe after the collapse of the western part of the Roman Empire. One area where it survived was Ireland, which has led to the Irish claim that they saved Western civilization. Greek manuscripts of the New Testament were preserved and copied, and while they were not very numerous, Erasmus was able to find at least a handful when he was preparing his edition of the New Testament. Furthermore, the Renaissance Humanists recovered a sense of Greek as a language and the difference between good Greek and bad Greek. The famous printer Aldus Manutius had a rule in his household that everyone should speak Greek—classical Greek, that is.

Two printed editions of the Bible were to play a part in the publication of the Bible in the languages required for scholarly study. The first was the Complutensian Polyglot, and the second was Erasmus's edition of the New Testament. The Complutensian Polyglot, named for the Spanish city of Alcalá de Henares, whose Latin name was Complutum,[34] was produced at the instigation of Cardinal Francisco Ximenez de Cisneros (1436–1517).[35] Ximenez led a very eventful life, which at one time included imprisonment and, at another, regency over the whole of Spain; but in the midst of his concerns he maintained a love of scholarship,

---

[34] The Renaissance Universidad Complutense was founded by Cardinal Ximenez in 1486. The Complutense was subsequently moved to and is still located in Madrid.

[35] There is some variation in the spelling of his name. Spanish sources refer to him as Cisneros, Francisco Jíímenez de; English sources tend to prefer Ximenez de Cisneros, Cardinal Francisco. Those searching for information should look under Cisneros, Ximenez, and Jíímenez, allowing for minor differences in how Ximenez and Jíímenez are rendered.

especially biblical scholarship. He conceived the plan of an edition of the complete Bible, which would include the texts of the Bible printed out in their original languages. His polyglot (literally "many languages") edition, edited at the outset by Elio Antonio de Nebrija (1441–1522) with the collaboration of other Spanish Humanists, was to be the first in a series of four outstanding polyglots. The others were the *Biblia Regia* or Antwerp Polyglot (1572) of Arias Montanus; the Paris Polyglot (1645) of Guy Le Jay; and the Oxford Polyglot (1657) of Brian Walton. One can see the development of the scholarly knowledge of ancient languages as each polyglot made improvements on its predecessors.

The Complutensian Polyglot consisted of the text of the Old Testament in Hebrew, Aramaic, and Greek, as well as the text of the New Testament in Greek and Latin. Its method of publication robbed it of the distinction of being the first published edition of the Greek New Testament. This curious fate came about because, although the printing began in 1514, the whole work was not completed until 1520 and was not actually published, that is to say, released for sale, until 1521. In the meantime Erasmus had already published his edition of the New Testament, which included the Greek text in 1517.

The Complutensian edition of the Bible was a good start to what was going to be a long process of experiment and refinement. In particular, its Greek text was certainly as good as that of Erasmus, as is shown by the number of corrections Erasmus made to his text in later editions based on the Complutensian edition. The drawback to large polyglots was that they were very expensive folios, whereas Erasmus's editions were in a smaller format and therefore less expensive for the average student or scholar and represented less of a financial risk to a printer contemplating a new edition.

Erasmus's edition was originally made up of the Latin text, probably from an edition of the Vulgate, along with his annotations, and the Greek text.[36] As the work underwent new editions, not only did Erasmus make improvements to the Greek text, but he also worked on the Latin translation, so by the time of later editions he had in fact produced a new Latin translation of the New Testament independent of the Vulgate. Erasmus claimed that he was not trying to replace the Vulgate but only

[36] See H. J. de Jonge, "Novum Testamentum a Nobis Versum: The Essence of Erasmus's Edition of the New Testament," *Journal of Theological Studies* (n.s. 35, 1984) 394–413. The University of Toronto's *Complete Works of Erasmus* has a section devoted to Erasmus's writings on the Bible, a wealth of research on the subject.

to provide a translation that would make it easier for scholars to understand the problems presented by any translation from the Greek into the Latin.[37]

It is interesting to see how Erasmus soon ran into problems that were to bedevil almost all later editors of the biblical texts. The fact is that people are naturally conservative about books they consider holy. This was not a new situation, for Jerome had run into this problem when in his new Latin translation he contrived to locate Jonah sitting under an ivy plant rather than a gourd while Jonah was sulking outside the gates of Nineveh.[38] This caused rioting in the streets.

Erasmus, too, encountered trouble when his translation became too accurate. One example is from the letter to the Romans. The Western doctrine of original sin, which states that Adam's sin was imputed to every descendant, started life as a translation mistake of Augustine. In Romans 5:12 there is a passage that reads, "Wherefore, as by one man sin entered into the world, and death by sin; and so death passed upon all men, for that all have sinned" (KJV). In the Greek the words translated "for that" (or "because" in some translations) are *eph hō*, which is a well-known expression whose strictly philological meaning is "in whom," but whose idiomatic meaning in Greek is "because," "so that," and similar words to indicate cause and effect. Duffers ignorant of the finer points of language are tempted to translate this as "in whom," in much the same way as they are tempted to translate *coup de grâce* as "lawn-mower." Now Augustine, for all his good points, was a duffer at Greek, and he did translate this expression literally and wound up with the observation "in *whom* [Adam] all humans sinned." This led Augustine on to the idea that somehow all humans were physically present in Adam at the time of the Fall, and therefore all humans are guilty of his sin. Erasmus did not deny the doctrine, but he objected to the translation. Not everyone was pleased.[39]

---

[37] On the subject of Jerome and the Vulgate, see H.F.D. Sparks, "Jerome as Biblical Scholar," *The Cambridge History of the Bible*, 3 vols. (Cambridge: Cambridge University Press, 1970) 1:510–541.

[38] Jonah 4:6. Augustine's account of the matter is found is his Letter 71 to Jerome. The reaction of the parishioners was caused, not by pure antiquarianism, but because of their affection for the paintings of Christian artists, who had linked the story of Jonah to the popular pagan image of the bower of gourds. Turning the gourd into ivy would be like saying the Christmas tree should be replaced by a dandelion.

[39] It is interesting that the translators of the King James Version did not make this mistake.

One of Erasmus's decisions about the text of the New Testament was to be fought over for several centuries, namely, a reading in 1 John 5:7, which included the italicized words in the following quotation: "For there are three that bear record *in heaven, the Father, the Word, and the Holy Ghost: and these three are one. And these are the three that bear witness in earth,* the Spirit and the Water and the Blood: and these three agree in one" (KJV). The italicized words were obviously useful in proving the scriptural basis for the doctrine of the Trinity; the only problem is that they are not found in most Greek manuscripts, including the ones Erasmus had to work with. This verse became known as the *Comma Johanneum.*[40] Erasmus did not include it in his earlier editions, for which he was criticized by the Englishman Edward Lee and Diego López Zúñiga (Stunica), one of the editors of the Complutensian Polyglot. Eventually, on the basis of one Greek manuscript that actually had the text, Erasmus restored the passage, not without reservations.[41] After several centuries of debate, this decision was to be overturned.

Erasmus's text of the Greek New Testament was the parent of a long line of editions.[42] After his death his already amended text was revised by various hands, including the French printer Robert Estienne (Stephanus) and the Swiss reformer Theodore de Bèze (Beza), who had access to one of the great uncial codices, which he eventually gave to the University of Cambridge. Others added to the improvements, and it was this text that was used as the basis for the King James Version of the Bible of 1611. In 1633 the Dutch Elzevir brothers produced their second edition of this text, in which the introduction referred to it as the *Textus Receptus.* Who had done the receiving was not quite clear, but the name itself gave a patina of holiness that made further textual emendations essentially impossible. Even today there are those who defend the *Textus Receptus* in the face of all reasonable evidence.[43] This is only one example of how irrationality is the occupational hazard of those who take the Bible seriously rather than learnedly.

[40] The spelling varies: "Comma ianneum," "Comma Joanneum," etc.

[41] See Bruce M. Metzger, *The Text of the New Testament,* 3rd ed. (New York: Oxford, 1992) 291, where he revises his acceptance (on p. 101) of the suggestion that a forged text was used to force Erasmus's hand.

[42] See Metzger, ibid., 103–06.

[43] For a discussion of this matter, see Gordon D. Fee, "A Critique of W. N. Pickerings' *The Identity of the New Testament Text,*" *Westminster Theological Journal* 41, no. 2 (Spring 1979) 397–423.

Arias Montanus (1527–1598), the editor of the Antwerp Polyglot, set a moral example to the scholarly world by turning down a bishopric but then accepting the directorship of a library, showing that knowledge is preferable to power for a wise man. His polyglot, published in eight volumes in 1572, was meant to be a corrected edition of the Complutensian Polyglot. It represented improvements over the Complutensian in that it contained a Targum for most of the books of the Old Testament and the Syriac for the New Testament (printed in both Hebrew and Syriac characters). To do this, he drew on various scholars, including the singularly learned and singularly eccentric Guillaume Postel, possibly the best Semitic linguist of his day.[44] However, even Arias Montanus could not escape the criticism of the enthusiasts for a narrow interpretation of the Tridentine emphasis on the authority of the Latin and for paying too much attention to non-Latin texts, thereby diminishing the authority of the Vulgate.

5. *Some Renaissance exegesis*[45]

The easiest way to get a taste of how Renaissance commentators dealt with the Bible is to take a few crucial passages from various parts of both Testaments and see how they dealt with them. The scholars we shall be discussing are:

Sebastian Munster (Munsterus; 1488–1552), astronomer, mathematician, geographer, and Hebraist. In 1529 he went over to the Reformation and taught at the University of Basel for the rest of his life.

Paul Fagius (1504–1549), a good Hebraist who was a student and a personal friend of Elias Levita. In 1549 he left his teaching position at Strasbourg to become professor of Hebrew at Cambridge, where he died in the same year as a result of either the cooking or the heating.

---

[44] Postel is not mentioned in the text.

[45] Most of the material cited can be found in the Genesis commentary in volume 1 of Pearson's *Critici Sacri: Sive Doctissimorum in Ss. Biblia Annotationes & Tractus* (London: Jacob Flesher, 1660). For Pererius, see his great Genesis commentary, *Commentariorum et Disputationum in Genesim* (Louvain: 1594–1602). Those who wish to check these passages will find the *Critica Sacra* in microform in the University Microform Collection of Early English Books Published (1641–1700) ##894–897. Pererius's commentary is available from IDC Publishers in Leiden; however, the IDC labeling gives the date 1601 and the place of publication as Cologne, although the microfilm itself gives the place and date as above.

Thomas Cajetan (Jacob de Vio; 1469–1534), a Roman Catholic cardinal and the great opponent of Luther.

Johannes Drusius (van den Driessche; 1550–1616), graduate of Cambridge and eventually professor in Leiden and Franeker.

Benedictus Pererius (Pereira; 1535–1610), a distinguished Jesuit theologian who taught Galileo and was renowned in England for his treatise against astrology.

i. THE OLD TESTAMENT

a. *The Pentateuch:* (considered the most important part of the Old Testament because it was the most ancient and was written by Moses, the antitype of Christ).

A source of more than one dilemma was the different names used for God in the Pentateuch. In the first chapter of Genesis and up to Genesis 2:4a, God is referred to as "elohim"and by no other name. An initial problem is that this word is plural in form; in fact, when reference is made elsewhere in the Old Testament to a god or the gods of other nations, the same plural form is used. There is a singular form meaning "a god" in Hebrew, but it is rare. Then in the second half of Genesis 2:4 the proper name for God in the Old Testament, namely, the Tetragrammaton JHWH, is introduced. There are some places in Genesis where "elohim" appears to be the preferred word for "God"; in others JHWH or both names are used. There are two places in the book of Exodus (3:13-15 and 6:3) where the name JHWH is revealed to Moses as something hitherto unknown. How, then, do the Renaissance commentators deal with what can only be called a confused situation?

Both Munster and Fagius were well aware that "elohim" is a plural and that in Genesis 1, while the verbs used with elohim often take the third person singular ("God created," etc.), they can also be in the first person plural ("let us make"). Munster went with the traditional Christian interpretation that the Trinity[46] is hinted at here, though he was aware of the Jewish explanation that this plural is simply what is usually referred to as a plural of majesty. Fagius mentioned these alternatives, as well as Ibn Ezra's suggestion that in cases where the first person plural is

---

[46]Curiously enough, Calvin is very suspicious of the Trinitarian explanation of the plural of the divine name. While not an outstandingly original exegete, Calvin knew his subject well and showed excellent, if not infallible, judgment in the decisions he made.

used, this simply marks where heavenly angels are summoned to help with the creation.

On the sudden appearance of the name JHWH in Genesis 2, Munster commented that the Jews had various suggestions; the one he gave is that once God's creation was perfected, it was appropriate to use God's perfect name. Fagius's answer, where again he cited Jewish opinion, was that here the emphasis is on God's mighty power. He supported this from Kabbala, where God's mercy is shown by the Tetragrammaton.

But the problem of JHWH occurs again in Genesis 4:26, where it is stated that "at that time people began to invoke the name JHWH." This does not fit well with the two passages in Exodus where the name is revealed for the first time. One can sympathize with Drusius, who admitted, "This passage has always tormented me and always will."[47] He was aware that some scholars had tried to link this with the "sons of God" in Genesis 6:1, but he pointed out that while this is indeed said in 6:1, where is it said they are sons of Jahweh? Pererius noted that Genesis 4:26 is hard to reconcile with the revelations in Exodus, because Exodus 6 states bluntly that patriarchs had not known God by that name, and he therefore rejected Cajetan's argument that Enoch was the first to call on God by special name JHWH. Therefore, said Pererius, what is more likely here is that Enoch was described as the first to invoke the name of the Lord as an indirect way of showing that he was above all his ancestors not only in his duties toward God but in promoting piety among others. Pererius also mentioned another possibility offered by the Targum: "Men at that time began to profane the name of JHWH." This comes from the ambiguity in the Hebrew verb *huchal*, which could mean "profane" as well as "begin," so this interpretation was not an arbitrary device.

By modern standards these men were not doing too badly, and to be honest, they had pointed out most of the difficulties any competent modern commentary tries to explain. What of course is the problem here and where we today are a little further on is that Drusius and the others assumed that the Pentateuch is the work of one author—Moses—and therefore everything should be expected to fit together.

In contrast, we have learned to allow for a combination of different sources that may have had no original connection. The Renaissance critics set out honestly what they noticed in the text and pointed out alternatives, although they had a tendency to make direct links between the Hebrew Bible and specifically Christian doctrines.

---

[47] "Diu me torsit hic locus, & etiam *torquet*."

Obviously, those critics were nowhere near more recent ideas of different documents or strands of tradition behind the two stories, but they were facing up to problems in a critical, that is to say, a rational comparative way, and were not necessarily opting for traditional Christian explanations. What one can say of their work is that thanks to both their patristic and rabbinical predecessors, these men had the Pentateuchal machinery in pieces on the floor. They were not so successful in putting it back together again, for the context in which they were working—the Pentateuch as divinely inspired—did not provide a sufficiently ample workspace for their theories. In fact, their situation was not altogether different from that of scientists today who discover anomalies that do not fit their theories; this does not always lead to the revision of theory, for approximation is more widely practiced in science than is usually known to the general public.

However, in the case of the Mosaic authorship of the Pentateuch, some Renaissance scholars got further than is generally recognized, and they began, albeit tentatively, to experiment with the idea that the Pentateuch is not a unified book, but rather a combination of different books.

The evidence that they noticed was that, first, there is the reference to the Book of the Wars of the Lord in Numbers 21:14. Does this suggest that there were written sources that existed before the time of Moses? Second, there is the recurring reference in the Pentateuch to "this day" in a manner that suggests that the time of the writing is much later than that of the events it describes.[48] Since these events were more or less in the time of Moses, might "this day" be an indication of a later scribe adding to the Pentateuch? The question then was, In what period of Israel's history was this addition made? Third, there is the account of Moses' death and burial in Deut 34:6, which is a little hard to explain as an account he wrote himself; and even if one opts for the long shot and invokes an inspiration, the question still remains: When it is said "no one knows his burial place to this day," which is the day that is meant?

Abraham Ibn Ezra had, in fact, danced around this problem very gingerly, but it was the Renaissance scholars who faced up to its implications. Andreas Carlstadt von Bodenstein, Luther's talented but mercurial friend, had a brief reference to the situation in his small work on the canon,[49] but it was the Flemish Semitic philologist Andreas Masius who

---

[48] Gen 19:37, 38; 22:14; 35:20; Deut 10:8.

[49] Andres Bodensten von Carolstadt, *De canonicis scripturis libellus* (Wittenberg: apud Johannem Vkidi Montanum, 1520). German translation: *Welche Bücher Biblisch seint* (Wittemberg, 1520).

faced the issue head-on and suggested that others had added to the Pentateuch after the time of Moses:

> My own position as I consider it, is this, Ezra, either by himself or together with others equal to him, men of distinguished piety and learning, inspired by the heavenly spirit, compiled not only this book of Joshua but also the books of Judges, Kings, and other books which we read among what are called the holy books. He compiled them from various records preserved among the church of God and edited them and placed them in the same order that already existed before. Moreover, plausible conjectures can easily be made that likewise the very work of Moses, which they call the Pentateuch, was edited a long time after Moses' death. It was, so to speak, stuffed and rendered altogether more intelligible by occasional insertions here and there of phrases and sentences.[50]

In the article on Pentateuchal criticism in the *Dictionary of Biblical Interpretation*, it is suggested that Richard Simon was the first to pay attention to Masius's arguments. This is demonstrably not the case. In the introduction to his work on Genesis, Pererius not only discussed the problems Masius raised, but he copied Masius word-for-word without acknowledging him.[51] Pererius was very well-known,[52] and it was through him that most people probably became familiar with the problems of the composition of the Pentateuch. This, I suspect, is true in the case of Hobbes, for 90 percent of what Hobbes had to say about the Old Testament could be easily derived from Pererius's introduction, which of course was based on Masius's work.

The Renaissance commentators even got close to one matter that we think of as quintessentially modern, namely, the relationship between the Bible and the scientific description of our world. That the world is a globe and not a flat disk was a well-known and often accepted idea in

---

[50] Preface to his commentary on Joshua (text in *Critici Sacri*, 1:xlv). Translation mine, with thanks to the Rev. T.C.G. Thornton for his help.

[51] Lapide also discusses these questions in language reminiscent of Masius, but he may well have derived them from Pererius, whom he had read and to whom he refers, but not in this context. See *Commentaria in scripturam sacram*, Tome I: *In Pentateuchum Moisis* (Paris: Vives, 1859) 28.

[52] Thomas Browne refers to him in *Pseudodoxia* Epidemica, VII:vi.

medieval times.[53] That the earth moves around the sun was a somewhat different matter, but as will be discussed in the next chapter (pp. 81–83), this was not necessarily a shock for the public. But Pererius, who incidentally condemned astrology as a vulgar superstition, set out as a principle of interpretation that no interpretation of Scripture should contract what was known from philosophy, which, of course, at that time could mean science as it then existed. Now Galileo and Bacon had similar views about the relation of the Bible to scientific truth, namely, that the Bible is not necessarily absolutely accurate in every detail; whether Pererius, who lectured to Galileo and whose work was known to Bacon, is the link I cannot prove, but the possibility is there.

b. *The prophets*

In the case of the prophets, the Renaissance commentators I have examined showed no interest in how, where, or by whom the books were gathered together. A good example is Hector Pintus, a very competent Portuguese scholar (1528–1584?). He was aware of the historical context where it is unmistakable, such as the case in Isaiah 7, where Judah is about to be invaded by Israel and Syria, and Isaiah goes to see Ahaz, the king of Judah, accompanied by his son Shear Jashub. Pintus was also aware of the symbolic significance of the name "Shear Jashub," which means "a remnant shall return," but he assumed that this was a prophecy of a remnant of the Jews being converted to Christianity.[54] One wonders why, in the midst of an invasion, this message about events at least eight centuries away would have been of much comfort to the king. But the New Testament was never far from Pintus's attention, for he argued that the "Lord" seen in Isaiah's vision (Isaiah 6) was Jesus; he proved this by referring to John 12:45. To be fair to Pintus, Isaiah 6 is quoted in that chapter of John, but his argument here only begs the question.[55]

Pintus's approach was typical of the lack of historical perspective in the sixteenth century. For example, it is quite clear that Isaiah 40–48 reflects the experience of the Jewish exiles in Babylon in the sixth century

---

[53] See Allison Peden, "The Medieval Antipodes," *History Today* (1995) 27–33. Sir Thomas Browne was very scornful of those who believed such nonsense, and he was not alone in seeing this sort of belief as the sign of a backward and ignorant person.

[54] Hector Pintus, *In Esaiam Prophetam commentaria* (Lyon: apud Theobaldum Paganum, 1567) 87.

[55] It is a curiosity of Pintus's commentary that he does not give verse references, only chapter references. It would be interesting to know if this was simply his style or whether he was unwilling or unable to use what was, after all, a Protestant invention.

B.C.E.[56] The fact that the sixth-century Persian king Cyrus is mentioned in Isaiah 45:1 makes this assumption very evident. However, for Munster and others, Isaiah (and there is no hint of Deutero-Isaiah here) is talking about the messianic era and/or the experience of the Christian church. Munster, in fact, dismissed as silly the Jewish argument that chapter 40 refers to deliverance from Babylon and return to Israel. It is the Gospel writers who teach the real sense, and Vatablus and Forerius agreed. Even the mention of Cyrus by name later on, although a real prophecy of Isaiah about Cyrus, is only an analogy used by the prophet to illustrate his real meaning.[57]

Pintus remarked about Daniel, whom he saw as both a prophet and a historical person, that Daniel prophesied the destruction of the Babylonians, the deliverance of Hebrews from Babylonian servitude, the four kingdoms—Babylonian, Persian, Greek, and Roman—and deadly wars between Assyrians and Egyptians. But Daniel's principal intention was to predict the mystery of the redemption of humanity through Christ our God. He tells of Christ's coming into the world, of his priesthood and eternal reign, and of his painful death; of abrogation of the old law, of preaching the gospel in the whole world, of the obstinacy and perfidy of the Jews, of the Antichrist, of return of the dead to life, of final and supreme judgment.

The Christian commentators were aware of possible criticisms of what they felt was important, such as the rabbinic awareness of the possibility that in Isaiah 7:14 the word translated "virgin" was much more probably "young woman." They also were aware of Porphyry's attack on the historicity of Daniel, but they treated these unwelcome suggestions in much the same way that modern scientists who are attached to a pet theory ignore anomalous results that crop up in a small number of experiments.

It is interesting to ask why something that appears to be self-explanatory to us completely escaped the notice of Renaissance commentators. The reason is that we all have some sort of scheme of interpretation through which we see texts. In scholarship we moderns assume that the prophet was talking primarily to his own contemporaries and that unless he had

---

[56] Most modern scholars would agree with the theory that at least these chapters in the latter part of the book of Isaiah were written by an anonymous prophet of the sixth century. This theory was first put forward in Christian scholarship in the eighteenth century.

[57] This is the interpretation behind the opening aria of Handel's *Messiah*.

at least this audience in mind, no one would have bothered to preserve what he might have said or written. The Renaissance commentator, on the other hand, assumed that the reason for a prophet's preservation was that he had something to say that would turn out to be important for the New Testament or for a later period in the church's history; otherwise the Holy Spirit would neither have inspired the prophet nor preserved his oracles.

c. *Wisdom literature*

Renaissance commentators faced certain problems with the Old Testament books traditionally attributed to Solomon. They were tempted by the rabbinic suggestion to see the Song of Songs as a book written by Solomon as a young man with the usual hormonal surges, Proverbs as the product of his middle age and his hard-won knowledge of human nature, and Ecclesiastes as his reflections as an old man weary of the ways of the world. The Song of Songs presented the most obvious challenges, for while the goal was to present it as an allegory of Christ and the church, commonsense interpretation found the subject elsewhere. Calvin hounded Castellion out of Geneva because Castellion did not find the allegorical meaning convincing. Munster, having a good knowledge of the rabbinical arguments, argued that while the Song appears to be a duet between Solomon and the daughter of the king of Egypt intermixed with two choirs—one of young men, the other of virgins—it can be turned without too many distortions into an account of the love of God and his people.

ii. The New Testament[58]

In the case of the New Testament, Christian Renaissance Humanists found themselves on slightly more familiar ground. Whereas the relatively new study of Hebrew and Aramaic had something of the exotic in

---

[58] There does not appear to be a full-length treatment of the history of the interpretation of the Bible in the sixteenth century later than Richard Simon's *Histoire critique des principaux commentateurs du Nouveau Testament depuis le commencement du Christianisme jusques à nôtre tems* [sic] (Rotterdam: 1693; repr. Frankfurt: Minerva, 1969), and Gottlob Wilhelm Meyer, *Geschichte der Schrifterklärung*, 5 vols. (Göttingen: J. F. Römer, 1802–1809). However, see Jerry H. Bentley, *Humanists and Holy Writ: New Testament Scholarship in the Renaissance* (Princeton: Princeton University Press, 1983). The lack of attention paid generally to Roman Catholic commentators is unfortunate. (L. Diestel, *Geschichte Des Alten Testaments in Der Christlichen Kirche*, 5 vols. [Jena, 1869] does, of course, cover the Old Testament scholars.)

it, with Greek they were more at home. But improvement in their knowledge of the grammar and style of classical Greek led to a certain embarrassment when they confronted the New Testament. Apart from Luke
and the author of the letter to the Hebrews, New Testament Greek style
was to try the patience of the new specialists who had learned to recognize good Greek when they saw it.

a. *Dogmatic considerations*

Once the Reformation had caused a split within the Western church,
certain texts with possible dogmatic implications tended to be treated
extensively on a frequent basis. One dogma often sought in New Testament texts was the Calvinist doctrine of double predestination, especially as set out at the Synod of Dort and summed up, not altogether
unfairly, by Burns's Holy Willy:

> O Thou, wha in the Heavens dost dwell,
> Wha, as it pleases best Thysel',
> Sends ane to heaven and ten to hell,
> A' for thy glory
> And no for ony guid or ill
> They've done afore Thee!

In fact, this subject was not confined to Calvinists or even Protestants;
it was one of the fascinations of the era, thanks to the influence of
St. Augustine, who had adherents on both sides of the Reformation
divide.[59] Milton poked fun at this obsession by describing how some of
the fallen angels in hell form a theological society:

> Others apart sat on a hill retired,
> In thoughts more elevate, and reasoned high
> Of providence, foreknowledge, will and fate,
> Fixed fate, free will, foreknowledge absolute;
> And found no end, in wand'ring mazes lost.[60]

A lot of effort in New Testament commentaries was devoted to texts
such as Romans 9, where Paul does seem to imply that the Jews at least
had been predestined to deny their messiah, a situation complicated by

---

[59] To what extent this doctrine in its strongest form was identical with the views of
Augustine and/or Calvin is not part of the argument of this book.

[60] *Paradise Lost*, Bk. 2, ll. 557–561.

the fact that in the next two chapters of the same epistle Paul might well be offering two other, themselves mutually contradictory, explanations of the same situation. Few of these doctrinal discussions produced useful biblical exegesis, and one can sympathize with Richard Simon's praise for the Protestant scholar John Cameron that he was "not of the number of those melancholy Calvinists who have gone on and on about the questions of predestination, grace, and free will."[61]

One of the more interesting exceptions to this practice was Joachim Camerarius, who devoted his commentary on the Bible to questions of the exact meaning of the text rather than its theological (mis)applications. Simon's opinion of Camerarius was that he would have done better had he known Hebrew and the pagan classical authors better, but that he deserved credit for avoiding contentious issues and instead acting on his claim to be a grammarian by profession. Camerarius also received credit for admitting that he did not know everything and that Scripture is not always completely clear and self-evident. It is interesting that when the eighteenth-century scholar Johann Semler was looking for a counterweight to publish with his edition of Lodewick Meyer's treatise on how philosophy would be sufficient to settle the problems of exegesis, he chose Camerarius's *De forma orationis scriptorum evangelicorum, et aliis quibusdam consideratione non indignis.*[62]

b. *The Gospels*

The basic problem with the interpretation of the Gospels is that there are four of them, and they do not always agree. If one insists that they are infallibly inspired, one is hard pressed to explain the disagreements among them. On the other hand, if you hold that the Gospels are not infallibly inspired, how can you sort out what is historical and what is not? This does not mean they are without value, but what sort of value can you expect and how do you find it?

Examples of text-critical difficulties in Gospel interpretation are the authenticity of some passages not found in all manuscripts, such as the "longer" ending of Mark's Gospel and the story of the woman taken in

---

[61] "Quoi que Cameron ne soit pas du nombre de ces Calvinistes melancoliques, qui ont outré les matieres de la prédestination, de la grace & du libre arbiter. . . ." *Histoire critique . . . Nouveau Testament,* 782. He does not, however, exempt Cameron from all prejudice in exegesis.

[62] J. S. Semler, ed., *De forma orationis scriptorum evangelicorum, et aliis quibusdam consideratione non indignis* (Halle: 1776).

adultery in John's Gospel, or the Lukan narrative of the Last Supper, where there appear to be two cups. Examples of differences between the Gospels are the genealogy of Jesus as found in Matthew and Luke and the problem of the dating of the crucifixion, where the Synoptics disagree with John.

The most extensive early evidence about the writing of the Gospels is the fragment of Papias that was included in chapter 39 of Eusebius's *Ecclesiastical History.* Since this was the text that Renaissance scholars had to begin with, it is worth looking at the sections dealing with the authorship of the Gospels (Eusebius is talking of Papias in the third person):

> It is worth while observing here that the name John is twice enumerated by him [i.e., Papias]. The first one he mentions in connection with Peter and James and Matthew and the rest of the apostles, clearly meaning the evangelist; but the other John he mentions after an interval, and places him among others outside of the number of the apostles, putting Aristion before him, and he distinctly calls him a presbyter. This shows that the statement of those is true, who say that there were two persons in Asia that bore the same name, and that there were two tombs in Ephesus, each of which, even to the present day, is called John's. It is important to notice this. For it is probable that it was the second, if one is not willing to admit that it was the first that saw the Revelation, which is ascribed by name to John. . . .
>
> Papias gives also in his own work other accounts of the words of the Lord on the authority of Aristion who was mentioned above, and traditions as handed down by the presbyter John; to which we refer those who are fond of learning. But now we must add to the words of his which we have already quoted the tradition which he gives in regard to Mark, the author of the Gospel. This also the presbyter said: "Mark having become the interpreter of Peter, wrote down accurately, though not in order, whatsoever he remembered of the things said or done by Christ. For he neither heard the Lord nor followed him, but afterward, as I said, he followed Peter, who adapted his teaching to the needs of his hearers, but with no intention of giving a connected account of the Lord's discourses, so that Mark committed no error while he thus wrote some things as he remembered them. For he was careful of one thing, not to omit any of the things which he had heard, and not to state any of them falsely." These things are related by Papias concerning Mark. But concerning Matthew he writes as follows: "So then Matthew wrote the oracles in the Hebrew language, and every one interpreted them as he was

able." And the same writer uses testimonies from the first Epistle of John and from that of Peter likewise. And he relates another story of a woman, who was accused of many sins before the Lord, which is contained in the Gospel according to the Hebrews. These things we have thought it necessary to observe in addition to what has been already stated.[63]

This fragment left a series of conundrums in its wake from Eusebius's time on. In the Renaissance it distracted attention from careful comparison of the Gospels by raising the issue of whether Matthew actually wrote in Hebrew and distracted scholars from the place of Mark in the composition of the Gospels. It was not until the eighteenth century that scholars were able to make an end-run around Papias.

The types of difficulties Renaissance critics met in the Gospels are shown in the perplexities of Josephus Justus Scaliger (1540–1609), generally admitted by his contemporaries to be the greatest scholar of the period.[64] As the foremost chronologist of his day, Scaliger had to deal with the different orders of events in the Gospels. His solution was to see John as the only evangelist who paid attention to the details of chronology and who assumed a ministry of three years for Jesus, since John records four Passovers (2:13; 5:1; 6:4; 11:55). However, Scaliger compared the Gospel accounts with the dates of Tiberius and concluded that if Jesus' baptism occurred in the fifteenth year of Tiberius (Luke 3:1), the crucifixion could only have taken place in the nineteenth year of Tiberius, when the first day of the Passover fell on a Saturday (John 19:14). Scaliger suggested that the missing fourth year was to be located between chapters 5 and 6 of John and that here was the location of the material recorded in chapters 4 to 14 in Matthew.

Scaliger is significant in that he was too honest an exegete to ignore the discrepancies between the Gospels, such as the different genealogies in Matthew and Luke or serious mistakes in historical data, such as the name of Herodias's husband. Yet he clearly assumed that the Gospels must have been free of error at the outset and that problems could be attributed to scribal errors or to deliberate insertions of incorrect material by monks trying to improve on a story.

---

[63] This translation is drawn from *The Post-Nicene Fathers*. This is not the place to discuss the Papias fragments in themselves, but the translation here is adequate to show the background of Renaissance discussions.

[64] For this discussion I am completely dependent on H. J. de Jonge, "Joseph Scaliger's Historical Criticism of the New Testament," *Novum Testamentum*, 38 (1996) 176–193.

What is interesting in Scaliger's approach is that he was using non-biblical sources such as Josephus to check and correct biblical data; it was not to be assumed automatically that in the case of a discrepancy the Bible was necessarily correct. Scaliger's thin edge of a wedge into biblical inerrancy was not something he cared to make publicly known, and there is at least a report that before his death he burned a work called *De insolubilibus Scripturae,* in which he discussed difficulties in the Bible that he could not resolve.

It is worth noting that among Arminians in the seventeenth century, there was a more relaxed attitude about possible errors in the Bible than among Calvinists. Scaliger's pupil Grotius was an Arminian and through him runs a line to Le Clerc and to Wettstein where one can see openings to a position that does not depend on absolute, utter, and uncompromised verbal inerrancy in the Scriptures. Perhaps even the authors of the Bible were not always correct. The solution proposed by Scaliger, namely, that the Gospels were originally problem-free but were then corrupted by poor transmission, was a useful but temporary bridge to a very different point of view.

There was also a wider implication to Scaliger's chronological studies. The centrality of the Bible as the reference point of European culture was a given for most Europeans in 1500. However, given the European desire for a system of knowledge that would include everything, the challenges to the accuracy of one of its foundation documents was eventually to lead to a shift in the perception about where certainty was to be found. While there was not an immediate crisis, the worrisome returns to the question that took place throughout the seventeenth century show an uneasiness about the centrality of biblical information about the history of the whole world. It is quite clear what the implications of such a shift would mean, as was demonstrated on a small scale in the eighteenth century and on a larger one in the nineteenth.

c. *A case study in New Testament interpretation:*
The Epistle to the Hebrews

In order to understand the impassable gulf that separates modern biblical exegesis from its predecessors, it may help to examine a dispute between Erasmus and Jacques Lefèvre (Faber Stapulensis, 1455–1536) over a passage in the Epistle to the Hebrews.

The Epistle to the Hebrews treats the Old Testament as if it were an undifferentiated whole where any useful phrase can be yanked out of its context to serve as a proof text. Thus Hebrews 2:6ff. quotes from Psalm 8:4-5:

> What is man that thou art mindful of him? Or the son of man, that thou visitest him? Thou madest him a little lower than the angels; that thou crownedst him with glory and honour, and didst set him over the works of thy hands [KJV].[65]

This psalm, which we today would consider a reflection on the human condition, was appropriated by the Epistle to the Hebrews as a christological prophecy, a move motivated by the phrase "son of man," which to a New Testament writer would recall a name used for Jesus in the Gospels.

The dispute between Erasmus and Lefèvre was caused by a textual divergence between the Masoretic Hebrew text and the Septuagint. Both Erasmus and Lefèvre agreed that this verse refers to Christ, not to mankind in general, as it did in the original psalm.[66] The difference between these two Renaissance scholars was that whereas Lefèvre felt that the passage in Hebrews should be interpreted according to the Hebrew of the Old Testament, namely, "Thou hast made him a little lower than elohim,"[67] which Lefèvre took to mean "God," Erasmus preferred the Septuagint Greek translation of the Hebrew, which read "Thou hast made him a little lower than the angels." As is the case in so many controversies, including those up to the present day, the personal element played a large part and led to a temporary estrangement between the two men, who had been good friends up to that point.

The extent of Erasmus's annoyance is shown by the fact that he gave seventy-two reasons why his interpretation was to be preferred; what is

---

[65] That other than philological considerations still skew biblical interpretation is shown by the NRSV's translation of the term "son of man" by "mortals" not only in Psalm 8 but also in Hebrews 2:6. This, of course, has nothing to do with accurate translation and everything to do with a dogmatically charged environment where "man" is now a three-letter word. The problem is that Hebrews' connection of Psalm 8 with Jesus, whether appropriate or not, is obscured, and this means that the translation is defective.

[66] This is also how the epistle interprets the verse.

[67] "Elohim" is a Hebrew word that could mean "God," "gods," "supernatural beings," or occasionally even the king of Israel (Ps 45:6). Actually the Septuagint translation of "angels" is not a bad attempt to convey the idea of heavenly beings in distinction to God properly speaking.

interesting is that most of them were not strictly speaking philological or critical, but rather doctrinal—which translation fitted in with a proper understanding of the two natures in Christ? The same can be said of Lefèvre's reasons for his point of view.[68] Here, then, is one area where we see the Renaissance interpreters unable to separate exegesis from dogmatics, or more properly, the original sense of a text from later theological developments. The question became "Whose Christology is faulty?" rather than "What is the textual evidence?"

For modern biblical interpretation, there is a strong sense that one can make a neat distinction between text criticism, philology, grammar, and exegesis. This means that one distinguishes between two different sorts of disciplines. The first one is made up of considerations that depend on objective elements, such as what is written in a manuscript, what a word means in various contexts, and how the syntax of a language determines the meaning of a text. The other sort of discipline is the more creative practice of theology proper, in which further implications of the text are worked out on the basis of the results of the relatively objective discussions. In fact, things are not necessarily that simple, but the principle remains: it is not permissible to declare a passage such as the *Comma Johanneum* a genuine part of the first Epistle of John simply because it is such a good proof text for the Trinity. Text-critical reasons have to be argued first. Now in fact, the objectivity of textual criticism and the other first type of disciplines is not nearly as objective as it first appears, but the principle remains: a word actually written in a text trumps a felt need for its existence in dogmatic theology. This distinction was not necessarily axiomatic for Renaissance scholars, and certainly Erasmus and Lefèvre did not hesitate to suggest that the other was weak in doctrine rather than in text criticism.[69]

---

[68] See the discussion of this debate in Helmut Feld, "Der Humanisten-Streit um Hebräer 2,7 (Psalm 8,6)," *Archiv fur Reformationsgeschichte* 61 (1970) 5–35.

[69] Ironically enough, in the matter of another text, namely, Romans 5:12, discussed above, Erasmus was criticized for rejecting the Augustinian translation, and when other interpreters followed his example, they were liable to be accused of Pelagianism. Similarly, certain critical conclusions were denied on ecclesiastical grounds. Cardinal Cajetan, who had played a large role in the attempt to combat Luther, came to the conclusion that the authoritative status of the Epistle to the Hebrews could be challenged on the grounds that it was not written by St. Paul. Happily for Cajetan, he wrote before the Council of Trent; had he lived longer and written after the Council, he would have been required to say something else that presumably he would not have really believed.

There is another detail of Renaissance interpretation of the Epistle to the Hebrews that is worth commenting upon. Hebrews 8:1-7 makes a clear contrast between the earthly tabernacle to be found in Judaism and the heavenly, eternal one associated with the equally eternal priesthood of Jesus. Our immediate reaction to this sort of imagery is to detect "Platonism," and Philo of Alexandria is the prime suspect.[70] Knowing that most Renaissance interpreters had read Philo as a matter of course, we turn to see what Erasmus made of the possible Platonism of the Epistle to the Hebrews. The fact is that he says nothing about this. Furthermore, while I have not been able to consult every commentary, even seventeenth-century commentators, such as Guilielmus Estius, Louis Cappel and his brother Jacobus, Cornelius à Lapide, and others, did not comment on what is to us a striking Platonic echo in Hebrews.

This is interesting in itself, but perhaps even more significant is the one possible exception we might have expected, namely, Grotius.[71] Grotius, who had what might be called an obsession with seeing parallels between the Bible and classical secular literature, indeed noticed the resemblance between Hebrews and Philo here, but he did not even suggest that Hebrews might have got its imagery from some form of Platonic philosophy.[72] In fact, it was not until 1750 that Johann Benedikt Carpzov (IV, 1720–1803) first argued that Hebrews was influenced by Philonic Platonism.[73] I suggest that the difference between the Renaissance scholars and an eighteenth-century exegete like Carpzov was not a

---

[70] To be fair, not all commentators agree that it is a question of Platonism here; for example, F. F. Bruce, *The Epistle to the Hebrews* (Grand Rapids, Mich.: Wm. B. Eerdmans, 1964). Nonetheless, Bruce has to take the suggestion sufficiently seriously to explain why a purely Old Testament background is sufficient to explain the allusion. Whether the Platonic imagery in the Epistle to the Hebrews was inspired by Philo of Alexandria can be disputed, but even if it does not, a Platonic tinge to the language can still be admitted. See Ronald Williamson, *Philo and the Epistle to the Hebrews* (Leiden: Brill, 1970).

[71] Grotius is obviously out of the time frame of this chapter, but he was in many ways the last of the Renaissance writers.

[72] Grotius comments twice on the resemblance to Philo. On verse 2 he says, "Philo de Mundi creatione Coelum vocat hieron katharōtaton." On verse 5 he says: "Exemplum illud in monte Mosi monstratum erat spirituale; corporeum, ejus figura. At illud spirituale significavit rem multo magis spiritualem: & mons, Coelum supremum. Hunc sensum esse loci istius in Exodo mysticum videre & veteres Hebraei." Citations from two works of Philo (*Critici Sacri*, IV, col. 1412).

[73] Joh. Bened. Carpzovius, *Sacrae exercitationes in S. Pauli Epistolam ad Hebraeos ex Philone Alexandrino* (Helmstadt: Weygand, 1750).

moment's inattention on the part of the former, but a new way of seeing the importance of history for the development of ideas on the part of the latter. This will be discussed further in chapter 4 (see pp. 127–29).

iv. THE SOCINIAN APPROACH

There was one group that was inching its way to seeing a more human component in the composition of the Bible. These were the Socinians or Anti-Trinitarians. The name "Socinian" comes from the Italian family name Sozzini of Lelio (1525–1562) and Faustus (1539–1604) Sozzini.[74] The Sozzinis were not the founders of the movement, but Faustus became sufficiently known that his name was given to the movement. Ultimately the Socinians were the spiritual ancestors of the Unitarians, but a certain amount of development in the movement has to be allowed for in history. In fact, the early Socinians were as "conservative" about the Bible as their opponents, with the possible difference that the Socinians were less interested in the Old Testament; it was in their approach to interpretation that they differed essentially.[75] Put very briefly, this group represented an attitude toward the Bible that it felt was more consistent in practice than that of other Protestants who claimed to take the Bible alone as the standard of doctrine, but who then, according to the Socinians, smuggled in other concepts.

One can see a growing appeal to reason in the Socinians, so that by the time of Sandius's discussion of the canon of the Bible in the latter part of the seventeenth century, it is clear, in his discussion of books that made it into the canon and those that did not, that the reasons he gave were linked to causes other than divine inspiration.[76] An earlier intimation of this document is found in Faustus Soccinus himself. To understand Faustus, one has to take into account the reasonably well-grounded report that when a crowd burned his possessions, the loss he mourned most was the manuscript of his refutation of atheism.

---

[74] Lelio (1525–1562) was the uncle of Faustus (1539–1604). Lelio spelled his family name "Sozini," but Faustus wrote it "Sozzini."

[75] Simon, *Histoire Critique*, 815–852, devotes a fair amount of space and certain respect to the "nouveaux Antitrinitaires," in part because they represented for him the *reductio ad absurdum* of the Protestant approach, but also because he was obviously interested in their suggestions.

[76] Christophorus Sandius, *Nucleus Historiae Ecclesiasticae Exhibitus in Historia Arianorum . . . Quibus Praefixus est Tractatus de Veteribus Scriptoribus Ecclesiasticis*, 2nd, rev. ed. (Cologne: apud Johannem Nicolai, 1676). The reference is to the *Tractatus de Veteribus Scriptoribus Ecclesiasticis*, the first work in this volume.

Faustus wrote a work called *De Authoritate* [sic] *Sacrae Scripturae,* which was essentially addressed to those who did not believe.[77] The chapter titles themselves indicate how Faustus set out his argument.[78] Chapter 1 deals with the first cause of doubt about the authority of the books of the Bible, namely, "First cause or pretence of Doubt taken from the Qualities of the Writers, confuted; by shewing, that they did not commit any Error, through Ignorance, Collusion, or Design." Chapter 2 is "A second Cause or Pretence of Doubt remov'd; by shewing, that we cannot be ignorant who the Writers of the New Testament were, though that is not absolutely necessary to be universally known." Chapter 3's aim is "to prove that the Books of the New Testament were never corrupted or deprav'd, in Things of any Moment at least. Chapter 4 shows "that no sincere Christians ever yet question'd the Truth of all, or the principal Books of the New Testament. Chapter 5's main point is "that those Books were never corrupted nor deprav'd by the Jews." Chapter 6 aims to convince those non-Christians who have some religion, "namely Jews, Mohometans, and Pagans." Chapter 7 is the same theme adapted to "Atheists and Epicureans." Chapter 8 is addressed to "all in general, that no just Cause can be assign'd why Faith should be with-held from the Books of the Old And New Testament." Chapter 9 shows that more faith is due to the biblical books "than is commonly given to other Books containing any Doctrine or History." Chapter 10 deals with those who want absolute proofs, and then, perhaps most significantly of all, chapter 11 is "The foregoing partly confirm'd by the Authority of the Italian poet Dante, which concludes the whole."

The significant character of the arguments that Socinus presented is that while historical record was appealed to, no attempt was made to impose the authority of the Bible by church discipline, as the Roman Catholic Church would have argued, nor was there an appeal made to supernatural inspiration guiding the reader, as was found in many Protestant circles. The basic appeal was to a reasonable person's weighed and rational judgment. The only authority invoked was Dante, whose words would obviously not have been given the same weight as those of the Holy Spirit. What is even more significant is that a generation later,

[77] The best source of this work is in his *Opera Omnia,* vol. 1 (Irenopolis [Amsterdam]: 1656) 265, in the *Bibliotheca Fratrum Polonorum.*

[78] I am quoting from Edward Combe's translation, *An Argument for the Authority of Scripture from the Latin of Socinius After the Steinfurt Copy. To which is prefix'd a Short Account of his Life* (London: 1731). I am indebted to Ms. Susan Killoren, the librarian of Harris Manchester College at Oxford for a reproduction of this work.

when Grotius was trying to present the claims of the Christian faith to an increasingly unbelieving circle of people, he made use of Faustus's work in preparing his own defense of the Christian faith.[79]

6. *Two misguided attempts that deserve mention*

Two misguided attempts to enrich biblical interpretation deserve mention. The first comes from that aficionado of the exotic, Giovanni Pico della Mirandola (1463–1494), who saw Hermes Tresmegistos as an ancient sage who was a contemporary of Moses and who also recommended the methods of scriptural interpretation of Jewish Kabbala.[80] The second is more a matter of farce than high drama, namely, the theory of the origins of language of the Flemish scholar Goropius.

Hermes Tresmegistos and Kabbala

In the fifteenth century the Italian scholar Marsilio Ficino (1433–1499) published a set of treatises ascribed to Hermes Tresmegistos ("Thrice-great Hermes"), which claimed to be the writings of an Egyptian writer from about the time of Moses. In fact, these were first-century C.E. neo-platonic documents, interesting for their own times, but scarcely wisdom from the remote past. Many scholars took these writings as ancient, including the Roman Catholic historian Cesare Baronius (1538–1607), whose rather less than impartial church history, *Annales Ecclesiastici*, made use of Hermes Tresmegistos as part of the evidence for Roman Catholic claims. The French Protestant scholar Isaac Causabon, in his refutation of Baronius, devoted his extraordinary scholarly ability to the Hermetic writings and proved their later provenance to the satisfaction of later historians, if not all his contemporaries. This did not prevent the Hermetic writings from enjoying a vigorous afterlife in esoteric circles, but they dropped out of consideration in serious biblical scholarship soon after Causabon's treatment.

Kabbala is not a subject that lends itself to easy summaries.[81] It is a portmanteau word to describe a series of mystical writings dating from

---

[79] Grotius's dependence on Faustus Socinus was not a modern discovery; it is stated plainly on the title page of the 1731 translation mentioned above.

[80] Giovanni Pico della Mirandola should not be confused with his nephew Gianfrancesco Pico della Mirandola (1469–1533), who was a member of Savonarola's circle and was influenced by Sextus Empiricus.

[81] The basic work is Gershom Sholem, *Major Trends in Jewish Mysticism*, various publishers and dates.

the early Middle Ages of the common era, when elaborate speculations were combined with a particular type of exegesis based on the signifi- cance of letters of the Hebrew alphabet. The attraction Kabbalistic writ- ings had for the Christian thinkers in the Renaissance was that, like the Hermetic documents, they too claimed to go back to ancient times, in this case to Moses himself, and to reveal doctrines hidden from the eyes of the less spiritual. The Renaissance held on to the conviction that there once existed an ancient wisdom that far surpassed what more degener- ate modern eras could attain to, so Kabbala as both a system of beliefs and a method of getting spiritual messages out of the most unlikely biblical passages fitted in with this predisposition.[82]

The result was a tradition of Christian Kabbala that persisted for about two hundred years. Christians found two advantages in Kabbala: first, some of its speculations could be interpreted as evidence for belief in Christian doctrines early on in Jewish history, and second, the tech- nique of finding special significance in the very letters of biblical passages meant that almost anything could be proved from almost any- where. Serious scholars such as Reuchlin and Guillaume Postel were attracted to Kabbala, although in the case of Postel there was a personal idiosyncrasy evident that some of his contemporaries were unkind enough to see as madness. Not everyone was convinced—Erasmus was notably silent about Reuchlin's Kabbalistic interests when he defended him—and serious scholars eventually recognized Kabbala as neoplaton- ist apocrypha. Nonetheless, even in the late seventeenth century, Henry More could still write a work extolling the ancient wisdom to be found in Kabbala, and a few eighteenth-century scholars were also tempted by it.[83]

Johannes Goropius Becanus (1518–1573)

All philologists live on the edge of a cliff, and every so often one of them falls off. This was the case of Becanus, who, in the midst of the sixteenth-century debates about whether Hebrew was the original

---

[82] François Secret, *Les Kabbalistes chrétiens de la Renaissance* (Milan: Archè, 1982). See also John Sandys-Wunsch, "The Influence of Jewish Mysticism on Renaissance Bibli- cal Interpretation," in *Mysticism: Select Essays; Essays in Honour of John Sahadat*, ed. Melchior Mbonipa; Guy Bonneau, and Kenneth-Roy Bonin (Sudbury, Ontario: Editions Glopro, 2002) 47–69.

[83] Henry More, *Conjectura Cabbalistica or, A Conjectural Essay of Interpreting the mind of Moses, in the Three first Chapters of Genesis, according to a threefold Cabbala* (London: William Morden, 1662).

language of humanity, argued that the original language was actually Netherlands (Dutch/Flemish) and in fact had been used by Adam and Eve in the Garden of Eden. This he proved to his own satisfaction on the logical grounds that the older a language is, the shorter its words. Since words in Netherlands are shorter than in Hebrew and in other languages, it follows that it must be the oldest language of all. Becanus added some very improbable etymologies to his argument: not only was the first language Netherlands, it was Netherlands as spoken in Antwerp, which just happened to be Becanus's native city. Thanks to his efforts, "Goropianism" became a byword for philological folly. Visitors to present-day Holland and the Flemish part of Belgium should bear in mind that Becanus is still a subject to be approached with tact, if at all.

Conclusion

The scholarly study of the Bible in the period 1450 to 1600 built on its heritage of critical methods and observations from the Graeco-Roman, the rabbinic Jewish, and the medieval periods. At their best, the Renaissance Humanists combined a vigorous effort to recover the past with an awareness of how their ideas might shape the future. Whether the Humanists should be described as precritical is a function of how one defines this term, but the Humanists were relentless in their recognition of what required explanation and did not shy away from difficulties. Many of their observations are still part of the staple of any biblical commentary. If we feel that they do not always satisfy us with their explanations, we should note that they did not always satisfy themselves. The fact remains that in the basic disciplines of textual criticism, philology, and the coherence of documents, they laid the foundations of the discipline, and in their publishing of texts and making them generally available, they preserved much. Apart from their contribution to the study of the Bible, by their sense of the unity behind all knowledge they also developed interests that eventually led to many of our modern humanities disciplines such as ethnology, linguistics, and archaeology.

Chapter 3

The "Baroque" Period (1600–1660)

In 1631 Robert Barker and Martin Lucas, the king's printers, published a Bible that has come to be known as "the Wicked Bible," for in the Ten Commandments it stated, "Thou shalt commit adultery." Then as now this typographical error must have caused some mirth, but not everyone was amused. Barker was fined two hundred pounds and Lucas one hundred. This incident is an indication of the changes that have taken place in the last four hundred years. The Bible is no longer a national sacred object protected by the law. This does not mean that we have ceased to have sacred objects altogether—witness the attempts to make flag-burning a criminal act in the United States or the prosecution in Paris of a tramp whose crime was to cook an egg over the flame on the tomb of the unknown soldier. But unless you are in a forest-fire danger area, you are free to burn Bibles all day long while your supply lasts.[1]

At the outset of the seventeenth century, it was considered appropriate that Barker and Lucas should be punished for their sacrilege, whether deliberate or otherwise. But by the end of the century, not only had the sacred status of the Bible been seriously challenged, but its hegemony across the spectrum of human knowledge and undertakings had begun to disintegrate. Like all generalizations, this statement is open to qualification, but even allowing for earlier, relatively isolated expressions of

---

[1] This, in fact, took place at the time of the introduction of the Revised Standard Version, when a fundamentalist group burned a pile of the new Bibles as an exercise in self-expression.

disbelief in small circles, especially in Italy, it was only in the seventeenth century that a multitude of discoveries, observations, and reflections were made that were to lead to the entirely different estimation of the Bible that we are familiar with in the modern world.

I. External Factors

1. The political situation

i. Holland: By the end of the sixteenth century, Holland had become independent of Spain, and while there was a large part of the population that retained its Roman Catholic allegiance, the politically dominant force was Calvinism, Calvinism of a thoroughgoing type as defined by the Synod of Dort in 1618–1619. A tolerant society—tolerant for the times—developed that welcomed refugees of various sorts—Huguenots from France, Marrano Jews from Portugal, and others who often added to its prosperity. The effect was to create a country whose importance was out of proportion to its size, for Holland became a leading trading nation with a powerful navy.

The new country needed an educated class to deal with the complexities of administration, and to create this class new universities were established. The wealth of these institutions meant that distinguished foreign scholars could be attracted to add luster to their reputation.[2] Students from elsewhere in Europe were attracted to the Dutch universities, especially medical students, such as Sir Thomas Browne. Dutch intellectual life blossomed, and Descartes preferred to live much of his life in Holland. Dutch printers were among the best in Europe in their techniques, but they also profited from a tolerant society, so that they could print, often at great profit, books prohibited elsewhere, even books not officially permitted in Holland itself. The best-known, nonresident foreign author to be published in Holland was, of course, Galileo, but at the end of the seventeenth century Richard Simon was able to publish in Holland what the censor had prohibited in France.[3] Jews, Socinians, and other radical writers

---

[2] A modern comment that Leiden was the Duke University of its day is an unkind cut aimed at both institutions, but it does not lack substance.

[3] Censorship could and did exist, and prosecution for heresy could take place. See Andrew Pettegree, "The politics of toleration in the Free Netherlands, 1572–1620," in *Tolerance and Intolerance in the European Reformation*, ed. Ole Peter Grell and Bob Scribner

were able to find a voice with relatively few restrictions. The intellectual ferment produced by prosperity and tolerance is the reason
the seventeenth century is referred to as the Golden Age of Dutch
culture, for from Holland flowed out books and later periodicals
that were to change Europe's thinking.[4]

ii. Belgium, culturally and linguistically closely connected to Holland,
had a long tradition of great scholarship that in the early seventeenth century continued in the works of Guilielmus Estius and
Cornelius à Lapide.

iii. France: The seventeenth century is generally referred to as *"le grand
siècle"* in France, not without reason, for in this period France established itself not only as the dominant Continental power but also as
the arbiter of taste and culture throughout Europe as French replaced
Latin as the language of diplomacy and even, to some extent, of
learning. In the Baroque period biblical studies flourished among
both Roman Catholics and Protestants, although the latter suffered
continuous acts of petty repression, despite their almost pathetic
loyalty to a royal house that was eventually to betray them.[5] One of
the Protestant seminaries, Saumur, was home to some of the more
distinguished scholars of Europe, most notably Louis Cappell. Intellectual life was also fostered by the learned salons of Paris, where
religious as well as other issues were discussed with great freedom.

iv. England was one of the major countries of Europe where Protestantism was dominant. The Roman Catholic minority was compromised in public opinion by attempts of foreign powers to use it for
political purposes. The Church of England was less doctrinaire and
more comprehensive than many churches, and some parts of it

(Cambridge: Cambridge University Press, 1996) 182–98; Jonathan I. Israel, *Radical
Enlightenment Philosophy and the Making of Modernity 1650–1750* (Oxford: Oxford University Press, 2001) 192–96. It is one of the ironies of history that despite the liberal
tenor of the Netherlands, Hugo Grotius, one of its greatest figures, had to live as an
exile from his native country, albeit for reasons more political than confessional.

[4] For an extensive treatment of this era, see Paul Dibon, *Regards sur la Hollande du
siècle d'or* (Naples: Vivarium, 1990).

[5] See François La Planche, *L'Écriture, le sacré, et l'histoire: Érudits et politiques protestants
devant la Bible en France au XVIIe siècle* (Amsterdam & Maarssen: APA-Holland University Press, 1986). Although the scope of Yvon Belaval and Dominique Bourel, eds.,
Le Siècle des Lumières et la Bible (Paris: Beauschesne, 1986), is European in its scope, its
articles on French scholars are especially useful.

worked to maintain its continuity with its Catholic past. Richard Hooker (1554–1600), whose learned and judicious discussion of biblical texts in his *Laws of Ecclesiastical Polity*, published at the end of the sixteenth century,[6] struck a mediating position between Roman Catholic appeals to church authority and Puritan demands for all questions to be settled from the Bible alone. His argument for a threefold source of authority, namely, Bible, reason, and tradition, was to be one of the themes in English church life from the seventeenth century on. The civil war, to the extent that it was religiously rather than politically motivated, provided the opportunity for extreme religious enthusiasts to assert uncompromising positions often based on eschatological hopes. Hobbes's political philosophy and its concomitant biblical criticism were one attempt to mitigate the social discord caused by an unbalanced interpretation of the Bible.

At the two English universities solid biblical scholarship of a technical sort continued in language and text, but it is interesting to see how few English contributions were included in the *Critici Sacri*, the great collection of critical works to be discussed below in the next chapter. At the same time, it is also clear that streams of antireligious thought were present in Britain, for much of Sir Thomas Browne's *Religio Medici* is written against the background of a perceived rising tide of disbelief.

v. Spain and Italy: The great Humanist tradition in Spain that produced the Complutensian Polyglot did not continue. One possible explanation is that the systematic repression of the Spanish Inquisition destroyed the freedom necessary for scholarly inquiry. In Italy the fragmentation of the country provided niches of freedom where good work could be done. In particular, Venice, being an independent republic, defended its autonomy against the pope, and its printers were relatively sheltered from the Inquisition by the Venetian republic.

vi. Germany: The Thirty Years' War left large parts of the country in ruin, and while the Treaty of Westphalia restored peace in 1648, recovery was to take two generations. While there were many universities within the empire, they and their students were naturally

---

[6] Books V–VIII were not published until after his death, and there are questions about the integrity of the textual transmission.

affected by the devastations of war, and some of the best scholars emigrated elsewhere, especially Holland. At the end of the seventeenth century, it was a well-known practice (to judge from remarks in learned journals) to make fun of German theologians, but this represented not a fair judgment but a misconception that the eighteenth century was to dispel.[7]

2. *Relations with the Near East*

One political development that was to influence biblical exegesis was the decision of the Ottoman Empire to encourage trade with western Europe. "Capitulations" were granted to European powers in the sixteenth and seventeenth centuries that enabled Europeans to establish trading stations where their nationals were governed by their own laws and had a great deal of opportunity to travel. This meant that not only could the knowledge of Semitic languages, such as Arabic, be improved, but manuscripts could be acquired, and reports could be brought back about the geography of Palestine and other areas mentioned in the Bible.[8]

One person who made use of this opportunity was Edward Pococke (1604–1691), the first professor of Arabic at Oxford, who developed an interest in Oriental studies from hearing the German Arabist Matthias Pasor (1599–1658) at Oxford and from lessons given by William Bedwell (1563–1632), the father of the study of Arabic in England. Pococke spent over five years as chaplain to the English merchants at Aleppo, during which time he collected Arabic, Hebrew, Ethiopic, and Armenian manuscripts, including a copy of the Samaritan Pentateuch. Edward Pusey considered that of all those who brought back manuscripts to the Bodleian, Pococke alone escaped being deceived or cheated by his suppliers.

3. *Printing*

A quantitative change in book production took place. The number of printers and their output increased throughout Europe, producing a

---

[7] See Rudolf Mau, "Programme und Praxis der Theologiestudiums im 17. und 18. Jahrhundert," *Theologische Versuche* 11 (1979) 71–91.

[8] See Robin A. Butlin, "A Sacred and Contested Place: English and French Representations of Palestine in the Seventeenth Century," in Iain S. Black, and Robin A. Butlin, eds., *Place, Culture and Identity: Essays in Historical Geography in Honour of Alan R. H. Baker* (Quebec: Les Presses de l'Université Laval, 2001) 91–131.

qualitative effect that should not be overlooked. Up to the beginning of the seventeenth century, it was possible for an educated European to have read almost every book published in Europe. By mid-seventeenth century this was no longer possible. Richard Burton's protest in *The Anatomy of Melancholy* about the number of books being printed is symptomatic of this new condition. Furthermore, the foundations of the collections of great libraries, such as the Bodleian at Oxford, were being laid even as an interest in the science of book collecting was addressed in various writings.

4. *Changes in thought in the Baroque period*

In the history of biblical interpretation, one has to keep an eye on two rather different areas of concern and therefore investigation. The most obvious is the actual exegesis of the Bible—problems such as textual transmission, language, dating, authorship, and translation. The other area consists of matters external to the Bible itself but which influenced biblical interpretation in the narrower sense of the word. In his work *The English Bible and the Seventeenth-century Revolution*, Christopher Hill coined the perceptive term "dethronement of the Bible."[9] While the time and circumstances of this dethronement are open to debate, the fact is that whereas at the beginning of the seventeenth century the Bible occupied a central position, not only in matters religious and ecclesiastical but also as a standard authority in matters of history, chronology, geography, politics, linguistics, and other forms of knowledge, by the end of the century we find the developments in the different types of knowledge that were to push to the sidelines the Bible as an encyclopedic work valid for all disciplines.

5. *Science and the Bible*

The roots of modern physical science go back to the Greeks, especially Aristotle. The reasons for the extraordinary development of science in western Europe from the seventeenth century on are open for debate, but the combination of the critique of older misconceptions, the growth of mathematics, and an experimental frame of mind are factors to be

---

[9] Christopher Hill, *The English Bible and the Seventeenth-century Revolution* (London: Allen Lane, 1993).

included in any explanation. The question here is what role did science play in the interpretation and subsequent dethronement of the Bible in the seventeenth century?[10]

It is important to bear in mind that occurrences of "science" as a word to describe an independent discipline are rare before the end of the eighteenth century. Up to that time, what we would call science was seen as a branch of philosophy, a situation best illustrated by the sign over an eighteenth-century shop in York that advertised "philosophical instruments," by which it meant telescopes, microscopes, and other forms of scientific instruments. The British Royal Society still publishes its work under the title *Philosophical Transactions*. The result of the inclusion of what we would call science within philosophy was that it was connected with the metaphysical problems of God, morality, and life after death to a degree unknown in the present day.

Astronomy and the Bible: It has been argued by good scholars[11] that the new picture of the solar system put forward by Copernicus and Galileo caused a "Copernican" or "Galilean" shock, comparable to the "Darwinian shock" that shook the later nineteenth century.[12] This has been regarded as almost self-evident to the point where careful evidence is not required. The problem is that the evidence of widespread dismay is hard to find. The usual proof given is the condemnation of Galileo by the Inquisition. The matter of the trial of Galileo is open to much dispute, but it is at least possible that he was condemned, not because he was out of bounds on the matter of cosmology, but because he refused to submit to the authority of the Inquisition.[13] It is also true that some of Galileo's personal traits, not least of all his habit of making fun of his

---

[10] A useful work that covers several centuries of debate about religion and science is David C. Lindberg and Ronald L. Numbers, eds., *God and Nature: Historical Essays on the Encounter Between Christianity and Science* (Berkeley: University of California Press, 1986).

[11] For example, Klaus Scholder, *Ursprünge und Probleme der Bibelkritik im 17. Jahrhundert* (Munich: Chr. Kaiser, 1966) 56–78. ET: *The Birth of Modern Critical Theology* (Philadelphia: Trinity Press, 1990) 46–64.

[12] For the case of Copernicus in the sixteenth century, see the relevant chapter in Richard J. Blackwell, *Galileo, Bellarmine, and the Bible* (Notre Dame: University of Notre Dame, 1991).

[13] The literature on this subject is extensive. See Annibale Fantoli, *Galileo: for Copernicanism and for the Church*, 2nd ed., Studi Galileiani 3, trans. George V. Coyne, S.J., (Rome: Vatican Observatory Publications, 1996), for a discussion of the matter and an extensive bibliography.

critics, provoked a certain amount of animus against him in ecclesiastical circles, where desire for revenge may also have played a part in his trial. But as far as Galileo's own position on religion and science was concerned, he himself seems to have remained a pious Roman Catholic, and he did not see his views as an attack on the Bible; in fact, even some cardinals agreed with his position. The beginnings of an outpouring of descriptions of Galileo as a martyr of science to obscurantist religion are not found until the late nineteenth century, when they were used as ammunition in the war between science and religion. What is also worth bearing in mind about the seventeenth and eighteenth centuries is that in lists of atheists and enemies of the faith, such as Jacob Friedrich Reimmann's *Historia universalis Atheismi et Atheorum*,[14] there is never any suggestion that Galileo was a threat to the faith, whereas for Reimmann even Sir Thomas Browne got off the "charge" by the skin of his teeth.

There were indeed some people who objected to Galileo's cosmology on religious grounds. In England, Alexander Rosse[15] wrote against him; in Holland, various theologians objected to the new cosmology, but here one has the suspicion that this was only part of the larger debate about Descartes' philosophy;[16] and in Germany, Abraham Calov dissented.[17] In contrast, however, there were a number of publications by authors who received the new cosmology with enthusiasm. William Derham (1657–1735), canon of Windsor, even wrote an *Astrotheology* on the basis of Galileo's work that went through many editions and was translated into various European languages.[18] A telling indication of the uncontroversial nature of Galileo's system was a "throw away" remark in Hobbes's *Leviathan*, where he said in part of his argument against the scriptural basis for belief in demonic possession:

[14] (Hildesheim: Ludwig Schroeder, 1725).

[15] Alexander Rosse, *The New Planet no Planet or, The Earth no wandring Star except in the wandring heads of Galileans* (London: T. Young, 1646). This is the Rosse mentioned in the opening of Canto 2 of Samuel Butler's *Hudibras:*
THERE was an ancient sage philosopher,
That had read ALEXANDER Ross over.

[16] For example, Jacob du Bois, *Dialogus Theologico-Astronomicus . . . et Ex Sacris Literis Terrae quietem, Soli vero motum competere probatur; adjuncta Refutatione Argumentorum Astronomicorum, quae in contrarium proferri solent* (Leiden: Petrus Leffen, 1653).

[17] Abraham Calov, *Commentarius in Genesin* (Wittemberg: Michaelis Meyeri, 1671) 175.

[18] William Derham, *Astro-theology: or, A Demonstration of the Being and attributes of God, from a Survey of the Heavens* (London: 1715).

To which I can give no other kind of answer but that which is given to those that urge the Scripture in like manner against the opinion of the motion of the earth. The Scripture was written to show unto men the kingdom of God, and to prepare their minds to become His obedient subjects, leaving the world, and the philosophy thereof, to the disputation of men for the exercising of their natural reason. . . .[19]

The force of the argument is that Hobbes expected his readers to be so much in agreement with the new view of the solar system that it could be used to illustrate another argument.

In fact, the initial effect of the new scientific enterprise was to provide in some cases a support for biblical religion in that the picture of an ordered universe was evidence of a beneficent Creator who provided a world suitable for all creatures, especially humanity, and whose providence could be seen at work in the physical world. The irony was that this natural theology, which is clearly biblically inspired, was to become the ground for the correction and criticism of the Bible itself by writers like Morgan and Tindale in the eighteenth century. But even here it was a case of a purer religion revealed by nature rather than no religion at all that was being argued.

There were two potential areas where an insistence on an orderly universe could be seen as problematical in a discussion of religion and the Bible. The first was the question of miracles. Putting aside the cruder notions of popular piety that survived from medieval Europe, what was the status of the miracles recorded in Scripture, given that the world was governed by the inexorable forces of natural law? But if the universe is completely controlled by predictable forces, how does one allow for any human freedom to make real choices? These two questions belong to a category that can be called philosophical dandelions; they crop up in different places, and there is no known way to extirpate completely the problems they pose.

As an afterword, it should be pointed out that there was one subject where there was general agreement about ecclesiastical obscurantism on a scientific matter, namely, the subject of whether the world is flat. Lactantius and St. Bernard were the two principal targets of scorn, such as that expressed by Sir Thomas Browne: "I have often pitied the miserable bishop that suffered in the cause of antipodes; yet cannot choose but accuse him of as much madness, for exposing his living on such a trifle,

[19] *Leviathan,* ch. 8 (p. 38 in the 1953 Everyman edition).

as those of ignorance and folly, that condemned him." It is interesting to find this example cropping up in different contexts.[20]

6. *The effect of world exploration:*
distance and ethnology and animal species

The new information that was pouring into Europe about the size and extent of the world and the number of peoples and creatures in it was beginning to inspire reflection about how all this could be included in such information as was available about world origins in Genesis. Attributing to Noah's sons Shem, Ham, and Japheth the origin of all the races of humanity meant that the argument got progressively more cumbersome as the number of known races increased. Where did the populations of the "new" world come from—could they be identified with biblical groups such as the lost ten tribes of Israel? How large was Noah's ark going to have to be to accommodate all the newly discovered animal species? How would the South American sloth have been able to cross huge distances and incredible obstacles in order to be on time to catch the last ark out? Isaac de La Peyrère was neither the first nor the last to argue that Genesis is not really as universal in its point of view as had been assumed, but was much more a document written from the limited perspective of a small people living in a restricted geographical area.

7. *Geography*

Geography, sometimes called the other eye of history, developed as new information came in from the European exploration of the world. Biblical exegesis was enriched by travelers' accounts of the Holy Land in works such as George Sandys' *Travailes* in 1615,[21] a work that went through nine editions (including translations) up to 1673 and the *Rélation d'un voyage fait au Levant,* published by Jean de Thévenot in Paris in 1664.[22] Samuel Bochart (1599–1667), not a traveler but a systematizer

---

[20] See the relevant footnote 53 in chapter 2, p. 59, above.

[21] George Sandys, *Sandys Travailes containing a History of the Original and present State of the Turkish Empire* (London: Richard Cotes/John Sweeting, 1652).

[22] Laurent d'Arvieux (1635–1702) spent even more time in the Levant and in 1670 even furnished information about Turkish dress for the production of Molière's *Le Bourgeois Gentilhomme.* However, d'Arvieux's memoirs were not published until the eighteenth century.

of information, published *Geographia sacra seu Phaleg e Canaan* in 1648, a painstaking examination of places and peoples since the Flood. The new spirit of this work, as described in its introduction by Villemandy,[23] was its determination to avoid older legends and concentrate on the facts in themselves. The critical diligence Bochart devoted to this work was extraordinary. Clearly he had a taste for careful investigation, for he followed the *Geographia* with his *Hierozoicon* in 1663, a catalogue of all the animals mentioned in the Bible. There are hints of the new seventeenth-century view about the world in Bochart's specific rejection of the interpretation of the Tower of Babel story as an attempt to build a tower literally up into heaven. Instead, Bochart put forward the view that what was meant was just a tall building that pandered to human pride. While Bochart did maintain the traditional view that Hebrew was the oldest language in the world, the pragmatic approach he took boded ill for some of the authority claimed for the Bible, because he was paving the way for more radical views that would conclude from geographical evidence that Eden was never a place that existed in human history.

8. *History and chronology*

In order to derive a coherent chronology from the Bible, that is, the dates of various happenings and the age of the world, one has to make a series of adjustments, for not all the systems of chronology within the Bible, in particular the dates of the kings of Judah and Israel, can easily be reconciled with each other. The Septuagint and the Hebrew Bible contain different chronologies, and some scholars were tempted to follow the Septuagint because it permitted the possibility of an earlier date of creation. Furthermore, reports that chronologies from other cultures, in particular China, recorded dates long before the time of the Hebrews were a cause of disquiet about the accuracy of the biblical numbers.[24]

To sum up, the beginnings of the process of the dethronement of the Bible as the ultimate source of knowledge about human culture and the physical world came not so much from dramatic discoveries or convincing arguments; rather, one finds a number of pinpricks from divergent

[23] I am using *Geographia sacra seu Phaleg e Canaan*, ed. Petrus de Villemandy, 4th ed. (Louvain: Cornelium Boutestyn et Jordanum Luchtmans, 1707). I presume that de Villemandy wrote the *Praefatio*.

[24] See Anthony T. Grafton, "Joseph Scaliger and Historical Chronology: the Rise and Fall of a Discipline," *History and Theory: Studies in the Philosophy of History* 14 (1975) 156–85.

sources of information, which by the middle of the eighteenth century had turned into the death of a thousand cuts.

9. *Belief and unbelief as separate issues from scholarship proper*

Having admitted that the growth of knowledge led inexorably to the dethronement of the Bible as a source of general knowledge, I would like to suggest that this rational process of gathering of evidence is separable, at least in theory, from the stream of outright disbelief that existed openly from the sixteenth century in Italy and was felt in France from the seventeenth century on.[25] The issue here is not the right or the wrong of a specific attitude toward the Bible, but how this opinion contributed in any way to the history of intelligent biblical interpretation.

In the early seventeenth century the group that was destined to have an influence, albeit an indirect one, was a loose group of friends known as *les libertins érudits*. They rejected Christianity as a belief, not as a result of the new philosophy via Descartes, but rather on the basis of older classical viewpoints that had been recovered. Their main attack was on what they felt were the superstitions of the Roman Catholic Church, whose basis in fact they delighted in debunking. Still the Bible came in for their criticism, such as in the verses of La Mothe:

> Messieurs encore un mot
> Avant que je me taise
> Je ne suis pas si sot
> De croire à la Genèse.

While *les libertins érudits* made jests of various things in the Bible, they did not produce much in the way of a serious treatment of the Bible as such. However, one of their acquaintances was Isaac de la Peyrère, who, possibly in reaction to their point of view, set out to defend the Bible against objections that sound like the sort of observations the *libertins* might have made. (His work will be treated below, pp. 101–107.)

Another author who was well aware of the arguments of the *libertins* or their Italian equivalents was Sir Thomas Browne, a man sufficiently modern to write a work called *Pseudoxia Epidemica: Enquiries into Vulgar Errors* (1646), but who remained unshaken in his loyalty to the beliefs of

---

[25] See René Pintard, *Le libertinage érudit dans la première moitié du XVIIe siècle*, rev. ed. (Geneva: Slatkine, 1983); Françoise Charles-Daubert, "La Bible des libertins," in J. Armogathe, ed., *Le Grand siècle et la Bible* (Paris: Beauchesne, 1989) 667–90.

the Church of England. Those who delight in the *Religio Medici* should recognize that it is in large part a defense of the Bible, albeit in an eccentric English mode, against the scoffers, whose points of view are easily visible underneath the text. As noted above, so clear was this to Browne's contemporaries that he was accused of himself being one of the number of those he criticized.

II. The Bible

1. *A note about clarifying terms*

The terms "revelation," "inspiration," "infallibility," and "authority" tend to overlap in meaning, and in general usage the confusion often produced makes the Cartesian ideal of clear and distinct ideas hard to realize.

i. *Revelation:* Strictly speaking, "revelation" refers to an act of God to reveal the divine nature to humanity. In one form of usage, revelation can stand for anything that suggests the divine; thus the created order of the universe can be seen as a revelation of the nature of God. Lapide's comment on this was that nature never indicates what transcends nature. In a different sense, when revelation is contrasted with "natural theology," revelation usually refers to specific and deliberate revelations of God at a given time or period to individuals or groups.

ii. *Inspiration* comes from the same root as "spirit" and can in common usage refer to any better than expected idea or creative impulse. In a theological discussion inspiration implies that such an idea or creative impulse is a revelation from God. What exactly is implied can vary; when one speaks of the prophets as inspired, does one mean that they speak with the voice of God in the same way that a telephone transmits a person's exact speech, or do inspired speakers/writers work under divine guidance, but within their own human limitations and styles? Whether in the seventeenth century or the present, discussions about inspiration turn as much on definition as on argument.

iii. *Infallibility* means free from error. If the word was not always used, the concept was clearly behind many arguments and statements. In a theological context it implies that the Bible—or for some, the church however defined—is preserved from error. The question is, what sort of error? Is every word in the Bible infallible in any context, so that even factual errors of a minor nature are not to be found in Scripture? In the nineteenth century the question was raised whether the Old Testament was scientifically accurate in classifying the hare as a ruminant; this led to a piece of doggerel of which the concluding lines are:

> Doctors, divines, beware!
> For frail is the faith
> Which hangs upon a hare.

As will be discussed below, in the seventeenth century it was an even more unlikely animal, the South American sloth, that troubled the faith of Europe. It is possible that infallibility was and is a theological will-o'-the-wisp that lures humanity with the illusion of certainty into the quicksands of despair.

iv. *Authority* is a word whose emotional overtones range all the way from the eminently desirable to the utterly detestable, from the enabling of a meaningful life to the high-handed abrogation of human dignity; one need only compare the difference between "authoritative" and "authoritarian" to see the different nuances found in authority. This is not a subject that can be covered fully in a few lines, but for our purposes, in assessing what a given scholar says about the authority of the Bible, it must be asked whether he or she is assuming that the Bible can only have authority if it enjoys infallibility in the strongest sense of the term; or does the Bible have authority in that at least some parts of it enable people to appreciate the world and themselves better? It all depends on what is assumed by "authority."

2. *Infallibility and inspiration in the seventeenth century*

In the sixteenth century the Roman Catholic Church and the Protestants had taken different routes to describe the authority of the Bible. I offer as a working hypothesis that some of the differences among scholars can be traced back, at least in part, to the different inadequacies of the starting points of their confessions. As discussed in the previous chapter, the Council of Trent in its fourth session issued a decree about the limits to methods for interpreting Scripture, which essentially made obedience paramount over argument, as the case of Galileo showed. Protestants, on the other hand, had appealed to the witness of the Bible, especially in its original languages. This was to make them prisoners of their own exegesis, and they were under pressure to perfect their instruments of grammar and lexicography in order to achieve a greater consensus among themselves.

Some Protestant theologians in the seventeenth century were faced with the dilemma that on one hand official Protestant bodies ratcheted up their position on the infallibility of the Bible in the interests of preserving its immediate authority, but on the other hand this intensifying of the definition of infallibility meant that they were more vulnerable to criticisms either on matters of fact, such as problems with chronology, or on questions of the appropriateness of the many unpleasant matters found in the Old Testament. Castellio a hundred years earlier could cope with the problem of repugnant matters in Scripture by shrugging them off with the observation that that is what life is like.[26] His general approach to problems in Scripture was: do not be concerned about what we cannot know, but do pay attention to what clearly concerns us. But for some in the seventeenth century it was too easygoing an attitude to the infallibility of the whole Bible. The *Westminster Confession* of 1646 is a good example of this emphasis on the centrality of the Bible:

> V. The authority of the holy Scripture, for which it ought to be believed and obeyed, dependeth not upon the testimony of any man or Church, but wholly upon God (who is truth itself), the Author thereof; and therefore it is to be received, because it is the Word of God.
>
> VIII. The Old Testament in Hebrew (which was the native language of the people of God of old), and the New Testament in Greek (which at the time of the writing of it was most generally known to the nations), being immediately inspired by God, and by his singular care and providence kept pure in all ages, are therefore authentical; so as in all controversies of religion the Church is finally to appeal unto them.
>
> IX. The infallible rule of interpretation of Scripture, is the Scripture itself; and therefore, when there is a question about the true and full sense of any scripture (which is not manifold, but one), it may be searched and known by other places that speak more clearly.

[26] Sébastien Castellion, *De l'Art de douter et de croire, d'ignorer et de savoir,* trans. Charles Badouin (Geneva: Jeheber, 1953) 57–60.

Even more significant were the second and third canons of the *Formula Consensus Helvetica*, which placed all bets of eternal salvation on the unreliable horse of Hebrew orthography:[27]

> Canon II: But, in particular, The Hebrew original of the OT which we have received and to this day do retain as handed down by the Hebrew Church, "who had been given the oracles of God" (Rom 3:2), is, not only in its consonants, but in its vowels either the vowel points themselves, or at least the power of the points not only in its matter, but in its words, inspired by God. It thus forms, together with the Original of the NT the sole and complete rule of our faith and practice; and to its standard, as to a Lydian stone, all extant versions, eastern or western, ought to be applied, and wherever they differ, be conformed.
>
> Canon III: Therefore, we are not able to approve of the opinion of those who believe that the text which the Hebrew Original exhibits was determined by man's will alone, and do not hesitate at all to remodel a Hebrew reading which they consider unsuitable, and amend it from the versions of the LXX and other Greek versions, the Samaritan Pentateuch, by the Chaldaic Targums, or even from other sources. They go even to the point of following the corrections that their own rational powers dictate from the various readings of the Hebrew Original itself which, they maintain, has been corrupted in various ways; and finally, they affirm that besides the Hebrew edition of the present time, there are in the versions of the ancient interpreters which differ from our Hebrew text, other Hebrew Originals. Since these versions are also indicative of ancient Hebrew Originals differing from each other, they thus bring the foundation of our faith and its sacred authority into perilous danger.

The difference in the sources of authority account for differences of emphasis between Roman Catholic and Protestant scholars. Protestants were free, indeed obligated, to go back to the original tongues of the Bible and discuss the exact philology of words and phrases. Even Richard Simon had to admit, somewhat grudgingly, that Protestants were on the whole better linguists, and Augustin Calmet, the eighteenth-century French exegete, at the outset of his studies, had to get permission to have language instruction from a Protestant. Roman Catholics had to tread lightly in matters of original languages lest they attract attention as

---

[27] Martin I. Klauber, "The Formula Consensus Helvetica (1675)," *Trinity Journal* 11 (1990) 103–23.

deniers of the authority of the Vulgate, for even Arias Montanus came under scrutiny for paying too much attention to the Targums in his Polyglot Bible.

But Roman Catholic scholars had their own advantages; it is interesting that Masius, Pererius, and Lapide felt free to discuss the possible sources Moses used or later additions to the Pentateuch, whereas Protestants shied away from this area. Furthermore, Roman Catholics felt more comfortable about pointing out difficult passages, since this would make the explanations of "mother church" all the more necessary and refute the notion of Scripture being easily interpreted from itself.

3. Debates about the text

i. OLD TESTAMENT

In 1631 Jean Morin, a Protestant convert to Roman Catholicism, wrote a treatment of the text of the Old Testament,[28] in which he argued that the Hebrew text was so corrupt and unsure that the only true form of the Bible must be the Vulgate. Needless to say, the Protestants were outraged and a debate ensued. Much to the joy of at least some Roman Catholics, a dispute had arisen within the ranks of Protestantism itself not so much about the text as the letters of the Hebrew Bible. The background to this debate was that Hebrew is written in a script that is essentially consonantal;[29] however, in most manuscripts there are marks called "points" that occur above, within, and below the letters to indicate vowels and other matters of pronunciation. At the beginning of the sixteenth century, Elias Levita (1469–1549) had written a treatise to show that this pointing was a device added in the Christian era. The potential conclusion was that if this was so, then it could be that Hebrew was sufficiently ambiguous to require the Vulgate to establish its real meaning, for if one can change the vowels at will in a text, one may get a different meaning.[30] For this reason Levita's argument was contested by various scholars already in the sixteenth century.

---

[28] *Exercitationes Biblicae de Hebraei Graecique Textus Sinceritate de Germana LXX Interpretum Translatione Dignoscenda, Illiusque cum Vulgata Conciliatione* (Paris: A. Vitray, 1633).

[29] This is an oversimplification; in fact, a few consonants, known as vowel letters, were sometimes used to indicate vowels.

[30] This is true in the case of Genesis 1:1, which, according to the vowels one inserts, one can get either "In the beginning God created . . ." or "In the beginning of God's

Seventeenth-century Protestant scholars were not pleased, then, when the *Arcanum Punctationis* of Louis Cappell appeared (published by the Dutch scholar Thomas (Van Erpe) Erpenius without Cappell's permission in 1624).[31] Cappell, one of the most eminent French expositors at the seminary of Saumur, set out a careful and exhaustive discussion of the evidence about the relative lateness of vowel points, an argument that was repeated in his *Critica Sacra,* published in 1650, which also treated the textual problems of the manuscripts of the Hebrew Bible.

Those who argue that Protestants inevitably favored freedom of thought would do well to examine the machinations used by Protestant scholars to prevent Cappell's *Critica Sacra* from being published in traditional Protestant strongholds such as the Netherlands or the Swiss Reformed cities of Geneva and Basel.[32] Eventually Cappell's work was published in Paris, thanks to the intervention of Jean Morin himself, who in a letter to Cardinal Barbarini published at the beginning of the work, expressed his opinion on how useful Cappell's arguments had been to the Roman Catholic cause, by which he meant that Cappell's textual studies could be used by Roman Catholic apologists to cast doubts on the integrity of the Hebrew text and thereby prove the superiority of the Vulgate.

Cappell was criticized by Johannes Buxtorf Jr.[33] (1599–1664) in his *Anticritica.* What is interesting is the tone of the introduction, especially his remark that his work "prepared a health giving antidote against the most pestilent poison handed to less cautious and resolute readers."[34] This is far from being the language of rational academic discussion, and it shows that more is thought to be at stake than a historical question to be solved in a rational way. The reason why Buxtorf was upset is that Cappell's work could cast doubt on the authority of the Hebrew text.[35]

---

creation . . ." The second alternative could suggest God working on preexisting matter rather than creating formless matter as the first step in the creation.

[31] See La Planche, *L'Écriture,* 212–24. has an excellent treatment of Cappell's work as a whole.

[32] La Planche, *L'Écriture,* 224–29.

[33] It is clear that Johannes Buxtorf Jr. inherited the cause from his father, about whom see Stephen G. Burnett, *From Christian Hebraism to Jewish Studies: Johannes Buxtorf (1564–1629) and Hebrew Learning in the Seventeenth Century* (Leiden: E. J. Brill, 1996).

[34] Johannes Buxtorf, Fil., *Anticritica seu Vindiciae Veritatis Hebraicae Adversus Ludovici Cappelli Criticiam Vocat Sacram, Ejusque Defensionem* (Basel: Sumptibus Haeredum Ludovici Regis, 1653).

[35] Buxtorf, *Anticritica,* 8.

Quite clearly he was afraid that Cappell was playing into the hands of the Roman Catholic controversialists, a view Morin himself agreed with, as his introduction to Cappell's work shows.

Now in fact most text critics today would be equally impatient with Buxtorf and Morin. Against Buxtorf they would argue that textual criticism makes its decisions after a careful and tedious comparison of different texts, compared to which accounting looks exciting, but it is tied to how texts are written and what they actually contain, and, like accounting, it is a study where the obligation is to search for the truth, not the convenience of the searcher. On the other hand, against Morin they would point out that in most cases the Hebrew text is reasonably clear even without the vowel pointing.

Cappell's *Critica Sacra* was one of the great exegetical works of the seventeenth century. It went beyond his original discussion of the origin of pointing in the Hebrew Bible; it was a painstakingly careful examination of different readings to be found in both the texts in the Masoretic and Samaritan tradition and the variants indicated in the various versions of the Old Testament. Much of what he discussed is worth attention today, providing one takes into account subsequent manuscript discoveries, not least of all the Dead Sea Scrolls. But there is one aspect of his work that cries out for comment, namely, the way he dealt with parallel passages in different historical books of the Old Testament, most notably between the books of Samuel and Kings on one hand and the books of Chronicles on the other. Cappell confined his discussion to possible textual variants, whereas a modern critic would immediately think of different types of material, different authors, and different dates of composition. The explanation for this apparent blank in the method of a brilliant scholar is that history as a factor in the origins of Scripture had not yet been recognized. This will be discussed in the next chapter (pp. 127–29), where this new development in European consciousness will be examined.

Apart from the importance of Cappell's work in itself, there are three points about the history of biblical interpretation that are worth making.

First, there is a lesson to be learned from the errors of competent men, for in the debate over Cappell's work, there is no doubt about the ability and the learning of all parties concerned. Both Johannes Buxtorf Sr. and Jr. were among the greatest Hebraists of the era, and, in fact, members of the family held the chair of Old Testament at Basel for a hundred and fifty years. Morin's competence was recognized even by Richard Simon, and he was asked to prepare texts for the Paris Polyglot. While it is easy to be critical of these men, it is more difficult to emulate their erudition. Their tragedy should inspire not scorn but pity and terror lest we, too, have tragic flaws.

Second, the afterlife of lost causes in the history of biblical interpretation is extraordinary. Nearly a hundred years after this dispute, the Enlightenment Orientalist Johann David Michaelis published a dissertation defending the antiquity of the Hebrew pointing, admittedly very early in his career, but he soon abandoned his position. Even in 1770 James Robertson, professor of Oriental languages at Edinburgh, published his *Clavis Pentateuchi*, which included a dissertation against the view that vowel points were later additions to the text of the Hebrew Bible.[36] Like graveyards, biblical exegesis is a popular place for the ghosts to walk.

Third, in the seventeenth century the debate about the accuracy of biblical manuscripts, reduced to the question of do we have the real Bible, spread from the Protestant-Roman Catholic debate into the wider sphere of philosophical discussion about the authority of the Bible.

ii. The Samaritan Pentateuch

The community of the Samaritans, who trace their descent from the inhabitants of the northern kingdom of Israel, survives even today. Their Bible is not the complete Hebrew Bible but consists of the Pentateuch alone. In the sixteenth century Guillaume Postel got wind of the existence of this manuscript tradition but was unable to procure a copy. In 1616 a French agent in Istanbul managed to acquire two copies, and by the end of the century there were roughly eighty manuscripts known in western Europe. The interest in the Samaritan Pentateuch was similar to the excitement about the Dead Sea Scrolls in the twentieth century, for it was hoped that in the Samaritan Pentateuch would be a Hebrew tradition predating the Masoretic Text, the text that lies behind rabbinic manuscripts of the Hebrew Bible.

iii. New Testament text

In the previous chapter the first hundred or so years of the history of the printed New Testament text was discussed, including how an introduction to an edition in 1633 accidentally created an authoritative status among Protestants for the *Textus Receptus*. As a result, whatever the rights and wrongs of this text may have been, from then on it was reproduced in various editions of the New Testament, and it was not until

[36] James Robertson, *Clavis Pentateuchi* (Edinburgh: Fleming and Neill, 1770).

Johann Jakob Griesbach (1745–1812) that a scholar dared to issue a Greek New Testament in which significant variants from the *Textus Receptus* were incorporated into the text itself rather than being indicated in the *apparatus criticus*. Even today there are defenders of the *Textus Receptus* to be found in the company of well-meaning advocates of lost causes in biblical studies.

iv. THE OXFORD POLYGLOT

The most important textual development of the Baroque period may well have been the publication in 1657 of the *Biblia Sacra Polyglotta* edited by Brian Walton.[37] The format of this work was to provide the text of each biblical book, along with the text of the various versions in parallel columns. Each text was printed in its own script and was accompanied by a Latin translation, so that those unable to read, say Arabic, could see from the Latin translation how the Arabic text differed from the Hebrew, at least in an approximate fashion.[38] Compared with the Complutensian Polyglot of the early sixteenth century, one can see the extent of the progress made both in collecting the ancient versions and in learning the relevant languages. However, what was still lacking was any method of sorting through and evaluating textual evidence in a coherent and systematic fashion. This was not to come until the eighteenth century.

4. *The Greek of the New Testament*

While Roman Catholics were theoretically committed to the authority of the Vulgate, Protestants had every interest in working from the Bible in its original languages. This meant that the Protestant scholars could get on with textual and philological studies of Greek and Hebrew with

---

[37] Although dated 1657, the work was printed between 1653 and early 1658. It was apparently published later in 1658, though some copies were not issued until after the Restoration in 1660. These copies have a variant form of the preface. [Note in Bodleian catalogue.]

[38] Richard Simon pointed out how Matthew Poole, discussed below (p. 134), in his summary of variations in the text and interpretation of the biblical books, made the mistake of taking the translation too seriously and finding differences between the versions that came not from the original texts but from the translations made of them in the Oxford Polyglot. An example may help clarify this matter. If I translate "le bateau est vite" as "the ship is fast," I am not doing anything wrong; but there is an ambiguity in English that is not in the French, namely, a ship may also be fast to the dock. This is a small example of how all translations are bruised reeds that can harm the hand of the user.

fewer *a priori* positions to hinder them. It was out of this interest that an interesting debate took place in Holland about the Greek of the New Testament. The background to this debate was that it is an inescapable fact that to anyone familiar with classical Greek as found in the best authors, the Greek of the New Testament is rather dowdy. There were only two writers in the New Testament who could write elegant, literary Greek—the author of the Epistle to the Hebrews, consistently, and Luke, who for the most part chose not to.

Furthermore, the Dutch universities in the seventeenth century required all theological students to learn Greek. This stipulation meant that there was a body of theologians who could appreciate the language, especially since knowledge of New Testament Greek had been greatly improved by the arrival of George Pasor (1570–1637), recognized as the founder of Greek New Testament philology, who came to Franeker in 1627 as a refugee from the wars in Germany and wrote the first New Testament Greek grammar as well as continuing to issue his Greek dictionaries. Shortly after his death a debate broke out in Leiden between Claudius Salmasius and Daniel Heinsius over the nature of New Testament Greek: Could one explain its strange forms as coming from its unique status as a special language of Greek words with Semitic meanings (Salmasius), or was it simply the everyday Greek spoken in a particular part of the Roman Empire (Heinsius).

Then there was also a debate between those who felt that New Testament Greek was like Mark Twain's remark about Wagner's music (not as bad as it sounded); it was just Greek enriched with Hebraisms to carry its meaning. Against these "Hebraists," such as Ludwig de Dieu, Heinsius, and Salmasius, there were those who argued that no barbarisms or solecisms existed and that the New Testament was using essentially Greek words once one tracked down the vocabulary.

The interesting feature of these debates was that they were argued out, not on the basis of doctrines of inspiration, but by reference to evidence from various sources that could throw light on the meaning of New Testament words—ancient Jewish sources in Greek, such as the LXX, and Josephus, ancient versions (translations) into other languages, and quotations from the Christian fathers. Here again there is the possibility of a new approach to the Bible; the New Testament is to be seen, not as a special source beyond comparison, but as a writing coming from a particular time and social context. Evidence and not orthodox doctrine was the standard of this part of biblical studies. Dr. Henk de Jonge has put forward a convincing argument that the renewal of biblical studies from the Enlightenment on can be attributed in part at least to debates in the earlier part of the seventeenth century about New Testament Greek.[39]

5. Translation

The most significant Bible translation into English in the seventeenth century was the Authorized or King James Version, first published in 1611.[40] It is sometimes stated that it was the *Textus Receptus* that was used for the New Testament. While not wildly inaccurate, this statement is at least anachronistic, for as noted above, the term did not come into use until some twenty years after the KJV appeared. The story of the making of this translation is often told, though apparently it is not quite clear by what authority it was recognized as the Authorized Version.

The KJV did not automatically become the Bible of choice in England, but it only gradually replaced the earlier Geneva and Bishops' Bibles. Its text was not adopted for the epistles and gospels in the Church of England prayer book until 1662, but even then in some of the services quotations from the Bishops' Bible were retained (e.g., the Comfortable Words in the communion service).[41] However, once established the KJV achieved a status in the English-speaking world more exalted than translations in other European countries; it not only replaced other versions in general use, its position made even thinking of new versions difficult. The only eighteenth-century English translation that had any public at all was Bishop Challoner's revision of the Roman Catholic Douai Version. This was in contrast to the situation in, say Germany, where Luther's Bible was challenged by Francke, and in the eighteenth century roughly a dozen major new versions were published. In England it was not until the late nineteenth century that even a revision of the KJV was possible, and even now, the KJV and its descendants (Revised Version, Revised Standard Version, New Revised Standard Version, New International

[39] Henk J. de Jonge, "The Study of the New Testament in the Dutch Universities 1575–1700," *History of Universities* (1981) 1:113-129.

[40] See Adam Nicolson, *God's Secretaries: The Making of the King James Bible* (New York: HarperCollins, 2003).This work is not a serious work about translation, texts, grammar, etc., but much more a human interest account about the clash of personalities behind theological infighting at a particular time.

[41] Interestingly enough, there was the same problem in the Roman Catholic Church with the introduction of new editions of the Vulgate under Sixtus V in 1590 and Clement VIII in 1592. Sixtus hoped to make his edition the standard text for Scripture readings at all services; Clement was less demanding in this regard.

Bible, etc.) still maintain a significant, perhaps even a dominant place in the English-speaking world.

6. *Biblical exegesis*

It is one of the suggestions of this book that in the work of exegesis, the distinctions between Roman Catholic and Protestant commentators were not as clearly defined as might be expected. It is arguable that after the seventeenth century the Roman Catholic tradition fell into decline and that the efforts of the eighteenth century to find new, creative approaches were mostly the work of Protestants. However, up till then Roman Catholic commentators were as esteemed as their Protestant counterparts, and not just in Roman Catholic areas. Thomas Browne had at least knowledge of Pererius's commentary on Genesis, and Milton complained that even Protestants used Roman Catholic works more than Protestant ones. It is only because histories of exegesis tend to be written by Protestants that this important fact appears to have been forgotten. For example, Campegius Vitringa, in his early eighteenth-century commentary on Isaiah, lists among older authorities he used not only Protestant scholars but also seven Roman Catholic authorities (Oleaster, Leo Castrius, Hieronumus Osorius, Hector Pintus, Francisco Forerius, Gaspar Sanctius, and Gabriel Alvarez).[42]

It may have been the overlap and mutual influence of Roman Catholic and Protestant commentators that led Hugo Grotius (discussed below, pp. 111–15) to conceive the idea of writing a commentary on the Bible in the hope of reconciling Protestants and Roman Catholics by trying to set aside proprietary interpretations that read specific doctrines into passages where they were not to be found in the original meaning of the text.

Two Roman Catholic commentators moving toward a more modern interpretation

A few samples from two Roman Catholic commentators should suffice to show a direction their work was taking and was to be developed more extensively by others. Guilielmus Estius (1542–1613) and Cornelius à Lapide (1567–1637) published their works in the first part of the seven-

---

[42] Campegius Vitringa, *Commentarius in librum prophetiarum Jesaiae*, vol. 1 (Herborn, Germany: Nicolai Andreae, 1715) Praefatio 4. I am reading the name "Pindus" as "Pintus."

teenth century. Lapide wrote an extensive commentary on the whole of the Bible; Estius took a different route and produced a book entitled *Annotationes in praecipua ac difficiliora sacrae scripturae loca*, that is, "Notes on the principal and more difficult passages in Scripture."[43] Neither author was exempt from criticism by Richard Simon[44] on the basis of their treatment of textual and grammatical problems, but for our purposes, what is interesting is that they were moving toward a historical rather than a theological interpretation of some passages in the Pentateuch.

Lapide had a series of preliminary observations on the Pentateuch. For him, Moses' sources of information consisted not only of direct revelation from God but also from what he had seen himself and what he had received from earlier written tradition. Following Masius and Pererius, Lapide stated that Moses wrote the Pentateuch simply in the mode of diaries or of annals; his work is to be distinguished from that of Joshua, who put the annals of Moses into order and added many additions and insertions. The evidence for these additions are references within the text itself, such as the one to the Book of the Wars of the Lord in Numbers 21:14.

In interpreting the Pentateuch, Lapide reminded his readers that Moses did not write the history of the world symbolically, mystically, or allegorically; rather, his history was in a plain and simple style because of circumstances at the time of writing, namely, the ignorant state of the Israelite people. While Augustine presented an elaborate philosophical argument about how light existed before the earth and sky, Lapide opted for the more obvious explanation, that is, the unlearned nature of the people of Israel, for whom Moses had to write an account they could understand.[45]

Lapide had an interesting solution to the problem of the divine name in Genesis 4:26, discussed in the last chapter (p. 56). He argued that while Moses knew full well that God was only known as "elohim" in Genesis, he nonetheless attributed the use of the name JHWH to earlier Israelites. Lapide also noted that Paul's style was informal, which meant that on

---

[43] (Douai: Patté, 1629). He did write a commentary on the Epistles of Saint Paul.

[44] Richard Simon, *Histoire Critique des principaux commentateurs du Nouveau Testament* (Rotterdam: 1693; unaltered reprint Frankfort: Minerva, 1969); on Estius, 641–49; on Lapide, 655–64.

[45] Cornelius à Lapide, *Commentaria in scripturam sacram*, Tome I: *In Pentateuchum Mosis* (Paris: Vives, 1859) 27–28. He wrote commentaries on every book of the Bible except Psalms and Job, which were published between 1616 and 1645.

occasion he let himself get carried away with remarks that had to be amended later. Simon praised him for this, since those who ignored Paul's style made up their own theology, which they attributed to Paul.[46]

Lapide also appears to have had a sense of humor that he allowed to enter into his writing. He referred to a certain scholar Dr. Thomas as not *"sanctus ille Angelicus, sed Anglicus,"* a neat Latin pun presupposing a certain knowledge of theology and English church history.[47]

Estius also followed Masius and Pererius in recognizing non-Mosaic strands within the Pentateuch. He admitted that it was possible that the additions were made by Ezra at the time of his reconstitution of the sacred books of Israel, though he was inclined to seeing Joshua rather than Ezra as the author of the account of Moses' death. But there was a rather endearing honesty to Estius. In response to a possible question of why Cain was afraid of being killed when there were only four human beings in the world, one of whom he had just killed, Estius's response was a refreshing "Veram non videtur," best translated as "I haven't the slightest idea."[48] In dealing with the New Testament, he similarly acknowledged that in Matthew's Gospel the genealogy of Joseph produces problems if it is meant to apply to Jesus.[49]

Obviously, any assessment of Lapide and Estius has to take into account that they have little to say to modern scholarship; they certainly did not have a modern understanding of the origins of the Bible, and the suggestions they made have long since been passed over. At the same time they showed erudition, diligence, and honesty in their efforts to make sense of the Bible. Lapide was aware that the ways of thinking of the seventeenth century were different from those of ancient Israel, or at any rate of most ancient Israelites. Estius was disarming in his frankness in admitting that there are texts he could explain fully. Both men saw the Bible as the product of human action in a historical context, and while they allowed for revelation, they did not permit this category to overwhelm their faculties of observation. One has to ask, In what sense is it fair to call them "precritical"? Certainly they recognized problems when

---

[46] Simon, *Histoire Critique,* 658.

[47] Puns are usually better left without explanation, but here Lapide's joke depended on his readers' knowing the story of the pope, who, seeing British boys (Latin *Anglici*) in a slave market, said that they were not *Anglici* but *angelici* and that Thomas Aquinas was known as "the Angelic Doctor." Since the Doctor Thomas was not Aquinas but simply an Englishman, Lapide could not resist the temptation.

[48] Estius, *Annotationes,* 7.

[49] Ibid., 443.

they saw them, and to this extent they were no less critical in intention than we are today.

La Peyrère and Hobbes:
two amateurs in biblical interpretation

It is only because those who write on La Peyrère and Hobbes have not read the works of the professional scholars of the sixteenth and seventeenth centuries that these two men are seen as far more innovative and original than they actually were. This situation may be due in part to the fact that many of the great exegetes of the times wrote in the then language of scholarly and diplomatic communication, namely Latin, whereas today Latin is less commonly used or understood.

Isaac de La Peyrère (1596–1676) [50]

Johannes Franciscus Buddeus, in his guide to theology,[51] published in the early eighteenth century, often links together as the great enemies of the Bible not only Hobbes and Spinoza but also Isaac de La Peyrère. His third choice may have been a mistake. Isaac de la Peyrère was a French Protestant who spent much of his life as a diplomat cum librarian in the service of the Condé family. His interests were wide, he was a genial companion, and he had many friends across the spectrum of belief and unbelief. La Peyrère acquired sudden notoriety by the publication of his *Prae-Adamitae*[52] (*Men Before Adam*) in 1655 and its companion volume, *Systema theologicae* (*A System of Theology*), which led to his imprisonment by the Inquisition and eventually to his more or less forced conversion to

---

[50] The spelling of the name varies; it can be Isaac La Peyrère, Isaac Lapeyrère, or Isaac de La Peyrère. The Bibliothèque Nationale at Paris spells the full name (mostly) the third way, but the last name is treated as La Peyrère. This is the usage followed in this work. The Latin form of the name is Peirerius or Peyerus, but care must be taken to distinguish it from Pererius, the Spanish scholar treated in the previous chapter.

[51] Jo. Franciscus Buddeus, *Isagoge historico-theologica ad theologiam universam singulasque eius partes*, 2 vols. (Leipzig: Fritsch, 1727) 1436.

[52] La Peyrère's work was in two volumes: *Prae-Adamitae sive exercitatio super Versibus duodecimo, decimotertio, & decimoquarto, capitis quinti Epistolae D. Pauli ad Romanos* (Leiden: n.p., 1655), and *Systema theologicum ex praeadamitarum hypothesi* (Leiden: n.p., 1655). Several subsequent editions were published with little material change. The English edition of *Prae-Adamitae* was published anonymously under the title *Men before Adam* (London: n.p., 1656). The English edition of the *Systema* was issued as *A Theological Systeme upon that Presupposition, that Men were before Adam* (London, n.p., 1655). These translations are usually accurate, but they tend to leave out phrases and sentences found in the Latin original and need to be checked against it.

Catholicism, along with a formal retraction of his work. In later life he still hung on to his ideas, with little interest in hearing objections to them, as shown by a letter to La Peyrère from Richard Simon, which exhibited a certain tone of exasperation on the part of that formidable critic, who was not known for suffering fools gladly even at the best of times.

R. H. Popkin published an extended work on La Peyrère,[53] in which he interpreted La Peyrère as part skeptic under the possible influence of Marrano Jews. With all due respect to Popkin's interesting works on skepticism in the seventeenth century, I consider his interpretation of La Peyrère as unconvincing; first, because I do not think he read La Peyrère accurately and, second, because he did not take into account the Renaissance tradition of biblical interpretation. Rather than comment on Popkin's work in detail, I will set out my argument and leave the reader to judge for himself or herself. *Caveat lector.*

La Peyrère's first theological publication was *Du Rappel des Juifs,*[54] which was addressed to the Jewish community and set out his own particular vision of the first stage of the end of the world, namely, of a reunion of Jews and Christians under the king of France and a return to Palestine. This work shows that La Peyrère was firmly rooted in the thought of seventeenth-century apocalyptic expectation, which expected the ingathering of Israel into the Christian church, for philo-semitism was a common theme in the Baroque period and was part of the motivation for the permission to Jews to return to England under the Commonwealth.[55] This early work of La Peyrère is vital for understanding the two later works that got him into trouble, namely *Prae-Adamitae (Men Before Adam)* in 1655 and its companion volume *Systema theologicae (A System of Theology)*, for it is clear that the eschatological expectation of the *Du rappel des Juifs* remained paramount for La Peyrère, for the *Prae-Adamitae* is addressed "To all the Synagogues of the Jews dispersed over the face of the Earth." There was a sense of urgency in this appeal, for he added:

[53] R. H. Popkin, *Isaac La Peyrère (1596–1676): His Life, Work, and Influence* (Leiden: E. J. Brill, 1987).

[54] Published anonymously in 1643 and not reprinted since then. A new edition is being prepared by Professor Elisabeth Quennehen.

[55] See Christopher Hill, "Till the Conversion of the Jews," in *Millenarianism and Messianism in English Literature and Thought 1650–1800* (Leiden: E. J. Brill, 1988) 12–36. The basic treatment of the subject is Hans Joachim Schoeps, *Philosemitismus im Barock* (Tübingen: J.C.B. Mohr, 1952). La Peyrère's choice of the king of France as the Messiah can be attributed to the royalism characteristic of French Protestants. See the discussion in La Planche, *L'Écriture*, 20–23.

I have spoken great things concerning you in this Treatise; wherein I have handled your election. Much greater are those which I shall speak in the next; where I shall handle our Restoration, which I certainly know shall be. And if God doth move here men's secret thoughts at all, I hope, and am confident, it shall be very shortly.[56]

This concern with the Jews was the reason for the subtitle of the *Men Before Adam*, which was *A Discourse upon the twelfth, thirteenth, and fourteenth verses of the Fifth Chapter of the Epistle of the Apostle Paul to the Romans*. This is the passage from which Augustine derived his doctrine of original sin, namely, that all human beings from the moment of their birth are guilty of Adam's sin, and baptism is indispensable for their forgiveness. La Peyrère was essentially trying to get around Augustine, for if Jews had to be baptized to enter into the eschatological community, La Peyrère envisioned that baptism was going to be a difficulty. To get over this problem, La Peyrère set out to reinterpret Romans 5:12-14. His argument was, to put it mildly, very complicated, but his logic can be summed this way. For Paul, the reason for physical death was sin; that is why all humans die. Paul then points out that without the law there is no sin, and before the law sin was not imputed. But La Peyrère pointed out that Adam was indeed under the law, for he had been commanded not to eat of the fruit of a particular tree; hence Adam had broken a law and appropriately died for his sin.[57] But who, then, were the people mentioned in Paul as those who were in the world before the law was given? Obviously, they could not have been Adam; it follows, then, that there must have been human beings who existed before him who were the only ones who could be described as not living under the law.

The initial conclusion that La Peyrère drew from this argument was that Adam was not the first man, but rather the first Jew, and therefore he was the father of the Jews, not the whole human race. La Peyrère then built up an elaborate argument to show why Jews did not have to be baptized on account of Adam's sins. Whether the logical structure of this position is valid is not of immediate importance; the fact is, La Peyrère

---

[56] *Men before Adam*, not paginated, but on first page of gathering A 4.

[57] La Peyrère was not the only one to notice that in fact Adam had been given a law to obey. This had been done by Bonaventura Cornelius Bertramus (1531–1594) in his *De Republica Ebraeorum*. I am referring to the edition by Constantine l'Empereur, in *Critici Sacri*, VI (1695 edition), col. 747. I have been unable to find any reference to editions of this work of Bertramus before that of Constantine l'Empereur, which was first published in Leiden in 1641 and therefore could have been available to La Peyrère.

thought he had proved his case and set out his conclusions on this premise.

Systema theologicae (A System of Theology), the second volume of his work, was La Peyrère's attempt to draw out the implications of his discovery that Adam was not the first man. He labored over this work for a number of years, and indeed it had the characteristics of an overwritten document; for to put the matter mildly, it was rather diffuse and formless. However, Book 4 of the work had a great deal to say about the Bible, and this was to give La Peyrère his trouble with the authorities. For example, he claimed that the Flood was not worldwide; that the Pentateuch was not entirely written by Moses; that the miracles of the sun going backward in Joshua and 2 Kings did not happen as stated; that Adam did not know everything when he was created; that the Israelites' clothes did wear out in the desert, notwithstanding Deuteronomy 29:5; that the world did not begin with Adam; and that not all humans are descended from the sons of Noah.

What happened was that La Peyrère allowed himself to become distracted from his original theme of the part of the Jews in the Palestinian messianic kingdom and went on to a different argument, namely, the defense of the Bible against some of the antireligious arguments he had heard, possibly in some of the circles he frequented in Paris. It is likely that he took this step because he noticed apologetic possibilities in his pre-Adamite hypothesis. Thus, were there two creation stories in Genesis? This was only to be expected, for the first was about men in general, the second about Adam, the well-known private person who was created at a later date and became the ancestor of the Jews. Is it impossible to see how all the races of humanity descended from one man? Of course, but then, given the creation of other men before Adam, it is not necessary to assume that only Adam had progeny.

However, La Peyrère felt impelled to extend his ingenuity into other problems. On the question of miracles, one gambit La Peyrère used resembled the excuse of the Victorian housemaid who, upon being scolded by her employer for having had a baby out of wedlock, defended herself with "It was just a little one, Ma'am." La Peyrère was adamant that the miracles recorded did take place and were indeed miracles, but not quite on the scale suggested. For example, consider the way he tackled the two most difficult from an astrophysical point of view: the standing still of the sun in Joshua 10:12-15 and the shadow going back on the sundial in 2 Kings 20:8-11. La Peyrère's explanation was that the sun and the universe neither came to a halt for Joshua nor reversed their motion for

Isaiah; rather, Divine Providence arranged for a special refraction of light to produce the extended daylight hours recorded in Joshua, and in the case of the sundial in 2 Kings, it was the shadow that went backward, not the sun.[58]

However, not all the criticism of the believability of Scripture arose from the miracles it recorded. Arguments from both geological considerations and the alleged antiquity of records from other peoples[59] had already been urged as reasons for denying the accuracy of the biblical chronology. Furthermore, within the Bible itself there were incongruities that demanded an explanation, such as Sarah being abducted at an advanced age by an amorous ruler (Genesis)[60] or Melchizedek apparently not having any natural parents. La Peyrère accounted for the problems of continuity by arguing that the Pentateuch was made up of different documents, not all of which came from Moses. It is sometimes stated flatly that La Peyrère denied the Mosaic authorship of the Pentateuch. Whether this is a fair statement depends on how you define your terms. La Peyrère did state clearly, "I need not trouble the Reader much further, to prove a thing in it self sufficiently evident, that the five first books of the Bible were not written by Moses, as is thought."[61] However, the qualifying phrase "as is thought" at the end of the sentence needs to be borne in mind, for further on La Peyrère said, "I do not doubt but that Moses set down very accurately the Jews going out of Egypt; God's Law deliver'd in Sinai; the Ceremonies prescrib'd in that Law; as also the History of Four hundred years, in which the Jews wander'd in the desert; as also that memorable mysterie of Deuteronomy." In other words, La Peyrère was saying that Moses did not write the whole of the Pentateuch, in the way supposed by popular opinion, but he nonetheless wrote large parts of it.

How original was La Peyrère then? Both Popkin and Grafton suggest that he was radically daring, even original. Popkin argues, "Only the wildest radical enthusiasts of the Puritan revolution and La Peyrère

---

[58] Popkin, *La Peyrère*, 90, interprets La Peyrère here to say that the sun went backward only in Palestine. I think La Peyrère himself would have been astonished at this explanation, but in fairness to Popkin, there is no doubt that La Peyrère was less than crystal clear at this point.

[59] Even John Donne accepted the suggestion that Zoroaster predated Moses.

[60] In fact, this happened twice: Genesis 12:10-20 and 20:1-17. To be fair, the stories themselves do not give Sarah's age, but if one follows the chronological pattern in Genesis, she is indeed an old woman in each case; cf. Genesis 12:4 and 17:17.

[61] *A Theological Systeme*, 208.

were willing to conclude that Moses was not the author of it all."[62] And Anthony Grafton states that an exegetical and scientific revolution had taken place between 1582 and 1692, which had deprived the Bible of some of its luster and perfection, and he attributed much of this to La Peyrère.[63] This is simply not so. Neither Popkin nor Grafton has taken into account the scholarship of the professional exegetes, such as Masius, Pererius, and others discussed above. La Peyrère himself was aware of his dependence on professional scholarship, for he cited John Cameron, professor at Saumur in the early seventeenth century, in his treatment of the reason why Melchizedek's parentage is not recorded in Genesis.[64]

The problem is, then, if La Peyrère's arguments were for the most part to be found elsewhere, why was there such an outcry and why was he jailed and more or less forced to retract and convert to Roman Catholicism? The answer has to be sought in the vagaries of public opinion, and it is important to take this factor into account in more than one incident in the history of biblical interpretation. A more recent example was the case of J.A.T. Robinson, who published a small book called *Honest to God*, which, as Robinson himself admitted, contained little that was original, yet it stirred up a great deal of public debate and outcry. One possible explanation is that while the works of the theologians Robinson quoted existed in heavy tomes in specialist libraries, Robinson made the ideas known to the general public in a popularly written text in an inexpensive format.

Similarly, the scholars from whom La Peyrère derived his ideas were published in folio editions expensive to buy and awkward to carry; La Peyrère's notorious works were available in a small, inexpensive format, and it was easy enough to smuggle them past authorities, so that anyone who heard of the scandal could get the documents for himself or herself. However, when all is said and done, this is not the whole explanation for public opinion, and there are times when there is no complete account-

---

[62] Popkin, *La Peyrère*, 50.

[63] Anthony Grafton, "Isaac La Peyrère and the Old Testament," in *Defenders of the Text: The Traditions of Scholarship in an Age of Science, 1450–1800* (Cambridge, Mass.: Harvard University Press, 1991) 204–05.

[64] *Theological Systeme*, 50. Actually Cameron's explanation is still conservative; compare this with Tirinus's suggestion that Melchizedek's parents are not mentioned because Genesis was not concerned with Gentile families. R. P. Jacobus Tirinus (1580–1636), *Commentarium in Sacram Scripturam*, 2 vols. (Lyon: Nicolaus & J. de Ville, 1723) 2:304. This point is echoed in Lapide's commentary on the letter to the Hebrews, 409.

ing for why irrationality combines with ignorance to overwhelm the judgment of the public and inflame its wilder impulses.

There is also another point to make about La Peyrère. At the beginning of this chapter, the dethronement of the Bible as a universal source of knowledge was discussed. The trend of La Peyrère's apologetics was to portray the Bible as a book concerned with one part of the world, not as a guide to the history of the globe. The Flood took place, but only in Palestine; Noah's children indeed fathered various peoples, but not all the different races and groups found by the European explorers since the fifteenth century. Whether La Peyrère was as original as he is sometimes portrayed is an open question, but he did make known to his contemporaries the possibility that the Bible was not the complete guide to human history, and echoes of his views persisted even in the nineteenth century, when they were turned around into bulwarks of biblical orthodoxy.

La Peyrère, then, was a talented amateur whose ingenuity was fueled by a type of hope for the immediate coming of the kingdom of God. However, he did combine a general knowledge of serious biblical scholarship with an interest in the changing shape of the world and tried to achieve a synthesis between the two. His efforts brought him close to the brink of disaster, because he woke the sleeping tiger of half-ignorant public opinion, but his efforts did not go unnoticed, for some of his observations found their way into Spinoza's work on the Bible and into the work of Burnet discussed below (pp. 140–46).

Thomas Hobbes was another amateur in theology who also brought disapproval on his own head, but his case was very different. Essentially, Hobbes was a political philosopher who was forced into biblical criticism in much the way some political scientists today are forced into economics; in both situations the results can be strange.

To see Hobbes in perspective, one has to remember the position of the Bible in his day as an encyclopedic source for guidance in many matters, not least of all politics, when it was a general assumption that any European state would be a Christian state. This is one of the reasons that a genre of biblical interpretation arose that can be called the *reipublica Hebraeorum*.[65] Works of this sort were written by Sigonio, Cunaeus, Bertramus, and others. In his preface to Bertramus, Constantine l'Empereur explained the importance of such an inquiry by saying that

---

[65] The Latin reipublica had a wider sense of meaning than "republic" as an alternative to monarchy; etymologically *reipublic* comes from "things" and "public," and in the period we are dealing with, it meant something like "political constitution."

while we cannot be bound by all the institutions of the Israelites—we should still try to get as close as possible to those institutions instituted by God.[66] What was sought in the Bible was not just general principles of a social gospel type; rather, there was a sense that guidance on particular matters could be sought, especially in the Old Testament.[67] For example, John Selden wrote his *Historie of Tithes* to discuss whether the Old Testament required people to pay tithes to the church; the fact that his answer was "no" explains why this work was suppressed.

In England of the seventeenth century, the place of the Bible as a guide to constitutional politics was a serious matter, as Charles I found out the hard way. Needless to say, just because people appeal to the Bible does not mean that their arguments are based on carefully weighed, sound exegesis, as a quick look at the so-called Christian right in the United States will demonstrate, but there is a real danger of people justifying their own preferences by identifying them with the will of God and therefore putting them beyond the bounds of discussion.

Hobbes had seen far too much of this in his day; it must be admitted that by nature he was not given to political courage. His was not the steely-eyed resolution of the martyr on his way to the stake, but then neither was he interested in sending anybody else to the stake. For Hobbes, then, the question was, How did one avoid the excesses of the religious enthusiasts and lay the foundations for a stable society? His first objective in *Leviathan* was to show how and why ordered commonwealths in general worked, but given that in his time a European country was by definition a Christian country, he then had to go on to devote a section to authority in a Christian commonwealth as one particular type of commonwealth among others. This task required a discussion of the Bible.

The key to Hobbes's discussion of the Christian commonwealth is that he saw himself fighting a war on two fronts. On one hand, the Roman Catholic Church claimed both temporal and spiritual power over the affairs of individual Christian states. For Hobbes, this was unacceptable, for it set up an independent source of power in opposition to that of the sovereign of a state. The other threat Hobbes saw was the radical Protestant, who claimed that one's duty to God as perceived by an individual's reading of the Bible or personal inspiration trumped one's duty to the

---

[66] Bonaventura Cornelius Bertramus, *De Republica Ebraeorum*, in *Tractatuum bibliocorum, Critici Sacri*, VI, cols. 741–42.

[67] Ibid., from the preface by Constantine l'Empereur, 740.

sovereign. Both approaches threatened the sovereign as the single source of government and left the way open to civil war. Much of the discussion of biblical interpretation in part 3 of *Leviathan* was the result of careful steering between the Roman Catholic Scylla and the Protestant Charybdis.

Hobbes skirted around questions of beliefs about the Scriptures and stuck to how these should become laws and require obedience. He dismantled the Protestant appeal to Scripture on the grounds that given that there are different canons of Scripture but nothing within Scripture that defines its contents, the canon has to be decided by the sovereign of a given Christian nation—in the case of England, the sovereign acting through the Church of England. Hobbes could then proceed to some observations about the books of the Bible in the interests of his political ideals. His discussion centered around the authorship of biblical books and their dates, and his conclusion was that by and large they were dependable sources, not because they were inspired but because they were written by honest, informed authors, a view set out in a way not far from the views of Grotius, to be discussed below (pp. 111–15). Having settled the question of the canon and authority by political rather than theological means, Hobbes then showed how biblical exegesis itself filled out and confirmed the position he had taken. Starting from the generalized eschatological hope of the kingdom of God found in the seventeenth century, Hobbes set out his most original, if not most convincing, interpretation of Scripture:

> I find the kingdom of God to signify in most places of Scripture a kingdom properly so named, constituted by the votes of the people of Israel in peculiar manner, wherein they chose God for their king by covenant made with Him, upon God's promising them the possession of the land of Canaan. . . .

Hobbes's position was that while God had a regular kingdom at the time of Abraham, which was renewed under Moses, this kingdom of God ended when the Israelites demanded that Samuel should get them a king like the kings of other nations. God's reaction in 1 Samuel 8:7 was: "Hearken unto the voice of the people, for they have not rejected thee, but they have rejected me, that I should not reign over them." This, then, was the end of the kingdom of God properly so named, and this kingdom has not existed on earth since that date. Hobbes argued that while it was part of the mission of Jesus to renew this kingdom, this renewal would not be accomplished until Jesus' second coming, when he would set up a kingdom of God on the earth once again. At that point there would be a general resurrection of all who had died; the circumstances of both the saved and the damned would be different, but when the kingdom of God is finally wound up and given back to his Father by Jesus, there would be a second death for the wicked and a new creation in which only the just would have a part.

The effect of Hobbes's proof of the nonexistence of the kingdom of God in his time was to make the laws of the kingdom of God as found in the Bible inapplicable to the contemporary situation, where people were still waiting for the reestablishment of this divine kingdom. This refuted the notion of the desirability of a biblical basis for all current laws. Furthermore, in the case where the sovereign was a Christian, it was his prerogative to decide on what was Scripture and who was to exercise the office of teacher in his kingdom. In this no outside power could claim authority over him (here the papacy was in mind), because there was no central Christian commonwealth that might claim such a right. In his refutation of Cardinal Bellarmine's *De Summo Pontifice*, Hobbes even took this so far as to claim that the sovereign had the right to ordain clergy and celebrate the sacraments if he so chose. Essentially, Hobbes had fought off, in his own opinion at least, the two challenges to a sovereign's authority, namely, the Protestant appeal to the law of Scripture and the papal claim to authority over all Christian nations.

There are many other questions raised about Hobbes's approach to Scripture, but the basic one for the history of biblical interpretation is, What difference did Hobbes make to this discipline? The immediate answer is "very little." What Hobbes said about the authorship of various biblical books, not least of all the Pentateuch, had already been said by professional scholars before him. Those who have credited great originality to his observations have only been able to do so by not taking into account authors such as Masius, Pererius, and Lapide, who were well enough known that their books or at least their arguments would have been familiar to Hobbes.[68]

It is possible, however, that Hobbes performed a work of *haute vulgarization* in making these views known to a general audience that did not read Latin, a group that of course includes many scholars who have interpreted the seventeenth century. What Hobbes did was to emphasize

---

[68] The evidence for the use of continental Roman Catholic commentaries in England is found in Arnold Williams, *The Common Expositor: An Account of the Commentaries on Genesis 1527–1633* (Chapel Hill: The University of North Carolina Press, 1948).

the weakness of the arguments of those who would claim biblical authority for measures they wished to introduce into the civil law of their day. He did not convince everybody, but the acuteness of some of his observations impressed even Johannes Franciscus Buddeus, who said of him: "While he was not very learned, he was nonetheless very ingenious."[69] However, if Hobbes did not contribute anything significant to exegesis proper, he contributed to the process of the political dethronement of scriptural law, which was finally achieved in the next century by Johann David Michaelis in his *Mosaisches Recht*.

The seventeenth century's most eminent exegete, Hugo Grotius (1583–1645)

To appreciate the biblical interpretation of Hugo Grotius, one has to begin with the decision in the University of Leiden, following the example of some Protestant universities, not to teach dogmatics as such, but only to teach the Bible in contrast to the traditional approach of the Roman Catholic universities. The latter offered courses not only in the Bible but also in dogmatic theology, usually based on the *Sentences* of Peter Lombard or the *Summa Theologiae* of Thomas Aquinas.[70] In fact, dogma was taught at Leiden under the guise of exegesis. That certain dogmas were not immediately derived from Scripture became apparent in the quarrel between the supralapsarians and the infralapsarians, that is, between those who felt that God had decided before creation who should be saved or damned and those who believed that this decision was not made until after Adam's fall.

Proving that either doctrine is found as such in the Bible was not easy, as was discovered by Jacob Arminius (1560–1609), who set out to defend strict determinism but was convinced by opponents of the doctrine. Now a strict Calvinist would have to admit that it is clearly predestined that some people will believe in free will, so it was no surprise when a year after Arminius's death, his followers drew up the five *Remonstrantiae* (literally "demonstrations," "advisements") based on his teachings. Calvinists made of sterner stuff were outraged, and at the Synod of Dort (1618–1619) Arminianism was condemned and the Remonstrants excluded from the Dutch Reformed Church. The Remonstrant Church that

[69] Buddeus, *Isagoge*, 311.

[70] See Henk J. de Jonge, "The Study of the New Testament in the Dutch Universities 1575–1700," *History of Universities* 1 (1981) 113–29.

emerged was to play an important role in the history of exegesis.[71] Its greatest representative in the Baroque period was Hugo Grotius, who was thrown into prison in connection with the Remonstrant controversy and who escaped from Holland to live the rest of his life a refugee from his own country.

Grotius, the marvel of erudition in seventeenth-century Holland, was arguably the last of the Renaissance universal geniuses. He is best remembered as a jurist, the author of *De Iure Belli ac Pacis*. He also wrote poetry and drama and eventually obtained a post as ambassador of Sweden to Paris. Yet he appeared interested neither in developments in what we would call scientific knowledge nor in the new turn philosophy had taken. Reventlow has described him well as someone who, on the threshold of a new era, seemed to be looking backward.[72]

Grotius, as a faithful student of his teacher Josephus Justus Scaliger, was committed to exact philological interpretation with as few dogmatic presuppositions as possible, but in his great works of exegesis on the Bible he also had another purpose in mind. In the face of growing opposition to the Christian faith in any form, he also hoped to reconcile the Roman Catholic and Protestant churches through the means of an exegesis that would not import denominational assumptions into biblical interpretation. At the same time, he used his extraordinary erudition in the classics to explain, illustrate, and elaborate biblical texts. In his efforts to achieve this goal, he aroused more antagonism among Protestants than among Roman Catholics, his principal antagonist being Andreas Rivet, a French Protestant who had become a professor at Leiden and who held to a strong doctrine of the inspiration of the Bible.[73]

The characteristics of Grotius's approach in dealing with Old Testament texts were that after discussing the significance of the syntax of sentences in Hebrew, Greek, or the languages of different versions, he

---

[71] In England, Arminianism, as it tended to be called, had a certain appeal to the Church of England's suspicion of hard and fast dogmatic assertions; this led to the *bon mot* of the times, "What do Arminians hold?" to which the answer was "All the best bishoprics and all the best deaneries."

[72] Henning Graf Reventlow, "L'exégèse humaniste de Hugo Grotius," in Jean-Robert Armogathe, *Le Grand Siècle et la Bible* (Paris: Beauchesne, 1989) 142. Reventlow's article is an excellent summary of Grotius's exegesis.

[73] Hans Bots, "Hugo Grotius et André Rivet: Deux lumières opposées, deux vocations contradictoires," in Henk J. M. Nellen and Edwin Rabbie, eds. *Hugo Grotius Theologian: Essays in Honour of G.H.M. Posthumus Meyjes* (Leiden: E. J. Brill, 1994) 145–55.

would go on to wider issues discussed in the church fathers, the rabbis, and other commentators, and then finally he would look for parallels in classical antiquity. Obviously, not every text would call forth all these categories, but a single verse could lead to a page of discussion, such as the prohibition of idols in Exodus 20:4. In this instance Grotius had a special interest in showing that the statues in Roman Catholic churches were not the idols forbidden in the Ten Commandments.

Grotius refused to strain after explanations that would invoke miracles not recorded in Scripture itself; his rather dry comment was that there were enough miracles in Scripture without adding more without good reason.[74]

Grotius's approach to exegesis was marked by a resolve to explain what is clearly in the text and to avoid reading into it what the author had not intended. He did, however, allow for later developments in the text that went beyond the original meaning of the author. Thus Grotius opted for the interpretation of the Song of Songs as a secular love song, being originally a duet between Solomon and the daughter of the king of Egypt, interspersed with two choruses, one of young men and the other of maidens who were attending the marriage. Yet he added that Solomon believed that once this writing had lasted many years, it would be possible to find in its art of writing, without the distortion of allegory, something of the love of God toward the Israelite people, which the Chaldean paraphrase both sensed and made apparent. Here we find several characteristics of Grotius's exegesis. It began with the clear sense of the text in its original meaning, which had to be brought out by careful examination, but then he allowed for the legitimacy of later development.

Another interesting observation of Grotius was an explanation of the two forms of the Decalogue in Exodus and Deuteronomy. The problem is that if you compare the form of the Ten Commandments in Exodus 20:1-17 with Deuteronomy 5:6-21, they differ in several important ways. Grotius accounted for this discrepancy by arguing that the Exodus version was the set of laws received from God; the Deuteronomy version was Moses' reminding the Israelites in a speech in which he exercised his liberty to change the wording of the Ten Commandments.

In his interpretation of the prophets, Grotius insisted on the meaning that a passage had at the time it was pronounced; thus the prophecies in Isaiah 9 and 11 did not refer to the messiah, but to Ahaz's son Hezekiah, and the servant in Isaiah 53 was Jeremiah.

[74] *Critici Sacri*, I, col. 557.

In his New Testament exegesis,[75] Grotius put the weight of his interpretation on the gospel of Jesus, not the four Gospels, that is, what was important was Jesus' commandment of love, which required a new life in the hearer. This teaching of Jesus was, of course, supplemented by his expiatory death and atonement for sin. Grotius's argument for the reliability of the Gospels was not based on their inspiration, but on the reliability of their authors, who had recorded the proofs of Jesus' divine authority in his miracles and his resurrection. Apart from the historical connection of the evangelists either as eyewitnesses of the events of Jesus' life or as being well-informed, the proof of the evangelists' accounts was found in the miracles they did or the miracles that took place near their graves.

Given the foregoing argument, Grotius was then freed from the necessity of accepting every detail in the New Testament as accurate. The evangelists might well have made incidental mistakes, such as in minor details of when a saying of Jesus was spoken or about geographical or historical details, but these mistakes did not threaten the Gospel as such.

A source of scandal to his Protestant contemporaries was Grotius's rejection of the identification of the pope with the anti-Christ figures in the book of Revelation. This interpretation, which in fact predated the Reformation, had been standard within Protestantism and remained so after Grotius. Clearly Grotius here was trying to get rid of a factor that poisoned relations between Protestants and Catholics, but more to the point, it was not in the text from a strictly exegetical point of view, and few competent scholars would wish to defend this interpretation today.

Obviously, Grotius's arguments were vulnerable in the debate over miracles that was soon to explode in the later seventeenth century, for he does not appear to have recognized the difficulty of attesting to the accuracy of the evangelists by citing the miracles that had taken place at their tombs. There is, however, another facet of his exegesis that was weak, namely, his tendency to see biblical texts as the products of individual authors, and therefore biblical books should be explained by the same methods used to treat other books by individual authors. Thus the differences between the Gospels could be smoothed out by assuming that the evangelists as separate authors had their own way of giving their material. It did not occur to Grotius that some incongruities might

---

[75] See Henk J. de Jonge, "Grotius' View of the Gospels and the Evangelists," in Nellen and Rabbie, *Hugo Grotius Theologian*, 65–74.

be explained by postulating that different documents had been combined into a single work.

The most perceptive summary of Grotius's work is by Ludwig Diestel. Diestel was talking of Grotius's Old Testament exegesis, but it holds true for his New Testament observations as well: "[Grotius] had an epoch-making effect on Old Testament exegesis, not in that he produced a great revolution, but that he brought a ferment into biblical research whose continuing effect gradually took on greater proportions."[76]

Two other important approaches to exegesis:

i. SOCINIANS

One group that had certain affinities with the exegesis of the Remonstrants was the Socinian church, somewhat to the embarrassment of the former. The Socinians, named after Lelio and Faustus Sozzini (Latin "Socinus"), were a group that insisted on the literal interpretation of the Bible, particularly the New Testament. It was for this reason that they denied the necessity of the traditional doctrine of the Trinity as it had been worked out in the patristic church, although at one point they were prepared to accept the so-called Apostles' Creed, if not the so-called Nicene Creed. If Roman Catholics, Lutherans, and Calvinists could agree on one thing, it was that Socinianism was to be suppressed, and indeed in the seventeenth century the Socinians were driven out of Poland, where they had had some success in setting up congregations and colleges.

Faustus Sozzini was appalled by the atheism that flourished in his native Italy, and much of his work was intended for unbelievers. When his manuscripts were burned by a mob, it is recorded that his greatest regret was the loss of his work against atheism.[77] As part of this concern, Sozzini wrote his de Authoritate [sic] Sacrae Scripturae, which argued for Scripture essentially on the basis of the reliability of the authors of biblical books as witnesses rather than on a doctrine of inspiration. Grotius,

---

[76] ". . . in der alttestam. Exegese epochemachend gewirkt, nicht indem er einen mächtigen Umschwung herbeiführte, sondern dadurch dass ein Ferment in die Bibelforschung hineintrug, dessen Wirkung nach und nach immer grössere Dimensionen annahm." Diestel, *Geschichte des Alten Testaments in der christlichen Kirche* (Jena: 1869) 430. My translation.

[77] Preface to Faustus Socinus, *An Argument for the Authority of Holy Scripture; from the Latin of Socinus, After the Steinfurt Copy. to which is prefix'd, A Short Account of His Life*, translation attributed to Edward Combe (London: W. Meadows, 1731).

in his *Truth of the Christian Religion,* borrowed Sozzini's argument without acknowledging his source, presumably because Sozzini's name of itself would have been enough to discredit the argument.[78] What is interesting here is that Grotius obviously preferred the argument from authorship because it gave him the freedom to acknowledge disturbances and even errors in the text of the Bible without detracting from its importance. It is possible that others may also have used Socinian writers as quarries for their exegesis, and this is a subject that invites further study.[79]

ii. JOHANNES COCCEJUS (1603–1669):
A SOMEWHAT DIFFERENT EXEGETE

To be fair, Coccejus still has his admirers.[80] He was another German (the non-Latin form of his name was Koch, and he was born in Bremen) who moved to Holland, and apart from his strictly exegetical work, he took part in the controversy over Descartes' philosophy as an enthusiastic Cartesian.

In Old Testament exegesis Coccejus was almost the exact opposite of Grotius. While he did reject allegorical interpretation, he interpreted texts in the Old Testament as referring to almost everything except their historical context; for example, he argued that Isaiah 33:7 prophesied the death of Gustavus Adolphus. His fondness for discovering messianic texts led to the witticism: "Coccejus found Christ everywhere in the Old Testament, Grotius found him nowhere." In Diestel's words, Coccejus saw prophecy as apocalyptic.

Coccejus also postulated a schema of history marked by specific covenants; hence his theology is sometimes referred to as "federal" theology

---

[78] Jan Paul Heering, "Hugo Grotius' *De Veritate religionis Christianae,*" in Nellen and Rabbie, *Hugo Grotius Theologian,* 41–52, discusses the evidence in detail. However, there is one small correction necessary; on page 46 Heering argues that Grotius's dependence on Socinus was not known until recently. In fact, in Combe's 1731 translation the title page has a note: "Grotius, in the composure of his Book of the Truth of the Christian Religion, was, among several other Authors, more especially assisted by the valuable performance of a writer otherwise justly of ill fame, viz. Faustus Socinus' little book de Auctoritate S. Scripturae." This quote is attributed to Dr. Smallbrook's Charge to the clergy of the Diocese of St. David's, 1729, p. 34.

[79] The basis source for the Socinian writings remains Christophorus Sandius, *Bibliotheca Antitrinitorium.*

[80] See H. J. Kraus. *Die Biblische Theologie: Ihre Geschichte und Problematik.* Neukirchen-Vluyn: Neukirchener Verlag, 1970, 20–24.

(from the Latin *"foedus,"* a "treaty" or "covenant"). What Coccejus offered was an interpretation of the Old Testament that saw it ostensibly as a book with its own schema rather than as a concatenation of proof texts. In this his attempt was interesting, and his federal theology even had followers among Lutherans, but too much was based on a fanciful reading of the text.

Conclusion to the Baroque period

Between 1600 and 1660, the façade of biblical authority remained standing, but there were cracks appearing whose seriousness might not have been immediately evident to even most scholars, but in hindsight the ground was giving way under the Bible as the most important monument of the past and most thorough guide to the present. A new trend in philosophy that discounted the past and looked to future discovery: a new view of the world and its peoples that expanded the evidence of antiquity and provided a wider landscape that the Bible could not always dominate; new knowledge within the study of the Bible that capitalized on old problems and noticed new ones; a new emphasis on grammatical and philological studies based more and more on concrete evidence rather than conjecture—all these were signs that neither Roman Catholics nor Protestants would be able to maintain appearances for ever. The final collapse of the structure did not take place in the mind of the general public until the nineteenth century, and even today there are people working in the ruins to reconstruct some semblance of the old edifice.

Yet there were also indications of something new that might come out of the ruins. Careful study was beginning to show how the biblical text might be improved, how its languages might be better understood, and how the sphere of the Bible's religious interests might be kept intact as more ambitious claims were discounted.

Chapter 4

The Early Enlightenment Period (1660–1700)

When Richard Simon's *History of the Old Testament* appeared in English, John Dryden included a review of it in his *Religio Laici:*

> A work so full with various learning fraught,
> So nicely ponder'd, yet so strongly wrought,
> As nature's height and art's last hand requir'd:
> As much as man could compass, uninspir'd.
> Where we may see what errors have been made
> Both in the copier's and translator's trade:
> How Jewish, Popish, interests have prevail'd,
> And where infallibility has fail'd.

Very few works of biblical scholarship are currently feted by major poets. Therefore, while I have found Christopher Hill's notion of the Bible dethroned helpful, one should keep in mind that at the end of the seventeenth century the Bible still played a large part in popular opinion. Dryden's reaction in the lines above illustrate that what Richard Simon had to say about the composition and transmission of the Bible was found by the public to be disturbing, but it was also worthy of public discussion. More significantly, the Bible's position as a basic authority in many matters was beginning to come under scrutiny in various areas, such as the accuracy of its transmission, the truth of its account of creation, and its soundness in matters of philosophical truth.

I. External Factors

1. *The Enlightenment*

Any attempt to divide history into periods is far from watertight.[1] Still, there is a need to acknowledge that within particular periods of time, there is a climate of opinion that makes some ideas more acceptable than others. One should also bear in mind that all epochs do not get their names in the same manner or at the same point in their history. Sometimes a period is defined by its successors in a manner that it would not itself have understood, for example, "Middle Ages," a term borrowed from Augustine long after his time and used in a way he would not have expected in order to describe a period after it was over. On the other hand, the Enlightenment, at least in its last phase, was defined in various ways by its own practitioners. For example, in 1788 in the *Berlinisches Journal für Aufklärung* the author of yet one more article on "Was ist Aufklärung?" began with the sentence "Ist denn aber nicht endlich genug von Aufklärung geschieben?" ("Has enough finally been written about Enlightenment?") His obvious answer was going to be no, but there is a certain defensiveness visible beneath the surface.[2] The Enlightenment in its later stages was self-conscious about its existence and its importance, even if there was no general agreement about what it meant to be enlightened.

For the purpose of the history of biblical interpretation, two serious mistakes about the Enlightenment are current. The first is an interpretation of the Enlightenment that sees it as a general conspiracy (the so-called "Enlightenment project") to deny the authority of the Word of God in the Scriptures. This is simply far too simplistic; even conventional eighteenth-century theologians such as Johann Christoph Doederlein could discuss "Enlightenment,"whatever they understood by the word, and pronounce it a good thing.[3]

---

[1] There is a useful discussion of the problem of periodization in Jonathan Rée, "The Brothers Koerbagh," in *London Review of Books*, vol. 24, no. 2 (2002) 21–24. This is in theory a review of Jonathan Israel, *Radical Enlightenment: Philosophy and the Making of Modernity 1650–1750* (Oxford: Oxford University Press, 2001), but it covers more than Israel's book.

[2] G. N. Fischer, "Was ist Aufklärung?" *Berlinisches Journal für Aufklärung* 1 (1788) 12–46.

[3] J. C. Doederlein, *Christliche Religionsunterricht nach den Burdürfnissen unserer Zeit* (Nuremburg: Nowrath, 1787) 213–15. Doederlein discussed the misuse of the term "Enlightenment" and the need for a proper definition of it.

Worse still is the second mistake made by some interpreters who go on to assume that because they have defined the Enlightenment, they have thereby refuted it. All that is needed henceforth is to label a scholar "an Enlightenment figure" and one has explained his or her motivation and method to the point where further discussion is not really required. Cultural history is not so simple, and honest argument even less so.

If one is to find a metaphor that gets anywhere near to understanding a period of human culture, one should not think of a group of soldiers marching in lockstep in a given direction until the order is given to change direction, whereupon they all suddenly veer left as one person. If anything, the Enlightenment is like a pileup on a freeway; everyone agrees that something significant happened, but exactly what it was is described very differently by the various people whom you ask for information.

There is no doubt that much of the modern approach to the Bible developed in the period usually assigned to the Enlightenment. While it is not the purpose of this book to discuss the Enlightenment in detail, it is important to take into account the very different streams of thought that are all very much a part of the climate of thought between 1660 and 1800, a period characterized by the dry, rational, penetrating analysis of Reimarus and Kant, yet also by the emotional expression of religious conviction across the whole range of European religions, such as the Pietists and the Methodists in Protestantism, St. Alphonsus Liguori in Roman Catholicism, and the Baal Shem Tov in Judaism; by the growth of toleration, yet also by the Gordon riots in London in 1780; by philosophical rejection of the importance of history, yet also by Herder, Vico, and Hamann, who made history the basic stuff of humanity; by emphasis on the rights of all humans, yet also by the slave trade across the Atlantic and by the preservation of slavery in the enlightened Constitution of the United States. I include below "A pack of useful lies" that capture some of the currents and countercurrents in European thought between 1660 and 1800.

2. *A pack of useful lies about the eighteenth century*[4]

This chart, adapted from one used by the late Professor Henry K. Miller of Princeton University, deliberately reduces the complexities of

---

[4] This is only one section of Professor Miller's list. In the full version there are also sections dealing with: social and economic, historical and political; literary and critical. I have taken the liberty to extend his time frame to the latter part of the seventeenth century.

eighteenth-century thought to artificial polar opposites or norms. The views in the left-hand column (Renaissance, Christian Humanist) might roughly be described as "conservative" or "traditional" during this period; those on the right (Romantic, Naturalist), as "radical" or "progressive." The dominant prestige or emphasis moves slowly and uncertainly from left to right during the years 1660 to 1800, but more often than not, the old and the new remain in uneasy juxtaposition.

The World Picture—Philosophy and Religion

1. *Conceptual Metaphor:*	The Great Chain of Being: The Hierarchy	The Mathematical Machine: The Organism
2. *Metaphysical Orientation:*	Ontological ("Being": relation to Universe)	Epistemological (Process Psychological individual)
3. *Question of the Universe:*	Why? (Rationalism: Religion: Synthesis)	What? How? (Empiricism: Science: Analysis)
4. *Cosmology:*	Meaningful, finite Universe (Purposeful interlocking Universals: Macrocosm-microcosm)	Scientific, Universe mechanical, infinite (Non-purposive Particulars)
5. *Highest Wisdom:*	Ethical contemplation: Knowledge leads to virtue	Scientific experiment: Knowledge leads to Power
6. *Philosophical Orientation:*	Theocentric (God-centered); but humanity at center of God's Universe	Anthropocentric ("Man the Measure"); but humanity not focus of neutral Universe
7. *Nature:*	The total spiritual, moral, material construct, structured by God	External, physical phenomenon, separate from the mind, but a stimulus to subjective spiritual experience
8. *View of "Reality":*	Metaphysical "Realism" (Universals are real): Lower explained in terms of the higher	Metaphysical "Nominalism" (only Particulars are real): Higher explained in terms of the lower
9. *Natural Law:*	Normative (defining norms) Duties of Man	Descriptive (describing effects); Rights of Man
10. *Psychological Emphasis:*	Intuitive Reason and the Conscious Mind: Identity as essence	Imagination and the (Unconscious) Irrational: Identity as state of mind

11. *Ethics:*	Christian: prescriptive: absolute	Benevolist, Utilitarian: descriptive: relative
12. *Ethical Emphasis:*	Reason: Motives: Ends	Emotion: Effects: Means
13. *Moral Truth:*	Extrinsic: objective (in Divine Will)	Intrinsic: subjective (in the Agent)
14. *Moral Faculties:*	"Right Reason" and the Will (the Head)	"Sensibility and the Will" (the Heart)
15. *Major Virtue:*	Caritas: Love of God and humanity for the image of God	"Natural Goodness"
16. *Major Sin:*	Pride	Sexual immorality
17. *Dominant Group in the Church of England:*	(Latitudinarian) Anglo-Catholicism	Evangelicism and "Broad Church"
18. *Leading Heterodoxy:*	Dissent; Deism	Methodism
19. *Science: major focus:*	Astronomy, Physics	Mathematics, Biology
20. *Test of truth:*	Congruity with basic norms	Experiment

3. *The role of the new philosophy of the Enlightenment in the interpretation of the Bible*

As the new philosophy[5] developed in the seventeenth century, it began to take over the position of universal standard that had been occupied by the Bible. Ostensibly the new philosophy's proofs of the existence of a beneficent Creator appeared to confirm the Bible, not least of all because that was where the idea had come from anyway. However, it was inevitable that the question would be asked which way the dependence ran: Was the Bible the guarantor of the idea of an ordered universe, or was it the truths of philosophy that revealed the nature of the world and not only confirmed the Bible but also corrected it in both matters of fact and even of faith and morals?

In contrast to the uncertainties, not to mention the disagreements about the interpretation of the Bible, the new ways indicated by Descartes and/or Bacon appeared to offer both a certainty and a practicality that

---

[5] This term denotes philosophy stemming from Descartes and Bacon, which was characterized by a self-conscious sense of being a new departure.

was preferable to endless theological disputes. It was only to be expected that even if Descartes did not discuss the Bible and its relation to the new thought, others influenced by Descartes might make the attempt. Once one is convinced, one has a sure and independent source of truth on which one can rely without hesitation, one has a standard by which the Bible can be judged in a manner independent of traditional attitudes. This was the basis for Spinoza's and the Deists' negative criticisms of the Bible.[6]

4. *Politics, political thought, and exegesis*

Apart from the question of an individual's personal belief, there was another facet of the human condition under discussion in a way that involved the Bible, namely, the improvement of political life. Reflection on the nature and art of government had its roots in classical antiquity; this was revived in the Renaissance in the hope that new approaches to statecraft might be a useful guide, whether this meant the gritty realism of Machiavelli or the hope of a perfect state in Thomas More's *Utopia*. But in the sixteenth and seventeenth centuries, the religious component of civil wars had made one thing self-evident to some philosophers: good order would remain threatened as long as some groups within the state could justify rebellion as a matter of conscience by appealing to the supreme authority of the will of God, whether founded on the interpretation of Scripture or as incorporated in a sacred institution independent of the state.

In France in the seventeenth century, it was the claims of the pope to interfere in French affairs that led Cardinal Richelieu to toy with the idea of setting up a national Gallican state church with the support of the Protestants. In England a large part of the justification of the civil war was based on conflicting interpretations of the Bible by Presbyterians, Independents, and other more radical groups, all of whom, in Samuel Butler's words, "proved their doctrine orthodox by apostolic blows and knocks." Hobbes, then, had to discuss the Bible in much detail in *Leviathan* in order to show that its authority, its contents, and its proper interpretation were matters not for the individual but for the sovereign,

---

[6] A superb book on the Deists is Henning Graf Reventlow, *The Authority of the Bible and the Rise of the Modern World*, trans. John Bowden (Philadelphia: Fortress, 1985). However, its focus is on how the authority of the Bible was criticized, not the history of exegesis properly speaking.

to whom subjects owed obedience in this matter as in others. Spinoza's motives for what, after all, he called his *Tractatus Theologico-Politicus*, were also as much political as exegetical, for a part of his argument was that the biblical history of Israel itself showed how a religious authority separate from that of the state led to disorder and downfall.

5. Science and the Bible

The question of cosmology was discussed in the previous chapter, but that most of the educated agreed generally about the new shape of the universe without any sense of religious difficulties was demonstrated in the 1654 debate between Jo. Webster,[7] a Puritan, and Seth Ward, a more establishment figure.[8] The argument turned on whether the universities were keeping up to date in their instruction, one principal bone of contention being whether students were instructed in the Ptolemaic or Copernican view of the universe. The point here is that both men were in agreement that Copernicus was correct; they differed on the issue of whether or not his cosmology was actually being taught.

Rather than astronomy, it was geology that was to be instrumental in raising concerns about the factual nature of the Bible. The matter that caused the difficulty was the story of the Flood. The logic of the situation was that if a worldwide flood as described in the Bible had occurred, the event would have been sufficiently catastrophic to leave undeniable traces. Fossils were taken into account as possible evidence of the Flood's destruction, but most fossils immediately available were shell-fish, leaving open the question of how you drown a clam.[9]

Various theories were put forward to explain the present shape of the earth's surface and the differences between the strata of rock formations, some of which assumed a huge flood of local importance at the very least. A flood sufficient to cover every mountain in the world would require more water than is currently available on the face of the earth, but how far could you deviate from the strict sense of the Bible, which

[7] Jo. Webster, *Academiarum Examen, or the Examination of Academies* (London: Giles Culvert, 1654).

[8] [Seth Ward], *Vindiciae Academiarum: Some briefe Animadversions upon Mr. Websters Book, stiled The Examination of Academies* (Oxford: Thomas Robinson, 1654).

[9] In fact, while fossilized teeth, miscellaneous bones, and even trees were also known, it was not until the nineteenth century that geologists reconstructed large and hitherto unknown animals.

says reasonably clearly that the whole earth was submerged? Isaac de La Peyrère had suggested that the biblical Flood was a local occurrence in Palestine, and though it was at first rejected, his theory had the virtue of being able to deal with the suggested water shortage, though the thrust of his argument was based on biology and geography rather than geological formation—how could all the land animals get to the ark in time, and where did Noah put them all?

It is not the purpose of this book to repeat what has been so well covered in Rhoda Rappaport's *When Geologists Were Historians*. Essentially her argument is that the basic weakness of geologists qua geologists was the failure to think in terms of far longer time spans than were permitted by a chronology that might be derived from the Bible, that is, they confined themselves to periods more appropriate to human history than to the process of geological formation.[10] In this respect the writings of Thomas Burnet will be discussed below (pp. 140–46).

6. *Chronology*

Reconstructions of human chronology based on biblical data were beginning to show cracks. It had been the ambition of the Renaissance scholars to integrate biblical data with records from other cultures, in particular the records of the dates of the Olympic games. On occasion a little creativity could be carried too far, such as Annius of Viterbo's (d. 1502) outright forgery of fragments he claimed came from Berosus, a Babylonian priest of the third century B.C.E.[11] Extended estimates of the antiquity of the Babylonians found in sixteenth- and seventeenth-century writings can usually be traced back to Annius. However, forgery was a symptom, not the cause of the problem, for to put the matter succinctly, there is no way of harmonizing the differing systems of chronology found within the Old Testament itself, still less how these are to be linked with nonbiblical systems.[12] The Septuagint version offered the possibility of another two thousand or so years in the life of the world,

[10] According to Prof. Rhoda Rappaport, *When Geologists Were Historians, 1650–1750* (Ithaca: Cornell University Press, 1997) 228–37, Benôit de Maillet's *Teliamed*, published posthumously in 1748, was the first serious publication to break out of this shell.

[11] There was a historical Berosus in the third century B.C.E. who wrote three books, of which fragments are preserved in quotations from other authors.

[12] See Anthony Grafton, "Joseph Scaliger and Historical Chronology: The Rise and Fall of a Discipline," *History and Theory* 14 (1975) 156–85.

but this did not help much. Attempts at working out a biblically based chronology grew fewer and fewer, and the genre finished out its day with a whimper rather than a bang.

7. A new factor in European thought—the creative role of history

There emerged at this time a new direction of thought that was to influence not only the study of the Bible but Western culture in general. This was a new perception of the importance of history for understanding ideas. In the previous chapter this was discussed in relation to the Epistle to the Hebrews, where it was shown that only when scholars began to think in terms of historical processes that the Platonism of the Epistle to the Hebrews was seen in terms of the history of thought.

It was this awareness of the history of development in thought that was to open up new possibilities in how European culture would look on all documents from previous eras. In the interpretation of the Bible, one could begin to apply a whole new set of explanations; earlier scholars trying to clarify difficult passages would try to locate the answer in terms of the deliberate meaning of a single author of a work who had something special in mind in creating what looked like a difficulty. Working from this assumption, the sudden introduction of the name JHWH in Genesis 2:4b might be explained as an effect of the author's sense of the appropriateness of only introducing this special name at the end of the work of creation. However, once scholars considered the possibility that perhaps Genesis 1:1–2:4a and Genesis 2:4b on came from different traditions from different times, then the contrast could be accounted for historically in a less strained fashion. This approach was suggested in connection with the Pentateuch by Henning Bernhard Witter in 1711, but while it was noticed by Valentin Ernst Loescher, only Johann Christoph Edelmann took it seriously in the first part of the eighteenth century.[13]

This application of history as a factor in intellectual investigation in the humanities began in the latter part of the seventeenth century. Stanley's *History of Philosophy*[14] came out in parts between 1655 and 1660, and other historical studies followed. In 1736 Stölle published his great

---

[13] In his *Moses mit aufgedecktem Angesichte* (n.p.: 1740) part 1, 111–12.
[14] Thomas Stanley, *The History of Philosophy* (London: Humphrey Moseley and Thomas Dring, 1656–1660).

work *Anleitung zur Historie der Gelahrheit*,[15] and in 1739 his smaller *Anleitung zur Historie der Theologischen Gelahrheit*. In biblical studies Richard Simon had a whole series of titles beginning with "Histoire." Obviously, many people had been writing history before this time, but there was something different in play now, that is, the attempt to see how ideas had been influenced by their past and how they played a part in the future.

It was during the Enlightenment that the search for explanations from cultural history spread into humanities research generally, where it has now become so dominant that it tends to overshadow other considerations, such as whether a philosophical statement might be true. Ironically, the historical origins of an idea have now come to be a means for evaluating it. Bertrand Russell remarked that Philo thought of himself as a Jew, but he was really a Platonist. The implication here is that Philo was not really Jewish in his beliefs. Philo's obvious reply would have been that if Platonism was good enough for Moses, it was good enough for him; or faced with the modern observation that Moses was unlikely to have known anything about Greek philosophy, Philo could have replied that if Plato's thought was an appropriate vehicle to explain the Jewish faith, why should its post-Mosaic origin prevent its use? Yet if one looks at modern commentaries on the Epistle to the Hebrews, there are plenty of examples of a similar discounting of its author's ideas purely on the ground that they came from Neoplatonist thought.

In the eighteenth century the historical approach to ideas and documents attracted progressively more attention as its usefulness came to be recognized. It had two effects on biblical exegesis. First, it broke many ancient logjams in interpretation; for example, Johannes Drusius's problem with Genesis 4, mentioned in chapter 2 of this book (see p. 56), is easily resolved if one assumes that the apparent contradiction was produced by the combination of two different ancient documents. Historical investigation of the text also provides a certain amount of "padding" between the text and the expositor; for example, it is much easier to explain the accounts of the Ascension in Luke and Acts as Luke's desire to include specific instances in his history work to mark points of transition in his narrative than to discuss whether the Ascension narratives describe something that took place and deal with the problem of whether Jesus was the first astronaut.

---

[15] Gottlieb Stölle, *Anleitung zur Historie der Gelahrtheit*, 4th ed. (Jena: Johann Meyers sel. Erben, 1736); *Anleitung zur Historie der Theologischen Gelahrheit* (Jena: Johann Meyers sel. Erben, 1739).

As a personal comment, I would like to suggest that the continuing appeal of the investigation of historical origins and influences has achieved a respectability in academic life that is now denied to earlier notions of evaluating whether ideas and values were right or wrong in themselves. Given that "research" has become the mark of a good academic, research in the humanities usually deals with origins, influences, and other noncombustible data. If an ancient people consumed human flesh in their sacrifices, it is somehow more respectable to account for this practice on the basis of a need for protein rather than decry the extent of the human cruelty involved in all features of the obtaining and slaughtering of victims. Historical sources are legitimate research; questions of truth tend to be smuggled in the back door. At all events, once one begins to become aware of the historical examination implicit in the discussion of many ideas, this whole trend in modern culture leaps out at even the most casual observer. This, I suggest, is one of the important factors that separate us from the Renaissance, during which historical examination was devoted to finding the use and meanings of words in their original context and whether manuscripts represented authentic documents faithfully transmitted.

II. The Bible

1. *The Bible and its original historical context*

As the authoritative encyclopedic source for its day, it would stand to reason that the Bible would have had to be linked with what was known from other sources about the ethnology, the languages, and the religions of the world. As more information, or what passed for information, came in, the problem became more acute. The initial approach was to assume that the Bible provided the framework into which the new information could be integrated. Thus in John Selden's *De dis syris syntagmata duo* of 1617, the explanation of other religious beliefs was simple—other religions were wrong and lost their power at the time of the Incarnation. In a similar fashion, Bochart assumed that behind the mythology of the heathens one could find traces of biblical stories. For example, if one looks at the stories about Saturn and his sons, one can still see their original source, which is the biblical account of Noah.[16]

---

[16] Samuel Bochart, *Geographia sacra seu Phaleg e Canaan,* . . ., 4th ed. (Leiden: apud Corenlium Boutesteyn et Jordanum Luchtmans, 1707) 1–3.

But the establishment of resemblances between the Old Testament and pagan religions could be made to cut both ways. In his *De oraculis veterum ethnicorum* of 1683, Anthony van Dale implied that the superstition and credulity induced by the pagan oracles were not altogether unknown in the main churches of his day, and the possible implications of his criticism for some of the practices of Israelite religion was not overlooked.

Furthermore, the weight of the cumulative empirical evidence about the size of the world and its animal population was beginning to have an effect on assumptions about the Bible's reliability in its accounts of people and cultures. Thus while Edward Stillingfleet, in his *De Originae sacrae* of 1675, might hold out in deriving pagan mythology and folk tradition from the Old Testament, even he, conservative as he was, had to take seriously, if unwillingly, the possibility that the whole world might not have been populated at the time of the Flood, and therefore a comparatively local flood would have been enough to get rid of human beings but leave far-off animals undisturbed.

Even the discussion about the origins of languages and ethnic groups was beginning to diverge from the simplistic pattern of details in Genesis. Could a given nation simply be descended from one man, and did all languages originate from an original tongue, which was usually thought to be Hebrew? What we now see is that the death of a thousand cuts had begun.

2. *Changes in religiosity that had an effect on exegesis*

For the genuinely religious, the Bible's authority and use could take different forms, especially in Protestant circles, where an appeal to the Bible alone without regard to the past could take some interesting deviations. An interesting example is an early Quaker, Samuel Fisher, whose writing reads like the transcript of a rant and makes heavy reading.[17] However, he was a university graduate, and he made interesting use of the technical theological commentaries he had studied, such as those of

[17] Samuel Fisher, *The Rustick's Alarm to the Rabbies*, first published 1660, reprinted in *The Testimony of Truth Exalted* (n.p.: n.p., 1679) 241. R. H. Popkin has argued for a link between Fisher and Spinoza in "Spinoza and Samuel Fisher," *Philosophia*, Ramat–Gan, t. 15, no. 3 (1985) 219–36, but the actual evidence he produces is rather slight for the weight of the argument. The probable explanation of any resemblance is that Fisher and Spinoza read the same books.

Buxtorf and Capellus.[18] The sort of conclusions he drew from the discussions about text, translation, and transmission were very different from those of his mentors. This is his comment on the text of the Bible:

> Yea, consider the naked Literal Aspect of the holy Scriptures, not in its highest, not in its Primitive best, and purest, as at first given forth, but in its moer [sic] derivative, in its lowest, meanest, and most adulterated Capacity, wherin it stand at this day, wrested and torn, and like a Nose of Wax twisted and twined into more twice, if not ten or twenty times twenty several shapes, by means untrue and tattered *Transcripts,* and *Translations* . . . yet as meer a Graven image as that is with Ink and Pen or Paper, or Skin of Parchment, . . . and as a dead Letter as it is . . . which may so easily, so endlessly be altered by the Wills of men. . . .[19]

Fisher then went on with the sort of objections to the Bible we have seen elsewhere: the canon of the New Testament is nowhere in the Bible, how does Moses record his own death, and so on. Presumably these considerations were part of the reason why Fisher left the Independents, whose whole life was centered on the Bible as the word of God, and joined the Quakers, where the Inner Light was a much more immediate, unblemished, and reliable guide to God's will.[20] Interesting here is the extent to which the accumulation of manuscripts of the Bible could be seen by Fisher and others, not as a means of getting a more accurate text of the Bible, but rather as a source of uncertainty about who, if anyone, had the real Bible. While Fisher found his refuge in the Inner Light, others similarly disturbed might well opt for the purified religion based on the light of reason offered by the new philosophy, or perhaps even no religion at all.

It was also possible that this new emphasis on the inner testimony of the spirit might lead to identifying the inner testimony with reason pure and simple, which then could be used to discover shortcomings in the Bible with regard to its coherence and even its morality. Such was to be the case in the next century with Edelmann.

---

[18] Ibid., 316.

[19] Ibid., 241.

[20] A similar attitude to the Bible is found in Madame Bourignon, who discovered that when she read the Bible, she found that it was a book she could have written herself and therefore gave up reading it.

3. *Enhanced opportunities for the communication of new ideas*

Ideas only have an effect on a general culture when there are facilities for diffusing them widely. Two institutions were to play a role in spreading new ideas about all areas of inquiry, namely, the learned journal and the learned society. A third factor was the practice of republishing past critical works.

i. In the latter part of the seventeenth century, the learned journal appeared as a natural extension of the international camaraderie of the Republic of Letters. The savants who had earlier carried on an extensive correspondence and acted as clearinghouses for books and ideas for individuals were replaced by editors of journals, whose many copies could be sent to anyone who wished to pay for them. It was not an accident that Pierre Bayle's journal was entitled *Nouvelles de la république des lettres*. The more serious journals were written in Latin, such as the *Acta Eruditorum*, published in Leipzig from 1682 to 1735. Others were written in modern languages, and eventually they dominated the trade, suggesting possibly that Latin was gradually losing its appeal and that there was a growing audience of reasonably well-educated people literate in their own tongue but not instructed in Latin. Among modern European languages, pride of place often went to French as the language of choice for international affairs in general. By the mid-eighteenth century, even journals outside of French-speaking areas were written in French, such as *La Revue Germanique*, edited by Jean Henri Formey, the secretary of the Berlin Academy.

The journals usually covered a wide range of subjects, but the very serious ones usually devoted a fair amount of space to theology and biblical interpretation. The German *Acta Eruditorum* had as its first section "Theologica et ad Ecclesiasticam Historiam spectantia," a feature that was given a great deal of attention throughout the journal's publication history.[21] In England *The History of the Works of the Learned* was published between 1699 and 1711 with much the same sort of interests as the *Acta Eruditorum*. Certain national preferences emerged in the eighteenth century; in Germany, while the wide-spectrum publications continued, most notably *Die Allgemeine Deutsche Bibliothek* (1766–1792 and 1793–1806), there were many journals devoted entirely to theology, such as Loescher's *Unschuldige*

---

[21] Other sections included "Juridica," "Medica et Physica," "Mathematica," "Historica & geographica," "Philosophia et Philologica Miscellanea."

Nachrichten (1702–1735), whereas in England the preferences seemed to be for more generalized publications, such as *The Gentleman's Magazine*.[22]

ii. The growing number of learned societies dedicated to the common pursuit of knowledge were another expression of the enthusiasm for discovery that led to the periodicals, and indeed their reports were really another type of learned journal. The Academy of Sciences in Paris (established 1666) and the British Royal Society (established 1660) were only two of the better known of such groups. While people have met for serious discussion on a regular basis for centuries, the learned societies provided the continuity necessary for sustained international discourse. In meetings the emphasis often fell on what we would call science, but as with the learned journals, the net was wider, and subjects dealing with the Bible, church history, and religious matters were broached.[23] This was not surprising, for even after some criticisms in the first part of the seventeenth century, the Bible was still seen as an object for further investigation even if it was no longer a source of final authority.

iii. Collections of "new" scholarly works

Whether or not they can be attributed to the developing sense of the importance of history or simply to the earliest skirmishes in the battle of the ancients and the moderns, there were several remarkable publications that republished and made available in a single edition the work of the more important Renaissance commentators. Jean de la Haye published his *Biblia Magna* in Paris in 1643 and an even more extensive *Biblia Maxima* in 1660. The *Biblia Magna* was a relatively modest six folio volumes, with some prefatory notes and then the commentaries of Estius, Menochius, and Tirinus (all Roman Catholic exegetes) arranged side by side. The *Biblia Maxima* was an elaboration of the *Biblia Magna,* with far more introductory material and added summaries about the comments of other exegetes. In nineteen folio volumes it was cumbersome and repetitious, and Richard Simon was justified in seeing it as rather overdone.

---

[22] The basic authorities for German learned journals are Joachim Kirchner, *Die Grundlagen des Deutschen Zeitschriftenswesens,* 2 vols. (Leipzig: Karl W. Hiersmann, 1928) 2:31; and *Das Deutsche Zeitschriftenwesenseine Geschichte und seine Probleme,* 2 vols. (Wiesbaden: Otto Harrassowitz, 1958–1962).

[23] For a useful discussion with extensive bibliography, see Rappaport, *When Geologists Were Historians,* 7–40.

Two English publications were more useful in that their choice of sources was wider and their arrangement relatively more concise. The first was *Critici Sacri,* a collection of scholarly works on the Bible since Valla. It consisted of commentaries on the Bible arranged in the biblical order, along with selected prefaces, dedications, notes, and separate articles. Published in nine folio volumes,[24] it was put out in three separate editions, namely, Oxford, Frankfort, and Amsterdam.[25]

An analogous undertaking was Matthew Poole's *Synopsis Criticorum* of 1669,[26] in which Poole summarized the opinions of the great commentators. His work was carefully done, but as was pointed out in the last chapter, he was guilty of one basic error in that he worked from the Latin translation of versions of the Bible as found in Walton's Polyglot rather than from the originals of Aramaic, Syriac, etc., and so his comparisons are not always supported by the original text. He also began a somewhat scaled-down English edition, which was completed by others and published in two volumes in 1683–1685.

The choice in both collections included both Roman Catholic and Protestant scholars. For the history of biblical interpretation, the appearance of these collections of excerpts is significant in that it indicated a feeling that there was a growing body of recent commentaries that was as authoritative as the patristic and rabbinic commentaries on which scholarship had relied upon up to that point.[27]

4. *Criticisms of the strong view of Bible infallibility and inspiration from within the Church of England*

i. JOHN SPENCER (1630–1693)

Spencer was one of the most careful and painstaking biblical interpreters of his day. Spencer had lived through the excesses and exaggera-

[24] This includes the two supplementary volumes published in Frankfort am Main in 1700.

[25] *Critici Sacri sive doctissimorum virorum in ss. Biblia Annonationes & Tractus,* ed. John Pearson, Samuel Bee, Richard Royston, Guilielmus Wells, Samueles Thomson, Thomas Robinson, Guilielmus Morden. The London edition is available in English Publications 1641–1700 (University Microfilms).

[26] Matthew Poole, *Synopsis Criticorum aliorumque S. Scripturae Interpretum* (London: Cornelius Bee, 1669–1682?). This work and its English translation are also available in microfilm format in English Publications 1641–1700 (see note 25 above).

[27] In the eighteenth century Ugolino in Venice put out a collection of works in twenty-five volumes that dwarfed the *Critici Sacri.* However, one needs to treat this

tions current in the time of the Commonwealth, and, like Hobbes, he recognized that the misuse of religion was a source of many social problems. In particular, he said in the preface to his earlier work *A Discourse Concerning Vulgar Prophecies:*[28]

> The soul of man was made for intimacy and converse with God, and therefore; in a tacit sense thereof, is continually reaching and aspiring after it. But Lust and Pride having blinded its Eye, it is apt to affect and seek it in fond and fantastick ways. Whereas good men . . . become familiar with God by holy practices, by profound Humility, by abstractions from the world and Lust: Men have conceited it is procured and maintained by going off from Reason, by Raptures, Visions, Prophecies, Enthusiasms, hot and vigorous impression of Spirit, and have verily thought . . . they are scarce ever full of God, till they are half beside themselves.[29]

In another earlier work, *A Discourse Concerning Prodigies,* Spencer also objected to a superstitious awe that interpreted natural phenomena as warnings or messages from God.[30]

His magnum opus, *De Legibus Hebraeorum Ritualibus et Earum Rationibus* ("The Hebrew Ritual Laws and Their Meaning") was a superb work unjustly neglected in modern discussions; perhaps had it not been written in Latin and run to over a thousand pages, it might have attracted more attention from historians of exegesis. Spencer continued to work at his masterpiece, and his personal copy of the work, preserved in the University Library at Cambridge, has numerous notes for planned improvements to a revised (and larger) edition. After his death Leonard Chappelow brought out this new edition containing material left in Spencer's literary remains.[31]

---

work with caution. Italian printers had a reputation for fine printing but bad proofreading, and Ugolino's edition would be part of the evidence for this statement.

[28] *A discourse concerning vulgar prophecies: the Preface* (London: 1663).

[29] Ibid.

[30] *A Discourse concerning Prodigies, wherein the vanety of Presages by them is reprehended, and their true and proper Ends asserted and vindicated* (London: 1663). Spencer here treated, among other things, comets, which tended to be seen by the more rational in the seventeenth century as the *pons assinorum* from ignorance to enlightened knowledge. See Don Cameron Allen, *The Renaissance Looks at Comets,* 1966 Wingspread Lectures in the Humanities, Johnson Foundation, Racine, Wis.

[31] John Spencer, *De Legibus Hebraeorum Ritualibus et Earum Rationibus, libri quatuor,* ed. Leonardus Chappelow (Cambridge: Cambridge University Press, 1727). On the

Whereas Hobbes's solution to inappropriate exegesis was to subordinate biblical interpretation to political power, Spencer approached the problem of interpretation from inside the examination of religion as such and from careful examination of the actual text of the Bible.[32] In undertaking this task, he was influenced by two non-Christian authors, Plutarch and Maimonides.

It was Plutarch (c. 46–c.120 C.E.) who gave Spencer his general framework for discerning between the use and the abuse of religion. Plutarch has been described as "one of the most attractive of the ancient authors writing with charm, geniality and tact."[33] For Spencer, what Plutarch offered was a rational guide for steering between the two extremes of superstition and atheism, which he felt were only too evident in the events of the seventeenth century. The opening of *De Legibus* began with a quotation from Plutarch's *De Iside et Osiride*, where Plutarch discussed the danger of the use of hallowed symbols that should direct human thought toward the divine:

> For some, erring completely, have slipped into superstition, and others, shunning it [superstition] like a marsh, have unwittingly fallen in turn over the precipice of atheism."[34]

In *De Legibus*, Spencer began with a *Prolegomena*, where he set out his four motives for his study.

First, he mentioned what has to be the marrow of scholarship, namely, *"jucunditatis nominee,"* which can be roughly translated as "the joy of finding out."[35]

Second, he discussed *Et multiplicis Utilitatis*, "the different advantages" of the results of such an investigation. He found three:

a. It would deal with the arguments of those who held Jewish laws in contempt. Here he had a reference to Herbert of Cherbury, who in *de*

---

basis of Spencer's notes, Chappelow added material to the original three books as well as a fourth book on the subject of the Jewish phylacteries.

[32] Hobbes indeed had comments that were both new and useful; but as the old jest has it, what was useful was not new and what was new was not useful.

[33] *The Oxford Companion to Classical Literature*, ed. Sir Paul Harvey (Oxford: Oxford University Press, 1937) 336.

[34] *Ad lectorem*, first page (not paginated) *De Iside et Osiride*, 378. Spencer quoted the Greek and gave a Latin translation. The text here is from J. Gwyn Griffiths, *Plutarch's de Iside et Osiride* (Cambridge: University of Wales Press, 1970) 225.

[35] Ibid., Prolegomena, 7.

Religione Gentilium ("concerning the religions of the nations") tended to see ritual as superstition impure and simple. Spencer argued that the proper understanding of the purpose of the law would rescue it from this prejudiced attitude.

b. The careful study of the Mosaic law would help to clarify difficult passages in Scripture.

c. The most important practical application was that knowledge of the original purpose of the Mosaic laws would help to reaffirm Christian liberty by eliminating superstitious practices in modern times, such as the fear of ritual uncleanness in relation to birth and menstruation, which were codified in the laws of the Roman Catholic Church on the basis of Old Testament regulations.

The third section of the book was *Honestatis etiam nomine*, namely, what was the truth of the matter, and the fourth section was *Et novitatis aut raritatis*, what was new and original in the laws.

In the body of *De Legibus*, Spencer raised the question of why God inserted so many laws about things neither good nor bad in themselves. Was this just to overcome the will of the believers, or was there more involved? The second alternative was to be preferred, for surely it was not likely that he who is called the Logos would give laws to his church without reason.[36] Spencer set out to find the origins and the meaning behind the Mosaic ritual laws in a way analogous to Plutarch's discussion of the sense behind the cultic practices of the cult of Isis and Osiris in Egypt. In this effort Spencer found a great deal of help in Maimonides, especially his *Guide of the Perplexed*, where Maimonides' goal—to explain the sense of ritual laws within Judaism—was very close to that of Spencer. Essentially, Spencer's argument was that Moses adopted Egyptian and other laws of a sort that would keep the Israelites from lapsing into paganism and polytheism.

The importance of Spencer's work is that he offered a way out of a difficulty inherent in the affirmation of the inerrant inspiration of the Bible. This difficulty is that in practice the Bible does not provide a unified system, and in the Christian tradition there is a particular complication in that parts of the New Testament denigrate the Old,[37] not least in the

---

[36] Ibid., Preface, 2.

[37] Within Judaism there is a long and honorable tradition of interpretation that aims at dealing with both ancient problems and modern applications.

matter of ritual practices the early church had declared to be optional. The absolute denial of the divine nature of some of the Pentateuchal laws was not open to Spencer, but by examining the human origins of some Israelite customs and by confining their relative validity to a particular set of historical circumstances, he could defend their original importance and deny their current applicability at a single stroke. Spencer was here in effect introducing into exegesis a criterion for evaluating different parts of the Bible, namely, the criterion of historical origins.

The strength of Spencer's method is shown in his discussion of a New Testament problem, the so-called apostolic decree of Acts 15:20. This was the decision of the church council in Jerusalem that excused the Gentiles from following all the laws laid down in the Old Testament, except that they should "abstain only from things polluted by idols and from fornication and from whatever has been strangled and from blood." This passage presents serious exegetical problems, for it not only mixes together moral and dietary prohibitions, but even the dietary prohibitions mentioned go nowhere near to meeting the sort of obvious ritual concerns of Jewish members of the Christian community, for one would have expected the prohibition of pork along with the prohibition of blood.[38]

Spencer devoted a long special section to this problem,[39] which, given that he did not have the modern option of explaining problems in Acts by blaming Luke, might well be read today not only for his method but also for the evidence he cited, both from classical antiquity and the arguments of interpreters up to his own day. Spencer argued that the reason for the particular list in Acts 15 is that the prohibition of particular acts and of eating particular foods might lead converts to fall back into pagan idolatry. The conclusions he drew from this position were that while the moral prohibition remained in force, the ritual prohibitions were no longer in force, because circumstances of the church have changed since the first century C.E.

Therefore, while Spencer did not challenge the verbal inerrancy of the Bible head-on, he was applying historical criteria, in this case the actual circumstances either of the Israelites in Egypt or of the Christians in the

---

[38] The distinction between moral and the ritual laws was one way the early church distinguished between what was valid and what was not in the Old Testament. This emphasis on morality was if anything emphasized in the Enlightenment and was certainly accepted by Spencer. It is possible that the first-century church did not make such a sharp distinction, but the fact remains that the selection of laws for the Gentiles in the Acts of the Apostles remains very curious.

[39] Spencer, *De Legibus*, 471–515.

Roman Empire, to show that certain laws were reasonable in their day and yet were no longer required in a world where circumstances were different. The assumption underlying this freedom in the interpretation of biblical laws implied that not everything in the Bible is the eternal word of God but rather the product of human decisions at a given time in history.

Not everyone agreed. Since the derivation of much of Moses' legislation from Egypt could lead to the conclusion that not all the Old Testament was directly inspired by God, Hermann Witsius, the great Dutch defender of what we can now see as lost causes, attacked Spencer in his *De Aegyptibus*, in which he argued that the dependence went the other way and that Israel influenced Egypt. It is worth noting that this gambit is often played whenever external influence on the Old Testament is suggested, such as the debates caused by the decipherment and reading of Egyptian and Babylonian texts in the nineteenth and twentieth centuries. Usually the gambit fails.[40]

Spencer's work was very influential in the eighteenth century, editions being brought out both in Tübingen and in Venice. In some discussions he tended, most unfairly, to be linked to the Socinians and Deists because of his implied limitation of the verbal inspiration of the Bible, and the sort of general reaction to him may be similar to that of Tristram Shandy's father (Stern was after all a Church of England clergyman with a degree in theology):

> Very well,—said my father,—nay, if it has that convenience—and so without stopping a moment to settle it first in his mind, whether the Jews had it from the Egyptians, or the Egyptians from the Jews,— he rose up, and rubbing his forehead two or three times across with the palm of his hand, in the manner we rub out the footsteps of care, when evil has trod lighter upon us than we foreboded,—he shut the book, and walked down stairs.—Nay, said he, mentioning the name of a different great nation upon every step as he set his foot upon it—if the EGYPTIANS,—the SYRIANS,—the PHOENICIANS, —the ARABIANS,—the CAPADOCIANS,—if the COLCHI, and TROGLODYTES did it—if SOLON and PYTHAGORAS submitted, —what is TRISTRAM?—who am I, that I should fret or fume one moment about the matter?

[40] To be fair to Witsius, little though he may deserve it, more recent opinion tends to see the influence on Israelite ceremonial customs as coming from "Canaanite" sources rather than Egyptian ones.

ii. THOMAS BURNET (1635–1715)

Another example of a chipping away at the throne of the Bible from within the Church of England was Thomas Burnet, whose views on the first ten chapters of Genesis aroused a certain amount of protest in his day. Sometimes his religious position is described as "heterodox," but this is to accept the valuation of his seventeenth-century opponents.[41] Burnet was an early example of the influence of emerging science on the interpretation of the Bible, though here again, as argued earlier in this chapter, of geology rather than astronomy. Ironically, Burnet's theory about the origins and history of the earth was not to endure either in its methods or its conclusions, but its intention was unmistakably scientific.[42]

Burnet is known for two works: *Telluris theoria sacra* (1681),[43] which he translated into English as *The Theory of the Earth,* and *Archeologiae philosophicae: sive doctrina antiqua de rerum originibus* (1692), known in translations (not made by Burnet) as *The Ancient Doctrine Concerning the Originals of Things.* The first work was a theory about the origins of the world; the second was a treatment of the history of the ideas about the earth's origins.

a. *Burnet's geology*

One factor that has been ignored in the history of biblical scholarship has been changes in aesthetic sentiment. This was discussed extensively in relation to the geological debate in theology in Marjorie Hope Nicolson's *Mountain Gloom and Mountain Glory,*[44] where she showed how aesthetic opinion about mountains played a role in the debates about the state of

---

[41] Thomas Burnet should not be confused with Gilbert Burnet (1643–1713), bishop and church historian.

[42] For more on Burnet, see Marjorie Hope Nicolson, *Mountain Gloom and Mountain Glory: The Development of the Aesthetics of the Infinite* (Ithaca: Cornell University Press, 1959); Rappaport, *When Geologists Were Historians 1665–1750,* 139–49; and Steven J. Gould, "The Reverend Thomas' Dirty Little Planet," in *Ever Since Darwin* (New York: W. W. Norton, 1977) 141–46.

[43] The work was first published in Latin in 1681 (books 1 and 2) and 1689 (books 3 and 4). Burnet issued an English translation entitled *The Theory of the Earth* in two parts, the first dealing with the Deluge and Paradise in 1684, and the second dealing with the burning of the world and the new heavens and new earth in 1690. The excellent prose of the translation made it one of the more-quoted books of the eighteenth century.

[44] (Ithaca: Cornell University Press, 1959).

the world before and after the Flood. Reduced and simplified, her argument was that if you see mountains as awe-inspiring monuments of incredible beauty, then their existence before the Flood was only part of the design of a benevolent Creator who wants us to have nice places to spend our holidays. This point of view comes easily if, having been whisked to the top of a mountain by a ski lift, you enjoy a beer on the restaurant terrace to be found on every high place in Europe. However, your view of mountains might be different if you were trying to make a living out of them, all the while enduring the obstacles they put in the way of your progress and trying to escape the deadly forces they unleash on you with little warning. Or again, if you were a good seventeenth-century Platonist like Henry More and you rejoiced in the perfect geometrical forms of the world of ideas, then a snowcapped peak was simply a very rough and imperfect implementation of the isosceles triangle. Burnet was such a Platonist; his basic assumption was that the earth in its primitive perfection must have taken the shape of pure Platonic forms, and its current rough and disfigured contours are due to the damages wrought by the Flood on the earth's original beauty and order.

In *The Theory of the Earth* Burnet argued:

> THAT there was a *Primitive Earth* of another form from the present, and inhabited by Mankind until the Deluge; That it had those properties and conditions that we have ascrib'd to it, namely, a perpetual Quinox or Spring, by reason of its *right* situation to the Sun; Was of an Oval Figure, and the exteriour face of it smooth and uniform, without Mountains or a Sea. That in this Earth stood *Paradise;* the doctrine whereof cannot be understood but upon supposition of this Primitive Earth, and its properties. Then that the disruption and fall of this Earth into the Abysse, which lay under it, was that which made the Universal Deluge and the destruction of the Old World; And that neither *Noah's* Flood, nor the present of the Earth can be explain'd in any other method that is rational, nor by any other Causes that are intelligible.[45]

The Flood, then, was the catastrophe that reduced the world to its present regrettable state.[46] Eventually, however, the imperfect earth

---

[45] *Theory,* book 2, chapter 9, 1692 edition, 287–89. The use of capitalization and italicization in the seventeenth (and eighteenth century) was not standardized.

[46] Burnet could say of this ancient earth: "In this smooth Earth were the first scenes of the world, and the first generation of Mankind; it had the Beauty of Youth and

would be destroyed by fire, and then the new creation would take place on more satisfactory lines.

There are several aspects of Burnet's theory that call for notice. First, it represented the continuing pressure of new discoveries on the credibility of the biblical accounts. La Peyrère's picture of the hapless giant sloth trying to make its way across four continents in time to catch a boat is a vivid image of the difficulties that many people felt despite themselves, even as the fanning out of the human race after Noah to populate the world was a notion that simply seemed less credible all the time. Burnet pointed out that his theory explained these difficulties: before the Flood there were no natural boundaries to human and animal migration. It was a populated and disparate world that was destroyed by the Flood; many human beings and animals survived in all parts of the world as best they could. Noah was simply one such survivor, but he and his ark full of animals were not the only ones. When Burnet argued that the Bible nowhere says explicitly that all humans descended from Noah, he was widening the scope of our understanding of the ancient world and implicitly reducing the Bible's role to one ancient document among other ancient traditions.

Second, while this theory was presented in a way we would call "scientific," Burnet was not quite a modern geologist, for he still assumed that human life was as old as the world, and there should have been human records of geological events. Therefore, while he could describe his theory as "drawn only by a thred of Reason, and the Laws of Nature,"[47] he clearly felt a need to discuss a possible objection that had such a catastrophic flood taken place, "All Antiquity would have rung of it."[48] His efforts in chapter 9 of book 2 to squeeze out evidence of fragmentary traditions which would confirm his theory and which could be found in such ancient documents that have survived the ravages of time and chance represent an interesting combination of learning and ingenuity but leave the reader with the impression of a man making heavy weather of an intractable problem. However, he closed his discus-

---

blooming Nature, fresh and fruitful, and not a Wrinkle, Scar or Fracture in all its body; no rocks nor Mountains, no hollow Caves, nor gaping channels, but even and uniform all over." See Marjorie Hope Nicholson, *Mountain Gloom and Mountain Glory*, 184–224, for an excellent treatment of the aesthetic component of Burnet's theory. While Nicholson's intention was to discuss aesthetics, her work is also invaluable as a contribution to the history of biblical interpretation.

[47] *Theory*, 274.
[48] Ibid., 276.

sion with a note that hinted at more ominous matters to be discussed at another time:

> Those places of Scripture which we have cited, I think, are all truly appli'd; and I have not mention'd *Moses's Cosmopoeia*, because I thought it deliver'd by him as a Lawgiver, not as a Philosopher; which I intend to show at large in another Treatise, not thinking that discussion proper for the Vulgar Tongue.[49]

Burnet and the nature of the Mosaic writings

In *Archaeologia philosophicae* Burnet was as good as his word on his promise mentioned in the above citation, and what he had to say might have had a creative effect on biblical exegesis had his contemporaries paid more attention.

In chapters 7 and 8 of book 2 of the *Archaeologica*, Burnet got to the heart of his thinking about the early traditions of Genesis.[50] He pointed out that "among the Ancients, but more especially the Orientals, there were two different ways of delivering their Divinity and Philosophy . . . a Popular and a hidden one."[51] This idea was scarcely original with Burnet. In 1567 Natalis Comes had published his *Mythologiae, sive explicationis fabularum*, in which, following Campeggio, he discussed the reasons for and behind myths or fables.[52] But Burnet applied this to the

---

[49] Ibid., 288–89.

[50] Burnet never translated this work into English himself. Reventlow lists an English translation of 1692 (*Authority*, 291), but he does not give details, and I have been unable to find evidence for any such book. The first English translations of the *Archaeologica* appear to be two published in 1736, one by the printer J. Fisher with the translator(s?) not named, the other by E. Curll, another printer, who gave Mead and Foxton as the translators. However, it is interesting that the Curll translation did not include the second part of the *Archaeologica*, which was the most explicitly critical of the historicity of the biblical accounts. There was, however, a translation of chapters 7 and 8 of the critical second part of the *Archaeologica* included in *The Oracles of Reason* (London: 1693), done by an anonymous translator at the behest of Charles Blount. I have compared this translation with the Latin, and while it skimps a bit on detail, it is a reasonably fair version, and since it is the one that would have been known to most readers of the day, I quote from it. I should add that I have not been able to reconstruct the publishing history of the *Archaeologica* to my own satisfaction.

[51] *Oracles of Reason*, 22.

[52] Natalis Comes, *Mythologiae, sive Explicationis Fabularum* (Geneva: Samuel Crispinus, 1620). There were a good number of editions of this work in the sixteenth and seventeenth centuries; the one listed is the edition I had available to me. Those who wish to investigate further should bear in mind that the author's name in non-Latin format is Natali Conti.

Bible, which used this style—by which Burnet meant a mixture typical of the ancients,

> of which dubious sort of style the Holy Scripture seems to make use in the explaining natural things; sometimes accommodating it self to the capacities of the people, and sometime to the real but more clouded truth.

In book 2 Burnet demonstrated the improbability of the story of the Fall by rewriting it as if it were "by a modern author." By treating the Garden of Eden story as if it were intended as a factual description of the origins of the world, Burnet had no trouble in showing its unlikely nature, for many of the details are simply unbelievable. Therefore, if one takes this story as a tale "adapted to the Vulgar," Burnet's comment is "I shall not think it amiss."[53] He then went on to demonstrate further problems inherent in the accounts of Adam and Eve, such as Adam's rib, the speaking snake, and so on. He suggested that while the punishment of the whole of humankind for so small a fault was perhaps Moses' attempt to "procure the greater Difference and Authority to his own Laws, which often Decree with the strictest Severity things Frivolous, and in their own Nature, Indifferent."[54]

At the end of this discussion Burnet's advice was:

> But upon these and the other Articles in Moses's Narration, let every one enjoy his own Sentiments, provided he do not destroy the foundation. Now by this Foundation I here mean the Doctrine of the Temporal Rise of Mankind, as well as of this Earth, the Degeneration of both and that Mankind will be redeemed by the Seed of a Woman.[55]

In discussing what we would call the first creation story, but which Burnet referred to as the Hexaemeron, he was, if anything, even more definite about the nonfactual nature of the account. Here again he treated the account as Moses' attempt to write for the "Vulgar" and not the learned, for "betwixt the Learned and the Vulgar there are two different Systems of the World, whereof one supposes the Sun to be the Center, and t'other the Earth."[56] Moses, said Burnet, "wrote not with the purpose

---

[53] *Oracles of Reason*, 32.
[54] Ibid., 49–50.
[55] Ibid., 50.
[56] Ibid., 53.

of describing the origins of the world "exactly according to the Physical Truth," but in order to "breed in the Minds of Men Piety, and a worshipping of the true God."[57]

Burnet and history

Burnet's treatment of the Old Testament was historical in both traditional and innovative ways. As noted above, he was still working in terms of the traditional world chronology, which based its estimate of the age of the world at several thousand years. Since the Flood had taken place in historical times, Burnet assumed that there must be traces of this in the documents of humanity. For him, this was proved by the recurrence of flood stories in many ancient traditions, one of which must have been available to Moses.

Yet in his *Archeologica* Burnet was close to foreshadowing Vico's argument, to be discussed in the next chapter (see pp. 186–87), that there is a historical progression in the ways people think. While Burnet still exempted Moses himself from the vulgar mentality, he felt that the people Moses had to deal with had not yet progressed to more philosophical insights. More important, this represented a countercurrent to the purely "representational" requirement of language lying behind Leibnitz's notion of a system of symbols that would enable all human beings to communicate, whatever their language might be.[58]

Burnet's work cost him the archbishopric of Canterbury. Refusing, with a few exceptions, to take his work seriously cost the Church of England far more. Burnet offered an opportunity to distinguish between scientific knowledge and biblical myth, and the chance was thrown away. Today Burnet's position would not be far from the majority view in many major denominations; even his admonition to be kind to the backwoodsmen among us would not be out of place. But the way to the

---

[57] Ibid., 74. In fact, Burnet makes an exegetical observation that is still a current possible choice that the reason for talking about the sun, moon, and stars in the creation story was to affirm that these were not deities in their own right but created beings subservient to the sublunary world and the use of human beings.

[58] I am aware that this statement represents a gross oversimplification in the interests of avoiding a long treatise on language. Let the reader beware. However, I do think that attempts to account for the intelligibility or even the truth types of discourse were part of an "anti-Enlightenment" current in the thought of Herder and others. Nor is this question yet solved, to judge from the fate of twentieth-century "logical positivism," whose search for "cash values" impoverished the scope of philosophy.

present situation would have been much less fraught with dispute and personal grief had not people insisted on defending an indefensible position.[59] However, this is only one more illustration of Immanuel Hirsch's observation that the heresy of one century becomes the orthodoxy of the next.

5. *Some radical views on the Bible*

i. LOUIS/LUDWEG/LODEWIJK MEYER (1629–1681)

Meyer was one of the interesting amateurs who played significant roles in the history of interpretation. A close friend of Spinoza and later one of the editors of his works, Meyer was by profession a physician, but he had wide interests, including, what is significant for our purposes, a taste for drama (including actresses). In the history of biblical interpretation, his significant work was *Philosophia Scripturae Interpres: exercitatio paradoxa*, published anonymously in Amsterdam in 1666 and edited and reprinted by Johann Salomo Semler in 1776.[60]

The tone set by Meyer's book is one recognized easily by most university teachers; this is the second-year student who, on the basis of a few survey courses, has discovered the secret of the universe, the solution to the world's problems, and the utter stupidity of all professional scholars, not least of all the one he or she is talking to. If this seems an unkind judgment, one need only look at the tone of adolescent glee in the opening phrase of the prologue, where Meyer exulted in the angry response he expected from the theologians: "As soon as the theologians cast their eyes on this work, they will look on its author without impartiality or good will; much more, some of them will fly into a temper—of that we are absolutely assured."[61]

Meyer then went on to explain how, having discovered the lack of agreement among theologians, he searched about until he found the

---

[59] Even *The Theory of the Earth* caused dispute because of its challenging of details in the creation story. Erasmus Warren, in *A Defense of the Discourse Concerning the Earth* (London: 1691) 2, could say: "Do we not plainly see, that if one single link breaks or drops off, the continuity of the Chain is quite dissolved? So if the least single passage of God's Word be false, it certainly shews the rest to be fallible; and a failure of truth in one of its periods, overthrows the credibility of all the other."

[60] There is a French translation by Jacqueline Lagrée and Pierre-François Moreau, *La Philosophie interprète de l'écriture sainte* (Paris: Intertextes, 1988).

[61] *Philosophia Scripturae interpres,* prologue (my translation).

philosophy of Descartes, which would bring the coherence of clear truth to the impenetrable jungles of theology. His pride in the innovation he was bringing is reflected in the very title of his work, where *paradoxica* is used, not in the sense of an apparent self-contradiction that enshrines a truth, but in its more philological sense of "against the teaching," perhaps now rendered as "unconventional" or even "innovative."

Meyer's basic argument was that philological methods are inconclusive in the interpretation of Scripture; otherwise scholars would agree on all important points, which obviously they do not. The conclusion he drew from an elaborate discussion of this theme was that it is philosophy which should provide the guide for the interpretation of Scripture. Just how a philosophical approach would result in more accurate biblical exegesis was not spelled out in detail in Meyer's work.

It would be interesting to know how Spinoza reacted to his first view of Meyer's book. Whether he waited until Meyer was not present for the moment to roll his eyes is not recorded, though he must have managed enough tact to retain Meyer as a friend. J. Samuel Preus has argued that in fact Meyer was one of the antagonists Spinoza was arguing against in the *Tractatus theologico-politicus*.[62] Whether or not this thesis is accepted, there is no doubt that if Meyer was one of the first to understand Spinoza, he was also one of the first to misunderstand him.

However, one cannot be an associate of Spinoza without learning something important, and there are two aspects of Meyer that should be commented upon even in a short treatment. First, the main thrust of his criticism was against the Reformed theologians in the Netherlands of his day.[63] His point that their strict notions of the nature of the inspiration of Scripture was a prejudice that acted as a barrier to the proper understanding of the Bible was not an unfair view of the situation.

Second, Meyer had one genuinely new observation about language, namely, that how language is spoken adds much to its meaning. The importance of bearing this in mind is shown by the interest we all have in

---

[62] Samuel J. Preus, "A hidden opponent in Spinoza's *Tractatus*," *Harvard Theological Review*, vol. 88, no. 3 (1995) 361–88. Preus's article is an indispensable source for observations and bibliography on Spinoza's biblical criticism.

[63] This point is made in a contemporary English criticism of Meyer by John Wilson, *The Scriptures Genuine Interpretation Asserted or, a Discourse concerning the Right Interpretation of Scripture wherein a late Excertation, Intitled, Philosophia S. Scripturae Interpres, is Examin'd, and the Protestant Doctrine in that Point Vindicated* (London: Boulter, 1678) 17. Wilson, although conservative in his own views, had a good understanding of the issues, and his work is omitted unjustly in many bibliographies of the debate.

hearing authors either read their own books or discuss them in public.[64] Conceivably, this observation came from Meyer's experience on the stage, where a change in inflection of a spoken line can reverse its written grammatical meaning. Obviously we cannot go back to hear biblical writers in person, but the orality behind many of the traditions should be a factor to be considered.

On the whole, Meyer's work was that of an enthusiast who had at best a secondary knowledge of the efforts of serious scholarship. He was republished by Semler in the eighteenth century, but more as an example of what was to be avoided. Semler added not only his own comments on the text but also the work of Johannes Camerarius (1500–1574), *De Forma Orationis Scriptorum Evangelicorum, et Aliis Quibusdam consideratione non Indignis*, which was one of the standard treatments of careful philological exegesis.[65]

ii. BENEDICT SPINOZA (1632–1677)[66]

It would not be altogether misleading to describe Spinoza's *Tractatus Theologico-Politicus* as a Dutch reedition of Hobbes's *Leviathan*. Neither man was interested in writing a work on biblical interpretation as such; rather, each was forced into discussing the Bible in the hope of keeping religious considerations out of the national decisions of his country so that public order, personal freedom, and security might all be preserved. The basic problem for each man was that the Bible as an authoritative "foundational" source could be appealed to by those who claimed its authority as their own, giving them the right to overthrow or at least disobey the sovereign power of a country. This entailed a discussion of the Bible itself in order to lessen its claims.

---

[64] I know this from my own experience. As a student I was very impressed by the Old Testament scholarship of a particular scholar. It was a great disappointment to me when I actually heard him speak; as a result, I never took him seriously thereafter.

[65] *Philosophia S. Scripturae interpres. Exercitatio Paradoxa. Tertium Edita, et Appendice Ioachimi Camerarii Aucta; cum Notis Variis et Praefatione D. Io. Sal. Semleri* (Halle: Hendel, 1776). Lagrée et Moreau, *La Philosophie*, 20 appear to suggest (the French is ambiguous) that only one copy of this work has survived. This is not correct; there is one in the Bodleian and I suspect there are others. The reason why the book does not show up in bibliographical searches is that Meyer's name is not mentioned on the title page, only the names of Semler and Camerarius.

[66] A reasonable bibliography for a major figure such as Spinoza would be too extensive for a general work. However, for those in search of basic information, a useful starting point would be the section on Spinoza in Israel, *Radical Enlightenment*, 159–74.

Hobbes took the approach that which books actually made up the Bible and how they were to be interpreted was the responsibility of the sovereign. Spinoza's appeal was not to pure political power in this matter, but rather to a more radical assessment of the Bible's philosophical standing, which led to a rejection of its infallibility or its perfection.

There were some differences in the approach of the two men; Hobbes was concerned, for the most part, with how government works; Spinoza was more interested in the freedom of serious thinkers to think and speak as they pleased. Hobbes saw his opponents in England not only in the Presbyterian clergy but also in various independent agitators who picked up bits and bobtails of scriptural quotations and spun them into "biblically warranted" demands. For Spinoza, the problem was the on-going conflict between secular politicians who preferred a pragmatic, generally tolerant attitude toward religious plurality and the hard-nosed Calvinist clergy who wanted tighter controls over heterodoxy.

It is reasonable to suppose that Spinoza had read *Leviathan,* but the Latin edition of Hugo Grotius's *De Imperio Summarum Potestatum Circa Sacra*[67] ("The Power of the Political Magistrate in Sacred Matters") was part of his library, and he may have derived some of his ideas about the powers of the state from this work. Grotius wrote his book in a French context, where Cardinal Richelieu was considering a reunion of Protestants and Roman Catholics into a Gallican church independent of the papacy in order to prevent papal interference in French affairs. Grotius's work could have served as a theoretical justification for the subjection of such a church to the French state, for he set out the rights of the state over the church by appealing to an exhaustive list of examples.[68] This in turn might have had some influence on Spinoza's thought about a "generalized church" subject to state control. Grotius, however, did not get into the problem of how one dealt with religious diversity.

From the viewpoint of the history of exegesis, Spinoza's discussion of the Bible can be seen to rest on three pillars.

First, basic to Spinoza's argument was his division of humanity into two parts: the intelligent, cultivated people, who could appreciate the clear and distinct ideas of philosophy, and the great unwashed multitudes, whose superstitious tendencies needed the control provided by

---

[67] I have only the French translation, *Traité du pouvoir du magistrat politique sur les choses sacrées* (London: 1751), as a download from Gallica.

[68] Much of Grotius's work is characterized by a gargantuan appetite for erudition but only a moderate taste for editing.

less refined ideas. This assumption about the need for beliefs that would keep untrustworthy people under control was common to many thinkers of the Enlightenment period, such as Voltaire, who declared that a man should make sure his wife, his tailor, and his lawyer all believed in a God who would punish bad conduct in another life. For Spinoza, the rough and ready guide for the masses was found in the Bible, whose unsophisticated language was at the level of the crowd's understanding. Superior intellects could find better guides in the rational world of philosophy.

Second, Spinoza mounted an attack on the absolute factual infallibility of the Bible. A great deal of the argument for infallibility rested on the nature of the inspiration of the prophets. Spinoza discussed the various types of prophets and argued that while the prophets had very good imaginations, their grasp of clear and distinct ideas was not as well developed. He went on to deal with inconsistencies and self-contradictions within the Bible, not to mention all the uncertainties of text and translation. For example, whereas Samuel thought that the Lord would not go back on anything he had decreed (1 Sam 15:29), Jeremiah says that God would not carry out the evil destined for evil nations or the good for righteous ones in the case of repentance or backsliding respectively (Jer 18:8-10). Spinoza pointed out that not all the dates in Old Testament chronologies can be reconciled; for example, 1 Kings 6 dates the building of the temple 480 years after the Exodus, but if one adds up the dates recorded in the history books of the Bible, the period comes to 580 years. The authorship of biblical books is not always what it seems; internal evidence shows that Moses did not write all of the Pentateuch; ancient books are missing, and so on.

More important for Spinoza, the conviction of the Hebrews expressed in the Bible that they were the chosen people of God is out of keeping with the truth that "Every man's true happiness and blessedness consist solely in the enjoyment of what is good, not in the pride that he alone is enjoying it, to the exclusion of others."[69] Here Scripture was speaking only to the understanding of its hearers, who, as Moses himself points out in Deuteronomy 9:6-7, knew not true blessedness.

Third, in the discussion of miracles Spinoza made the point that the common people imagined two different sources of power, divine will and natural causes, and could only adore God and refer all things to

---

[69] From *The Chief Works of Spinoza*, trans. R.H.M. Elwes (New York: Dover, 1951), vol. 1: *Tractatus Theologico-Politicus*, 43.

divine power by ignoring natural causes.[70] If, then, what are described as miracles in the Bible did happen as described, then it was a case of not describing their real causes accurately. On the other hand, one has to allow for the natural disposition of historians to get things wrong or at least to exaggerate them.

However, Spinoza was not prepared to deny any value to Scripture; on the contrary, he stated, "In so far as it contains the word of God, it has come down to us uncorrupted."[71] Given what he had been saying so far, this comes as a surprise, until one looks carefully at his meaning. Essentially, Spinoza saw the Bible as containing simple doctrines that are adequate for giving the masses proper direction for their lives. This does not mean the Bible is infallible, but even in its present imperfect condition, it does contain the basic outlines of what is necessary, and even if something important had been lost because of textual corruption, this missing part could be made up from reason alone. The simple doctrine of the Bible is good in that it is related to the personal conduct of its hearers, for its message is that God is supremely just and supremely merciful. Scripture teaches obedience rather than philosophical truth.

The difference between philosophy and theology—by which Spinoza meant the Bible—is comparable to the difference between a racing yacht and a rowboat: they both float, and they both will get you across the bay to get groceries, but if you are going on a round-the-world race, the rowboat should not even be considered. Thus there is no point in searching out great truths from the Bible; it is not built for that. Rather, the Bible provides the wherewithal for those incapable of philosophy to get on with their lives in a reasonable, if modest, way.

On the question of Spinoza's contribution to biblical studies, there are two points of view. The first asks the question of Spinoza's actual exegesis. Now Spinoza's method, in some cases at least, was to take over someone else's observations and turn them in a new direction. The opening of the *Tractatus Theologico-Politicus*, the discussion of prophecy, was heavily dependent on Maimonides, who emphasized the aspect of imagination among the prophets. But Spinoza turned Maimonides' argument around and suggested that while indeed imagination does characterize the prophets, this characteristic is simply a sign that they did not have excellent minds. Similarly, in the discussion of the miracle of the sun standing

[70] Ibid., 81.
[71] Ibid., 165.

still in the book of Joshua (Josh 10:12-13), Spinoza picked up a suggestion from La Peyrère, who argued that rather than reverse the motion of the whole solar system, God simply caused a special sort of after-sunset illumination that La Peyrère had once noticed himself. For La Peyrère, this was nonetheless a miracle in that it was a specific intervention of God in the universe. Spinoza took the same explanation a step further to suggest that what happened was a purely natural phenomenon that just happened to occur at that moment.

Spinoza dealt in a similar way with possible contradictions or incongruities in the Bible. As we have seen in earlier chapters, critics had made lists of these for a long time before Spinoza. However, the same critics sought answers within the framework of some sort of inspiration of Scripture, however fragile their constructions might have been, or if all else failed, they were content to leave the matter open rather than suggest a self-contradiction within the Bible. Spinoza emphasized that Scripture was simply wrong or self-contradictory. That parts of the Old Testament were a bit crude and irrational had also been noticed, but this was explained by the need to appeal to the crude nature of the Israelites at the time. Spinoza built on these observations but went on to describe the whole nature of the Old Testament as crude and simplistic compared with the new knowledge that philosophers had discovered in the seventeenth century.

Now in the matter of the fallibility of the Bible, Spinoza was not the first to come to this conclusion; the *libertins érudits* of the first half of the seventeenth century had made this point already. However, they do not seem to have argued their case out in detail; rather, their condemnation of the superstitions of religion in general was simply expanded to include the Bible. Where Spinoza was doing something new was to combine the conclusion of the *libertins* with the work of the biblical critics to produce a new, explosive assessment of the weaknesses of the Bible in the interests of cutting the Calvinist pastors off at the pass.

The real difference Spinoza made was to give a different framework of explanations to what had long been noticed, namely, that the Bible was not inerrant in all its details. Spinoza's conclusion was that while the Bible was not divinely inspired in any special way, nonetheless it did provide a basis for ordinary folk to live out their lives, even if it (and they) did not rise to the perception of the truth reserved for philosophers.

Many years ago I argued that Spinoza should be seen not as a brilliant biblical exegete but rather as a biblical theologian, that is, someone who used the basis of certainties provided by another system of thought to judge the nature of the contents of the Bible and to distinguish between what it contained of value from what was purely superstitious nonsense.[72] In effect, this was one more step in the dethronement of the Bible. However, here it was not a question of geology or geography, but it was in the Bible's heartland of theology that the case was being made.

iii. BALTHASAR BEKKER (1634–1698)

Bekker, a Calvinist preacher, attacked belief in the devil, in particular the devil's personal interference in the natural order of the world and the efficacy of sorcery and similar practices. His *Betoverde Weereld*, in four huge volumes (1691–1693), began, significantly enough for the argument of this book, with a historical overview of belief in the devil before launching into a refutation of the belief in his existence. Bekker's work was translated in whole or in part into French, German, and English and was the cause of a great deal of uproar at the time. Significantly, Johann Semler thought enough of the work to bring out a new edition of Bekker, but equally significantly, even Semler thought that some condensation of the work was required.

For biblical studies, the importance of Bekker's work was the break he was making both with the thought world of the Bible, where occasionally evil spirits and even Satan were part of the metaphysical landscape, and with the thought world of his own day, in which concerns with witchcraft had, if anything, increased during the seventeenth century. While Hobbes had preceded Bekker in this observation, it was now apparent that passages such as the exorcism narratives of the Gospels were open to serious objections or at least qualifications.

iv. L. P., AN ANONYMOUS POPULARIZER OF NEW VIEWS

That geological questions were beginning to put into question the factual reliability of the Bible is shown by an interesting anonymous publication that, despite its small size, created a furor at the end of the seventeenth century, namely, *Two Essays sent in a Letter from Oxford to a Nobleman in London* by L. P., Master of Arts.[73] From internal evidence it is reasonably sure that the author was educated at Cambridge, possibly as

---

[72] J. Sandys-Wunsch, "Spinoza the First Biblical Theologian," *Zeitschrift für die alttestamentliche Wissenschaft* 93 (1981) 327–42.

[73] L. P. has so far escaped detection; see Rappaport, *When Geologists Were Historians*, 162–63.

a member of Corpus Christi College, and was familiar with the work of Cambridge theologians such as Tillotson, Spencer, Stillingfleet, and with the biblical exegesis of Grotius, Le Clerc, and Simon. L. P.'s basic argument in the first essay was that, on the basis of Burnet's *Theory of the Earth,* the complexity of both human and animal populations of the earth, and an analysis of the essentially primitive literature found in Genesis, while Moses may be esteemed as a great moralist, his account should not be taken as scientifically accurate. This early shot in the so-called battle between Bible and science was a clear sign of the new problems exegetes were increasingly called upon to deal with.

In the second essay L. P. also dealt with the nature of Moses' writings, which he saw as part of the ways of writings of "the Eastern Nations, the Hebrew themselves not excepted," which he described as "mythological," a term that was to have an increasingly important place in exegesis in the following centuries.[74] His argument was close to Burnet's treatment of Genesis in his *Archaeologica* but he also got into demonology, which, on the same basis as Hobbes and Becker, he dismissed as ancient superstition.

6. *Two continental attempts at a balanced view of problems of exegesis posed by critical studies*

Let us finally turn to two men who, within the bounds of orthodoxy, generously interpreted, managed to break new directions in freeing the Bible from the restrictions usually expected within the Genevan Calvinist or the French Roman Catholic church. They had much in common. Both had troubles with their denominational authorities. Jean Le Clerc had to leave the Calvinism of Geneva to find a professorship among the Remonstrants in Amsterdam, while Richard Simon was expelled from the Oratory, one of the premier learned orders in the French Roman Catholic church. Both had to turn to Holland to publish their works, and both might have agreed easily on many points except for the fact that they could not stand each other personally.

i. RICHARD SIMON (1638–1712)

The French Roman Catholic Richard Simon was a scholar's scholar. Witness what even one of his more determined opponents had to say of

[74] L. P., *Two Essays sent in a Letter from Oxford, to a Nobleman in London* (London, 1695) pt. 2, 30.

him. Frederick [?] Spanheim[75] was a conservative Calvinist who wrote a severely critical review of Simon's work, but he had to admit that it had been a long time since he had read any book with such fascination, and it would be difficult to see how it could have been written better. In his opinion the book was a superb abridgement of many volumes—even a whole library—and indeed in Simon's references to other works, one could find the necessary information to build a new library. Spanheim went on to praise the order in which Simon set out his book and the good sense, discernment, erudition, candor, penetration, and judgment it exhibited.[76] Less enthusiastic about the book was Bossuet, one of the dominant ecclesiastics of his day, who banned Simon's work after it had actually been printed.[77]

Simon's *Histoire Critique du Vieux Testament* was a work unlike any other in its day. Part 1 dealt with the Hebrew text, but included were discussions of the origins of the form of the books of the Old Testament as well as about the transmission of the text; part 2 discussed versions, that is translations, of the Old Testament; and part 3 began with an outline of a project for a new version of the Old Testament, but then got into a discussion of how the Old Testament had been translated throughout history up to Simon's current times. Only by looking at the audience Simon had in mind can one understand his purpose.

One should begin by noting that the work was written in French, not Latin. In his response to Spanheim, Simon himself remarked dryly that his greatest crime may have been to have written in a language understood by the people.[78] Simon's public, then, was not just the learned professor

---

[75] Both Frederick (Jr.) (1632–1701) and Ezekiel (1629–1710) Spanheim have been suggested as the author of the extended critique of Simon in "Lettre à un ami . . . publié à Paris en 1678" included in Leers's edition of *Histoire Critique du Vieux Testament*, 563–622.

[76] "Lettre à un ami . . .," published as a supplement to Leers's 1685 edition of *Histoire Critique du Vieux Testament*, 565–66.

[77] Those with a taste for irony will appreciate that Simon, who admired Louis Cappell more than any other critic, was to suffer the same fate, for just as Cappell the Protestant was hindered from publishing by the Protestants, Simon was hindered by Roman Catholics.

[78] *Réponse à la lettre de Mr. Spanheim*, bound in Richard Simon, *Histoire Critique du Vieux Testament* (Rotterdam: Reinier Leers, 1685) 625. Nominally this is attributed to "un Théologien de la Faculté de Paris," but it is generally ascribed to Simon, even by Leers in his edition. As the author of a banned book, Simon was perhaps constrained to write anonymously, but it is clear that he took the occasion to have some fun with his remarks about himself.

but the educated reader, the person whose Latin was not up to tackling a long book in the language, but who was aware of Spinoza and others who had attacked the Bible on critical grounds. The sort of problems these people would have been aware of were: How can we be sure that translations of the Bible are accurate? Did Moses write the whole Penta-teuch? Were there errors of fact in the biblical chronologies and else-where? Were some incidents unbelievable, such as Sarah's beauty at an advanced age? What about repetitions in the Bible? Had the text been sufficiently well preserved, given the difference between the manu-scripts? What did the great critical scholars have to say about the Bible? These sorts of questions can easily be seen behind the answers Simon announced in his preface that he will give in the body of his work.

Essentially, Simon was setting out to provide a reasonable explanation of the sorts of difficulties intelligent readers have when they look care-fully at the Bible. Thus in chapter 1, where he gave an outline of his book, he cited Augustine's admonition that those who study Scripture should above everything else apply themselves to *la Critique de la Bible* and correct their copies. Simon also cited the example of Jerome's answers to the ques-tions of the German ladies Sunia and Fretila, in which Jerome applied all his learning "pour satisfaire à leurs doutes" ("to satisfy their doubts"). Like La Peyrère and others who had tried the same task, Simon found himself attacked as someone bent on destroying what he intended to de-fend. This is a pattern that continually repeats itself in church history.

However, there were other factors that attracted the wrath (disagree-ment is not quite the *mot juste* here) of Simon's critics. It is possible that part of Bossuet's anger was stirred up because Simon attacked Augus-tine's competence in remarks such as if Augustine had only known Hebrew, he would not have had to retract his opinions so often.[79] On the other hand, Protestant commentators objected to Simon's invocation of the authority of the church as defined by the Council of Trent to cover over gaps in the biblical doctrine at points where the Protestants were, in Simon's estimation at any rate, covered only with confusion.

ii. SIMON AND SPINOZA

Good scholars disagree on whether Simon knew Spinoza's work while he was writing the *Histoire Critique du Vieux Testament* itself or whether he only became aware of Spinoza shortly before he wrote the preface,

---

[79] See Patric Ranson, *Richard Simon ou du caractere illegitime de l'augustinisme en theologie* (Lausanne: L'Age d'Homme, 1990), esp. ch. 3.

which presumably would have been written after the main body of the work. It is true that Simon did not discuss Spinoza directly outside his preface, but he did refer to Cuperus's refutation of Spinoza,[80] which showed that he knew Spinoza's name at least and, Simon being the book enthusiast he was, probably much more besides. Why, then, did Simon not deal with Spinoza more extensively? One possible explanation is based on the fact that in his preface Simon referred only to chapter 8 of the *Tractatus Theologico-Politicus*, which set out Spinoza's observations on incongruities in the text of the Old Testament. This was the only area where the interests of the two men overlapped enough in method of approach for Simon to comment; Spinoza's philosophizing elsewhere was outside the interest, perhaps even the competence, of Simon the historian.[81]

My tentative conclusion in this matter is that since prefaces are written in the interest of selling books rather than advancing the cause of truth, it suddenly occurred to Simon, when he was writing his preface, that throwing in a reference to Spinoza might help to generate sales.

Much more interesting was the basic difference in approach between Simon and those like Spinoza who assumed that contradictions, incongruities, and inexplicable leaps within the Bible only show its philosophical inadequacies and the consequent distance from truth. Simon replaced the philosophical test with the historical explanation. Thus, if internal evidence shows that Moses did not write all of the Pentateuch, this is not a refutation of its importance but only an elucidation of how it was composed; if numbers do not add up or if genealogies differ, this is not a sign of a lack of truth but only a lack of a good secretary to keep scraps of paper rolled on sticks in the right filing order.

Simon's explanation was that throughout the history of Israel up to the monarchy, public records were kept by prophets, known as public scribes (in distinction to the private scribes who acted for individuals), who preserved records and edited the Pentateuch and other biblical books by adding and deleting records. This did not reflect on the authority of the Pentateuch, for all these scribes were inspired, not in the sense that they necessarily foretold the future but in the sense that divine inspiration kept them from making serious errors in the essentials of Israel's faith.

---

[80] *Histoire Critique du Vieux Testament*, 452.

[81] On this point see Henri Margival, *Essai sur Richard Simon* (Paris: 1900) 125ff., and Ranson, *Richard Simon*, 25–27.

Here is an example of how Simon used his hypothesis to explain matters in the first few chapters of Genesis.

> I question likewise whether one should attribute to *Moses* or to the publick Writers which were in his time the little order which is to be found in some places of the Pentateuch, it is more probable that as in those times the Books were written upon little Scrolls or separate Sheets that were sow'd together, the order of these sheets might be changed. And besides the Books of the Bible as we have now, being onely an abridgment, the order of matters contained in them has not always been regarded. . . . A great many places in the Books of the Law where the order is confus'd make me think that those Books were not originally compos'd in that method. For example, can any one believe that an Historian should write the History of the Creation of Man with so little order as there is in the first Chapter of *Genesis*, where the same things are several times repeated without method, and as it were beside the purpose? And moreover after the Man and Woman were created in the first Chapter and 27th Verse, the Woman is supposed not to be made, and in the following Chapter the manner how she was taken from *Adam's* side is described, nevertheless in the same Chapter it was before forbidden him, as he was her Husband, whom she accompanied in the Garden, to eat the fruit of a certain tree.[82]

The significance of Simon's approach was that he had given up attempting to reconcile difficulties that scholars had been breaking their teeth on for centuries. Instead, he admitted that there are many incongruities that do not fit in with the theory of Moses' sole authorship of the Pentateuch as it now exists. Thus the present format of the biblical books has to be explained in part at least by the historical processes by which they were preserved, for editing, addition, and mischance all have to be considered as parts of a larger explanation. It was for this reason that Simon has been credited as the originator of the fragmentist theory of Pentateuchal criticism: problems are to be explained as the result of an unconnected series of editorial actions and not as the result of the combination of different documents, each of which had its own opinions.

---

[82] *A Critical History of the Old Testament* (London, 1672) 40–41. I am quoting from the English translation of the 1678 Paris edition of *Histoire Critique du Vieux Testament* attributed to Richard Hampden, because this is the format in which Simon would have been known to many English readers.

The reason for Simon's freedom in this undertaking was that for him the authority of the Bible is not found in its literal truth but rather in the divine inspiration of the public scribes. This flows into the normative tradition of the Roman Catholic Church as set out by the Council of Trent.

> The Catholicks, who are perswaded their Religion depends not onely on the Text of Scripture, but likewise on the Tradition of the Church, are not at all scandaliz'd, to see that the misfortune of Time and the negligence of Transcribers have wrought changes in the holy Scriptures as well as in prophane Authours: there none but prejudic't Protestants or ignorant people that can be offended by it."[83]

For Simon, then, church tradition had the same function as philosophy had for Spinoza: it provided a backstop so that the process of examining the problems of the biblical text did not go over the cliff into the rocky pit of doubt and confusion. Not everyone, least of all Bossuet, found Simon's argument convincing or even reassuring.

Is it appropriate to call Richard Simon the father of biblical criticism? Simon would have rejected out of hand any suggestion of the latter designation; for him, and indeed for most of his learned contemporaries, biblical criticism was the careful examination of the text of the Bible in the interests of correcting, understanding, and translating it. This was a discipline that had been carried on by church fathers and rabbis alike, and Simon saw himself as standing within this discipline, not at its head. Although he was also sure that he had added to its sum total, his references to predecessors such as Jerome, Masius, Pererius, and others show how much he depended upon their work.

Simon was aware of the negative connotations of the word "criticism," so in his preface he warned his readers:

> Thus we shall often find in this Work the word Critick, and some other such like, which I have been forced to use the better to express my self according to the terms of the art I treated of. Besides persons who are Scholars are already us'd to these terms in our tongue.[84]

But the real question is, Did Simon liberate himself sufficiently from dogmatic presuppositions about the authority of Scripture to undertake

---

[83] Ibid., 9–10. Simon's choice of "prejudic't" is deliberate; he was quite clear in what follows that he did not consider all Protestants to come under this heading.

[84] Ibid., "Authour's Preface" (unpaginated).

a fully critical examination of the text in a manner comparable to Spinoza's? This requires a second question: How far from presuppositions was Spinoza? He had certainly liberated himself from any notion of the infallibility of the Bible, but had he done this by adopting a philosophy as dogmatic as the religious orthodoxies he rejected? It might be argued that in fact Spinoza was operating from his own faith perspective, for philosophers since Spinoza have not always been sure about being able to prove philosophically a morality integrally linked with an ordered nature. This matter is open to discussion.

Simon certainly appealed to the authority of the church and the church fathers in general. However, when one looks closely at his case, one can see why Bossuet was worried. Simon pointed out that the church fathers did not agree, that they did not know everything, and that Augustine was incompetent, so one had to take into account the parallel work of the rabbis before the way was open to new discoveries. Simon added that in all this no important doctrine of the church was threatened, but one might wonder whether there was a certain amount of window dressing here, such as the opening remark to his work: "No one can doubt but that the truths contained in the Holy Scripture are infallible and of Divine Authority. . . ."[85] In my opinion, Simon had cleared away all the elbow room he needed for an independent evaluation of the formation and the transmission of the text of the Bible.

Where Simon was important for the history of biblical interpretation was not so much in his radical observations, interesting as they might have been. Rather, his contribution was the introduction of history as a vital factor for understanding both the Bible and the works of its interpreters through the centuries. Simon was one of the first to carry out this sort of investigation in a systematic manner.

iii. JEAN LE CLERC (1657–1736)

Le Clerc was born in Geneva but studied theology at Saumur, the French Protestant seminary, which for its day had considerable "liberal" tendencies.[86] Le Clerc flourished in the atmosphere there, but on his

---

[85] Just how serious Simon's profession of Roman Catholicism was is open to debate, albeit not likely of solution. For the purposes of the history of biblical interpretation, it is justifiable to take him at face value, for this was how he appeared to his contemporaries and successors.

[86] On Saumur, see François La Planche, *L'Écriture, le sacré, et l'histoire: Érudits et politiques protestants devant la Bible en France au XVIIe siècle* (Amsterdam & Maarssen: APA-Holland University Press, 1986) 1–180.

return to Geneva he let enough slip out about his convictions to make himself *persona non grata* to the Genevan church, which at that time was in the grips of a rigid Calvinism. Le Clerc wound up teaching at the Remonstrant seminary in Amsterdam, where he found an ecclesiastical tradition much more in tune with his own convictions. The two figures who inspired him were Erasmus, whose works he edited, and Grotius, to whom he continually returned.[87]

Le Clerc's writing was extensive, ranging far beyond the boundaries of theology strictly speaking, possibly due to the necessity of supplementing his meager salary. Apart from his serious theological publications, he founded and to some extent edited three learned journals and wrote works of secular history. It is, however, misleading to characterize him as a "journalist," as Rappaport does. The problem is that words can escape their etymological roots. "Journalist" has acquired a certain negative overtone of someone whose speed is superb but whose accuracy often leaves much to be desired; thus the editor of a serious journal such as the *Journal of Theological Studies* might not consider it a compliment to be called a journalist. In any event, Le Clerc was one of the leading intellectual figures of his day and influenced British philosophy through his personal friendship and correspondence with John Locke, whom he had met during Locke's exile in Holland.

It has already been said above that while the tone of their disputes sometimes became shrill, Le Clerc and Simon had much in common in their assessment of how the Bible came to be. But apart from personal incompatibility of gargantuan proportions, there was a fundamental difference in their dispositions, summed up by Le Clerc's comment that Simon had shown "plus d'érudition que de solidarité ("more learning than solid judgment") in his work.[88]

That Le Clerc was correct in his judgment here is shown by comparing how each man treated the subject of the Hebrew language.[89] In *Histoire Critique du Vieux Testament*, Simon discussed the probable etymology of

---

[87] The most recent extended study of Le Clerc is Maria Cristina Pitassi, *Entre Croire et Savoir: Le Problème de la Méthode Critique chez Jean Le Clerc* (Leiden: E. J. Brill, 1987). Where I differ from her is the extent to which Le Clerc was influenced by Spinoza rather than by professional scholars such as Lapide and Grotius.

[88] *Sentiments de quelques théologiens de Hollande sur l'Histoire critique du vieux testament* (Amsterdam: 1685) 2.

[89] For Simon, see *Histoire Critique du Vieux Testament*, book 1, chapters 14 and 15 (pp. 83–91 in the 1685 French edition). For Le Clerc, *Twelve Dissertations out of Monsieur Le Clerk's* (sic) *Genesis*, trans. Mr. Brown (London: R. Baldwin, 1696) 1–50; 170–81.

the word "Hebrew" and then argued that Hebrew was essentially the same language as spoken by the Canaanites and the Phoenicians. Whether Hebrew was the first language of all was much more difficult to establish, for several peoples claimed this distinction for their own tongues. Most Christians accepted the Jewish claim that Hebrew was the oldest language on the grounds that it was the simplest, but then the simplicity of a language is not a proof of its antiquity, and Simon gave examples from Italian of words that had been simplified, that is, shortened rather than lengthened as time went on.

Simon then shifted to Gregory of Nyssa's *Answer to Eunomius' Second Book*, in which there was a discussion about language. Simon did not concur with Gregory's acceptance of the hypothesis that Hebrew was created for the Israelites during the Exodus, but he accepted the argument that God was not the Creator of the names of the sky and the earth, but rather the Creator of the sky and the earth themselves. However, God gave human beings an ability to reason, which they used to express their thoughts by inventing words. Simon sought support for this point of view from those ancient philosophers who attributed the invention of languages to nature, for nature and reason are the same thing.

Simon also invoked Gregory's argument that at the Tower of Babel God did not create new languages but simply confused the existing one in order to drive people apart and cause the populating of the whole world. To be sure, the worthy saint does not explain how one distinguishes between creating new languages and confusing an original one, but Simon attributed to both Gregory and Moses a dual way of describing events. If one speaks theologically, one attributes events to God's providence, but if one speaks historically, one looks for human causes of the same events.[90]

Simon then began another section dealing with how languages were invented, along with a digression about the origins of languages. He began with postulating the necessity people faced of inventing new words when they faced new things; this is seen in the Tower of Babel story, where the confusion was produced by men having to invent so many new words to cover new things. Then suddenly Simon moved on to observe that since nature begins necessarily with what is most simple and moves on to more complicated structures, it follows that the first

---

[90] Simon threw in a comment that this style of double explanation explains why in the Bible it can be said that God hardened pharaoh's heart and that pharaoh hardened his heart himself; it is simply two ways of explaining the same thing.

language must have been the most simple and with the least complications. Hebrew was the tongue that fit this description more than any other, and therefore Hebrew was the mother of Oriental languages; other languages developed as new letters and syllables were added. Simon then added a qualifier that threw into doubt this first position, for he added that Hebrew was no longer in its primitive form, since many words had been made more complicated over the centuries. What followed was a long series of examples, leading one to wonder where the argument is going, given the odd repetition, but even more so because Simon nowhere referred to the point made in the previous section that words can be shortened as well as lengthened in the history of a language. The net effect is that one is left confused about what Simon thought about the origins of language and whether he thought Hebrew was the oldest.

The contrast with Le Clerc's handling of the same topic is revealing. Le Clerc worked his way through the issues in a systematic way, beginning with the evidence for Hebrew as the original language, which he found inadequate. Then he discussed the one language that existed before the Flood and showed how the gradual changes that crept into usage eventually led to new languages developing from an older one, such as the emergence of Italian, French, and Spanish from Latin. The language that Abraham spoke before he entered Canaan was Chaldee (Aramaic), but his descendants spoke Canaanite, for they communicated with the Canaanites without the need of interpreters. Le Clerc then got on the subject of the nature of Hebrew, which, he argued, was a barren, ambiguous, and unrefined language in which only the poetry had any claim to excellence. He went on in some detail to defend his opinions that the Hebrew language was "Rude and Impolite." All this he distinguished from the importance of what was nonetheless said in Hebrew, namely, what was revealed to the Jewish prophets and communicated by them to the world. Finally he discussed the transmission of the Old Testament text very briefly.

Obviously, much of what Le Clerc said would no longer be received with patience by a learned group, but what he said was, by the standard of his day, a coherent and defensible discussion of the subject of Hebrew language where his own conclusions were set out in a reasoned way. The contrast with Simon's tortuous treatment is evident and shows, in my opinion, that while Simon was superb as a historian of what others had said, he was either uninterested or incapable of arguing out his own conclusions on the issues raised by those whose works he described so well.

This might well explain an interesting difference between Le Clerc and Simon, namely, that there were few places where their discussions of the Old Testament actually overlapped. Whereas Le Clerc tackled the new issues that were coming more and more to the fore in his day, Simon's interest was essentially in the writing of biblical books and their transmission and translation. Le Clerc, in his Genesis commentary, had sections dealing with what actually happened to Sodom—a lightning strike ignited naturally occurring bitumen; how Lot's wife became a pillar of salt—"the common belief of the Pillar of Salt, wholly proceeded from misunderstanding the words of Moses, and has been obstinately maintain'd by the Vanity of Some and the credulity of others";[91] the origins of the custom of circumcision—it was an Egyptian custom taken over by Moses; the extent of the Flood—it was a relatively local occurrence. What Le Clerc had to say was not always original,[92] but here we find a serious biblical scholar trying to incorporate arguments against the literal meaning of Scripture in a way that would not challenge the religious authority of the Bible. In contrast, Simon gave the impression of someone who once he felt he had explained why the text was in its present form, there was no need to discuss the problem of its truth, however truth might be defined.

There are two passages in Le Clerc that are worth noting. One was his opinion of miracles. In his discussion of the Flood, he said:

> Tis true, this could not be effected without a Miracle; but then there is no way to solve the Difficulties of so great a Cataclysm without a Miracle. However the less and fewer of this Kind we suppose, provided the rest may be conveniently explain'd, that Exposition uses to be accounted the most agreeable to Truth by all Interpreters, because God is never so prodigal of Miracles, as to have recourse to them where natural Causes are sufficient. . . .[93]

In his discussion of Lot's wife, Le Clerc pointed out:

> . . . the Stile of the Oriental Writers, who always affected bold and pompous Metaphors, is not to be expounded by our modern way of

---

[91] Le Clerc, *Twelve Dissertations*, 276–77.

[92] For example, in the case of Sodom, the Roman historian Strabo had already described the existence of asphalt in the Dead Sea area. Sir Thomas Browne knew of the suggestion of lightning as the immediate cause of the conflagration but looked on the idea as a temptation to be resisted.

[93] Le Clerc, *Twelve Dissertations*, 168. The influence of Grotius is evident here.

speaking, which is one of the greatest Faults the Interpreters of them have committed. When they wou'd find out the Meaning of any Word or Expression, they rather consider how they wou'd be understood if they spoke so now, than how those People who differ no less from us in Opinion and Fancy, than they are distant from us in relation to time or place, wou'd understand them.[94]

Le Clerc, then, was setting out to grapple with the problem of how to steer between the doctrine of biblical infallibility and the Deist opinion of the Bible as "a Work full of Falsities, and wherein there is nothing but what is purely human."[95] Just how narrowly biblical infallibility was defined can be seen in the extreme form of hard-boiled Calvinism, namely, the two canons of the *Formula Consensus Helvetica* cited in the previous chapter (p. 90). Le Clerc's alternative viewpoint was that in the Bible

it is only in Prophecies, and some other places, as in the Sermons of Jesus Christ, and where God himself is introduc'd speaking, that the Matter or Things have been immediately reveal'd to those who spoke them: That the Stile, for the most part, was left to the liberty of those who spoke or writ: That there are some Books that are not inspir'd, neither as to the Matter nor Words, as Job Ecclesiastes, &c.[96]

Le Clerc went on to admit that there were occasions that writers wrote from bad temper ("passion"), such as the curses in the psalms, that the historians made minor mistakes, that the apostles in their teaching were not ordinarily inspired but had recourse to their own memories and judgment and might in some cases be mistaken. Yet despite these qualifications about the accuracy of the Bible, Le Clerc urged against what he considered the Deist position that the apostles were "not deceiv'd in any Point of Doctrine . . . because Christian Religion is easy and compris'd in a few Articles." The appeal here was implicitly to Grotius and Erasmus, as was made explicit later on.[97]

Essentially, Le Clerc was working from an assumption analogous to that of Richard Simon. For Simon, the tradition of the church was enough to compensate for weaknesses in the text, whereas for Le Clerc the simple nature of the Christian faith as shown in its practice was clearly

[94] Ibid., 271.

[95] *Five Letters Concerning the Inspiration of the Holy Scriptures: Translated out of French* (n.p.: 1690) 137.

[96] Ibid., 134–35.

[97] Fifth Letter, *Five Letters*, 201.

visible behind the rough and awkward documents of the Bible. This was the way of Grotius in his efforts to reunite divided Christendom, and this resemblance was not lost on Richard Simon, who accused Le Clerc, not completely without reason, of having derived his views from Grotius's *Votum pro Pace Ecclesiastica.*

7. *Summary on the intention, influence, and history of interpretation*

On the basis of the evidence produced above, I propose the following interpretation of the outlines of developments in biblical scholarship in the second part of the seventeenth century.

The scholars: These were the people who worked at learning languages and compiling dictionaries and grammars or who compared manuscripts and edited editions of the biblical text. Obviously, no one is completely objective, but it is in this sort of work at its best that there is the highest proportion of rationality in the decisions made. Of these men in this period, Walton, Mill, Vossius, Fell, and others, the most distinguished was Richard Simon, who is best seen as a pure research scholar. It is true that to the modern reader Simon gives an impression of someone almost modern in his convictions, but Simon himself only claimed that he was continuing to practice *critica sacra* as part of a long tradition.

The reason why Simon appears more modern lies in an accidental convergence of two different impulses. Both Simon and modern commentators are reluctant to stray from how the text was transmitted and its exact philological meaning to wider questions of theology and philosophy. However, the reasons for this common approach are different. Modern critics, for the most part, are not tempted to find the site of the Garden of Eden, defend the historicity of the Flood story, or explain the unexpected emergence of a wife for Cain, because for them the Bible has been dethroned as a source of general knowledge about the origins of the world. Simon ignored these issues, because he was of the opinion, rightly or wrongly, that attention to the text alone would answer all the problems of the sort raised by critics in antiquity or La Peyrère and Spinoza in his own day.[98] Simon defended himself vigorously against the charge of being an innovator introducing *Paradoxe dans sa Critique*, "new things into his criticism," by appealing quite rightly to predecessors such as Masius and Pererius.[99]

---

[98] See the course of his argument in *Apologie pour l'auteur de l'histoire critique du vieux testament* (Rotterdam: Leers, 1689) 79–84.

[99] *Apologie,* 77. The word paradoxe in this context meant "against the usual teaching."

Simon's strength was his immense erudition in matters of text and translation, not only about the matter of biblical readings and manuscripts but also about the secondary literature in the field. He had a gift for summing up authors clearly and at the same time a generosity of spirit that could show itself even in his treatment of those with whom he disagreed. But Simon was no radical and not even an innovator, and when it came to the wider questions that were being raised in his day, he showed little interest. That his views were seen as radical is only one more example of the public's failure to understand the niceties of biblical studies.[100]

Radical thinkers: By this term I mean those whose commitment to new philosophy or to inherent skepticism[101] led them to reject not only the credibility of the Bible but also of religious affiliations—Roman Catholic, Protestant, or Jewish—that appealed to the Bible. Here I include not only the better-known figures, such as Meyer and Spinoza, but also the *libertins érudits,* such as Vanini, from the first part of the seventeenth century, as well as later writers discussed thoroughly by Jonathan Israel.

From the point of view of the history of biblical studies, one has to treat the issues of the radicals' originality and their influence. The originality of the radicals did not lie in noticing problems that had been overlooked before; a look at the great commentaries of the church fathers, the rabbis, and the Renaissance commentators shows that very little escaped the critical faculties of these men. What the radicals did was to put the problems in a new context, where solutions were to be found in rejecting the authority of the Bible and seeing it as a book second rate at best, or definitely immoral at its worst. While the influence of these persons is open to debate, there is no doubt that they contributed to the dethronement of the Bible during the eighteenth century. They did not, however, contribute a great deal to the understanding of the nature and origins of the Bible itself.

The innovators: Le Clerc, along with Burnet, has to be given credit for tackling the obstacle of biblical inerrancy, not from a position of denying the authority or even the value of the Bible, as Spinoza did, but with the

---

[100] I think Rappaport misses the point in lumping Simon and Spinoza together, and she is plain wrong in saying "Few European scholars . . . commanded the knowledge of ancient languages displayed by both writers." *When Geologists Were Historians,* 75.

[101] It is important to distinguish between those who reject religious beliefs on the basis of an inverted "blind faith" and those who do so from a carefully thought-out position.

intention of trying to interpret the Bible rationally in the face of what reasonable people could see as insurmountable problems within the Bible as long as it was seen as infallible. In the *Five Letters Concerning the Inspiration of the Holy Scriptures,* Le Clerc argued consistently and ably that support for his position could be found in many of the church fathers, as well as in the writings of Erasmus and Grotius. While Le Clerc might have been taking these eminent authorities a little further than they themselves might have found comfortable, it is clear that he was trying to interpret the Bible from what is in it rather than from a preconceived schema that is not itself biblical. The immediate tradition in which he stood came from the great Arminian scholars Simon Episcopius and Hugo Grotius, but in all fairness it should be admitted that the Socinians had also started on this way, as is evident from Christoph Sandius's *Tractatus de Veteribus Scriptoribus Ecclesiasticis,* which is notable for discussing the canon of the early church from the point of view of history rather than dogmatic theology.[102]

If one has a stronger taste for irony than detail, one might sum up the results of the history of biblical interpretation in the latter part of the seventeenth century as follows. Simon, who argued justifiably that he was anything but an innovator or an attacker of the Bible, was looked upon as both by the officialdom of his own church, whose authority in matters of biblical interpretation he had hoped to preserve. Conservative Protestants continued to defend a doctrine of the inspiration of the Bible that was not really claimed within the Bible itself. More liberal-minded Protestants, in their efforts to show that what was factually or morally wrong in the Bible was not vital to its authority, were decried as virtual atheists. More radical critics of the Bible, such as Spinoza, based their criticism on a philosophy of reason which was nominally clear and undisputed to any right-thinking person but which was itself in the long run not demonstrable by reasoned proofs in a universally convincing way. Omar Kháyyám and the author of Ecclesiastes would both have been delighted at the spectacle.

---

[102] Christophorus Sandius, *Nucleus Historiae Ecclesiasticae exhibitus in historia arianorum . . . quibus praefixus est Tractatus de veteribus scriptoribus ecclesiasticis,* 2nd rev. ed. (Cologne: Johannus Nicolai, 1676) 1–12.

Chapter 5

1700–1750

It was in the eighteenth century that the balance tipped away from the conservative norms of interpretation, whether among Protestants or Roman Catholics. The argument of the next two chapters, then, will be that in the eighteenth century the basis for the modern approach to the Bible was worked out, especially in Germany but also to a lesser extent in England. There were two important factors that made this process both necessary and possible.

First, as has been discussed in previous chapters, the logic of mainstream biblical exegesis was that it was less and less possible to present the Bible as a book that had somehow fallen down direct from heaven. Rather, it had to be understood as a book whose origins took place within human history and which was subject to the vicissitudes that history visits upon the composition and transmission of all documents. How far you wished to carry this observation varied, but it was not only those who attacked the Bible who were aware of these matters; on the contrary, it is a contention of this book that most of the observations of problems with the Bible came from professional scholars who had—usually—some sense of loyalty to their churches.

Second, the question of the Bible was influenced by political changes, in particular a nominal secularization of the state. Allowing for almost unpardonable oversimplification, the matter can be described this way. The heritage of Christendom in Europe was the idea of a Christian society under divine guidance whose instruments were ecclesiastical—the national church of a country—and whose secular administration was in the hands of a sacral monarchy chosen by the will of God. It was allegiance to the sacred dynasty that often defined what a state was. Different languages and cultures were administrative problems, but not of theoretical importance; hence the curious nature of the empire the Hapsburgs built up. An example of how seriously some people took this matter was the decision of the Nonjuring Church of England bishops and clergy who refused the oath of obedience to William of Orange and Mary after the glorious revolution of 1688, on the grounds that James II, having been chosen by God, could not legitimately be deposed. In this system the Bible was the central foundational document, any criticism of which could be seen as a crime against the state. Thus it was considered normal that interpreters of the Bible who pushed their observations to unacceptable lengths might well find themselves in jail for criminal behavior.

The emerging new political order was a putting aside of this older conception of a theocratically constituted order in favor of a new source of legitimacy, namely, the will of the people, however defined, and the foundational documents—usually "axiomatic" ideas embodied in national constitutions—are often expressed in terms of self-evident rights of humanity. Political changes are seldom complete and consistent; thus the revolting American colonists preserved the British eighteenth-century monarch in the figure of their president, except that the president is elected every four years by the people's votes, nominally counted in a fair and nonpartisan manner. Where monarchies still survive in the modern world, they do so as a desirable appurtenance rather than as the essence of the state and are subject to removal if their appeal to tourism falls off.

Once again, the reader is warned that the foregoing is a simplification of an almost unpardonable sort, except that it is important to realize that the change in the political view of what was sacred also played a role in creating a situation where biblical scholars could work freely. As state interest waned in the matter of making sure the Bible was treated in a proper way, scholars were freer to express new views. The question they then faced from the mid-eighteenth-century on was, If the Bible is to be treated as any other document in how it is interpreted, is there anything in that exposition that suggests it is authoritative for shaping Christian religious belief, and if so, how is this to be expressed? Increasingly as the eighteenth century went on, there were scholars who tried to produce a synthesis between the new modernity of thought and social structure that was gradually eroding the "fallen down from heaven" respect given to the Bible and new methods of understanding the Bible, which, while accepting its human origins, nonetheless tried to maintain its enduring religious significance. In the next chapter the origins of biblical theology will be discussed, and in the final chapter of this work we will come to Martin Kähler, who, in the opinion of this author, provided a useful triangulation point to steer by in any search of the religious importance of the New Testament.

I. External Factors

1. *The general background*

One aspect of a great deal of eighteenth-century thought was the conviction that the human condition should be improved intellectually, morally, and physically. The taste for improvement of any sort was not a new human experience, but what was novel in modern times was the feeling that improvement should be continuous and cumulative, and that it should cover many aspects of society, such as individual behavior, social norms, and technological advance. Progress was to include advances in the knowledge of truth, in technology, in the shape of society, and in personal moral responsibility. In what was to come to be known as science, the achievements of the seventeenth century were pursued by an increasing number of enthusiasts, and by the end of the century, lectures in science had begun at Göttingen from where they spread to Berlin.[1] New attempts in philosophy were made to think through the problems raised in the previous century, and there was a gradual shift in the balance between rediscovering what the ancients knew and discovering or creating what they did not know. The importance of this for theology was that here, too, people expected knowledge to increase as theology incorporated into itself the new knowledge coming from other fields, and by the end of the century there was a widespread though not universal conviction that theology had indeed widened its horizons in many ways.

In order for the study of the Bible to work out new approaches, it was first necessary to accept that the Bible's centrality and its infallibility were compromised by the new ideas and discoveries that were being made. As we have seen, Renaissance scholars were quite aware of many

---

[1] One of the more bizarre examples of this sort of interest in scientific discovery was the fashionable lady who kept a corpse in her coach so that she might perform dissections as she rode.

problems of biblical exegesis, but while they faced up to these problems in detail, at least to the extent of recognizing them as difficulties, for the most part they were willing to see these as interesting puzzles, but not as the raw material for new overall frames of interpretation.

In contrast to this earlier attitude, Spinoza was the most impressive among those who offered new assumptions about the Bible, for he had treated the Bible as an ancient document to be discussed in the same way as other ancient documents and judged by the same standards. What made his argument unacceptable to many was his conclusion that the Bible was a second-rate guide to truth compared with philosophy. Still, while he did not win immediate acceptance, he was nonetheless read; even a fairly conservative Dutch Reformed scholar like Campegius Vitringa was aware of Spinoza peering over his shoulder as he wrote his monumental commentary on Isaiah.[2] It was not long before other radicals were espousing negative interpretations of the nature of the Bible. The question was whether this issue was to be left in abeyance or whether on its side theology might not recast its assumptions to take into account both the value of the Bible and the new perceptions that were pouring in.

2. *A shift in balance—Germany and its universities*

In the eighteenth century the center of gravity in biblical research and theology shifted gradually from other parts of Europe to Germany. Whereas German theologians and scholars were the butt of jokes at the end of the seventeenth century, from 1750 on Germany was the most interesting and exciting country in Europe for intellectual discourse. In this the universities played a central role.

In the seventeenth century, German universities had suffered from the devastations of the Thirty Years' War. There had been good German scholars during those times, but many had had to move elsewhere to survive, never mind continue their careers. Georg Pasor, Daniel Heinsius, and Johannes Coccejus are all examples of Germans who succeeded in Holland. The state of German universities in the period of the war was lamentable, especially for students, who were often forced by economic necessity to enlist in army service, from which they returned crippled

---

[2] *Commentarius in Librum Prophetiarum Jesaiae* (Herborn: Johann Nicolai Andreae, vol. 1, 1715; vol. 2, 1722).

and broken, if they returned at all. However, by the end of the seventeenth century the area[3] had recovered, and in 1694 Prussia founded Halle, which has been called the first modern university.[4] The leading personalities were Christian Thomasius, a "radical" philosopher, and August Hermann Francke, a leading Pietist and friend of Philipp Jakob Spener. These two men, different as they might have been in other respects, had one thing in common, namely, a dislike of Lutheran orthodoxy. Halle soon became the leading university of Germany; its example and success provoked improvements in German Protestant universities elsewhere. It was at Halle that many of the outstanding scholars of the day either taught or studied,[5] and it was not until the founding of the University of Göttingen that Halle found itself overshadowed.

The intellectual ferment of eighteenth-century Protestant German universities was extraordinary. Even the encyclopedist Jean le Rond d'Alembert, not a great friend of theology, was impressed. One way of measuring the seriousness with which theology was studied in Germany is to compare the advice given to students there with what was said in England. At Oxford Edward Bentham published for theological students a short guide of about fifty pages, consisting of advice and including a couple of pages of bibliography.[6] His recommendation was that "the books here proposed are plain and easy: and that indeed was the reason which determined the Tutor to the choice of them."[7] Bentham admitted that writing more than one or two discourses a week was "a tax of labor too great for men of common industry and common genius to pay," but some writing was nonetheless required.[8] In other words, to expect English gentlemen at Oxford (or Cambridge) to work too hard was just not done. In a similar vein, John Randolph's *Enchiridion theologicum*

[3] Germany as a unified state did not exist until 1870, so the use of the word in connection with earlier periods should be taken as a geographical/cultural expression, not the name of a specific regime.

[4] See Friedrich Paulsen, *Geschichte des Gelehrten Unterrichts* (rprt.; Berlin: de Gruyter, 1965) 1:534ff. Further, see Rudolph Mau, "Programme und Praxis des Theologiestudiums im 17. und 18. Jahrhundert," in *Theologische Versuche* 11 (Berlin: Evangelische Verlagsanstalt, 1979) 71–91.

[5] Christian Wolff, Johannes Buddeus, Johann Edelmann, Siegmund Baumgarten, Johann Semler, Johann David Michaelis, to name only the most outstanding for the subject of this book.

[6] *Reflexions upon the Study of Divinity* (Oxford: Clarendon, 1771).

[7] Ibid., viii.

[8] Ibid., xxxi.

or a Manual for the use of Students in Divinity [9] was a convenient collection of a few works that might be useful, none of which was exceptionally challenging.

The contrast with what teachers in Germany required is striking. Johannes Franciscus Buddeus put out an annotated bibliography for the use of those who wished to study theology.[10] It has about two thousand pages, and while it can be lifted with one hand, two are recommended. At the end there is an additional list of other important works published in the interval between the completion and the printing. While it is unlikely that Buddeus meant this as a reading list for his students, there must have been some demand for such a work, for Michael Lilienthal, Christoph Matthaeus Pfaff, and Johann Georg Walch published similar works about the same time.[11] A work especially for students was Valentin Ernst Loescher's[12] *Breviarium theologicae exegeticae* of 1715, which certainly had high expectations of what the students should cover, and later in the century Johann August Noesselt published a work of several hundred pages intended as a guide to students' reading; that it went through several editions shows the importance given to it.[13] Presupposed by these publications was an enthusiasm for scholarship both from the past and what might be going on in the present, for Noesselt's later editions took account of recent important works.

The great historian of German higher education Friedrich Paulsen ended his discussion of the eighteenth-century German Protestant university with a fine rhetorical flourish, pointing out the eighteenth-century disparity in size between the endowments of Oxford and those of Halle and the equal disparity in the other direction of the achievements of the two institutions. A certain chauvinistic glee can be detected in this statement, but at the same time even this member of Oxford has to admit that he does have a point. The best that can be said in rejoinder is that in his autobiography Johann David Michaelis credited his time at

[9] (Oxford: J. Fletcher, 1792).

[10] *Isagoge historico-theologica ad theologiam universam singulasque eius partes*, 2 vols. (Leipzig: Fritsch, 1727).

[11] See Edgar M. Krentz, *Essays on Theological Librarianship* (Philadelphia: American Theological Library Association, 1980) 47–66, for a treatment of similar works by Lilienthal, Pfaff, and a little later Walch.

[12] *Breviarium theologicae exegeticae, regulas de legitima scripturae sacrae interpretatione* (Frankfort: Gaarmann, 1715).

[13] *Anweisungen zur Kenntniss der besten allgemeinern Bücher in aller Theilen der Theologie*, 1st ed. (Leipzig: Weygand, 1779).

Oxford as crucial for his escape from the narrow Pietism of his student days at that excellent university at Halle.[14]

3. *Universities elsewhere in Europe*

Reasons for the comparative lack of intellectual ferment in the English universities are open to discussion, but two possible factors were, first, the lack of competition when there were only two universities in all of England, and second, the requirement that fellows of Oxford and Cambridge colleges were not allowed to marry, so many preferred to move on to non-university positions.[15]

In France the Protestant college at Saumur, which had produced such excellent scholarship, was forced to close in the seventeenth century, and the Roman Catholic universities in France, as indeed elsewhere in Europe, had much of their originality despoiled in part by the oppressive censorship but also by an attitude represented by De Malesherbes's opinion of theology: "L'erreur, come j'ai déjà dit, est un crime. D'ailleurs, ce n'est point une science susceptible de progrès. L'unité, la simplicité, la constance, sont ses principaux attributs. Toute opinion nouvelle est au moins dangereuse et toujours inutile."[16] ("Error [i.e., in theology], as I have already said, is a crime. Besides it [theology] is not a science capable of progress. Unity, simplicity, and its unchangeable nature are its principle characteristics. Every new opinion is at least dangerous and always useless.")[17]

In Holland the university tradition continued with excellent scholars such as Compegius Vitringa and Albert Schultens, so that the highest praise that could be heaped on Johann August Ernesti was that at last Germany had a philologist who was equal to the Dutch; nonetheless, some of the excitement of the Golden Age of Dutch culture had abated.

---

[14] Johann David Michaelis, *Lebensbeschreibung von ihm selbst abgefasst* (Rinteln and Leipzig: 1793) 30ff.

[15] The advantage of this system was that since many fellows died without leaving close family, they often left their books to the college library.

[16] *Mémoires sur la librairie et sur la liberté de la presse* (Paris: 1809; rept. Slatkine, 1969). Translation mine. This work was a report written about 1759 and reprinted after the author's death in 1794. It was about the principles of censorship, but it shows how establishment figures saw theology in contrast to other subjects. De Malesherbes later showed great courage in undertaking the defense of Louis XVI at his trial, an action that led him also to the guillotine.

[17] See Marie-Helène Cotoni, *L'Exegèse du Nouveau Testament dans la philosophie française du dix-huitième siècle* (Oxford: The Voltaire Foundation, 1984).

4. *Learned periodicals*

Learned periodicals had emerged in the latter part of the seventeenth century, but in Germany there were a relatively large number of specialized journals. For the first third of the century the most significant was Valentin Loescher's *Unschuldige Nachrichten von Alten und Neuen Theologischen Sachen*.[18] The title of Loescher's journal can be translated as "accurate, unbiased news about . . .," and indeed, while Loescher was a staunch advocate of old-fashioned Lutheran orthodoxy, that is, Orthodoxy in contrast to Pietism, he tried to give a fair summary of what authors had to say before letting his own opinions show.[19]

Another useful series was *Acta Ecclesiastica Nostri temporis*, which was a useful indicator of particular German concerns in the amount of space it devoted to various matters; for example, it had far more to say on the Herrnhuter community than on radical criticisms of the Bible, a notable difference from England, where nonconformist groups were accepted, not always cheerfully, as part of national life.[20] This did not mean that more generalized periodicals ceased to take an interest in theology; the *Acta Eruditorum* had sections on theology up to the end and in the second half of the century. Friedrich Nicolai's *Allgemeine Deutsche Bibliothek* was invaluable for its reviews of important theological works in the latter half of the century.

The importance of the journals was that even those who did not have access to good libraries could nonetheless keep abreast of what was going on in theological discussion. Some journals, such as Loescher's above or Siegmund Jacob Baumgarten's two periodicals,[21] also discussed older works to fill in their readers' knowledge of the history of the discipline, a practice seldom met in present-day publications. Johann Christian Edelmann, discussed below (pp. 212–16), was thus able to keep up with developments even when he was tutor to a family in a relatively remote area.

[18] The first issue came out as *Altes und Neues aus dem Schatz Theologischer Wissenschaften* in 1701. From 1721 to 1731 the journal was not under Loescher's editorship.

[19] It would be interesting to have a study of the history of the word "unpartheyisch" at this time, for its sense is not far from "unschuldige" in denoting a desirable virtue. Compare the title of Gottfried Arnold's *Unpartheyischen Kirchen-und Ketzer historie* (1699–1700).

[20] The basic work on German periodical literature is Joachim Kirchner, *Die Grundlagen des Deutschen Zeitschriftenswesens*, 2 vols. (Leipzig: Karl W. Hiersmann, 1928) 2:31.

[21] *Nachrichten von einer Hallischen Bibliothek* (1748–1751) and *Nachrichten von Merkwürdigen Bücher* (1752–1758).

5. *The Deists' criticism of the Bible*

"Deism" was a contemporary term used to describe the position of somewhat more radical English thinkers before and after the turn of the eighteenth century.[22] These men had a creative effect on the reinterpretation of the Bible that later took place in Germany, for works both by and against them were translated into German and disseminated their views. To understand the extent of their importance, one has to separate in theory two matters that in practice are inextricably intertwined, namely, exegetical observation and the framework in which it is interpreted. The first approach can be called "objective" (with all the qualifications this word should have) and the second "evaluative."

  i. "Objective" problems are problems about the origins and exact, original meaning of the Bible. In this category would fall the philology of the different languages involved, the transmission and subsequent correction of the text, and the processes through which the biblical material passed on its way to its present form. Here would also be the question of the relationship of various books in the Bible to their historical context, including chronology, history, religious and political institutions, and any other subject one might include under the "background." In theory this is a type of discussion into which religious and philosophical preferences do not intrude.

 ii. "Evaluative" problems are questions such as how the Bible is to be seen as authoritative in the way we live our lives in the world as we find it today: In what sense does the Bible provide guidance in matters of belief and practice? Is the Bible to be seen as a whole, or may one ignore parts of it like old lumber to be taken away? What is the relation of the Bible to science?[23] What sort of truth might the Bible lay claim to? What sort of ethical judgments does it still provide?[24]

[22] The best work on the Deists is Henning Graf Reventlow, *The Authority of the Bible and the Rise of the Modern World,* trans. John Bowden (Philadelphia: Fortress, 1985).

[23] This word hides a number of problems on its own. How science is done and how it has made changes throughout its history are matters of considerable debate. Science has long since ceased to be a matter of "common sense" or even common understanding. The lack of comprehension that exists among scientists, even those nominally in the same discipline, raises question of how one can talk about the unity of science.

[24] The modern period is not the first time the Christian church has had to face a pluralistic world, for the church fathers found themselves in a sophisticated world in

To some extent, it was the better understanding of the Bible that contributed to its loss of position as an infallible book, because some of the critical work, such as the arguments for the only too human origins of the Bible's parts, could easily be used as arguments against the claims of the suprahuman inspiration of the Bible as a whole; in other words, the "objective" study fed into the "evaluative" process. The more important factor in the decline of the authority of the Bible was the emergence of another source of authority, namely, reason. As we have seen, basic to Spinoza's discussion of the Bible was that reason—his to be sure—provides an absolutely firm and secure source of guidance that both replaces the Bible and provides the means of evaluating it. What exactly reason is or is not and its relation to science, still less its own validity, are far beyond the scope of this book and its author.[25] However, for many thinkers in the age of Enlightenment, the advocacy of reason as a guide superior to the Bible did not necessarily imply atheism or even moral laxity.[26]

It is important, then, to be aware of the difference between biblical criticism and biblical authority in discussing the history of biblical interpretation. Reventlow's *The Authority of the Bible* is thus properly named, for his interest is basically in the vicissitudes of the authority of the Bible, whereas an example of a misunderstanding of Reventlow's book is found in its preface by another author, who from the outset of his remarks talks about the origins of biblical criticism. Reventlow's argument

---

which the Bible appeared very unsophisticated indeed, and the creative achievement of the fathers was the reinterpretation of the Bible in this new cultural context. Their success is ironically one of the problems of a church that is always tempted to defend the fathers' solutions rather than follow their examples.

[25] John Toland (1670–1722) pointed out that "we find by Experience, that the word *Reason* is become as equivocal and ambiguous as any other," but he immediately affirms "though all that are not tickl'd with the Vanity of Singularity, or Itch of Dispute, are at bottom agreed about the Thing." *Christianity not Mysterious or a Treatise Shewing that there is nothing in the Gospel Contrary Reason, Nor Above it: and that no Christian Doctrine can be properly call'd a Mystery* (London: Sam. Buckley, 1696) 8.

[26] It is true that some of the *libertins* discussed in *Les Libertins Erudits* were *libertin* in more than one sense of the word. However, Anthony Collins showed a certain annoyed sensitivity about this being said about himself and others. He had a quotation on the title page of *A Discourse of Free-Thinking*: "Fain would they confound Licentiousness in Morals with Liberty in Thought, and make the Libertine resemble his direct Opposite" and he takes great pains to show that free thinkers have been "the most understanding and virtuous people in all ages." *Discourse*, Section 3: 6th Objection.

for the importance of the Deists[27] only makes sense if it is the authority of the Bible that is the focus of the work, not the history of criticism. The Deists contributed very little to biblical criticism as such, although they appealed to some of its practitioners, but they did a great deal to contribute to the discussion of the place of the Bible critically understood vis-à-vis the claims of reason.

John Toland's *Christianity not Mysterious* was a treatise aimed at proving that reason and revelation are complementary, with the proviso that reason is what confirms revelation, not vice versa.

> For as 'tis by reason we arrive at the Certainty of God's own existence, so we cannot otherwise discern his *Revelations* but by their Conformity with our natural Notices of him, which is in so many words, to agree with our common Notions.[28]

Toland buttressed his argument that the gospel is meant to be clear rather than mysterious with the observation that its style "is also most easy, most natural, and in the common Dialect of those to whom it was immediately consign'd."[29] Lurking behind this argument was the controversy about the nature of New Testament Greek that was fought out in Holland in the first part of the seventeenth century, but this was scarcely an original observation on Toland's part.[30] Toland argued that whereas Jesus taught that the purest morals, reasonable worship, and a "just Conception of Heaven and Heavenly things" stripped the truth of all the "Types and Ceremonies which made it difficult before," it was the human taste for abuses and the desire of the emperors and priests for power that led to the complexities of mysterious Christianity.[31]

While Toland tended to be very gentle with the Bible, such was not the case in the work of Matthew Tindal, *Christianity as Old as the Creation*, and Thomas Morgan, *The Moral Philosopher*. Tindal was scornful of the attempts of the church fathers to allegorize away the more shocking parts of the Old Testament, such as:

[27] One has to be careful in assigning labels to authors. "Deism" was indeed a word used in seventeenth- and eighteenth-century England, but not all authors who are classed as Deists in modern discussion would have claimed this designation for themselves.

[28] Toland, *Christianity not Mysterious*, 31.

[29] Ibid., 50. He contrasted this with the folly of trying to speak in proper English to the country people in Scotland.

[30] See the discussion of this matter in chapter 5 above (pp. 95–97).

[31] Toland, *Christianity not Mysterious*, 151–74.

> And how can we depend on any Thing said in the Scripture, if we can't on its Facts? One wou'd think nothing was a plainer Fact, than that of *Lot's* lying with his two Daughters, yet St. Irenaeus allegorises That away. . . .[32]

Morgan was, if anything, more scathing about the Old Testament. On the conquest of Canaan by the Israelites, Morgan commented:

> But to put women and children to the sword, without any provocation, who had never injured them, and who were quietly and peaceably enjoying their own, in order to enter upon their possessions and properties, and to plead a divine commission and authority from God for all this seems to be the highest complication of outrage, bloody cruelty, superstition and profanation of the holy name and awful authority of God that human Nature is capable of.[33]

What is interesting about the Deists is that on the whole they were not arguing against religion as such—and by religion they meant Christianity, albeit a less doctrinal, moralistic Christianity of their own making. Their criticism of the Bible sprang from an earnest concern about faith and morals, not from lighthearted contempt.

6. *German philosophical developments*

Another intellectual current that was to influence the development of biblical studies among other disciplines was the extraordinary flowering of philosophy in Germany from Leibnitz on. In the universities philosophy was more or less a handmaid of theology, and the close links between philosophers and theologians in Germany meant that the latter could not fail to be influenced by developments in philosophy. It is sometimes argued that it was philosophy that drove theology in the eighteenth century. While this may be an overstatement, links between theology and some types of philosophy were often close. (Yet there were notable exceptions, such as Johann Ernesti.[34])

[32] Matthew Tindal, *Christianity as old as the Creation: or, The gospel, a Republication of the Religion of Nature* (London: n.p., 1730) 226.

[33] Thomas Morgan, *The Moral Philosopher in a Dialogue between Philalethes a Christian deist, and Theophanes a Christian Jew* (London: n.p., 1739) 2.

[34] Ernesti wrote a monograph on the vanity of philosophizing in the interpretation of the Bible and championed solid, philologically based exegesis as the way to understand it. "De Vanitate Philosophantium in interpretatione Librorum sacrorum" reprinted in *Opuscula Philologica et Critica* (Leiden: 1764) 233–51.

The philosophy commonly espoused by theologians at the beginning of the century can be called eclectic, a mixture of Aristotelian and other influences seen, for example, in Buddeus. New directions were taken by Christian Thomasius and Christian Crusius, but one philosopher in particular, Christian Wolff (1679–1754), had an influence that was to affect theology and biblical interpretation. Wolff was a philosopher influenced by Leibnitz, but also by Locke and Descartes. Wolff saw mathematics as the model for philosophical inquiry, that is, knowledge should be set out as a logical whole, in which subordinate parts were derived logically from preceding truths. On this basis Wolff managed to discuss a wide range of subjects, including religion, in a way that brought all knowledge together. This taste for orderly systematization was one of his gifts to German philosophy. He also wrote much of his work in German, and by so doing he created a German vocabulary for philosophical discussion. His thought was even popularized in a novel, Jean Henri Formey's *La Belle Wolffienne* (6 vols., 1751–1756), which introduced Wolff's philosophy into France.

Wolff argued that the basic doctrines of Christianity, God, revelation, and even miracles could be shown by this method. Some theologians, especially Baumgarten, were influenced by the "mathematical method," whereas others objected to it strongly on the grounds that it seemed to imply determinism and was too close to pure rationalism. Wolff was much more moderate than many of the English Deists, for he even allowed the possibility of miracles. However, the effect of his providing a basis for belief apart from the Bible was to make the Bible subject to philosophy, and thereby he contributed to removing the Bible from its privileged position. Another weakness introduced by the nature of Wolff's arguments was that a strictly logical, deductive system has little place for the importance of history, and it was this weakness that apparently led to Baumgarten's disenchantment with Wolff's thought.[35]

7. The beginnings of German theological Enlightenment

On the whole, the opinions of English philosophers/scientists were less threatening to traditional beliefs than the positions of more radical thinkers elsewhere. John Locke tried his hand at biblical commentaries,

---

[35] This is the argument of Martin Schloemann, *Siegmund Jacob Baumgarten: System und Geschichte in der Theologie des Überganges zum Neuprotestantismus* (Göttingen: Vandenhoeck und Ruprecht, 1974). Schloemann's work is an excellent piece of scholarship and should be read by anyone interested in early eighteenth-century thought.

Robert Boyle endowed a lectureship to discuss religious matters, and The Royal Society was generally positive in its attitude to rational theology. In his *History of the Royal Society*, Thomas Sprat included a section on the relation of the new knowledge to the Christian faith:

> I will now proceed to the weightiest, and most solemn part of my whole *undertaking;* to make a defence of the *Royal Society,* and this new *Experimental Learning,* in respect of the Christian Faith.[36]

The fact that a moderate person such as John Tillotson could become archbishop of Canterbury showed that learning, new ideas, and episcopacy were not incompatible alternatives in those days.

The tone set in England carried over into Germany, where the first signs of latitudinarian Lutheranism emerged a little later. Two of the earlier figures were Christoph Matthaeus Pfaff and Johannes Franciscus Buddeus, who inched carefully toward a less traditional attitude to the Bible, although Buddeus in particular was very critical of Wolff's philosophy.[37] Pfaff was able to travel widely and had met many of the more influential theologians of the day. He was well aware of the problems met by those who read the Bible:

> The Bible is in no way clear by itself. The clarity ["perspicuitas"] claimed by older writers is very problematic. There are so many historical, genealogical, geographical, and chronological difficulties in it, so many questions that raise doubts that even Alexander's sword would not be able to solve, indeed they will remain to some extent unresolved until the end of the world.[38]

Pfaff made a few tentative stabs at reinterpreting problems in the Bible, such as attributing Jonah's rescue to a ship called "Whale," and the darkness at Jesus' crucifixion not to an eclipse but to a cloud. The sun standing still in Joshua was not really a cessation of the earth's rotation but an extension of the light available.[39] Stolzenburg argued that Pfaff

[36] Thomas Sprat, *The History of the Royal-Society of London* (London: J. Martin, 1667) 345.

[37] The best work on this subject is A. F. Stolzenburg, *Die Theologie des Jo. Franc. Buddeus und des Chr. Matt. Pfaff* (Berlin: Trowitzsche und Sohn, 1927). Stolzenburg does not give a bibliography of his subjects' works, and his use of abbreviated titles in his footnotes is a trial to the patience.

[38] Nöth, *Unterr.*, 241, as quoted in Stolzenburg, *Die Theologie*, 91.

[39] Stolzenburg, *Die Theologie*, 109. Stolzenburg does not appear to have noticed the reliance on La Peyrère (or perhaps even Spinoza) for the last suggestion.

and Buddeus had a good claim to a crucial role in the changes that eventually took place in German theology, and it is possible that their importance in this matter is a question that should be revisited.[40]

Siegmund Jacob Baumgarten (1706–1757) was one of the most influential theologians of the first part of the eighteenth century in Germany. He was a professor at Halle but escaped its Pietist leanings under the influence of Christian Wolff's philosophy. His influence was felt not only for what he produced in scholarship but also for the large number of brilliant students he produced who were to take part in the recasting of all parts of theology in the latter part of the century, men such as Johann Semler, Johann Michaelis, Johann Töllner, Gotthelf Zachariae, and Johann Noesselt. He also influenced Johann Joachim Winckelmann, the aesthete who did not complete his studies at Halle, and Johann Joachim Spalding, one of the great Enlightenment preachers, who was not at Halle as a student but who was often a guest of Baumgarten's during an extended visit he made there in 1745. Baumgarten was able to inspire his students with a love of learning and yet left them free to follow their own natural impulses, shown by the fact that Gotthold Lessing's most insistent and orthodox opponent, Johann Melchior Goeze, was also a Baumgarten student. Semler, who loyally edited many of Baumgarten's writings after Baumgarten's death, left a vivid and sympathetic portrait of his teacher in his memoirs, showing the affection and admiration he inspired in his students.[41]

Baumgarten was instrumental in helping to make foreign theology known in Germany, especially the debates about the Bible that had been taking place in England. In his two periodicals, *Nachrichten von einer Hallischen Bibliothek* (1748–1751) and *Nachrichten von merkwürdigen Bücher* (1752–1758), he discussed many works he considered worthy of notice and made foreign thought known to the provincial world of German theology of his day. It must be admitted that he did not always catch the nuances of British humor. In his *merkwürdigen Bücher* [42] he discussed an older English publication entitled *The Difficulties and Discouragements which Attend the Study of the Scriptures in the Way of Private Judgement; Represented in a Letter to a Young Clergyman*, which he denounced as the greatest danger to true belief. In fact, this was a satiric piece written by

---

[40] It must also be admitted that Pfaff was not without his weaknesses. Adolf Harnack showed that Pfaff forged a reputed Irenaeus fragment, a fact inexplicably mentioned more often in English than German treatments of the period.

[41] Johann Semler, *Lebensbeschreibung von ihm selbst abgefasst* (Halle: 1781, 1782).

[42] Vol. 8 (1755) 138–41.

Francis Hare, a bishop of the Church of England, as a means of showing the limits of scholarship.

Martin Schloemann argued that it is possible to see a change in Baumgarten's interests in mid-career.[43] If his theory is correct, it would mean that Baumgarten personally illustrated the great shift in biblical exegesis of the eighteenth century, namely, the change from a reliance on proofs derived with geometric precision from previous postulates to the examination of history to solve many of the hitherto unexplained irregularities and problems in the interpretation of the Bible.

Baumgarten's actual works on the Bible did not break new ground in themselves, and in fact his theological opinions did not differ from those of many orthodox theologians of his day. However, hidden at the heart of his theology was a change in direction that was to become better known in the next generation. Rather than beginning with the Bible as a given that stood as one of the foundation stones of religion and society, he argued that the inspiration of the Bible was something to be proved. In his *Evangelische Glaubenslehre*, Baumgarten attempted this feat in a long argument in which every section branched into two subsections, which in turn may have had two more subsections. The cogency (or lack of) of Baumgarten's arguments is not as important as the fact that it set an example: issues such as in what sense is the Bible the word of God, or what might be the difference between inspiration and revelation and how all this might relate to the generally accepted results of reason were now a goal of inquiry, not its starting point.

Furthermore, the emphasis Baumgarten put on the importance of history fitted in with a growing interest in the subject among educated people generally, if one is to judge by the number of historical periodicals. *Critica sacra* was expanding to become the historico-critical approach.

On the whole, in the eighteenth century German philosophy was more conservative in its attitude toward religion than some philosophy elsewhere. Immanuel Kant, for all his critique of most of the traditional proofs of God's existence, could still find a place for deity somewhere in the sphere of morality, though it must be admitted that Kant himself, when he acted as rector of the university, would lead the academic pro-

---

[43] Schloemann, *Siegmund Jacob Baumgarten*, 96–170. Schloemann presents a good case that Baumgarten gradually lost interest in Wolff's system and instead became interested in history. Schloemann's work is very well done and belongs to that class of book one wishes one could have written oneself.

cession up to the formal church service but would then duck out at the church door. It was only after Kant that the atheism debate broke out.[44] This did not mean that the German intelligentsia were ignorant of materialist French thinkers, such as the Baron Paul Henri Thiry d'Holbach or Julien de La Mettrie, not to mention scathing critics of established religion, such as Voltaire, who was welcomed for a while at the court of Frederick the Great. The Germans were simply not impressed, and they worked out their own approach to the Enlightenment.

It also helped that the fragmentation of Germany produced a certain amount of intellectual freedom, almost as an accident of history. It is true that censorship and official disapproval did exist in Germany in a way that would be unacceptable today.[45] Nevertheless, regime change might produce an improvement, for under Frederick the Great, Wolff returned to Halle in triumph, after having been exiled for his views. Actual toleration emerged at the University of Göttingen, which was the first to establish academic freedom as a policy.

8. *History and human culture*

The philosophy of history is as fascinating as the history of philosophy, but both these matters are best examined in the works of those competent to discuss them. For the purposes of our study, it will be sufficient to indicate where different notions of history have had an effect on the interpretation of the Bible. In the previous chapter I pointed out the growing use of historical criteria in the seventeenth century to catalogue and explain ideas. This, I suggested, is something now so endemic to modern thought that just as *Burke's Peerage* was the reference point for the nobility to decide precedence among themselves, the record of the genealogy of an idea in the modern period is of itself often sufficient to establish or discredit a concept. In the eighteenth century the progression and the family relationship among ideas certainly flourished as a theme in the various histories of learning, but history also had larger applications.[46] For the study of the Bible, two of these larger applications

---

[44] Self-conscious atheism was nonetheless known in Germany before that time, shown by the incident around Matthias Knutzen in 1674.

[45] See Gunther Franz, "Bücherzensur und Irenik, in M. Brecht, *Theologen und Theologie an der Universität Tübingen* (Tübingen: Mohr, 1977).

[46] The eighteenth century was not the first time that larger roles for history were thought of. For Thucydides, history was the way one learned about the ways of the world; in the Renaissance history could be interpreted as the hand of God visible in

were history as a guide to different ways of thinking and history as the recognition of the process that takes human nature ever upward and onward.

Giambattista Vico (1668–1744) was an example of a thinker ahead of his time. He was not generally recognized during his lifetime, and the irony is that by the time he became well-known, ideas analogous to his own had been developed by others.[47]

Vico's importance is that he offered a new frame of reference for interpreting the past. Up to his time, two basic assumptions that had informed the approach to antiquity had been behind many of the ideas we have already looked at in the history of exegesis.

The first assumption was that all cultural constructs branch out from a single stem. Thus Egypt was the country that taught civilization to Greece, and from Greece this achievement was passed on to others; some even suggested that Moses derived his ideas and laws from his experience as an Egyptian administrator. Language, too, started in one place at one time in history, and one can trace the origins of languages as individuals went off and became the ancestors of various peoples who gradually changed the form of the ancestral tongue, but eventually all languages are to be traced back to a common original, whether Hebrew or Antwerp Dutch, or some other. This point of view made it easy to see the Bible as an important, if not the only, source of our ancient culture and language, so it made sense to derive Greek mythology from biblical narratives. That culture might develop independently along parallel lines was not a working hypothesis.

The second assumption, common to the Renaissance and for some time afterward, was that any society was divided between the minority elite on one hand, who had education, manners, and a clear view of the world, and the vulgar multitude on the other, unwashed, unlettered, and incapable of an interest in anything better than beer, bawds, and brawling. However, it was assumed that the leaders of antiquity, Moses for example, were much the same as the educated people of the Renaissance; these ancient leaders only wrote crudities because of the audience they had to communicate with. Assumed by this view was that if Moses

---

human affairs. For Coccejus, history was the working out of patterns already foretold in the Bible.

[47] A useful guide to Vico is Peter Burke, *Vico* (Oxford; New York: Oxford University Press, 1985).

could return to earth, he would admit quite freely that his version of creation was singularly inadequate, but would then excuse himself by arguing that the work of vulgarization is seldom elegant. Even radical thinkers saw things this way—for example, Spinoza, whose preface to the *Tractatus Theologico-Politicus* was quite clear that he did not want the multitude reading his book; in fact, the theme of the *Tractatus Theologico-Politicus* might be that if they had no philosophy, let them read the Bible, which is all they were capable of.

Vico broke with the temptation to see people in the past as modern people in funny clothes; instead, he saw several stages of the development in human culture, which happen more or less as a natural process, wherever human beings might be. In the beginning were the giants or stupid beasts, incapable of almost anything human. Then followed three stages—gods, heroes, and men. In the age of the gods, humans explained everything as caused by the gods or some suprahuman force. In the age of the heroes, human beings acted more by force than principle, which explains why the behavior of characters in Homer's *Iliad* is often so juvenile and unprincipled. Finally came the age of reason, when human beings became capable of abstract thought and consistent argument. The drawback of this new stage in humanity was that the quality of poetry declined along with the vividness of the imagination and the sense of the sublime.

Vico was arguably the first in the eighteenth century to think of human culture in this way. He was not the last, and the extent to which he influenced others is open to a great deal of dispute. However, whether or not his particular ideas influenced biblical scholars directly, the approach to human history exemplified in his work was to have an extraordinary effect on biblical studies. First, it showed a past that was not necessarily better or worse than the present, but different from it and to be judged by its own outlook rather than ours. Second, the growing sense of a connection between myths outside the Bible and stories within it was to be explained, not by the influence of the Bible on other peoples, but by the nature of all cultures to generate similar images at a given point in their development. Finally, these myths were not to be taken as philosophical ideas in folkloric dress; they had their own meaning and should be explained in terms of it. By the same token, poetry, more typical of earlier cultures than our own, should be appreciated for its imagery rather than analyzed for its doctrinal implications. What all this meant was that a sense of difference among cultures was being worked out that was to produce a new appreciation of the Bible.

9. *Geography*

Geography and biblical studies have always had a close affinity, both in their general interest in human experience and in their particular overlap in the ancient Near East. Edward Wells wrote two extensive works on the geography of the biblical era: *A Historical Geography of the New Testament* (1708) and a three-volume *Historical Geography of the Old Testament* (1710, 1711, 1712).[48] Wells never visited the areas he was describing in these works, so his accounts lack the immediacy of personal experience, but he nonetheless made a solid attempt to put together what was known, and his work continued to be influential throughout the eighteenth century. Wells's sources were ancient authors such as Strabo, Eusebius, and Josephus, as well as contemporary authorities such as Athanasius Kircher (1601–1680), Samuel Bochart (1599–1667), and Paul Rycaut. He also used the firsthand accounts of travelers such as George Sandys; in particular, he used the relatively recent account of Henry Maundrell, chaplain to the British factory at Aleppo, *Journey from Aleppo to Jerusalem at Easter*, A.D. 1697. However, careful, meticulous surveys of the land with mathematical precision were going to have to wait another hundred years.

In his treatment of the Old Testament, Wells is an example of the extent to which a literal understanding of the factual content of the Old Testament was a hindrance to understanding its geographical setting and the historical geography of various cultures. Wells devoted attention to pre-Deluvian geography, especially those two hardy perennials, the site of Eden and the resting place of Noah's ark. He was also hampered, at least from a modern point of view, by taking seriously the Genesis account of the repopulation of the world after the Flood. For example, for Wells, Japheth was the father of the European nations, a cliché of the times but now an outmoded view that comes nowhere near to accounting for the movement of peoples and the development of cultures and languages.

In geography the Bible still held its central scientific significance, at least for Wells and others like him. The breaking of the notion of the

---

[48] I am indebted to R. Butlin, "Ideological contexts and the reconstruction of Biblical landscapes in the seventeenth and early eighteenth centuries: Dr. Edward Wells and the historical geography of the Holy Land," in Alan Baker and Gideon Biger, eds., *Ideology and Landscape in Historical Perspective* (Cambridge; New York: Cambridge University Press, 1992) 31–62. Butlin discusses Wells in the context of the history of geography.

factual infallibility of the Bible in the eighteenth century was to release not only the interpretation of the Bible but also the study of geography from their swaddling clothes.

II. The Bible

1. *The Pietist contribution*

In the development of the modern understanding of the Bible, it is easy to see the role of those who attacked its infallibility or its direct inspiration, such as Spinoza or the Deists. But that German Pietism arguably had as much influence is perhaps less immediately obvious, yet no treatment of the subjects of the text, translation, and interpretation of the Bible can be complete without discussing the role of Pietism. While not all the figures to be treated in this section were Pietists, even those who were not were linked to the work of Pietism to some extent and have to be understood in the context the Pietists created.

i. THE ORIGINS AND NATURE OF PIETISM
AND ITS CONTRIBUTION TO BIBLICAL SCHOLARSHIP

Pietism began as a movement within Lutheranism that attempted to reinvigorate the church by stressing the importance of a personal, experiential religion based on the meticulous study of the Bible under the guidance of the Holy Spirit. The central figure in this movement was Philipp Jakob Spener (1635–1705), whose *Pia Desiderata* was a call to a return to simplicity and the study of the Bible. Unlike groups which were essentially outside the established church from their beginnings, Pietism was, in intention at least, a movement within established Protestantism, although its criticism of things as they were soon brought it into hefty conflicts with orthodox Lutheranism. Pietists occasionally hived off into separatist groups, of which Count Ludwig von Zinzendorf's community at Herrnhut was the most notable and contentious, but on the whole they managed to keep within the bounds of the state churches despite the tensions they generated.

Eventually, after the first third of the eighteenth century, orthodox and Pietists managed a sort of truce, possibly because they found a common enemy in the form of the rationalist Enlightenment. Pietism also had an appeal outside Lutheranism; some of the Calvinist churches felt its attraction, but Pietism's most notable success outside its own realm was triggered by John Wesley's meeting with German Pietists in America, and Methodism can be seen as an English branch plant of the Pietist movement.

It is tempting to see Pietism as a type of Fundamentalism,[49] but while there are historical connections and some resemblances, German Pietism never lost its connection with solid learning, in contrast to some Fundamentalist churches whose theological sophistication was not notable. As mentioned above, when the University of Halle was founded, one of its most prominent figures was the Pietist August Hermann Francke (1663–1727), friend and disciple of Spener.[50] Francke was a solid scholar whose *Praelectiones Hermeneuticae* (1717) was sufficiently influential to be republished in an English version in the early nineteenth century.[51]

ii. AUGUST HERMANN FRANCKE

Francke was one of those astonishing figures in the history of scholarship whose extraordinary qualities require some mention. When he went to Halle as professor, there was no salary attached to the position, so he was also put in charge of a parish. The sort of person he was is shown by his custom of not just giving food to the needy who came to his door but of inviting them into his house and talking kindly to them. From his conversations he decided that what was needed was more attention to children, so he established an orphanage and a school to go with it. He cared enough for the quality of the instruction in the school that eventually even well-to-do families began sending their children there. While keeping this foundation going was not easy, Francke possessed the incredible energy to undertake yet other projects. He established what was in fact a biblical institute and was active in sending out missionaries to foreign lands.

Francke took as another part of his calling making the Scriptures available to ordinary people who could read but who found copies of the Bible too expensive. He set up his own printing house and in fact

---

[49] "Fundamentalism" is an early twentieth-century word used to describe an American Protestant phenomenon. Its usage has been widened to include many groups other than the first ones to use the term. Like many such words, it tends to be more evocative or even pejorative than descriptive in any accurate fashion.

[50] The counterweight to Francke at Halle was the rationally inclined philosopher Christian Thomasius, which led to the saying among students that if you went to Halle, you emerged either as a Pietist or an atheist.

[51] *A Guide to the Reading and the Study of Holy Scripture* (London: William Jacques, 1815).

improved printing technology to lower the price of books, creating the greatest surge in Bible ownership since the Reformation.[52]

iii. FRANCKE AND THE TEXT OF THE BIBLE

Francke was of the opinion that theological students should know the Bible in its original languages if they hoped to understand it thoroughly, so he also provided critical editions of the Old and New Testaments in their original languages.

In the case of the Old Testament, what Francke achieved is best seen by reviewing what had happened to the text of the Old Testament since the invention of printing.

The first complete Hebrew Bible was printed at Soncino in 1488, a second at Brescia in 1494 by Gerson ben Mose of Soncino. Both of these editions were far from accurate; however, the second was used by Luther in making his translation of the Old Testament. There was also a folio Hebrew Bible printed about 1500, possibly in Istanbul. There were also other editions, but they added little to these, on which they tended to be based. Better efforts were the Old Testament text of the Complutensian Polyglot and the second edition of Daniel Bomberg's *Biblia Rabbinica* (1525–1526). Subsequent Bibles up to and including the London Polyglot tended to mix the Complutensian and *Biblica Rabbinica* texts. During the seventeenth century, attempts were made to get beyond this approach, beginning with John Leusden, whose work was published by the Amsterdam printer Athias (1661, 1667). One of the better attempts was the *Biblia Hebraica* of Daniel Ernst Jablonski, the first edition of which appeared in 1699.

Jablonski's edition was a solid attempt to provide students with a useful text. It was a medium-sized, well-produced volume, with the Hebrew text well printed in an easily read font. Jablonski had a fifty-nine-page introduction with notes on various editions of the Hebrew Bible, the reasons for mistakes in the transmission of the text, a careful explanation of the convention of Hebrew, and he even included musical notation in European format for the chants in the synagogue service as provided for him by David de Pinna, a learned Jewish medical doctor in

---

[52] The most useful article on Francke is Kurt Aland, "Bibel und Bibeltext bei August Hermann Francke und Johann Albrecht Bengel," in Martin Geschat, ed., *Orthodoxie und Pietismus*, Gestalten der Kirchengeschichte 7 (Stuttgart: Kohlhammer, 1982) 89–147. It is unfortunate that as far as I can discover, this excellent treatment has not been made available in other languages. On the success of Francke's publishing, see pp. 90–92.

Amsterdam. While the text itself did not include manuscript variants, it had running marginal comments in Latin to summarize what the Hebrew text was dealing with at any given point.

Francke arranged for Johann Heinrich Michaelis (1680–1764) to bring out a Hebrew text based generally on Jablonski's.[53] This was the first Hebrew Bible to include important variants, which Michaelis put at the bottom of the page. The general opinion is that Michaelis was not as careful as he might have been, but it could be argued that this was at least a new departure in its format.

Francke also printed a Greek New Testament. His choice fell on John Fell's 1675 Oxford edition of the *Textus Receptus*,[54] which Francke re-issued in 1702 with a preface by himself. Fell's edition was the most scholarly of its day, for he attempted to take into account the evidence of variations among the manuscripts that had been collected up to his time, and in his preface he claimed to have consulted more than a hundred manuscripts or collations. Fell's arrangement of his edition was well suited to serious students. While Fell reproduced the *Textus Receptus*, where there were textual variants he tagged the text with an identifying mark from the list given in his preface. Then the actual variant and its source were put at the bottom of the page. In the margin, references were given to parallel or connected passages elsewhere in the Bible.

One unexpected drawback to the text put out by Francke was that the number of differences between the manuscripts noted by Fell might give substance to the arguments of those who claimed that the text of the Bible was so corrupt that we could not be sure about anything it contained. One such person worried by these variants was Johann Albrecht Bengel, discussed below, who eventually set out to tackle the textual problem for himself.

iv. FRANCKE AND THE TRANSLATION CONTROVERSY

Francke was aware of the problems inherent in translating the Bible accurately into a European language. Although there had been one or two translations done by Lutheran scholars since Luther's, in Francke's day it was Luther's Bible that was central for Lutherans. But even with Luther's translation itself there were problems, for there were variations in the text of its printed editions. Francke, who was after all a learned

---

[53] Johann Heinrich Michaelis was the great uncle of Johann David Michaelis, discussed in this chapter (see pp. 236–38).

[54] John Fell (1625–1686) was dean of Christ Church, Oxford. He published this text anonymously.

and conscientious man, openly discussed these matters in a series of monthly *Observationes biblicae*. In the first issue the subtitle was:

> Notes on several passages of Holy Scripture in which the German translation of the late Luther is compared with the original text, with an appropriate suggestion of where a better understanding of the words may be found, as would serve edification in Christian doctrine and application in prayer.[55]

There is a strong combative strain within Lutheranism, and it made itself felt in no uncertain terms. Johann Friedrich Mayer, an Orthodox pastor and professor in Hamburg, lost no time in expressing his opinion of Francke's proposal (Francke was after all a Pietist). Having read through the first issue of the *Observationes*, he wrote:

> I was profoundly pained to recognize how Satan, feigning the deepest reverence and sanctity, has once again contrived to bring misfortune to the poor, distressed, and universally persecuted evangelical church by confounding her tongue, with which she has for so long read the Scriptures in unity in the congregation of the Lord in accordance with the spirit of God, and converting it into a veritable Babel. . . . Where do they learn such proposals? I weep to write the truth: in the school of Satan.[56]

One may well wonder whether Mayer was recording tears or attempting to induce them. There is little doubt about the sincerity of his concern about order in the church, but it must be admitted that signs of Christian charity were rather less notable. I have already mentioned in previous chapters the riots that attended Jerome's attempt to change a gourd into ivy or the Bible bonfires that marked the first edition of the Revised Standard Version. Mayer's reaction is a good example of the intemperate irrationality about change, even reasonable change, which has disfigured the Christian church throughout its history, and one may well wonder whether the appropriate discipline to discuss this matter is theology or psychology.

Eventually, Francke had to stop issuing his *Observationes*, let alone proceeding to a new German translation, but it is possible that he may

---

[55] I am indebted here to another article of Aland's, "The Text of the Church," *Trinity Journal*, n.s. 8 (1987) 131–44. The translations of Francke and Mayer are from this article, 132 and 133.

[56] As translated in Aland, "The Text of the Church," 133.

have had more effect than he suspected, for there is one aspect of German Protestantism that is singularly different from its British cousin. In the English-speaking world in the eighteenth and well into the nineteenth century, the King James Version retained its dominance, with very little competition from the Roman Catholic Douai version revised by Bishop Challoner in the eighteenth century. There were other English Protestant versions published, but they remained without serious appeal. By contrast, in the eighteenth century in Germany a relatively large number of translations of various types were produced, and it is reasonable to assume that it was due in part at least to Francke's *Observationes* having had an effect among calmer and more reasonable people in the long run.[57]

v. The legacy of Pietism for the development of biblical interpretation

The net effect of Pietistic Halle on the study of the Bible was the seriousness it brought to bear on the subject. Francke's own exegesis might have been more spiritual than critical, but the sort of conscientious accuracy he wished to instill in his students was to produce interesting results in the Halle of the last two-thirds of the century. Part of Pietism was to cast doubt on the biblical basis or the necessity of many doctrines dear to the heart of orthodox Lutheranism, and as a consequence, Pietism opened the way to a more rigorous examination of the text to find its exact meaning. Heirs to this approach were not always Pietists; but radicals such as Johann Lorenz Schmidt and Johann Christian Edelmann or the liberal theologians who were students and/or professors at Halle throughout the eighteenth century owed much to the Pietists, who had weakened the foundations of rigid orthodoxy.

2. *Two masters of textual criticism of the New Testament: Bengel and Wettstein*

Erasmus had only a handful of New Testament manuscripts, but since his first edition a great deal of labor had gone into locating and often acquiring other manuscripts and collating different readings. After

---

[57] In translating the Bible, one is always caught between an exact literal translation that is usually hard to understand and an almost Targumic paraphrase that may have more appeal but is sometimes more interpretative than accurate. For two relatively recent examples of each genre, compare the original Revised Standard Version with The Living Bible.

two centuries this effect had had a qualitative success, so that when John Mill[s?][58] (1645?–1707) published his Greek text of the New Testament in 1707, he had over thirty thousand different readings. This situation produced a general problem and a series of technical questions. The general problem was felt by those working on the assumption that the Bible had to be infallible, for even given that the original autograph manuscript of a biblical book had been perfect, where were the contents of that perfect manuscript to be found in the midst of a large number of copies, all of which had errors? The technical problems revolved around the choices that had to be made in any preparation of an edition of the text. When one chose a reading, how did one justify one's choice? Were some variants more likely than others, and were there any principles one could follow? Was there any pattern to the occurrence of variants? Were some manuscripts dependent upon or related to others?

At this juncture Johann Albrecht Bengel (1687–1752) took up the challenge. The Pietist movement, like all reformist movements, had its fair share of saints, zealots, and scallywags. Bengel belonged to the saints. He was an intelligent, very diligent scholar, but he was also honest about what he saw in the Bible, and in his personal life he remained untouched by the snares and delusions of the world of "advancement." He was very conservative in his view of Scripture, but it was not based on ignorance, for as a student he had been required to read enough of Spinoza to defend the *Tractus Theologico-Politicus's* ideas as an exercise in debate.

It is worth noting that as in the case of many other eighteenth-century scholars, Bengel's publications arose from his teaching. He did not hold a university appointment, though he was offered two, which he declined, but he taught at Denkendorf, in what can best be called a theological preparatory school. In the interest of his classroom instruction, he put out an edition of Cicero's letters, because this was the guide to Latin style, and an edition of two Greek church fathers, because they were basic to Greek instruction; then he proceeded naturally to editing and commenting upon the Greek New Testament. Bengel's approach of using research to improve teaching presented a significant contrast to the later history of the university, where it was to be research that determined the instruction—or lack of it, as the case may be—to the point where in some institutions research is today the *sine qua non* of professional appointments and advancement. Bengel had himself been disturbed as a student by the number of variants in Fell's New Testament

[58] The name is spelled both Mills and Mill in discussions of the subject. Mill appears to be the correct version.

issued by Francke, so much so that he bought another edition that was text only. However, as head of a school he had to account to his students why there were variations in the New Testament texts they were using, so in the methodical manner of an honest Schwabian, he set out to produce a scholarly edition of the Greek text, which was published in 1734.[59]

Bengel's work was notable for several advances he made on his predecessors. First, he fulfilled a promise he made in the *Prodromus* to his work that he had published in 1725, namely, to reduce a large number of rules to a single statement. He did this in a pithy Latin sentence: *Proclivi scriptioni praestate ardua,* which can be translated "The hard sentence excels the easy one." Later scholars preferred the wording *Difficilior lectio potior*—"The more difficult reading is preferable"—but the basic sense of Bengel's rule still applies, that is, one has to prefer the reading that is hardest to explain because the natural tendency of a scribe is to "correct" a manuscript to give an easier or less offensive reading.

Bengel did not produce his own text to incorporate what he felt were better readings; instead he printed the *Textus Receptus* but listed variant readings along with it.[60] To give his reader some guidance in sorting out the different variants, he classified them into five groups according to their probability. Bengel used the first five letters of the Greek alphabet to show his considered opinion, starting from alpha, which denoted a reading that he considered superior to the *Textus Receptus,* through to epsilon, which marked a reading that was highly unlikely to be correct.

The work was well produced in a medium-sized format with good margins. Parallel passages were given. However, the layout of his text was rather curious. He indicated variant readings and their likelihood at the foot of the page but put the source of such variants in another part of the book. Possibly his early preference for a text without variants influenced him here.

Bengel's judgment in matters of text was conservative but honest. One obvious test case for any scholarly edition is the ending of Mark's Gospel in 16:9ff., which is not found in all manuscripts. Even more suspicious is that some manuscripts have a shorter ending, raising the problem of whether either ending was an original part of the Gospel. Bengel

[59] Johann Albrecht Bengel, *He Kaivn diēthēkē, Novum Testamentum graecum, ita adornatum ut textus probatarum editionum medullam margo variantium lectionum. . . . Apparatu subiunctvs criseos sacrae millianae praesertim compendium, limam, supplementum ac fructum exhibeat* (Tübingen: J. G. Cotta, 1734).

[60] He did, however, make some changes to the text in the book of Revelation where the *Textus Receptus* was corrupt to the point of unintelligibility.

indicated this problem and even gave the text of the shorter ending as recorded by Richard Simon, but he remained with the view that the longer ending was likely a genuine part of Mark's Gospel. On the matter of the *Comma Johanneum* (1 John 5:6-7), mentioned in previous chapters of this book (see p. 53), Bengel discussed the problems thoroughly but opted for the genuine nature of the verses, yet interestingly enough he reversed their order.

Finally, Bengel made an advance that was to prove a basic principle of textual criticism for the next two hundred years. He arranged manuscripts according to their "nations," in this case Asiatic and African. Essentially, what Bengel was doing here was separating manuscripts and versions according to their specific historical origins. This classification did not endure as he described it, and there is now some dispute about whether the number of "cross-pollinated" manuscripts did not make the process more complicated than was first thought, but his use of historical criteria to resolve manuscript problems is an interesting example of the growing importance of history as a way of explaining difficulties in the Bible.

Bengel's textual work was part of his larger plan of making the Bible better known, which would include producing a new translation that would meet the needs Francke had described, issuing a harmony of the Gospels, and writing a work he called *Gnomon* to help in understanding the grammatical structure and the words of the Bible by commenting line by line on all the books of the New Testament. His translation and his harmony did not enjoy a great success, but his *Gnomon*, discussed below, in its various editions has long proved its worth to students and is still in print.

While Bengel developed some important new methods in text criticism, his work was overshadowed by the text put out by Johann Jacob Wettstein (1693–1754). Wettstein, a very different personality from the peaceable Bengel, was Swiss, but because of questions about his orthodoxy, he followed Le Clerc's example and moved to Holland, where he eventually succeeded Le Clerc in the Remonstrant seminary. Wettstein had been an assistant to the English scholar Richard Bentley (1662–1742), who never managed to finish his proposed edition of the New Testament text,[61] but Wettstein's work for Bentley meant that when he produced his

---

[61] It was a part of the traditions of the Republic of Letters that Wettstein was kindly received by Roman Catholic scholars in Paris when he was working on New Testament manuscripts. Even the irascible and unconventional Jean Hardouin treated him

own text, he was able to consult and collate more manuscripts than Bengel. He also made extensive use of quotations from the New Testament that are found in the fathers.

Wettstein published his work in 1751.[62] It was superbly produced and was a marvel of erudition, to the point that even today it is worth consulting. In a Prolegomena extending over two hundred pages, Wettstein went through the work of his predecessors and outlined the problems involved in textual criticism. The main body of the work had three sections to a page: the first and smallest was the text; the second contained the variants; the third was made up of extended notes often going beyond what is usually in an *apparatus criticus* today; for example, he included an extended note discussing whether Matthew wrote originally in Hebrew, an ancient opinion about which Wettstein was far from convinced. On the whole, Wettstein's judgments on the text were far less conservative than Bengel's, such as rejecting the *Comma Johanneum* outright. Other notes included rabbinic material, possible classical parallels, biblical parallels, short analyses of complex texts—much of the sort of material that would today be included in a learned commentary rather than in an edition of the Greek text. Bengel had covered this sort of material in his *Gnomon*, but Wettstein included it with the text and discussed it more fully and less piously.

Wettstein also invented a significant classification method still in use. Greek New Testament manuscripts are written in two types of script: uncial, the more stately forms that are roughly the equivalent of capital letters, and minuscules, often less-expensive productions written in a smaller and faster cursive script that is the equivalent of handwriting. Wettstein devised the convention of using capital letters to denote the uncials and arabic numbers to refer to the far more numerous minuscules.

3. Biblical languages

a. *Hebrew:* A person who approaches Arabic on the basis of a knowledge of Hebrew is likely to be surprised by the overlap between the two languages and sometimes of the difficulty of keeping them separate in

---

kindly. See Anthony Grafton, "Jean Hardouin: The Antiquary as Pariah," reprinted in *Bring Out Your Dead* (Cambridge, Mass.: Harvard University Press, 2001) 187–207.

[62] *Novum Testamentum Graecum*, 2 vols. (Amsterdam: 1751–1752).

his/her own mind. The utility of consulting Arabic for the understanding of Hebrew was recognized by Thomas Erpenius (1584–1624) and Edward Pococke (1604–1691), but Albert Schultens (1686–1750) carried on their work.[63] In the history of language study, Schultens is credited with showing that Hebrew was simply a Semitic language among other Semitic languages.[64]

For this, Schultens was criticized by some theologians, who accused him of detracting from the sacred and unique nature of the Hebrew tongue. Of itself this is a controversy long dead, but the fact that this controversy broke out at that particular time is significant. In the history of biblical interpretation, a point of view seen as "radical" tends to attract the most opposition not when it is put forward, but when it appears to most people to be probably true, especially to those who wish the case were otherwise. At this point conservative condemnation becomes most frantic. That Hebrew was not the original language of humanity had been argued for at least fifty years before Schultens, but the convincing quality of his arguments caused the trouble. This pattern is one that repeats itself in the history of exegesis.

b. *Greek:* The most useful treatment of New Testament Greek in this period was a work of pedagogy rather than of research. As noted above, part of Bengel's plan for providing tools for understanding the Bible was a work he called *Gnomon,* which is among the most successful works for students studying the New Testament closely. The word *gnomon* means literally a "finger" or a "pointer," and the purpose of the work is to point out features of the language and the text of the New Testament books that a student might miss. While Bengel's very conservative attitude to the New Testament is clear, the incidental observations about text, the meaning of words, and the links with other biblical passages are still very useful to the beginning student.

---

[63] See J. van den Berg, "The Leiden professors of the Schultens family and their contacts with British Scholars," *Durham University Journal* 1982 (751) 1–14. Van den Berg clarifies the work and dates of Schultens' son Johann Jacob (1716–1778) and grandson Henry Albert (1749–1793), both of whom in succession held his chair at Leiden.

[64] Schultens, *Origines Hebrææ, sive, Hebrææ linguæ æantiquissima natura et indoles, ex Arabiæ penetralibus* (Franeker: 1724); the 1761 Leiden edition added his treatise *De defectibus hodiernis ling. hebr.* See Jan Nat, *De studie van de Oostersche talen in Nederland in de 18e en de 19e eeuw* (Purmerend: J. Muusses, 1929). [I have not been able to consult any of these works myself.]

4. *Hermeneutics*

"Hermeneutics" is derived from the Greek word *hermeneutikos,* which means an expert in interpretation. The proper method of interpreting, that is to say, making appropriate sense out of any written material, became a problem that can be dated accurately from the first day after writing was invented. However, from the early eighteenth century on, it came to be discussed with greater and greater frequency, to the point where a late-twentieth-century student is reported to have said, "I came to university to study theology, and all I did was eight semesters of hermeneutics."

It was in eighteenth-century Protestantism that many of the discussions about interpretation originated, possibly as a result of a basic weakness in the doctrine of the verbal inspiration of Scripture. If you argue that every word of Scripture is directly inspired by God, how then do you deal with the inevitable problem that parts of Scripture are difficult to understand, or worse still, difficult to explain when they are only too clear? Roman Catholic commentators could take great comfort from appealing to a long tradition buttressed by the present authority of the church, which could deal with any important difficulty. Protestants were vulnerable to the problem of what happens when different qualified scholars come to different conclusions about how to interpret the Bible. The Protestant ideal was to find a method that would produce results as reliable and as uniform as results to mathematical problems.

It is important to bear in mind that hermeneutics was not a problem for theology alone. In 1742 Johann Martin Chladensius (1710–1759), in his introduction to correct interpretation, had his eye on the interpretation of all documents, though he did admit that a general method of hermeneutics would be a help in interpreting Scripture. (He did, however, allow for different procedures when it came to biblical mysteries and prophecies.[65]) Even the philosopher Christian Wolff had a short piece on the use of the demonstrative method in the interpretation of Holy Scripture.[66]

---

[65] Johann Martin Chladensius, *Einleitung zur Richtigen Auslegung von Vernünftigen Reden und Schriften* (Düsseldorf: Stern Verlag, 1969, repr. of 1742 edition) 106.

[66] Christian Wolff, "Von dem Gebrauche der demonstrativischen Lehrart in Erklärung der heiligen Schrift," *Kleine Schriften* (Halle: Renger, 1755) 234–61. This article was originally published in 1731.

To show where Protestant biblical hermeneutics stood at this time, it is useful to look at the principal points made by Johann Jacob Rambach (1693–1735), a very good Pietist scholar of the era whose works on interpretation were basic to many discussions of the subject in the eighteenth century.[67] Rambach began with a look at the history of the hermeneutical tradition, listing Lutheran, Reformed, and Roman Catholic scholars, but then he went on to comment on the progress that had been made.[68]

> Just as all parts of theology today have gained a different shape from the one they had a century ago, so are sacred hermeneutics (*hermeneutica sacra*) and exegetical studies so constituted that new discoveries are always being made, and so that enriched with new advantages they stand today on a completely different footing than before.[69]

This note of progress to be expected in scholarship contrasts sharply with the attitude of De Malesherbes, cited above (p. 175). Here one finds what was distinctive about German theology in the eighteenth century, namely, dissatisfaction with repeating past formulas and a sense that there were important and exciting discoveries to be made. It is all the more significant that a Pietist like Rambach endorsed this hope. By the end of the century there was an unmistakable triumphal note in some writings about how much had been found out, not just in discoveries about the past, but how much had been learned about truth itself.

Rambach's criteria for interpreting a text required asking the question about who was the author or speaker, to whom the text was addressed, and what was the date, place, and occasion. He also warned against deriving speculative doctrines from texts, for preaching should concern

---

[67] Quotations and references from Rambach's *Erläuterung über seine eigene Institutiones hermeticae sacrae,* ed. E. Neubauer (Giessen: Philipp Krieger, 1738).

[68] The names Rambach gave were: *Evangelisch* (i.e., Lutheran): Flacius, Glassius, Gerhardus, Franzius, Hunnius, Calovius, Dannhauer, Pfeiffer, Learius (2), Finkius, Reinhardus, Herm. V. der Hardt, Franckius, Carpzovius, Baier, Schmidius, Loescher, Werner, Maius Mirus, Segers, Langinus, Chladenius, Grosham, Scharammius, Raupius; *Reformed:* Rivetus, Chamier, Gulechius, Hottinger, Heigegger, Netemus, Vitringa, Turrentini, Clericus; *Pontifical* (i.e., Roman Catholic): Sanies Poignance, Situs Sinensis; Jack Greasers, Cornelius Lapide, Serarius, Bonfrerius, de la Haye, Johann Martin Ellies du Pin, Menochius, Heitius, Simon, Calmet, Marcilli, Ascosta (pp. 27–42).

[69] Rambach, *Erläuterung,* 45–46. The translation is mine.

one's way of life. The fact that Rambach's criteria were anchored to the historical origins of a passage and that unnecessary speculation was to be discouraged shows that he was in the tradition of a rational, but not rationalist, interpretation aimed at getting the essence of a text in a sensible way.

However, Rambach had presuppositions that were to be challenged in the course of the century. The first is found in a passage where Rambach discussed mistakes in interpretation, namely, those who rely on reason *(ratio)*. The users of reason were Socinians and rationalists.[70] The *lumen rationis* is not nearly as perfect as the *lumen revelationis,* for there are many things in Scripture that reason does not know. The implication is that one does not have the option of invoking reason to contradict the plain meaning of Scripture. Presumably, the implication is that if a passage in the Bible says an ax head floated, then that is what the fact of the case was.

The second presupposition is the principle of the *analogia fidei,* which Rambach based on the doctrine of the *theopneustos,* the inspiration of the Bible by the Holy Spirit.[71] "The whole system of the Holy Scripture is to be grasped as one book that has a single author, namely, the Holy Spirit, who used all the sacred writers as his amanuenses and edited all their concepts of things and words."[72] This means there can be no possible disharmony in Scripture.[73] Rambach extended this principle to the admonition that one should always refer to the Mosaic writings, which are an infallible norm that forms the basis of revelation. Neither the prophets nor Christ taught anything that is not in Moses. Clearly, Rambach was not willing to push the criterion of historical circumstances to their logical limits, and this meant that he was left behind when exegetes in the later eighteenth century worked out new methods of interpretation for which the historical meaning of a text was basic, even if the conclusion did not fit in with what is said elsewhere in the Bible.

[70] Ibid., 325–26. The rationalist given as an example appears to be Lodewijk Meyer. The other error Rambach described was that of those who relied on tradition, that is, Jews and Roman Catholics.

[71] The term is found in Romans 12:6, which does not necessarily mean that it had there all the meaning attributed to it by Rambach and others.

[72] Rambach, *Erläuterung,* 321. My translation.

[73] Rambach was fully aware that not everyone would have agreed with him; for answers about possible self-contradictions within the Bible as suggested by Spinoza and Hobbes, he referred his readers on page 95 to Godof. Hofmann, *Diss de Dubiis Scripturae.* I have not been able to locate or consult this work.

5. *Prophets and prophecy*

In the history of interpretation, how the prophets are seen is often a useful indication of where exegesis is going. Before discussing this matter in detail, it is important to set out first the different ways "prophecy" can denote aspects or books of the Old Testament.

In the traditional rabbinic division of the Bible into Law, Prophets, and Writings, the prophetic books are divided into Former and Latter Prophets.[74] The Former Prophets consist of Joshua, Judges, 1 and 2 Samuel, 1 and 2 Kings, and Ruth; the Latter Prophets are made up of Isaiah, Jeremiah, Ezekiel, and the twelve "Minor" Prophets, which include Jonah but not Daniel. Obviously, there were prophets whose words and actions were not included in the prophetic books, such as Moses himself, who is called a prophet in Deuteronomy 34:10, Balaam in Numbers 22–24 and elsewhere; Miriam, the sister of Moses, in Exodus 15 and also Numbers 12, where she got herself into a certain amount of trouble.

In modern discussions of the prophets, the distinction is between the writing prophets, that is, those who have a book of their oracles which they themselves may or may not have written attributed them (for example, the book of Amos), and other prophets, a very numerous group in Old Testament times, of which only a small number are mentioned by name in other Old Testament books. However, in New Testament usage the whole of the Old Testament is treated as a prophetic work from which prophecies and explanations of New Testament events and beliefs can be derived. The use of the figure of Melchizedek in the Epistle to the Hebrews is an example of this.

At this point it is appropriate to say something about prophecy in the Old Testament. The fact of the matter is that we do not have enough evidence to reconstruct the social history of ancient Israel, of which prophecy was an important institution. We do not know precisely what role prophets played in Israelite society, we do not know what changes may have taken place during the times of the Old Testament, and we do not know when or indeed whether prophecy died out. In short, we do not really understand prophecy "from within," but what we do know is that prophecy is something far beyond our ken. Take one example: in Isaiah 20 it is recorded how Isaiah walked naked and barefoot through town for three years. In modern Europe or North America it would not

---

[74] "Law" means the first five books of the Bible (the Pentateuch); "Writings" is a catchall term for anything not in the Law or the Prophets, such as Psalms, Ecclesiastes, Song of Songs, etc.

be long before either the police or the weather would put an end to that sort of activity. Those who wax enthusiastic about the prophetic office of the church would do well to wonder how close to some Old Testament examples they would choose to model their own activities.

In the history of biblical interpretation, it is no wonder, then, that modern exegetes have tended to read different interpretations into the prophets, such as Richard Simon's picture of the prophets as inspired scribes whose additions to the Pentateuch were as authoritative as its earlier parts. Most of the interpretations that have been suggested about the roles of the prophets can be supported by an appeal to one text or another, but no one approach can get the whole picture. There are even possibilities yet to be explored; for example, in 1 Samuel 9, Samuel as a prophet is introduced as someone well-known for finding lost animals, but to the best of my knowledge no one has so far suggested that prophets should be seen as dogcatchers.

Traditionally, both within the Bible and in later interpretation, the prophets were cherished for their ability to foresee the future or at least their willingness to try.[75] In the New Testament the fulfillment of Old Testament prophecies in the details of the life of Jesus is a constant theme, and up to the eighteenth century this is how prophecies tended to be interpreted. However, there are problems with how at least some Old Testament passages are interpreted in the New. For example, the identification of John the Baptist with the voice crying in the wilderness in the Gospels rests on a mistake; the Hebrew of Isaiah 40 (which is probably not by Isaiah but by an anonymous prophet more than two hundred years later) should be read as "A voice cries, prepare the way of the Lord in the wilderness." In other words, it is the road out of Babylon back to Judah that is located in the wilderness, not the prophet. Similarly, the opening aria of Handel's *Messiah*, "Comfort ye, comfort ye my people," has really nothing to do with the promised Messiah; it is the promise of the deliverance of the Jewish exiles in Babylon from their captivity, something that took place in the sixth century B.C.E. The nature of this deliverance is not the coming of the Messiah but an invasion by a foreign power, and while there is indeed a messiah named in a subsequent chapter, that messiah is Cyrus, the sixth-century B.C.E. king of Persia, that is, Iran.

---

[75] In 2 Kings 22, Huldah the prophetess prophesies that King Josiah will be gathered to his fathers in peace. But as 2 Kings 24:29 shows, Huldah was completely wrong.

What is opening up is a gap between not only the Old and New Testaments but also between the traditional Christian approach to interpreting the prophets and the new sense of the importance of historical setting in understanding a biblical text. The beginnings of this sort of problem were already apparent in the seventeenth century in the contrast between Johannes Coccejus's interpretation of the prophets and that of Hugo Grotius. Coccejus found in the prophets all sorts of exact foretellings of events that occurred not only in the New Testament but long after, up to the time of seventeenth century C.E. Grotius, for his part, admitted practically no exact prophecies of New Testament events in the Old Testament, let alone subsequent ones in church history. The difference was that whereas Grotius insisted on the historical situation of the prophets, which meant that their messages had to be understood as addressed to the circumstances of their own times, Coccejus saw the prophets as people whose foreknowledge extended over many hundreds of years. Grotius did not deny the application of Old Testament prophecies to the New Testament completely, but it was a case of a general resemblance in the nature of the divine action rather than a direct reporting of what exactly was to happen.

Caught by this problem, more than one scholar in the seventeenth century (and indeed since then) tried to have his cake and eat it by suggesting, for example, that while indeed the Immanuel prophecy in Isaiah 7:14 referred to a coming king of Judah in the eighth century B.C.E., it also referred to the birth of Jesus, as Matthew said it did. In 1707 William Whiston touched off a controversy on the question of the multiple meanings of biblical prophecy in his Boyle lectures entitled *The Accomplishment of Scriptural Prophecies*.[76] In this work Whiston stated that the inspired writers "do not in their Expressions at all belong to the time wherein they were written, but are accommodated to those, for which they were designed by the Spirit of God. For example, the 2d Psalm is to be understood as spoken at the beginning of the Gospel, when the Heathen raged, and the people imagined a vain thing." Whiston was arguing that the biblical prophecies refer to one thing and one thing only, namely, their fulfillment in events yet to come some hundreds of years after they were spoken. This meant that Old Testament prophecies are only to be interpreted in terms of their eschatological fulfillment and had no real relationship to the times of the prophets who spoke them.[77]

[76] London, 1708.

[77] Whiston was an interesting mixture of what are to us contradictions. While his view of prophecies was literal in the extreme, he could also say, "The prophetic stile

Whiston, protégé and successor of Newton at Cambridge, was yet one more example of a mathematician bewitched by the computational charms of millenarian predictions, which will be discussed in relation to eschatological hopes in the next chapter (pp. 266–70). His approach was literalistic and unhistorical to an extreme, to the point where one wonders why the prophets' contemporaries would have been interested in what the prophets had to say if it were not relevant to their own times.

While more conservative critics such as Samuel White attempted to attack Whiston's one meaning per prophecy,[78] another, more radical approach to the prophets was provided by Anthony Collins (1676–1729), who was a fervent anti-clerical writer and considered a Deist, and yet who remained a practicing member of the Church of England to the end of his life. Collins argued that indeed prophetic sayings referred to one event only; his difference from Whiston was that the events foretold in the Old Testament prophets were not the New Testament occurrences, but events expected in the time of the prophets and their hearers. Furthermore, Collins rejected as prophecies of the Messiah texts from non-prophetic parts of the Old Testament, such as the saying about the woman's seed bruising the serpent's head in Genesis 3:15. Collins also had a certain fame coming to him in connection with his opinion on the book of Daniel as a second-century B.C.E. work. Nominally, Daniel was written in the time of the Babylonian Captivity, that is, sometime in the sixth century B.C.E. This was not of itself a new theory; it had been proposed by Porphyry in the third century C.E., and Porphyry's views were mentioned by various exegetes, such as Pererius, but Collins was the first modern writer to accept the pseudonymous nature of Daniel and its later date.

While the details of the debate are rather convoluted and only of antiquarian interest, the whole debate turned on the assumption that prophecy consisted in foretelling the events of the future in accurate detail. The fact of the matter was that none of the arguments got very close to understanding prophecy as a cultural phenomenon in ancient Israel.

---

is not always intire, continued, and coherent through one Series of Reasoning or Succession of Events," and that this may well have been the result of serious dislocations of blocks of material within the Old Testament books in the accidents of history. Advocates of the infallibility of the Bible would not find this comforting, and they might object that if Whiston was correct about dislocations, how can one be sure about the accuracy of the Bible? For a recent treatment of Whiston, see James E. Force, *William Whiston: Honest Newtonian* (Cambridge: Cambridge University Press, 1985).

[78] Samuel White, *A commentary on the Prophet Isaiah wherein the Literal Sense of his Prophecy's briefly explained* (London: Arthur Collins, 1709).

Any discussion of prophecy should mention the commentary on Isaiah by Campegius Vitringa.[79] Dutch scholars were renowned for their linguistic standards. Vitringa was no exception, and his huge, two-volume folio commentary is such a superb work that even modern scholars do well to consult it for its philological notes and suggestions. Vitringa is an interesting example of an essentially conservative scholar who, despite himself, felt the attraction of the new, more historical approach, such as his willingness to agree with Le Clerc about the existence of non-Mosaic material in the Pentateuch. Vitringa was convinced that no Israelite prophet would have attracted any attention had he only talked about events to come in a remote future; any prophecy had to be related to the prophet's own times.

However, Vitringa also suggested that prophecies might well have had two meanings—one for the times of the prophet and another for a later period. In fact, when it came to more difficult questions, Vitringa gave the impression of someone stepping back from the brink. For example, in the exegesis of Isaiah 40 it had been recognized by critics for some time that this made more sense as a prophecy for the Babylonian Exile, but Vitringa took it primarily as a prophecy of the vicissitudes of the church in general and only secondarily applicable to the exilic period. The impression one might get is that this was a way of avoiding the obvious question of why Isaiah, living in the eighth century B.C.E., would have dealt with the exile in the sixth century B.C.E. if, as Vitringa had argued, the first thing any prophet did was to speak to his own times.

In the history of biblical interpretation since the times of Whiston and Collins, a great deal will turn on the understanding of the work and the achievement of the prophets.

6. *Two less conventional views of the Bible: Johann Lorenz Schmidt, Johann Christian Edelmann*

Francke might well have had second thoughts about opening the Pandora's box of new Bible translations had he lived to see Johann Lorenz Schmidt's *Die Göttlichen Schriften von der Zeiten des Messie Jesus,*[80] a translation of the Pentateuch that was to be the first part of a proposed

---

[79] Vitringa, *Commentarius in Librum Prophetiarum Jesaiae.*

[80] *Die göttlichen Schriften von der Zeiten des Messie Jesus. Der erste Theil worinnen Die Gestetze der Israeliten enthalten sind nach einer freyen Übersetzung welche durch und durch mit Anmerkungen erläutert und bestatigt wird* (Nehr: Wertheim, 1735).

new translation of the Bible, published anonymously in 1735. Since it was published in Wertheim, it acquired the name Wertheimer Version from that day forward. It was not long before Schmidt's authorship was revealed, and for a time he was even put in jail for his efforts and had to live under assumed names for the rest of his life. Schmidt intended to translate the whole Bible, but no more of his translation was ever published, nor does it appear to have survived in manuscript. What is certain is that for several years his translation of the Pentateuch was the center of a storm of controversy remarkable even for German theologians always ready to hammer a colleague until he was scarcely visible above the ground. In all this Schmidt defended himself with great vigor, and we are fortunate that much of what he said and what was said about him survives in Johann Sinnhold's 1739 collection of the documents.[81]

Schmidt's basic starting point was Christian Wolff's philosophy, which he had embraced with great enthusiasm. Hirsch summed up Schmidt's approach as the application of Wolff's system "with a pedantic exactness and thoroughness that went beyond Wolff himself."[82] Schmidt's introduction shows his dependence on Wolff for his notion of a deductive system held together by clear definitions. This by itself was a red rag to the theological bulls of his day, but Schmidt took a step that Baumgarten never made explicit, namely, it was philosophical thought that was to explain the Bible, not vice versa. In his introduction he put forward a theory of cultural development that argued that the Hebrews were really too uncultured to put biblical truths into a coherent form; the Greeks might have done it, but for various reasons did not. But now this can be done in the dawning world of the new philosophy that provides a certain basis for all knowledge, even theology. While Schmidt was clear that the origins of the biblical books lay in a revelation of God to humanity, he was also clear, in a way that outraged his critics, that the resulting documents could have been expressed more clearly. In effect, this was to turn the Bible into a document marked by human misunderstandings and failures.

Schmidt also got something from Wolff apart from a philosophical basis, namely, a theory of translation. In 1731 Wolff, never at a loss to

[81] A useful collection of the relevant documents is found in Johann Sinnhold, ed., *Ausführliche Historie der verruffenene sogennanten Wertheimischen Bibel* (Erfurt: Johann Heinrich Nonne, 1739).

[82] Emmanuel Hirsch, *Geschichte der neuern Evangelischen Theologie,* 3rd ed. (Gütersloh: C. Bertelsmann, 1964) 2:419 (my translation). Hirsch's discussion of Schmidt (417–438) is very good, and I have only a few details to add to his conclusions.

find uses for his system, published three articles on how his philosophy was also a guide to translation and interpretation, especially the translation and interpretation of the Bible.[83] Wolff made the point that the philological equivalent of an expression does not always give the best translation of the sense of the author, such as the statements in the first part of Genesis about God seeing that parts of creation were good, for grammatically this could imply that the creation could have been better, which was not the original author's intention. Wolff also pointed out that deviating from the literal sense of the text can be carried too far, such as Hermann von der Hardt's reinterpretation of the Flood story as the account of an invasion in which the ark became a fortress.[84] However, there are times when words (*Wörter* or *Ausdrücke*) are to be distinguished from ideas *(Begriffe)*, for the same idea can often be adequately expressed in different words.

Seizing on this distinction with a determination worthy of a pit bull terrier with a steak, Schmidt elevated it into the principle behind his new translation of the Bible, which he called a "free translation," in contrast to a literal one. This translation was to communicate the ideas of the Bible rather than the philological equivalent of its words. At the same time he aimed to avoid the exaggerations of a complete reformulation *(Umschreibung)*, which he does not explain in detail, but it is possible that he might have been thinking of something like von der Hardt's rewriting of the Flood story.

But Schmidt also combined what he had borrowed from Wolff with a concept of his own concerning the history of language. He argued that the problem of interpreting Scripture is that it is written in a sort of language very different from Western languages. In ancient times people began by using such words as were necessary to distinguish among

---

[83] Christian Wolff, "Von Üebersetzungen," "Von dem Gebrauche der demonstivischen Lehrart in Erklärung der heiligen Schrift," and "Von dem Nutzen der beweisenden Lehr-Art zu Lehr-Büchern von der geoffenbarten Theologie," reprinted in *Kleine Schriften* and *Einzele* [sic] Betrachtungen zur Besserung der Wissenschaften (Halle: Renger; 1755) 209–33, 234–61, and 349–87 (aus dem Früh-Jahrs Quartal der *Marburgischen Neben-Stunden*, 1731).

[84] Hermann von der Hardt (1660–1746) was a Pietist professor at Helmstedt, whose drift into rationalist ideas got him into trouble with the university authorities. When the first volume of his commentary on Job was banned, he burned the manuscript of his second volume and took the cinders to the university library with the comment, "These are the ashes in which Job sat."

physical objects necessary to maintain human life. A new situation arose when human beings then went on to discuss things that were not material. The best they could do was to reapply the old words that described material things to nonmaterial concepts, and this was the origin of abstract speech. When one tries to translate ideas correctly, one has to use terms current in one's own world, not the world of the original writer, particularly when his words for abstract ideas are simply recycled from concrete expressions of earlier times.

Schmidt was not very good at illustrating his argument from examples, but a possible example is the Latin adjective "sincere." Its basic philological meaning is "without wax," a reference to the practice of dishonest masons who would fill imperfections in stone with wax to hide them from customers. Thus a translator might be philologically correct in rendering the Latin adjective "sincere" as "wax free," but it would be very short of an accurate translation if the original author's intention had been to indicate that a particular man was honest.

Schmidt was arguing that when he did this in translating the Bible, he was not trying to improve on the Bible; the terms it used were in their time quite ample to express the ideas intended, but now things have changed and different words are required to get the original idea across. An example from his own work is his translation of Exodus 4:24, where it is said that God sought to kill Moses. Schmidt translated this as "Moses fell sick," which, according to Schmidt, was the original idea behind the expression.

However, what was tied up in Schmidt's linguistic theory was a concept of cultural development. Unlike the Hebrews, who could not, and the Greeks, who would not, put statements into mathematical-like structures, modern Europe—at least those who had read Wolff—was now in a position to reach a better understanding of truth. This was somewhat like Vico's theories on speech, but there was a long way to go to reach the complexity of the theories of Johann Herder and others. Nonetheless, this was a beginning of a way of understanding the Bible as a book that reflects human variations rather than divine dictation. This did not mean that Schmidt was denying the inspiration of the Bible any more than Wolff; both considered themselves orthodox Lutherans, but they allowed an equal weight to natural and revealed theology. This approach was to create trouble ahead.

What Schmidt hoped to achieve in his free translation, then, was to render the original Hebrew in such a way that the ideas it contained were made clear and distinct, in contrast to the literal vocabulary in which they had been expressed in ancient times. To do this one could not stick slavishly to either the exact words and word order, or even the formal verse and chapter divisions within the Bible. This is how he rendered the first verses of Genesis:

> All the parts of the Universe and our Earth itself were made in the beginning by God. In the case of the Earth, it was in the beginning entirely a mess; it was surrounded by a thick cloud and completely sodden with water over which strong winds began to blow. Soon however it cleared up a bit according to God's plan. And because this was very necessary and useful, it took place according to the ordinance that God had made at this time, that from then on light and darkness would alternate, and this was the origin of day and night. This night and day together made up the first day.[85]

Schmidt was trying to reconcile the Genesis creation story with the Galilean universe. For example, the words recording the creation of the heavens were designed to record the creation of all the heavenly bodies apart from the earth; the subsequent creation of the sun and moon was simply the clearing of the thick cloud so that they could be perceived. Given that the basic idea was creation, its meaning was better carried by this free translation than the older, more verbally correct translation that got people arguing about incidental details, such as the composition of the solar system. On the whole, Schmidt was making a heroic effort to rescue the Bible from its more radical critics by producing a clearer, more up-to-date translation. He succumbed occasionally to the temptation to round off the sharper corners of explanations. An example of this is his rendering of the strange story in Genesis 6 of the sons of God seeing that the daughters of men were fair. He interpreted this as a story about the sons of the *Rechtgläubige* ("orthodox," or even "virtuous" in this context), being allured by the daughters of *das rohe Volk* ("common, rough people")—in other words, nice boys getting mixed up with girls from

---

[85] Alle Weltkörper, und unsere Erde Selbst, sind anfangs von Gott erschaffen worden. Was insonderheit die Erde betrifft; so war dieselfbe anfänglich ganz öde: sie waren mit einem finstern Nebel umgeben, und rings herum mit Wasser umflossen, über welchem heftige Winde zu wehen anfingen. Was wurde aber bald auf derselben etwas helle, wie es die göttliche Absicht erforderte. Und weil dieses sehr nöthig und nützlich war: so geschahe es nach der Einrichtung, welche Gott dissfalls gemacht hatte, dass von an Licht und Finsternis beständig abwechselten; und dies ist der Ursprung von Tag und Nacht. Diese Nacht und Tag zusammen machten den ersten Tag aus (*Gesetze* 3; my translation).

less respectable families.[86] While one may consider his attempts a bit far-fetched, his intention was quite clear: he wished to defend the Bible against a gathering storm of negative criticism of the Old Testament text by making use of what might be considered more "rational."

At any rate, this was how Schmidt saw matters. His critics begged to differ—to be precise, they lined up to denounce him. They felt that he was breaking the links between the Pentateuch and the New Testament. For example, he did not find the Trinity foreshadowed in the plural form *elohim*; rather, he interpreted the plural form of *elohim* as Moses' condescension to the usage of his day, since all the peoples about Israel were polytheists.[87] And he denied the Holy Spirit's part in creation by translating *ruah elohim* as simply "a terrible wind." Similarly, he did not mention that there was a christological prophecy in Genesis 3:15, nor was there a prophecy of the messiah in the blessing of Jacob in Genesis 49.

To be fair to Schmidt, his innovations were for the most part neither new nor daring. Calvin himself was not convinced that the plural form *elohim* in Genesis implied the Christian doctrine of the Trinity, and the possible translation of *ruah elohim* as "wind" had been recognized by Christian scholars for two centuries. Schmidt's approach to the Old Testament and the New here is not really very different from that of Grotius, and he may well have been using Le Clerc's commentary on Genesis as the source of his interpretations.

Why, then, did the Wertheimer Bible provoke such a reaction? Schmidt's originality lay in the type of translation he was attempting, not the exegetical observations that lay beneath it. Many of his opponents simply did not recognize the scholarly tradition on which he was relying. But the violence of the storm was also the fear any challenge to accepted norms evokes when the challenger points out a weakness that defenders of the norm would prefer to forget. Schmidt was simply at the wrong end of a lightning rod. As was remarked thirty years after its publication, had Schmidt produced his work later in the century, no one would have taken much notice of it.

Had they only known, the orthodox defenders of the faith might have done better to have settled with Schmidt, for ten years later they were

---

[86] This was, in fact, an interpretation that had been proposed by some Renaissance critics and still survives today in some conservative commentaries.

[87] So *Gesetze*, note 2, p. 4. Schmidt numbered his notes consecutively throughout his translation. The printer did not always manage to get the note on the same page as the text commented upon.

faced with an antagonist who capitalized on all the weak areas Schmidt was trying to defend. Johann Christian Edelmann, like Schmidt a Bible translator,[88] was also seeking certainty.[89] But for Edelmann, certainty was found not by shoring up the Bible but by destroying any claim it had to absolute authority, in order to reach the certainty elsewhere, namely, in reason.[90]

Edelmann studied theology at Halle, where he considered Buddeus his great guide. He was also impressed by Valentin Loescher's *Unschuldige Nachrichten*, which he used as the source of much of his knowledge of current theology. When he produced his own journal, his title imitated Loescher's; his title was *Unschuldige Wahrheiten* ("unbiased truth"). In his theological position, Edelmann was a sort of hybrid; he maintained all the religious intensity of his Pietist roots along with the Pietist weakness for a sense of self-righteousness that could extend into a sense of one's own perfection, yet he found in Spinoza's radical monism the source of all certainty.

Edelmann's *Mose mit aufgedeckten Angesichte*[91] was his work that aroused the most controversy. It was a dialogue between two brothers, Lichtlieb ("lover of light") and Blindling ("blinded"). A figure often referred to in the discussion was an archetypal Lutheran pastor called Stockfinster ("pitch-black darkness"). One may be tempted to see in the names where Edelmann's own sympathies lay.

[88] Edelmann had worked for some time on the Berleberg translation of the Bible, the work of a small group of separatist Protestants.

[89] We are indebted to Walter Grossmann for his work on Edelmann. See his *Johann Christian Edelmann: From Orthodoxy to Enlightenment* (The Hague and Paris: Mouton, 1976). Grossman has also produced an edition of Edelmann's writings, some of which had not been published before.

[90] In the *Unschuldige Wahrheiten*, preface to vol. 13, Edelmann's terse comment on the Wertheimer translation is that the author does not want his writings compared with such stuff ("mit solchen will der Auctor seine Schriften nicht verglichen wissen"). On the other hand, in his frontal onslaught on the Bible in *Die Begierde nach der vernufftigen Lautern Milch* (Neuwied: 1744) 167, he says of Zinzendorff's translation and the Wertheimer Bible that while they are not perfect everywhere, "da doch nicht zu läugen ist, dass beyde den Sinn der biblischen Schrieber . . . doch am meisten Orten, viel besser ausgedruckt, als all andre Übersetzungen die wir haben"—"It is not to be denied that in most passages both have expressed the meaning of the biblical writers better than all other translations that we have."

[91] The first three volumes were published in 1740. Three more parts of this work were completed by Edelmann but not published until 1972. Since they played no part in the debates of the eighteenth century, they are not commented upon here.

While not a book about Scripture in itself, a great deal of the volumes consists of discussions about the Bible in which Edelmann shows a wide breadth of knowledge about what had been said about the Bible in Europe over the past eighty years.[92] His position was analogous to that of Spinoza in that while parts of Scripture have their merits, the Bible itself is too unreliable to provide absolute certainty. Therefore, for certainty one has to go to the light of reason that is within oneself, something Edelmann argued was recognized by the Bible itself once one understands the preface to John's Gospel correctly and sees "the word" as one's own innate reason.[93]

For our purposes, namely, the history of exegesis, Edelmann's Spinozism is less important than his approach to the interpretation of the Bible. His radical departure was similar to Schmidt's in one way but not in another. Both men agreed that the key to understanding Scripture must be found in large part outside Scripture, that is, in what we consider to be true for reasons not found in Scripture. For both of them it was the new knowledge offered by the Enlightenment that gave them a position from which they could assess what was either lacking or important in Scripture, for whether it was Wolff or Spinoza who supplied the guide to absolute truth, both philosophers were in fact variations on a theme in their approach.

The difference between Schmidt and Edelmann is apparent in how they made use of this new standard. Schmidt tried to explain or interpret Scripture in such a way that the crudities of the simple-minded Hebrews were obviated by giving the sort of meaning that these Hebrew writers would undoubtedly have given had they only had the talent to do so. This was in effect one strategy to blunt radical criticism that was used from John Spencer through to Johann David Michaelis, and since then. Edelmann took the more daring position; for him the reason why so much in the Bible appeared crude, barbarous, and unbelievable was because in many places the Old Testament really was crude, barbarous, and unbelievable, and no amount of clever explanation was going to get

---

[92] It is clear that he was a devoted reader of Loescher's *Unschuldige Nachrichten*, and he gave useful references to the articles in this journal that showed the support available for more radical interpretations of the status of the Bible. The very orthodox and conservative Loescher would have been shocked, but not altogether surprised, at this inverted use of his unfavorable reviews and articles.

[93] Faust's struggles with translating John 1:1 in Goethe's play may owe something to Edelmann's attempt to face the problem in his own life. Such are the unexpected connections between exegesis and literature in the eighteenth century.

one out of this difficulty. Instead, one had to forge ahead to God's revelation to oneself in one's reason, where one could be sure of finding absolute assurance, on the basis of which one could judge the Bible, condemning its weaknesses and confirming the many good things it nonetheless had to say.

For instance, here is an example of Edelmann's attack on the believability of the Bible: In the first volume Edelmann devoted a great deal of somewhat ill-organized attention to the Mosaic authorship of the Pentateuch. He gave a fairly standard list of objections to be found in the early Enlightenment, such as how did Moses record his own death; if Moses claimed direct inspiration from God, how do we account for other prophets who made similar claims such as Zoroaster, Minos, Lycurgus, or Mohammed; or why did God not spend as much time with the copyists of the text of the Bible as he is supposed to have expended on its authors? Even the supposedly ignored book of Henning Witter[94] on the criteria of Mosaic sources is cited to show that Moses was not directly inspired but worked from older documents. The final form of the Bible is due to Ezra, not Moses. Edelmann took an impish glee in pointing out that it is generally admitted that it was in the time of the patriarchs that the purest religion flourished, a time when neither Bible nor exegetes existed.[95]

Edelmann's view of the Bible essentially relativized it. If it contained truth about God, albeit in imperfect form, it was not the only book to do so. Truth was truth wherever it is to be found. This is one of the earliest incidents in Germany of a sort of thinking that showed itself not only in Lessing's *Nathan the Wise* but also in the educational experiments of Johann Basedow. The Bible was on its way to being one of many estimable religious documents, but for the moment religion itself remained estimable.

Is there a moral to this story apart from the innocent pleasure it provides to the harmless drudges like myself who prefer to live in the eighteenth

[94] Witter published a work, *Jura Israelitarum in Palestinam terram Channaneam* (Hildesheim: 1711), analyzing a part of Genesis, using the criteria of the divine names and doublets in the narrative in order to show the existence of two sources behind the present form of the book. It is not true to say Witter was forgotten; apart from Edelmann, Gabler refers to Witter in his edition of Eichhorn's *Urgeschichte*, I, 2. See the article by Adophe Lods, "Un précurseur allemand de Jean Astruc: Henning Bernard Witter," *Zeitschrift für die alttestamentliche Wissenschaft* 43 (1925) 134–35.

[95] *Moses*, vol. 2, p. 5. This remark is curiously similar in tone to Goethe's idealization of the patriarchs in *Dichtung und Wahrheit*.

century rather than their own times? First, evaluations of the contents of the Bible presuppose some authority external to it—even the narrowest creationist presumes a standard of scientific, factual accuracy. Second, in their search for certainty, Schmidt and Edelmann started from similar assumptions but wound up in different places. Schmidt's certainty was achieved through a hermeneutical process that purged the Bible of its incidental dross; Edelmann's, by a more radical excision of large parts of the Bible in the interests of exalting the individual reason. Yet the criterion remained rational truth, that is, a certainty whose truth would be apparent to all readers of goodwill and adequate competence, a truth that was to be found in demonstrable form somewhere. For a hundred years this mirage led on the majority of creative religious thinkers until it was abruptly ambushed by Kierkegaard.[96] But that is another story.

7. *Two interesting scholars with glaring weaknesses and a note on eminent skeptic*

i. AUGUSTIN CALMET (1672–1757)[97]

On the library of the University of Strasbourg there are reliefs of great figures from literature and scholarship. Built in a time of one of Alsace's attachments to Germany, it is perhaps significant that the building features in its reliefs the Oratorian Augustin Calmet, a French-speaking citizen of Lorraine, who had lived part of his life in Alsace. Calmet, one of the most notable Roman Catholic scholars of the eighteenth century, wrote two great works on the Bible, his multivolume commentary and his biblical dictionary.

Calmet was a diligent, honest scholar who was familiar with most of the problems presented by biblical texts. He had obtained permission to take language lessons from a Protestant whom he felt was a better instructor in biblical languages than anyone he could find in his own communion. His erudition was respected even in Germany. In his introduction to his commentary, Calmet explained that he was writing in French because he wished to produce a work for those not able to read

---

[96] See *Concluding Unscientific Postscript*, trans. David Swenson and Walter Lowrie (Princeton: Princeton University Press, 1968 [1st ed.1941]) 97–98.

[97] See Patrick Marsauche, "Présentation de Dom Augustin Calmet (1672–1757)," in Jean-Robert Armogathe, *Le Grand Siècle et La Bible* (Paris: Beauchesne, 1989) 233–53; Bertram Eugen Schwarzbach, "Dom Augustin Calmet: homme des lumières malgré lui," *Dix-Huitième Siècle* 34 (2002) 451–63.

Latin commentaries full of citations in Greek, Hebrew, and Arabic. For this audience he discussed problems with great clarity and openness. But at this point his weakness was that he really did not attempt to explain or deal with the problems he laid bare. Whatever his reason may have been, Calmet was leaving the door open to those who wished to argue that the Bible was a flawed document whose problems and contradictions put into question its divine origins. One of those who walked in was Voltaire. Ernest Renan, the nineteenth-century biblical skeptic, remarked, "Richard Simon did not leave a single disciple; Calmet had only one—Voltaire."

ii. WILLIAM WARBURTON (1698–1779)

No one ever accused William Warburton of lack of ingenuity in defending the Bible. Warburton, an autodidact who had not been to university and was a member of the Scribblerian club of Pope and Swift, eventually became bishop of Gloucester.[98] He is remembered for his *Divine Legation of Moses Demonstrated on the Principles of a Religious Deist, from the Omission of the Doctrine of a Future State of Reward and Punishment in the Jewish Dispensation*, which was written as an answer to Anthony Collins's observation that there is no hope of life after death in the Old Testament.[99] Collins was, in fact, correct for the most part, and Warburton had the wit not to challenge his starting point. Instead, he argued at great length that it was the purpose of divine Providence to preserve the true doctrine of God among the Hebrews; therefore Providence provided for a theocratic state to be set up that could make heresy a state crime. While a belief in an afterlife was not part of this theocratic establishment, Providence provided that during this period human beings received just rewards and punishments for all their misdoings, thereby making rewards and punishments in a future life unnecessary.

Warburton's book, sometimes called the worst defense ever made of a good cause, was not as bad as one might expect. It was diffuse and wordy, but its arguments were not always silly, and there was a great deal of erudition displayed. One interesting unexpected influence this book enjoyed was that the section which contained a lengthy treatment of Egyptian religion (part of an argument too complex to discuss here)

[98] He is the same Warburton whose cook is infamous in the history of English drama for using parts of her employer's collection of British playscripts as liners for pie plates.

[99] Five vols. (London: 1738–1749).

was translated into French where it became part of the eighteenth-century French fascination with things Egyptian.

iii. VOLTAIRE (1694–1778)

The omission of a serious discussion of Voltaire from this chapter will attract debate. Voltaire was a just-minded man outraged by what he saw in the French Roman Catholic Church. Incidents such as the execution of the Chevalier du Barry for scoffing at a religious procession were part of the reason for his famous "écrasons l'infâme," and there is no doubt that his outrage was to his credit. Voltaire saw the Bible as a weak chink in the church's armor and devoted a significant part of his writing to this attack, in which the wit and moral intensity he showed are part of the French literary heritage. However, the question remains, What was his contribution to understanding the Old Testament? If one looks at the basic assumptions of his anti-biblical writings, one finds an urbane, humane eighteenth-century *philosophe* who was constantly surprised that the people of the Old Testament did not think as he did. He was the equivalent of the tourist who accused kilted Highland Scots of cross-dressing.

Essentially, Voltaire did not understand the Old Testament and mined the helpless and hapless Calmet for information to back up his superficial, if well-written, scorn for things Jewish past and present. Nor was Voltaire's weakness in understanding other people confined to his view of the Bible. Montesquieu commented succinctly about Voltaire's history writing:

> Voltaire n'écrira jamais une bonne histoire. Il est comme les moines qui n'écrivent pas pour le sujet qu'ils traitent, mais pour la gloire de leur ordre. Voltaire écrit pour son couvent.

> Voltaire will never write a good work of history. He is like the monks who never write for sake of the subject they treat, but only for the glory of their order. Voltaire writes for his monastery.[100]

---

[100] My translation.

Chapter 6

1750–1800

I. External Factors

1. Changes in political and personal attitudes

Between the accession of Frederick the Great in 1740 and the crowning of Napoleon as emperor in 1801, an extraordinary series of changes and events took place in Europe. Kings and aristocrats flirted with Enlightenment ideas until French aristocrats during the Revolution found that they were cut short, not by the arguments of the reactionaries, but by the guillotines of the revolutionaries. Napoleon was to go on to play ducks and drakes with the boundaries and the thrones of Europe, erasing a thousand years of traditions as he went, but in so doing he called forth the nationalism that was to wreak havoc on France and the rest of Europe for the next century and a half. To get a sense of the rate of change, one need only consider the life of Goethe, who experienced the coronation of the last Holy Roman Emperor as an adolescent in Frankfort, but by the time of his death, Karl Marx was already a schoolboy.

What happened was that the center of gravity had shifted across the spectrum of human interests, endeavors, and perceptions. Not everyone went along with these new developments, and attempts would be made to turn back the clock, but the general shape of the modern world had emerged to stay, and the whole planet would never be the same again. The guardianship of the past was no longer the overarching guide for human endeavor, and from now on it was to be the future that would be the standard for the present. The change is shown in a trivial way in an exchange between two officials in the court of Napoleon. A traditional aristocrat with a line traced back to a protoplasmic amoeba declared to one of the new nobility whom Napoleon had appointed from humble origins, "Look at me, look at my ancestors!" The other exclaimed, "Look at me, I am an ancestor!" In the modern world our origins may be irrelevant, but we are all ancestors.

2. *Enlightenment and its critics*

The eighteenth century is well-known as the Age of Enlightenment— of the throwing off of old prejudices and the shining forth of reason from behind the clouds of superstition and prejudice. But as the list of "lies" at the beginning of chapter 4 (p. 121–23) makes clear, one should not confuse important movements of thought with the whole of a culture and assume an unruffled harmony of outlooks. There are always those who are behind the times and those who are ahead of them. Even within ourselves we are seldom completely consistent, and we should not be too critical of the framers of the U.S. Constitution, whose list of self-evident rights somehow did not include black slaves.

Movements in human thought tend to call up their own opposition, and the Enlightenment was no exception. In the latter part of the eighteenth century, even as the Encyclopedistes appeared to have seized the intellectual high ground, the criticisms of reason, order, common sense, and predictability emerged; even horticulture felt new influences in France as the style of the formal, rational garden was challenged by the irregular meanderings of the "jardin anglais," whose wandering lines had more in common with Mandelbrot than Euclid.

Throughout the Enlightenment period there had always been a rearguard resistance to the new world of Enlightenment thought and physical philosophy, but devastating as Swift's satire on the Royal Society had been, even he could not prevent serious people from trying to get sunbeams out of cucumbers. In the sphere of religion, the rational postulate of a divine watchmaker faced competition from a movement of piety almost its opposite, namely, a surge of enthusiastic movements within Christian churches and even within Judaism. For example, Pietism and Methodism among Protestants, St. Alphonsus Liguori and his Redemptorists within Roman Catholicism, and the Baal Shem Tov in Judaism have a certain family resemblance. These enthusiastic movements were to have an influence on theology and biblical studies and on the wider community as well.

Later on it was to be within the very citadel of reason that signs of unrest made themselves felt. For a good example one need only to turn to Emanuel Swedenborg. He was a Swedish engineer with considerable technical accomplishments, but he then became a visionary of note whose influence extended not only to Blake but arguably also to the Mormon leader Joseph Smith. Kant was appalled at Swedenborg and wrote his *Reveries of a Ghost Seer* in reaction to him, but the specter was not laid to rest. Another rebel was Johann Georg Hamann, a friend of Kant's, who eventually turned away from Enlightenment philosophy for his own form of enlightenment.

Things were changing. Imagination, a word used as a rebuke of the Hebrew prophets in Spinoza, suddenly became respectable, and color, creation, and feelings made their return. Color itself was defended by Goethe, for whom the dry and rational experiments on the refraction of light were a joke in bad taste. In *Maria Stuart*, Friedrich Schiller, who was not religious himself, created a character who converted from Protestantism to Roman Catholicism because there he found the pageantry and excitement that appealed to his imagination.

Some well-established assumptions were turned on their heads. Rousseau's *Discours sur les sciences et les arts* (1750) and *Discours sur l'origine et les fondements de l'inégalité parmi les hommes* (1755) were essentially rejections of much of what the Enlightenment had treasured.[1] In critical writings disguised as travel memoirs, the figure of the urbane rational observer of the follies of European culture changed into the noble savage, far from urbane but possessing virtues not to be found in civilization. Montesquieu's Persian of *Les Lettres Persanes* was replaced by James Fenimore Cooper's Mohican. Even the lower classes of Europe became interesting, and Marie Antoinette had Little Trianon built to provide a retreat from the sophistication of Versailles, where she and her ladies could play at being shepherdesses. The Middle Ages ceased to be barbarian, and Gray turned from his elegiac description of a country churchyard to Welsh chieftains wont to shout "Ruin seize thee ruthless king" at visiting English monarchs. Suddenly peasant art from the past became respectable and admirable; Percy's *Reliques of Ancient Poetry* was a collection of folk poetry; and where such art of the people was in short supply, Macpherson could supply *Ossian* for an eager public in both England and Germany.

[1] Yet Rousseau had a great influence on Kant, who kept Rousseau's portrait in a prominent place in his house.

3. *Goethe and the Bible*

Johann Wolfgang Goethe was far too imposing a figure to be classified, but he read the Bible with pleasure, if not religious conviction. His experience is worth examining, for it shows the emergence of a new type of sensitivity—the person who appreciates the Bible as literature. In his autobiographical *Dichtung und Wahrheit*, Goethe discussed his relationship with Scripture. In his boyhood he had taken a great interest in the Bible, even to the point of trying to learn Hebrew. He implied that his teacher, Dr. Albrecht, rector of the gymnasium, was more critical about the Bible than he preferred to let on, something suggested by a taste for Lucian, the classical author most ironic about all manner of sacred things. Goethe himself noticed early on that there were passages in the Bible that strained credulity, such as the sun going backward in Joshua and passages that contradicted other parts of the Bible.[2] This did not, however, destroy his fascination with the Bible, for later on in the same chapter, Goethe retold in great detail, but with obvious pleasure, the stories about the patriarchs in Genesis. At the end of it all he explains why he did this:

> Perhaps some one may ask why I have so circumstantially narrated histories so universally known, and so often repeated and explained. Let the inquirer be satisfied with the answer, that I could in no other way exhibit how, with my life full of diversion, and with my desultory education, I concentrated my mind and feelings in quiet action on one point; that I was able in no other way to depict the peace that prevailed about me, even when all without was so wild and strange. When an ever busy imagination, of which that tale may bear witness, led me hither and thither; when the medley of fable and history, mythology and religion, threatened to bewilder me,—I liked to take refuge in those Oriental regions, to plunge into the first books of Moses, and to find myself there, amid the scattered shepherd tribes, at the same time in the greatest solitude and the greatest society.[3]

---

[2] *The Autobiography of Johann Wolfgang von Goethe*, trans. John Oxenford (New York: Horizon, 1969) 131–33 [Book 4 in the work]. Those who wish to consult other editions of Oxenford's translation or Goethe's original German (preferably in the Weimar edition) will find it relatively easy to locate the passage mentioned in this and subsequent notes by following the book numbers given. (Each "book" is the equivalent of a chapter.)

[3] Ibid., vol. 1, 145 [Book 4].

For Goethe, the Bible had become not a source of doctrine but a literary work that inspired him with its images and its poetry. He was quite aware of the emerging historical-critical interpretation among scholars, but his conclusion on the matter was that this was a matter of the outer form of the material that should be left to the critics; for himself, he was interested in the meaning, the direction, the inner core of the work, which no external concern could destroy.[4]

Now even generations of doctrinal sermons had not hidden from people that the Bible was interesting in its own right. From the York cycle of mystery plays to Milton, the Bible had provided the imagery and the narratives that go to make up a basic education. In Goethe it had come loose from its doctrinal surroundings, for while Goethe's attitudes to Christianity throughout his life can be summed up as variations on lukewarm, his friend Ernst Langer, who initiated him into much of the historical-critical method, would rebuke him for having too emotional an attachment to the Gospels.[5] It is interesting that Goethe's attachment to the Bible was such that he refused to countenance any scornful attitude toward its contents, and he said, "I still perfectly remember, that in my childishly fanatical zeal, I should have completely throttled Voltaire, on account of his 'Saul,' if I could have got at him."[6] (*Saul* was a play in which Voltaire expressed his usual contempt for the contents of the Old Testament.) The Bible had become part of secular literature.

Here there is an indication of a general shift in opinion that started more or less in Goethe's time and continues to the present. Up to the mid-eighteenth century, "literature" was almost anything written; discussions of the literature of various peoples included whatever documents a people had left behind—not just stories, but histories, laws, religious texts, and so on. With a few exceptions,[7] literature today refers to artistic creations such as plays, poetry, and novels—matters referred to earlier as "belles-lettres."

Born along by this rising tide, novels in the nineteenth century came to have a prestige they had not earlier enjoyed, for they became a serious way of commenting on life, whereas in Sheridan's 1775 play *The Rivals*, the passion for novels shown by some of the characters was a sign of

[4] On the historical-critical method, see ibid., vol. 1, 295–98 [Book 7]; on the real meaning of the Bible, ibid., vol. 2, 131–34 [Book 12].

[5] Ibid., vol. 1, 362–63 [Book 8].

[6] Ibid., vol. 2, 132 [Book 12].

[7] It is still usual to refer to academic and scientific publications as the "literature" on a given subject, although no one would accuse these of artistic merit.

their superficiality. The stage and even more its celluloid derivative, the cinema, have also become much more respectable, and the sort of general public support for subsidizing and attending performances and showings today is not too different in psychology from the sort of public support that can be expected for church/synagogue attendance and upkeep.[8]

4. *Discussions of the nature and origins of language*

That language is as much a constraint on our thinking as well as a means of expressing our ideas is a philosophical theme whose charm is that the subject discussed and the means of discussion are identical. In the eighteenth century the theory of language, both its nature and its origins, attracted a great deal of discussion. Several theologians made contributions that were important outside the realm of theology.

In the seventeenth century it was assumed that language was simply the expression of more or less complete ideas already formed in the brain. Ideally, according to this theory, it would be possible to formulate a language of symbols that would represent ideas in any language, since clear and distinct ideas would be the same in educated speech the world over. It was assumed that Egyptian hieroglyphs were one possible model for this universal script. In a world where clear, distinct ideas had the psychological advantage in evaluating human experience, poetry could take on a somewhat prosaic tone. Pope's couplet sums up one strain of thought:

> True art is nature to advantage dressed;
> What oft was thought but ne'er so well expressed.

In some ways this theory of language fitted in with a view of the Bible as a series of doctrinal statements which were consistent with one another and which could be arranged into a logical, harmonious whole. The Bible provided the building blocks for the factually exact statements of dogmatics.

---

[8] Carl Jung suggested that movie stars are the reincarnation of ancient gods and goddesses. Without going this far, the cult of the stars, with an accompanying erudition about their lives and morals to the point of devotees knowing when their favorites got their false teeth, clearly provides the sort of images by which many people live and which Goethe found in his picture Bible, among other sources. (Goethe, *Autobiography*, vol. 1, 30–32).

But poetry, even Pope's, has always been more than philosophical truth in verse form, and while Molière's Monsieur Jourdain might well be correct that he had been speaking prose all his life, some people felt that poetry carried a dimension of evocation, color, and meanings beyond the grasp of logic that distinguished it from prose. At all events, this was what Robert Lowth thought, and he tried to show, in his *De Sacra poesi Hebraeorum ("Lectures on the Sacred Poetry of the Hebrews"),* that this should be borne in mind when we try to appreciate the Bible.

i. Robert Lowth (1710–1787)

Lowth had a distinguished career as a scholar and bishop. As professor of poetry at Oxford, he gave a series of lectures in Latin on the poetry of the Old Testament between 1741 and 1750, which he published in two volumes in 1752–1753.[9] While Lowth devoted much of his lectures to the analysis of Hebrew poetics, a complicated subject at best, what is interesting is his insistence both on the nature of poetry and how it was typical of earlier stages of culture. In lecture 4 he begins:

> The origin and first use of poetical language are undoubtedly to be traced into the vehement affections of the mind. For what is meant by that singular frenzy of poets, which the Greeks, ascribing to divine inspiration, distinguished by the appellation of enthusiasm, but a style and expression directly prompted by nature itself, and exhibiting the true and express image of a mind violently agitated? When, as it were, the secret avenues, the interior recesses of the soul are thrown open; when the inmost conceptions are displayed, rushing together in one turbid stream, without order or connection. Hence sudden exclamations, frequent interrogations, apostrophes even to inanimate objects: for to those, who are violently agitated themselves, the universal nature of things seems under a necessity of being affected with similar emotions. Every impulse of the mind, however, has not only a peculiar style and expression, but a certain tone of voice, and a certain gesture of the body adapted to it. Some, indeed, not satisfied with that expression which language affords, have added to it dancing and song; and as we know there existed in the first ages a very strict connection between these arts and that of poetry, we may possibly be indebted to them for the accurately

---

[9] *De sacra poesi Hebraeorum,* published in 1753 and in various editions thereafter. The lectures were translated into several languages, including French and German. The English translation, *Lectures on the Sacred Poetry of the Hebrews,* was made by G. Gregory in 1787, along with notes from J. D. Michaelis and others.

admeasured verses and feet, to the end that the modulation of the language might accord with the music of the voice, and the motion of the body.

Poetry, in this its rude origin and commencement, being derived from nature, was in time improved by art, and applied to the purposes of utility and delight. For as it owed its birth to the affections of the mind, and had availed itself of the assistance of harmony, it was found, on account of the exact and vivid delineation of the objects which it described, to be excellently adapted to the exciting of every internal emotion, and making a more forcible impression upon the mind than abstract reasoning could possibly effect; it was found capable of interesting and affecting the senses and passions, of captivating the ear, of directing the perception to the minutest circumstances, and of assisting the memory in the retention of them.[10]

Lowth was introducing an aesthetic criterion into the interpretation of the Bible, arguing that the artistic form of a passage should be appreciated before one goes on to exegesis. Obviously, what Lowth was saying would apply especially to the writings of the prophets, whom he saw as primarily poets.

ii. JOHANN DAVID MICHAELIS (1717–1791) ON LANGUAGE

Michaelis, who had run into Lowth's ideas during his stay in Oxford, wrote an essay which received a prize from the Berlin Academy on the subject of *De l'influence des opinions sur le langage et du langage sur les opinions* ("On the influence of ideas on language and of language on opinions"), in which he argued that rather than speech merely linking the mind to the outside world, it would be more appropriate to allow for the influence of the nature of a language on what was going on in the mind. An incomplete language restricts the ability of the mind to think. Michaelis did not break entirely with the old tradition of the mind finding words to express its perceptions on reality, for he assumed that the expressiveness of a tongue is limited by the number of words in its vocabulary, but it was an early attempt to show a reciprocal relationship between language and thinking.

iii. CHRISTIAN GOTTLOB HEYNE (1729–1812)

A more imaginative approach to language was that of Christian Gottlob Heyne, who argued in a Vico-like manner that there are different sorts of

[10] Lowth, *Sacred Poetry* (Gregory translation).

language that correspond to various developments in the history of human culture. Heyne applied this to the Greek writings, which he saw as beginning with myths. This use of "myth" was a deviation from its traditional usage (for example, in Comes[11]) to describe pagan and untrue stories about the gods, which had been derived from historical stories in the Old Testament. Heyne was in fact reversing the order of how myth was explained; instead of explaining the origins of myth from Old Testament stories as in Comes, the origin of accounts in the Bible were explained from myths. It soon became clear that this category of myth could be applied to material in both the Old and the New Testaments.

A closely related issue was the question of the ultimate origins of language. Without actually confronting the issue directly, more and more this question tended to be divorced from the story of Adam and Eve in general discussion. Rather, it was assumed that language developed by natural processes in the early history of the human race. One idea that was revived was the story from classical antiquity about Psammeticus II of Egypt, who decided to test the belief of the Egyptians that their language was the oldest in the world. Psammeticus instructed that two children should be separated at birth from all human language to see what they would produce on their own. One day the attendant came in with their food, and they called out "becos." Inquiry was made to see where this word occurred among known languages, and it appeared to be the same as the Scythian word for "bread," so the conclusion was reached that the Scythian language was the oldest and Egyptian only the second oldest language.[12] Whether this account was historical is an interesting question, but in the eighteenth century some people, such as Jean Formey (1711–1797), suggested that this experiment ought to be tried out again, possibly using orphans in public care.[13]

---

[11] Natalis Comes (1520–1582), *Mythologiae, sive Explicationis Fabularum* (Geneva: Samuel Crispinus, 1620). This was the edition available to me; there are numerous editions.

[12] Herodotus, *History*, Book 2.

[13] Jean-Henri Formey, *Abhandlung über dem Ursprung der Gesellschaft und der Sprache* (Berlin: Pauli, 1763) 14–23. [This is described as a translation from the French, but I have not been able to find the title of the original.] Formey (1711–1797) was a pastor of the French-speaking Hugenotte community in Berlin. He had wide philosophical interests and on the recommendation of Pierre-Louis Moreau de Maupertuis became secretary of the Berlin Academy. There are records of actual attempts in earlier centuries to replicate this experiment of Psammetichus.

iv. JOHANN GOTTFRIED HERDER (1744–1803)

Johann Gottfried Herder will be discussed under various headings in this chapter. Herder's meeting with Goethe in a tavern in Strasbourg in 1770 and their subsequent friendship were some of the important events that were to influence the outburst of German creativity in the late eighteenth century, for Herder inspired others, as well as being himself a fount of exciting ideas, not all of which he was able to develop as fully as he wished.[14] Herder was not a technical scholar in the mold of Semler or Ernesti, but he nonetheless had a great influence in the interpretation of the Bible. He ignored the concentration on details of academic investigation and luxuriated in the wider world of the aesthetic appreciation of works of art and the intoxicating property of great ideas. At the same time, he found the source of his theology, not in a supernaturally imposed source to be given special and reverent treatment, but within the creations of humanity at its best. This meant that his approach to religious matters was marked by an exuberance that denied both the exaggerated reverence of orthodox interpreters and the reasoned but somewhat bloodless standpoint of the *philosophes*. Herder's prize essay, *Abhandlung über den Ursprung der Sprache (Essay on the Origin of Language)*, can be interpreted both as a rejection of a supernatural explanation as put forward by Süssmilch and of an over-rationalized purely instrumental interpretation as in Condillac. The combination of historical inquiry and aesthetic awareness was to provide one way for biblical interpretation to escape from the looming crisis it faced.

5. *Changes in Protestant theology*

There can be no doubt that between the seventeenth and the nineteenth century, Protestant theology underwent extraordinary changes, as indeed did almost every other facet of life in western Europe and its cultural extensions elsewhere. In predominantly Roman Catholic countries, theology tended to follow a different pattern, which deserves its own treatment, but it was to be mainly within a Protestantism with the burr of Judaism under its saddle in which modern biblical studies were

---

[14] In the case of Goethe, it is regrettable that he appears to have woken up one morning to discover that he had undergone a sort of metamorphosis, not into a cockroach, which might have been bearable, but into an institution, which made him even less of a human being. His meanness to his old friends in his latter years showed that while he was a great writer, he was not a great man.

worked out. For various reasons the great Roman Catholic tradition of biblical scholarship that was so important in the Renaissance was allowed to languish.[15]

Even at that time the changes that had taken place were obvious to many. Carl Friedrich Stäudlin's *Geschichte der Theologischen Wissenschaften*[16] is a superbly written account on the part of a Kantian who had seen theology change. In the twentieth century, the most elaborate attempt to explain the changes within Protestantism was Emanuel Hirsch's *Geschichte der Neuern Evangelischen Theologie.*[17] It is unfortunate that this work has not been made available in other languages, possibly for reasons due to its author's personal history.[18] Still, Hirsch's work is very important, for he connected changes in theology with changes going on in politics, philosophy, and society in general. In particular, he devoted a section to the creative breakthrough in German intellectual and spiritual life ("Geistesleben"), which he situates in the second half of the eighteenth century.

In order to understand some of the changes of emphasis in biblical exegesis over the past three hundred years, one has to bear in mind the differences between what most Protestants thought at the beginning of the eighteenth century and what their modern descendants are likely to believe. (Roman Catholics may find parallels in their own experience.) Some perceptions are seen as less important; God is less likely to be seen as a terrible, vengeful authoritarian figure visiting eternal and excruciating punishments on those who deny him; the present world is not seen as a vale of tears but as a place well worth our attention and capable of improvement; Christians of other confessions are not necessarily going to hell for not belonging to the true church, and even unbelievers or members of other religions may show up in heaven without upsetting us

---

[15] I would like to make clear that this observation is not to be interpreted as Protestant triumphalism but as a historical fact that needs investigation.

[16] Carl Stäudlin, *Geschichte der theologischen Wissenschaften seit der Verbreitung der alten Litteratur.* (Göttingen:Vandenhoek und Ruprecht, 1811). See also Christian Heinrich, *Versuch einer Geschichte der Verschiedener Lehrarten der Christlichen Galubenswahrheiten* (Leipzig: Weidmann, 1790).

[17] Gütersloh: Güterslöher Verlags Haus Gerd Mohn, 1949; 5 vols.

[18] To be blunt, Hirsch was an enthusiastic member of the Nazi party, much more openly than Heidegger. As a result, his work has been under a shadow; several of those who helped him complete it preferred to remain anonymous. That a professor of Christian theology should be caught up by something so evil is a warning of the weakness of human nature to those of us who have not been similarly tempted—so far.

too much; ghoulies and ghosties and long-legged beasties and things that go bump in the night are not seen as real threats,[19] but viruses and various pollutants are; the devil as the personal incarnation of evil has faded, but evil itself is as real as ever; there is a variation of concern with creeds and items of belief across the spectrum of the Christian churches, but even among churches that take their theoretical theology seriously, about 99.5 percent of the members, especially the clergy, would be incapable of explaining the traditional doctrine of the Trinity adequately; sexual mores are less stringent, and divorce (or its equivalent) is generally tolerated; illegitimate children do not carry a lifelong stigma, and a man may marry his deceased wife's sister without scandal.

But if some things have been relaxed, other matters are taken more seriously. Racism of any sort is a major sin, and slavery is something to be stamped out; our responsibilities have increased as the world has become more accessible; social and economic structures are to be scrutinized and if necessary reformed; women's rights to equal treatment, even down to the last grammatical detail, are a holy object that must not be profaned.[20] Obviously, this list could be extended much further, but the point remains: things have changed a great deal in Protestantism.

In more recent historical studies of the eighteenth century, it is usual to distinguish between three general groups among Protestant theologians: the orthodox, the neologians, and the rationalists.[21] The orthodox were those who chose to swim against the tide and hold on to the traditional formulations of orthodox dogmatics, including the infallibility of the Bible and its verbal inspiration. The rationalists were those who felt that while revelation might have been a step up, once one reached a view of religion in conformity with reason, this viewpoint was self-authenticating and required no further support from revealed truth. The neologians occupied a mediating position; revelation was indeed neces-

---

[19] Ghosts, rather than being threats, have become curiosities. There is one ancient library in Britain, which will remain anonymous, where the librarians are quite convinced there are two ghosts around all the time. There was a third ghost, but it was upsetting people and was exorcised for bad behavior. Even ghosts must obey library rules about courtesy to other readers.

[20] In the late nineteenth century it was appropriate to sum up the gospel as the brotherhood of man and fatherhood of God, expressed in the acronym BOMFOG; now we are more used to the motherhood of God and the sisterhood of women, or MOGSOW.

[21] Karl Aner, *Die Theologie der Lessingzeit* (Halle/Salle: Max Niemeyer, 1929).

sary, but it was never out of step with reason, which was the standard by which material could be judged to be revealed or not.

There are two points to bear in mind about this classification. First, like all classifications it obscures differences among members of various groups even as it obscures connections between those within and those without. This means that there is always the problem of who belongs in which classification; for example are Michaelis and Semler to be classified as neologians? Second, this classification was done after the fact. Thus while the word "neologian" was indeed in use in the eighteenth century, it tended to be almost a word of contempt for anyone who deviated from pure orthodoxy. Therefore, while the distinction between orthodox, neologians, and rationalists is useful for understanding history, it is not itself historical.

Furthermore, members of all three groups considered themselves to be members or near-members of a Protestant church. Even the rationalists such as Lessing were very far from being outright opponents of the Christian faith in the manner of the French philosophes. And while Lessing eventually became a follower of Spinoza, the determinism he espoused was not the same as the mechanical determinism of La Mettrie or the Baron d'Holbach.

Another change in theology in the course of the eighteenth century was the growth of a spirit of toleration. At one time polemical theology, the refutation of the claims of other groups to be considered Christian, was part of the honor of being the senior professor in a theological faculty. As time went on, the level of the rhetoric declined, and even polemical theology changed its name. In a figure like Johann Bernhard Basedow (1723–1790), one finds a pan-religious tolerance to the extent that other religions were known, and in his schooling system Basedow created prayers that could be used by Christians, Jews, and Muslims together. Lessing's play *Nathan the Wise* was a far more literary and effective discussion of the same theme. Here one has the inversion of the *Story of the Three Imposters*; instead of all religions being false, each was in its own way true.[22]

For our purposes, how have these changes affected the understanding of the Bible? Since 1750 to 1800 is the turning point of biblical studies,

---

[22] *The Three Imposters* was a title of a book often mentioned in the seventeenth century. It was alleged to have shown that the founders of the three religions (Moses, Jesus, and Mohammed) had simply deceived gullible humans about religion for their own interests. It is possible that the title circulated long before someone wrote a book by that name, but the whole matter is complicated and far from resolved.

what happened in this period that represents a shift in attitude on the part of some of the leading thinkers of the day?

II. Biblical Scholarship

1. *The situation from 1750*

It has been the argument of this book so far that people had been aware of problems within the Bible from the time of the church fathers on. For the most part, defenders of the Bible had adopted the strategy of either an ad hoc defense of each problem or an admission that a problem did indeed exist, but the fact that they could not explain the reason for the difficulty did not exclude the possibility of a solution being found. In the meantime, texts were accumulated and compared, knowledge of languages was increased, and various solutions were tentatively tried out in the hope of getting a better understanding of the Bible.

Among the major issues at stake were revelation and the inspiration of the Bible (was this a question of its authority or its factuality?) and the *analogia fidei* (was the Bible consistent within itself?). What was the relation or indeed the relevance of this ancient book to new views of the physical world and new discussions of the inner world we humans experience as our constant companion? In fact, there were variations in how individual scholars saw the matter; for some, inaccuracies were due to Moses' need to explain matters in terms understandable by his audience; Andreas Masius could explain irregularities by Moses' combination of different, older documents; some authors allowed for an inspiration that did not erase the style of the author; others allowed for errors in matters that were not that important. If all else failed, one could always explain problems as the result of incompetent scribes or, in the case of the Old Testament, even malicious alterations made by the Jews to spite the Christians. However, for many scholars in the mid-eighteenth century, the whole structure of holding up the special nature of the Bible as a book deserving special treatment simply fell over from the weight of the problems where explanations only generated new difficulties.

However, there were two relatively new ways of dealing with passages that presented problems of morality, consistency, or believability. The first way was the history of documents. If one had documents from different eras that discussed the same subjects, then it was not surprising if they differed in their perceptions and presentations. For example, 2 Samuel 24:1 says, "Again the anger of the LORD was kindled against

Israel, and he incited David against them, saying, 'Go, count the people of Israel and Judah.'" In 1 Chronicles 21:1 the same incident is introduced by the words "And Satan stood up against Israel, and provoked David to number Israel." There is an insuperable inconsistency here, but if you take into account the different times in which each passage was written, then the problem can be explained as the result of the author of Chronicles trying to smooth over a passage that might give offense.[23]

The second way of dealing with inconsistency was to invoke the history of culture. "Culture" as a word began to appear from 1750 on to describe the sum total of a nation's attributes, perceptions, and amusements. Given that Israelite culture differed from one era to the next, it was only to be expected that documents from different periods of Israel's history might well have had a different slant on law, morality, and theology.

In the second half of the eighteenth century, some German biblical scholars made substantial progress toward finding a creative solution to how the Bible could be treated on the same basis as any other ancient book in accounting for its history, and yet at the same time preserving its significance for religious faith. It was on this basis that the scholars in the nineteenth century were able to work out a place for a reasonable understanding of the Bible in a situation where discoveries in ancient history and modern science challenged many of the traditional structures that had formerly appeared to support the importance of the Bible. Needless to say, not everyone was convinced, but then in the modern world we live in a situation where beliefs that are universally convincing are no longer possible.

2. *Two giants in the land: Semler and Michaelis*

Two particular scholars were influential in so many ways during this period that it is easier to treat them first, namely, Johann Salomo Semler and Johannn David Michaelis.

i. Johann Salomo Semler (1725–1791)

Semler is usually seen, and properly so, as the person who incarnated the spirit of the new theology of the period. The extent to which he was responsible for every new idea of the time is a debate that can be left to

---

[23] In the Old Testament the figure of Satan occurs only in Job and Chronicles; the identification of Satan with the snake of the Garden of Eden story is a postbiblical interpretation.

more detailed studies. One can say that had Semler not existed, it would have been necessary to invent him. He summed up in his work the application of historical and cultural criteria to both the shape and the truth of theology. His published output was as prodigious as it was cloudy, even by German standards. His contemporaries vied with each other to describe the prolix and less than lucid nature of his prose, as well as the fascinating but not always completed or consistent nature of some of his positions. Perhaps their undertaking was doomed from the start; only a master of French such as Jean Le Clerc or Pierre Bayle could have achieved a succinct summing up. Despite his stylistic weaknesses, Semler was nonetheless a guiding spirit of the theology of his day and even participated in the wider enthusiasm for natural science when in his old age he took up botany and made several interesting contributions to the subject.[24]

Semler's distinctive approach in biblical exegesis, doctrine, and church history was to ask, What were the historical circumstances that led to the origin of a document and in what ways were the cultural assumptions and immediate concerns that motivated writers different from the thought world of the current interpreter? The effect of this question was to remove any a priori assumptions about the authority, the value, and the mode of interpreting the document in question. Even when a document was valuable, its truth was not necessarily established for all time, for theological statements were limited in the extent to which they were useful beyond the times when they were written, and no theological work could hope to be as valuable for ever as it was for its time of origin.

In order to appreciate Semler's position, one has to bear in mind that Semler, like others such as Johann Philipp Gabler, made a clear distinction between theology and religion. Religion is the essential part of a living faith; it is an individual's personal commitment to God and a devout life. Theology is simply the formal, academic description of the nature of religion. As such, theology is a professional matter for the scholar, whose task it is to explain the origin and the meaning of various theological statements and documents. This distinction led Semler into a curious

---

[24] The most useful treatment of Semler is Gottfried Hornig, *Die Anfänge der historische-kritischen Theologie: Johann Salomo Semlers Schriftverständnis und seine Stellung zu Luther* (Göttingen: Vandenhoeck und Ruprecht, 1961). Hornig's work is as much concerned with Semler's Lutheranism as his scholarly methods, but to be fair, Semler himself was almost as concerned as well.

dichotomy he saw between the public statements of a given faith and the private expression of this faith in individual members.

It is beyond the purpose of this book to discuss this facet of Semler's thought in detail, but a short note is appropriate. Official religions have different forms which are human constructions but which are politically useful. For Semler, it was his duty as a Lutheran to leave the public theological statements of his confession inviolate. His own personal faith was beyond the control of the authorities, and in fact it was not in their interest to interfere so long as a citizen he continued to endorse the official statements. Semler's position tends to escape our modern comprehension and certainly our sympathy; still, it explains why he opposed Karl Friedrich Bahrdt's appointment to a university. Bahrdt was a radical in theology, but it is an open question whether in the matter of private religious opinions Bahrdt and Semler were all that widely separated. What Semler objected to in Bahrdt's theological position was that Bahrdt wished to change the statements of public religion.

Semler's emphasis on seeing texts in their historical and cultural settings was the thread running throughout his work throughout his life. In his 1764 work[25] *Historische und Kritische Sammlung Über die so genannten Beweisstellen in der Dogmatik,* Semler argued that it is not accurate to find the doctrine of the Trinity in the Old Testament on historical grounds. In his advice to students published in 1757, he pointed out that the Bible consists of many books, which were not all written at the same time by one author under identical circumstances, and this must be taken into account in making sense of them.[26] Respect for the actual meaning of an original author is paramount, and the ignorant Bible user who finds personal guidance everywhere in Scripture is no different from the learned scholar who finds his own ideas confirmed by Scripture.[27]

Whether or not one agrees with Semler in every detail, one must admit that he was making a reasonable attempt to cope with the obvious argument that not everything in Scripture is improving, inspiring, or even tasteful. The arguments of the Deists or Voltaire that the contents of the Bible are not always admirable can be met with the explanation that the Bible is the product of historical processes in the life of a small

---

[25] (Halle: Hemmerde, 1768?) part 2, 17–23.

[26] *Versuch einer nähren Anleitung zu nützlichem Fleisse in der ganzen Gottesgelersamkeit für angehende Studiosus Theologiae* (Halle: Justinus Gebauer, 1757) 175.

[27] *Vorbereitung zur theologischen Hermeneutik zu weiterer Beförderung des Fleisses angehender Gottesgelerten,* 4 vols. (Halle: 1760 vol.) 1, 7.

Middle Eastern nation whose actions and beliefs did not always correspond with the nature of the God whom they worshiped.

Furthermore, an awareness of the historical circumstances behind biblical ordinances can help us see that laws laid down for particular circumstances are not binding on the church for all ages. Similarly, on matters of doctrine one can take a local situation into account, for Semler pointed out that St. Paul did not write the same sort of letters to the Galatians as he did to the Corinthians. Indeed, even within the New Testament in general, one sees different sorts of theology, such as the tension between followers of Peter and followers of Paul.

What Semler, along with others of similar opinions, provided was an attitude toward the Bible that freed the theologians from trying to pretend that the Bible was other than it was and from trying to make their opinions conform to a book that was not completely coherent within itself.

ii. JOHANN DAVID MICHAELIS (1717–1791)

Another figure who contributed to the new attitude toward the Bible was Johann David Michaelis, who, while not as daring as Semler in his evaluation of the contents of the Bible, nonetheless made some interesting contributions to biblical studies. Michaelis was an excellent language scholar and introduced Robert Lowth's lectures on language to the German public, but he also made three contributions toward changing the perception of the Bible.

First, he wrote a work on the laws of the Bible.[28] This subject was scarcely new, but rather than starting from the Bible and then going on to discuss law in general, Michaelis took as his model Montesquieu, whose *Esprit des Lois* tried to sum up how laws and constitutions worked.[29] Instead of assuming divine intervention in the laws of Israel, Michaelis sought naturalistic explanations based on matters such as cultural differences, health reasons, and tradition. By taking this approach, he was able to show why Israelite conceptions of law should not determine what

---

[28] Johann David Michaelis, *Mosaisches Recht*, 6 parts (Frankfort a.M.: Garbe, 1770–1775). Reprinted at various times in the eighteenth century.

[29] Montesquieu was to have a great influence on the thinking of the framers of the United States Constitution, whose form was based on Montesquieu's distinction between the legislative, the executive, and the judicial functions of government. Much of Montequieu's thought was based on his perception of the limited monarchy in England, which is why the United States got rid of George III but preserved the system he represented.

eighteenth-century European states ought to do, but understood in relation to their own times, the Israelite laws were quite reasonable.[30]

Second, Michaelis developed a new form of the presentation of scholars' opinions. Collections of the works of different scholars, such as the *Critici Sacri* of Pearson, the works of Jean de la Haye, and the huge volumes of Ugolino, were well-known, as were learned journals that provided overviews of what scholars were doing. But in his *Einleitung in die göttlichen Schriften des neuen Bundes*, Michaelis developed the format that we associate with "introductions" today, namely, a counterpoint of problems encountered in biblical interpretation, along with the approaches taken by various scholars. As his work went through various editions, Michaelis refined and expanded it. It was translated into English both in its earliest and latest forms, in the latter case by Herbert Marsh, who smoothed over Michaelis's somewhat inelegant style and made developments in German scholarship available for the English-speaking world.[31]

Third, Michaelis was responsible for one of the more rigorous explorations of the Near East undertaken up to his time. Travelers had been bringing back accounts of biblical lands for centuries, and scholars had made visits to learn languages or accumulate manuscripts, but Michaelis proposed a more rigorous undertaking in which a series of questions written by himself would form the agenda for the investigation to be undertaken by a group of trained observers. This captured the imagination of many, and during the occupation of Göttingen during the Seven Years' War, the occupying French army was under strict instructions not to interfere with his person or his project. Not everything works out as it should: the questions Michaelis prepared were not ready by the time the experts sailed and had to be sent after them. Of the five experts in different fields, only one, Cartsten Niebuhr, returned alive from the trip, but he brought back a great deal of material, including drawings of cuneiform inscriptions accurate enough to be used as sources when the key to the script was finally found in the nineteenth century.[32]

---

[30] It is now almost impossible for us to really understand those who felt that the removal of James II was an act of impiety, however much they regretted the direction his rule was taking.

[31] *Introduction to the New Testament*, transl. Herbert Marsh (Cambridge: Archdacon 1793–1801). The translation of the first edition was published in 1759 and 1761.

[32] An English abridged translation of his account is *Niebuhr's travels through Arabia* (Edinburgh: 1792).

Michaelis published his questions in German, and a French translation followed swiftly after.[33] He did not wish to let too cryptic a style obscure the finer points he wanted investigated, so for one hundred questions there are several hundred pages of commentary (nearly five hundred in German, six hundred in French). He gives instructions about how the investigators were to proceed, such as the keeping of journals; the buying of manuscripts (biblical preferred; important rather than the beautiful); attention to social conditions, such as the effects of polygamy; and at the end of the book is a table of the dynasties of Yemen with instructions for further investigation. The questions themselves cover a great number of topics: what is the depth of the Red Sea where the Israelites crossed; do flying fish exist in the Red Sea, and are these identical with the "quails" of the Exodus story; what is the leprosy of houses and clothing; are fields sown with only one type of seed today as required in Leviticus 19:19; is there a wood that sweetens water; what are local terms for various items and peoples; and so on. Michaelis made it clear that it was facts, not theories, he was interested in. The whole undertaking had every right to be considered the first strictly scientific expedition to gather information about the geographical setting of the Bible.

3. *The Old Testament text*

Michaelis in his memoirs recalled that when he went to Oxford, everyone took for granted that there were no problems with the Masoretic Text of the Old Testament. One should always be suspicious of human memory, especially in autobiographical accounts, but Michaelis was correct to the extent that not as much work had been done on the Old Testament as on the New, and even the learned Johannes Buxtorff (Senior) relied on already printed texts for his edition of the text. Benjamin Kennicott set out to remedy this situation both in his own work and in the work of collaborators in various parts of Europe. In 1776 and 1780, Kennicott published his *Vetus Testamentum Hebraicum cum Variis Lectionibus*, based on six hundred and fifteen Hebrew manuscripts, sixteen Samaritan manuscripts, and fifty-two previous editions.

---

[33] *Fragen an eine Gesellschaft gelehrter Mäner, die auf Befehl ihro Majestät des Königes von Dänemark nach Arabien reisen* (Frankfurt am Main: bey Johann Gottlieb Garbe, 1762). *Recueil de Question, traduit de l'Alleman* (Franfort sure le Mayn: Jean Gottlieb Garbe, 1763). Only the French edition was available to me.

Kennicott's work had some weaknesses in its approach, such as his ignoring the evidence of the differences in pointing, and he did not have many older manuscripts to work from, but he did stimulate interest in a better Old Testament text.

4. *Documents in the Pentateuch*

It had been suggested from at least the time of Masius that Moses had made use of preexisting material when he wrote the Pentateuch. Richard Simon had even postulated the existence of prophetic scribes who added material after the time of Moses. Nobody had raised the question of whether one could see patterns in the material behind the Pentateuch until Witter's *Iura Israelitarum in Palaestinam* was published in 1711.[34] It is not correct to say that Witter was ignored completely; he was reviewed in Loescher's *Unschuldige Nachrichten* and mentioned with approval by Johann Edelmann. Johann Gabler, in his edition of the *Urgeschichte* to be discussed below (p. 251), mentions Witter in a footnote. However, Witter did not attract a great deal of attention,[35] and instead it was to be a French medical doctor, Jean Astruc (1684–1766), who was to be credited with founding the documentary hypothesis in his work *Conjectures sur les Mémoires Originaux Dont il paroit que Moyse s'est servi pour composer le Livre de la Gènese.*[36]

Astruc made clear in his introduction that his purpose was to defend Moses' authorship of the Pentateuch but that he was at first reluctant to publish his work because "les esprits forts" might take it as an attack on the Bible. However, he had submitted the work to a learned man, who told him that the same ideas had already been discussed by Fleury and Le François. Given that there still exist people who exhibit a stultifying ignorance by suggesting that any attempt to find sources in Genesis is necessarily a deliberate attempt to reduce its authority, it is a historical fact that, whether you agree with Astruc or not, he intended to defend the Bible.

Astruc argued, on the basis of the different names for God in Genesis, the dislocations in chronology, and the repetitions of material that Moses had at least four recognizable documents before him, along with fragments

---

[34] Henning Witter, *Iura Israelitarum in Palaestinam terram Chananaeam commentatione in Genesin perpetua sic demonstrata* (Hildesia: Schröder, 1711).

[35] *Urgeschichte*, 1:2.

[36] Brussels: 1753.

from up to eight others. Some of these documents may even have been from non-Israelite sources. This suggestion of Astruc's about sources in the Pentateuch was to be a seminal idea in Old Testament criticism from then on. Michaelis, it is true, did not agree with his theory, but Michaelis was very conservative in his defense of Moses as an original writer. On the other hand, Johann Eichhorn took over Astruc's ideas, and the debate began about the relative age of each document. It was not until Karl Graf made his suggestion to Julius Wellhausen later in the nineteenth century that an explanation emerged that satisfied a significant number of scholars.

5. *The New Testament*

i. JOHANN JAKOB GRIESBACH (1745–1812)

Griesbach, a pupil of Semler's, produced a notable edition of the Greek text of the New Testament in which he was the first to deviate in more than incidental ways from following the *Textus Receptus* in his edition of the text.[37] Building on the work of Wettstein, he added to the number of manuscripts consulted and attempted to work out the recensions of the text that lay behind the various manuscripts that survive. Griesbach refined the classification of families of manuscripts and further refined the rules for judging which were the better readings.

Compared with Wettstein's work, the actual format of the Griesbach edition is rather disappointing. It does not contain the additional evidence that Wettstein put in the third section of each page, and the printing is cramped and of indifferent quality. It is possible that this was an edition meant more for students than for scholars, libraries, or collectors to purchase.[38]

But apart from his textual work in itself, Griesbach added a new dimension to the criticism of the first three Gospels. If one compares the four Gospels, the first three have more in common with each other than they do with John, which differs markedly in style, order, chronology,

---

[37] A brief explanation might clarify. When a scholar publishes a scholarly edition of a biblical text, he or she has at the top of the page the text he or she thinks most likely. Exceptions are noted in the *apparatus criticus* below this text. Previous scholars had followed the 1634 *Textus Receptus*—more or less—even though they felt quite strongly that it was less accurate than their best guess. Griesbach was taking a risk in deviating from this text.

[38] I have only been able to consult the edition printed in Halle by Curt in 1776.

and material presented. In fact, the resemblances in Greek are so close in the actual wording of the text that if the Synoptic Gospels were answers on separate examination papers, the examiner would immediately assume collusion, and the only problem would be to find out who copied from whom.

However, the resemblances between Matthew, Mark, and Luke only become clear when you have them in parallel columns. The way the Gospels were compared traditionally was in harmonies of the Gospels, that is, attempts to produce a single coherent account of Jesus' life and actions out of four different books. Such works had been produced in the church from the time of Tatian, whose *Diatessaron* was written in the second century C.E. This tradition was carried on in Renaissance times by scholars such as Nicholaus Mercator (1620–1687), but Jean Le Clerc added a new twist, for in his harmony of the Gospels, instead of homogenizing the differences, he printed out the Gospels in parallel columns so that the reader could easily compare both the order and the wording of the four Gospels.[39] His work was superbly printed in a handsome folio volume; the passages from the Gospels, opening with Luke's, are set out in the order in which they occur in their original works, and where they overlap with each other; there is plenty of white space in the layout.

The shape of written materials is more important for their interpretation than is often realized. When the early church pioneered the codex, that is, the book as we know it in contrast to the scroll, it opened the way for a more accurate and assiduous comparison of biblical passages. Anyone who has worked with the modern scroll, that is, the microfilm roll, knows how tedious the task is of switching back and forth from one page of a work to another. The Complutensian Polyglot is an example of how this can be taken further; it printed on one page the same biblical text in different versions so that the readers could compare different renderings without having to shuttle back and forth to where they had stuck various fingers into different parts of the work.

Le Clerc's harmony went that much further to show as never before how much the first three Gospels have in common and how hard it is to integrate John into the pattern. He also made some shrewd observations in the course of his work. He was convinced that Luke and John and even Mark followed the order of events more accurately than Matthew, an observation he may have derived from Scaliger. Le Clerc was also

---

[39] *Harmonia Evangelia . . . auctore Joanne Clerico* (Amsterdam: Suptibus Huguetano-rum, 1699).

convinced that while all the evangelists mention deeds and words of Jesus in a satisfactory way, they often disregard the circumstances and the exact wording. He felt that neither one nor all of the evangelists have all the deeds and words of Christ, and he gave up the attempt to make them agree.

While Griesbach was clear that he was not trying to write a harmony of the Gospels, it is evident that he was following Le Clerc's layout in his work, except that he gave up the unequal task of trying to integrate John into the picture. Griesbach entitled this first part of his edition of the Greek New Testament *Synopsis Evangeliorum Matthaei Marci et Lucae una cum iis Joannis pericopis quae omnino cum caeterorum Evangelistarum narrationibus conferendae sunt.* "Synopsis" originally meant "overview," but his form of arrangement has become by extension a description of the contents, so the first three Gospels have since been known as the Synoptic Gospels.

Griesbach eventually decided that Mark was not an abridgement of Matthew, as had usually been assumed up to that time; rather, Matthew wrote first, Luke came later, and Mark's was the latest Gospel, copied from both Matthew and Luke. Griesbach's theory did not command general assent, though in the history of New Testament interpretation his solution is revived periodically. The irony is that the most popular explanation among scholars today, namely, that Mark was the first Gospel, was proposed by Gottlob Christian Storr (1746–1805) in his 1786 book *Über den Zweck der evangelischen Geschichte und der Briefe Johannis,* though it would be some time before anything like a majority consensus on this matter was achieved. The irony consisted in the fact that Storr was a rather conservative scholar whose other work was in retrospect less than exciting. To be honest, it is possible that no completely convincing explanation will ever be offered because we have no reliable contemporary witnesses about the writing of the Gospels, and it is possible that unrecorded and therefore unrecoverable particular circumstances lie behind what actually happened.

However, Griesbach was the first to raise the question of the literary relationships between the Gospels, especially the Synoptics, and this represented a new departure that sprang from the increasingly historical questions asked about the origins of the Bible.

ii. JOHANN AUGUST ERNESTI (1707–1781)

Ernesti was in the tradition of Erasmus and Camerarus in his writings on hermeneutics. For Ernesti, the way to understand ancient documents was to pay careful attention to grammar, style, and the meanings words had at particular periods in their history. His view of the Bible was very conservative; he assumed that careful philological interpretation would elucidate all necessary doctrine. In particular, in his monograph "De Vanitate Philosophantium in Interpretatione Librorum S.[acrorum]" ("The Vanity of Philosophizing in the Interpretation of Sacred Scripture"),[40] he rejected the importation of philosophical ideas into biblical exegesis. His introduction to the principles of biblical interpretation, *Institutio interpretis Novi Testamenti*, was reedited after his death with comments from both Samuel Morus and Christof von Ammon and was translated twice into English along with the additional comments.

Ernesti also contributed to biblical studies in Germany by editing two influential theological journals, *Neue Theologische Bibliothek* (1760–1770) and *Neueste Theologische Bibliothek* (1771–1775). He wrote most of the reviews himself and maintained a position of conscientious fairness tinged occasionally with an ironic comment.

6. The Life of Jesus

i. Herbert Samuel Reimarus (1694–1768)

Up to the eighteenth century, although there had been debates about the ontological status of Jesus, there had been no real discussion about what he would have been like as a human being, although there was general agreement that he was at least that. Reimarus wrote a work called *Apologie oder Schutzschrift für die vernünftigen Verehrer Gottes*, which tried to get behind dogmatic accretions to what Jesus' words actually meant in the first century C.E. and what Jesus' goal really was. Reimarus never published his work, but his widow gave the manuscript to the German writer and radical theologian Gotthold Ephraim Lessing, at that time librarian of the library at Wolfenbüttel, who published at intervals two selections from the work. Lessing called the extracts "Fragments of an unknown work," and in the hefty debate that followed, the author was referred to simply as "the Fragmentist." The Fragmentist controversy became one of the most celebrated of all the *causes célèbres* in eighteenth-century Germany.

Reimarus's own views about theology are best described as thorough-going Deism. In a work he published during his lifetime entitled *Die*

---

[40] First published in 1750, reprinted in *Opuscula Philologica et Critica* (Leiden: Luchtmans, 1764) 233–51. This collection was reprinted several times.

Vornehmsten Wahrheiten der natürlichen Religion[41] ("The Most Important Truths of Natural Religon"), he set out a belief in God, morality, and eternal life with rewards and punishments without any reference to the Bible. He obviously felt that this sort of belief can be established from reason alone, so it is clear that after very conservative beginnings, he was free of reliance on the Bible in later life. Two incidental features of this work worth noting are: first, Reimarus's academic title was professor of mathematics and Oriental languages, a combination of disciplines seldom attained today, and second, his criticism of Rousseau did not lack for humor and irony.

Obviously, one has to make a clear distinction between what was in Reimarus's work as a whole and what was excluded from the partial publication in the eighteenth century. In fact, the manuscript tradition is somewhat complicated, and a complete version was not published until the twentieth century. However, it is clear that in the nineteenth century David Strauss had access to a more or less complete copy.

Reimarus's discussion of Jesus, as set out in the selections Lessing made of his work, consists of two parts; the first deals with the historical Jesus and the second with other New Testament figures and writers.[42] In his reconstruction of the historical Jesus, Reimarus made the point that one has to get behind the centuries of accretion in the Christian tradition and see Jesus as a Jew of his time. One also must rely entirely on the Gospels for information about Jesus, for while the Gospel writers tried to record what Jesus actually did and said, by contrast the apostles, that is the writers of other New Testament books, considered themselves teachers, with the right to work out their own doctrines.

Reimarus showed that some of the terms assigned to Jesus in the tradition, such as "Son of God," had entirely different meanings in the context of first-century Judaism. From uses of this term in the Old Testament, Reimarus showed convincingly that it did not mean the second person of the Trinity but rather someone whose life was fashioned according to God's will. He went on to produce a portrait of Jesus as a man who indeed criticized the superficial legalism of the Pharisees and emphasized the necessity for true obedience, but who in no way intended

---

[41] First published in 1754, 1755[2], 1766[3]; reprt. Hermann Samuel Reimarus, *Die vornehmste Wahrheiten der natürlichen Religion* (Göttingen: Vandenhoeck und Ruprecht, 1985).

[42] For this discussion of the Fragments I am using George Wesley Buchanan, *The Goal of Jesus and His Disciples* (Leiden: E. J. Brill, 1970).

to abolish the Jewish Law as such. Reimarus argued that Jesus, however, did see himself as the coming messiah of Israel as expected in his day, that is, the successor to David. This was the sort of kingdom of God that occurs regularly in Jesus' preaching, and the fact that Jesus never describes it in detail shows that he was not proclaiming a new idea that had to be explained to his audience. It was in his unsuccessful attempt to seize control of this earthly kingdom, that is, of the Judah of his day, that Jesus perished. Reimarus argued that there is nothing to be found in this portrait of a savior and redeemer of the world.

In the second part of the work Reimarus then argued that after his death, Jesus' disciples, having become accustomed to the comforts of living off people's offerings, introduced a second sort of belief about Jesus that then led into Christianity as we know it traditionally. It is possible, then, to see parts of both the old and the new systems in the New Testament.

Whether Reimarus's argument was justified or not, it has certainly influenced many since his time. It did, however, rely on his reconstruction of the New Testament, which involved eliminating as a later addition anything that contradicted his picture of the historical Jesus. It might be suggested, then, that while he accused others of begging the question by a circular argument, he himself was as guilty as they in this respect.

However, Reimarus set in motion two trends that were to influence New Testament interpretation from then on. The first was the vogue for the Lives of Jesus; the shelves of libraries groan under the weight of various attempts to write a Life of Jesus from the eighteenth century on, until Albert Schweitzer's book *The Quest of the Historical Jesus*[43] showed up many of the weaknesses of the genre. The problem is, On what grounds does one adopt a standard of authenticity on which a Life of Jesus can be erected out of the various elements in the Gospels? Personal preferences about what one wants to see as authentic inevitably play a large part in one's selection. This difficulty is illustrated by the story of an Oxford tutor who remarked to a student, "I have just read X's [a well-known British liberal theologian] autobiography. It is a very good book, really, but he has given it a strange title. He calls it *The Life of Jesus*."

The second trend that Reimarus set in motion was the driving of a wedge between the teachings of Jesus and those of the disciples. While Reimarus assumed that all the apostles were involved in this reinterpretation of the message of Jesus, in subsequent discussions Paul in particular

---

[43] Published in 1906 as *Von Reimarus zu Wrede: eine Geschichte der Leben-Jesu Forschung.*

was usually selected as the one who refounded the Jesus movement according to his own view of the universe. Here again, this may be right or it may be wrong.

ii. GOTTHOLD EPHRAIM LESSING (1729–1781)

Lessing was far more than Reimarus's champion. He was one of the great literary figures of his day, whose plays are still performed. His religious faith was far from orthodox, and he considered himself in agreement with most of Spinoza's ideas. However, Lessing championed the cause of tolerance and indeed understanding among adherents of different religions, and in his play *Nathan the Wise* he wrote one of the most enduring literary works on this subject.

Lessing had studied theology and was in a position to argue theological problems. One of his observations was the theological equivalent of Fermat's third theorem in mathematics, that is a question that is not easily answered. In the article "On the Proof of the Spirit and of Power,"[44] he posed the problem, How can the contingent events of history be taken as part of the necessary proofs of reason?[45] This is the [in]famous ugly ditch of how do you get from the biblical accounts, which, after all, are only what people reported, to a certainty that transcends the notorious uncertainty of historical reports?[46] Essentially, his position was similar to that of Spinoza's defense of the infallibility of Scripture, where reason

[44] "Über den Beweis des Geistes und der Kraft (1. Schreiben)," in *Sechs theologische Schriften Gotthold Ephraim Lessings,* introduction and commentary Wolfgang Gericke (Berlin: Evangelische Verlagsanstalt, 1985).

[45] "Zufällige Geschichtswahrheiten können der Beweis von notwendigen Venunfts-wahrheiten nie werden." Lessing, "Über den Beweis des Geistes," 116. The distinction between "contingent" and "necessary" is an important part of philosophy and perhaps even life itself. Contingent events are happenings that occur at much the same time, for example, if I hung a red shirt on a clothesline visible to the general public just before the leader of my country resigns, these are contingent events. However, if it turns out that I am a secret agent and I am giving a signal that documents proof that the leader's deceptive practices have just been leaked to the press and he has to resign to avoid disgrace, then there is a necessary connection between the two incidents. In the case of Lessing, it is interesting that the example he chose is from mathematics—he argued that a mathematical solution is true independent of the mathematician proposing it. But is there a philosophical problem here, namely, do beliefs about the significance in our lives (or its lack)—religious, social, etc.—represent the same sort of discourse as mathematical proofs?

[46] Lessing's term for this in German was *"der breite garstige Graben"* (Lessing, "Über den Beweis des Geistes," 117), an illustration of how theological terms are often more impressive in German than in English.

could be called on to fill in anything that was missing. Reason would supply the truths; Scripture may well have true things in it, but they are true because they coincide with reason, not because they are in Scripture. Thus in an editorial remark, Lessing could defend the authors of the New Testament against Reimarus's strictures with the observation that the truth of what the evangelists said does not depend upon their having said it.

Yet Lessing also wrote a work called *The Education of the Human Race*, which is essentially an optimistic view of human progress as the human race learns how to be fully human. This is useful as an illustration of how all religions can then be true in their own way, but it does raise its own problem: how can this process, which is by definition historical, be itself a necessary proof of anything? Some have suggested that Lessing had his own *garstige Graben*, which required more than good literary style to leap.

7. The "first modern" scholar:
Johann Gottfried Eichhorn (1752–1827)

With Eichhorn we see the emergence of a new type of biblical scholar. Up to his time most biblical scholarship was carried on by professors (often of theology) who were usually clergy. Michaelis, it is true, was not ordained, but he insisted on writing a dogmatic in which he discussed matters of theology as distinct from philological or exegetical problems. For Eichhorn, it was his research into history ancient and modern that drove him; his attachment to the church was at best conventional, and he had no interest in discussing the theological implications of his work. His interest was wide-ranging—he lectured on European history among other subjects—and his taste for work was prodigious. He would get up several hours before anyone else in his household and study, with a heavy coat around him, since the fires had not yet been lit. He is famous for his advice to two American students that since they were not used to the sort of work German students did, they should not try to study more than ten hours a day, seven days a week.[47]

Eichhorn may also deserve credit for two of the terms that held sway for over a hundred years and are still encountered, namely, "lower criticism"

---

[47] For a discussion of Eichhorn (and Michaelis), see the entertaining article of Rudolph Smend, *Theologie in Göttingen: eine Vorlesungsreihe* (Göttingen: Vandenhoeck und Ruprecht, 1987) 58–81.

and "higher criticism." Lower criticism concerns matters of fact, such as manuscripts, textual criticism, and grammatical matters. Higher criticism refers to attempts to date documents, separate sources, and other matters that can never be quite as factual as the subjects of lower criticism.

In assessing the English horror of "German theology" in the next chapter, we note that it was not just the exciting radicals like David Strauss who were denounced, but industrious, if less aggressive men like Eichhorn, who seemed to be not so much cataclysms that flattened the bulwarks of traditional biblical infallibility in a single night as they were termites boring slowly but relentlessly into the supporting beams in the cellars. It should be borne in mind that Eichhorn had had Edward Pusey as a student at Göttingen, where, according to his contemporary Samuel Davidson, he was anything but a distinguished student.

Eichhorn and the prophets

As discussed in the last chapter, prophets tend to be a useful form of scholarly litmus paper to indicate what is going on in scholarship, since sooner or later interpreters are tempted to find what they are looking for, especially if they treat all biblical prophets as if there were few differences among them. For Eichhorn, the starting point was not the exegesis of prophecies of the future in the Old Testament, but prophecy as a cultural phenomenon. The awareness that human beings can think and use language in different ways began to be applied systematically to biblical interpretation in the eighteenth century. This interpretation of the history of civilization tended to be arranged on an evolutionary scale that culminated in the modern enlightened European.

Eichhorn began his discussion of the prophets with a discussion of what primitive humanity was like. Eichhorn himself admitted that evidence for this development of the human species does not and cannot come from firsthand sources but is based on the situation and ways of thinking of contemporary emerging peoples. Whether his assumption is really correct is best left to anthropologists to discuss, especially since there is very little hard evidence to justify any given hypothesis.[48] The important thing to keep in mind is that this is how late-eighteenth-

---

[48] The problem is that when we refer to "modern Stone Age peoples," we mean peoples whose technology is fairly rudimentary to the point of not having metal tools or weapons. We assume, with a certain amount of evidence, that these peoples are living in much the same way as humanity as a whole fifty thousand years ago. But when we go on to extrapolate from their beliefs and customs to what was believed and observed in that remote period, we are making assumptions that are hard to verify.

century scholars saw the matter, and this viewpoint persisted almost unchallenged for at least a century.

> As long as humankind lived in its primitive crudeness in a happy/unhappy unawareness of what lay outside it, it remained caught up in the present alone and let the future look after itself. A nasty shock that cannot be endured for long is necessary to wake humanity from its deep sleep; it is only when its carelessness revenges itself and leaves humanity even once suffering from some terrible threat that the first thoughts about the future occur to it and lay the basis for all its future experience.[49]

Eichhorn attributed to the work of the prophets much in the development of any primitive human society into a cultured people. Prophets emerged as older and wiser members of the community who reminded their people that if things were going well, they might get worse; if things were bad, they would eventually get better. Their wisdom so impressed their hearers that, as trusted confidants of the gods, the prophets appeared to have a higher-than-human knowledge, and this was the simple origin of prophets and their messages from the gods. Careful not to be too precise in their foretelling of the future, these early Poloniuses and Poloniesses managed to maintain their authority even when matters did not turn out as promised, a stratagem perhaps not unknown to political commentators today. Furthermore, the message of these prophets was delivered in a form designed to impress, namely, in poetry, which Eichhorn took as the oldest form of human speech, and accompanied by extraordinary actions and gestures to add a little corroborative detail, intended to give artistic verisimilitude to an otherwise bald and unconvincing narrative. In other words, Eichhorn was offering a completely naturalistic explanation of prophecy, describing it as an office that occurred in every society on its way to higher things.

In short, when Moses founded the Israelite nation, he established prophets, whose basic task was to maintain the monotheistic system he had founded. In Old Testament times, then, one can see the prophets all more or less proclaiming the same message, even as they felt the duty to preserve and edit the oracles of their predecessors. They were responsible for maintaining the high moral tone typical of Israel's faith and guiding the people through their vicissitudes by warning them in the midst of prosperity and comforting them in the face of disaster.

[49] Eichhorn, *Einleitung ins Alte Testament*, 2nd ed. (Leipzig: Weidmans, 1787) 3:1. My translation.

Whatever else Eichhorn saw in the prophets, he did not see them as guided by direct, divine, individual illumination that opened the mysteries of the coming messiah to them. It is possible that Eichhorn might have admitted that there was some general providence behind developments in Israel, but this was a far cry from traditional interpreters, who saw an unbroken and direct link between what the prophets foresaw and what the New Testament recorded.

Voltaire saw the prophets as examples of unmitigated lunacy; Eichhorn gave them a place in the development of civilization generally, and in particular as preservers of Israel's moral legacy.

8. *Myth as a tool for interpretation:*
Eichhorn's "Urgeschichte" and Johann Philipp Gabler (1753–1826)

In one view of the stages of the development of human thought, it was argued that an early stage was marked by the creation of myths.[50] Christian Heyne passed the idea on to both Eichhorn and Gabler, who made use of the concept to argue for an entirely different and more sympathetic view of the creation stories in Genesis, whose crudity had been a problem for many critics. This is how Eichhorn began his seminal work "Urgeschichte," which was a study of the early traditions of Genesis.

> Even now stands an ancient pantheon, the oldest, most beautiful, and simplest of them all, a gift of artless nature, despite the storms of wasting time, untouched and almost without sign of age. A temple full of nature and simplicity, only here and there enlivened by art, sets off the entrance. A single and narrow path leads up to it, but the path is overgrown and without trace that it was ever passable, because art for more than a thousand years has built new ways, which have since then been used. The old path is short but simple; the new ways are longer, but full of sights of many works of art. The old path leads direct to the temple, the new ones to magnificent fortifications and palaces. Since these were built, interest has only been on them; few know the temple that lies behind them and if you ask their shape, you are usually shown one of the fortifications.[51]

[50] "Myth" is one of the most multifaceted of words, and whenever it occurs, the critical reader is advised to see what definition, if any, the author is using. Roughly speaking, there is a spectrum of meaning, ranging from outright lie, through primitive mentality, to an inescapable aspect of human thought in the present.

[51] *Repertorium für biblische und Morgenländische Litteratur* (1779) 126. Translation mine. The complete article is found on pages 129–72 and 172–256.

In a prose tinged with the deepest shade of purple, this is a fine example of eighteenth-century sentimentality about ancient creations whose beauty is untouched by the refinements of civilization. But if "artless" is used, it means that "crudity" is rejected, and this puts a new interpretation on the primitive. Down with Voltaire and long live Rousseau.

Eichhorn published his "Urgeschichte" as a two-part article in his periodical *Repertorium für biblische und Morgenländische Litteratur.* Gabler was very impressed by it and suggested that Eichhorn publish it in longer form as a book. For various reasons Eichhorn declined, so Gabler edited and annotated the work and published it in three volumes. He retained Eichhorn's text but added a large number of notes, which he was careful to distinguish from Eichhorn's own. Gabler's interest in producing this edition is clear: he saw Eichhorn's approach as a completely new way of defending the Bible from the scorn of its enemies in a completely reasonable way.[52]

One other difference between Eichhorn and Gabler was that Gabler was much freer in his use of the word "myth." Clearly, he saw it as a useful tool for deflecting criticism of the Bible that was based on a rational rejection of factual error or unbelievable incident. Gabler was prepared to apply the concept of myth, for example, to explain incidents in the New Testament, such as the appearance of angels. His contribution to the notion of biblical theology will be discussed below (pp. 261–62).

9. *The authority of the Bible in the new theology*

i. THE BACKGROUND

There is an unavoidable tension in exegesis between seeing the Bible as an ancient book and the Bible as an authoritative book, in the sense that it is normative for how one interprets and lives one's life. The first is a statement of fact that few would doubt; the second is a response of faith of some sort that not everyone might wish to make.[53] What the Bible contains as an ancient book is logically prior to the second question of whether it should provide guidance to us; serious discussion, then,

---

[52] J. G. Eichhorn, *Urgeschichte,* ed. J. P. Gabler, 3 vols. (Altdorf and Nürnberg: Monat und Kussler, 1790) 1:v.

[53] "Faith" is used here in the most general sense of the term. This whole sentence covers over a multitude of questions that could take up a whole book—only not this one.

has to begin with the ancient book. Thus, when the church fathers had to defend the Bible against critics such as Porphyry or Faustus the Manichean, they were forced to argue on the Bible's integrity as a book; when the Renaissance Humanists defended their study of the Bible against the scholastic traditionalists, they had to appeal to the proper understanding of the text as written in its original languages. New perceptions of the Bible as an ancient book do have an effect on its authority; one good example is the apostolic command for women to cover their heads in church in 1 Corinthians 11:5ff. Do we see this regulation as a response to a particular situation that no longer exists, or do we see this as an eternal principle to be followed forever?

In the latter part of the eighteenth century, an increasing number of scholars came down decisively on the side of seeing the Bible as a book written over a period of time and reflecting the different attitudes, stages of culture, and immediate problems of the various centuries in which it was written. Given what had been discovered in the various sciences and in the exact scrutiny of the contents of the Bible, many educated people felt that it was no longer possible to accept the Bible as the infallible Word of God direct from heaven in its origins, if somewhat less sure in its transmission.[54]

The contrast between Eichhorn and Gabler illustrates how two scholars who agreed upon much in their research could have had different motives for undertaking it. For someone like Eichhorn, it was scholarly research for its own sake that was his driving passion; how research affected the wider matters of religious belief was clearly not an issue he wished to investigate, which is why he declined Gabler's suggestion to reedit the *Urgeschichte*. Gabler, on the other hand, was an example of those who were concerned about the implications of scholarship for how faith was to be set out in theology.

Within Christianity there had always been a problem in deciding how much of the Old Testament law was applicable to those who lived in later and very different times.[55] For example, in the early church one way of getting clear of the demands of the Old Testament ritual law was to argue that while the moral laws of the Old Testament were still in force, the ceremonial laws were not. While this is, of course, a distinction for-

---

[54] To be accurate, it was not just the Bible that was in question, but religion in general. Hence the title of Schleiermacher's *Speeches on Religion to its cultured Despisers*.

[55] There is a similar problem within Judaism, but the route for the Jewish faith was the reinterpretation of law rather than annulment.

eign to the Old Testament, it was effective in giving an explanation of why the Christian church chose to ignore many Old Testament regulations. Other questions nonetheless still remained, such as whether the Old Testament laws against usury applied to the new economic system of capitalism. In the sixteenth century this biblical law had to be explained as no longer in force, thus paving the way for Christians to enter the banking profession.

In the eighteenth century the growing awareness of the historical circumstances behind the Bible's origins had become a factor that could be taken into account. Might it be possible to distinguish between what in the Old Testament applied to the historical conditions of ancient Israel and what applied to humanity in general? But for Protestants a complicating factor was the collection of so-called symbolic books, a term that comes from the ecclesiastical use of *symbola* in Greek to describe creedal statements.[56] In Protestantism the symbolic books were collections of doctrinal statements such as the Forumula Concordiae, the Westminster Confession, or the Anglican Thirty-Nine Articles. In effect, these were church traditions based largely on sixteenth- and seventeenth-century biblical exegesis. Now the Roman Catholic Church could argue that tradition was how the Bible ought to be understood, so there was no possible contradiction between Scripture and authorized doctrine. Protestants could not appeal to this sort of backstop.[57]

How authoritative the symbolic books were was a problem that perturbed Protestant Europe in different ways. In trying to come to terms with the view of the Bible presupposed in the symbolic books, there were in Protestantism at least three different routes that could be followed in the effort to distinguish between what was valuable from what was less so in the Bible, namely, the examination of the biblical canon, the discussion of the nature of inspiration and revelation, and the new discipline of biblical theology.

ii. JOHANN SEMLER AND THE CANON

The first route was taken by Semler in his discussion of the contents of the canon. Despite what is sometimes suggested, Semler was scarcely

---

[56] A convenient list of Protestant symbolic books can be found in K. Heussi, *Kompendium der Kirchengeschichte* (Tübingen: Mohr, 1960) 379–81.

[57] There were one or two suggestions to give the symbolic books final authority in the eighteenth century, but they never attracted a great deal of support. Even in England the Thirty-Nine Articles of the Church of England came under fire in the Blackstock controversy.

the first to raise this issue; as we saw, Luther made some tentative moves in this direction but later abandoned them. Christof Sandius, the Socinian, had presented the history of the canon in a very historical fashion without endorsing or rejecting the superior value of the books that had gotten accepted into it;[58] and Anthony Collins had certainly raised matters about the canonicity of various biblical books, not to say the authenticity of creedal documents.

As will be discussed below, Semler began by taking aim at the book of Revelation, but he went on to declare various other parts of the Bible, such as the historical accounts of the Old Testament, as having no legitimate place in the canon, for they did not exhibit the appropriate moral concern. It has been argued by Gottfried Hornig that "moral" here did not mean just "ethical," but rather was the counterweight to "physical," so in modern parlance it would be more appropriate to understand Semler's use of "moral" as much the same as the vague sense of "spiritual."[59] Indeed, it is hard not to admit that Semler had a point, for the story of the Levite's concubine in Judges 19 and the account of the machinations and subsequent assassinations surrounding Solomon's accession to the kingship in 1 Kings 1–2 are not often mined for Sunday School lessons in behavior or forgiveness, still less for spiritual insights.[60]

iii. Töllner on inspiration

The second route—inspiration and revelation—was taken by Johann Gottlieb Töllner (1724–1774), who published a work entitled *Die göttliche Eingebung der heiligen Schrift*[61] ("The divine inspiration of Holy Scripture"). Töllner was a pupil of Baumgarten's and a "neologian" in conviction, that is, someone who rejected the infallibility of the Bible but who admitted the reality of divine revelation. He began his work with a careful discussion of the history of different opinions on inspiration, including Luther's, who confined inspiration to the meaning, not to the

---

[58] *Nucleus Historiae Ecclesiasticae exhibitus in historia arianorum . . . quibus praefixus est Tractatus de veteribus scriptoribus ecclesiasticis*, 2nd rev. ed. (Cologne: Johann Nicolai, 1676).

[59] Gottfried Hornig, *Die Anfänge der historische-kritischen Theologie Johann Salomo Semlers Schriftverständnis und seine Stellung zu Luther* (Göttingen:Vandenhoeck und Ruprecht, 1961) 106–11.

[60] T. H. Gaster had a vivid summing up of the Levite's sending parts of his concubine to the tribes of Israel: "They won't let you send things like that through the mail these days."

[61] Mietau & Leipzig: Hinz, 1772.

words themselves. Töllner was ready to admit that perhaps no single explanation of the problem had the whole truth of the matter, but his approach was to distinguish between the inspiration that leads a biblical author to write and revelation, which is truth about God. It is necessary, then, that the divine reputation of the teaching in the Bible is not bound up with the question of the inspiration for the writing of the books. All Scripture is inspired; not everything in it is a revelation of God.

There was a long and complicated history behind this sort of discussion, and Töllner's work was not to be the last time that a book on inspiration would discuss the problem of distinguishing between the important and unimportant in the Bible, but it was to be in the next approach that the whole issue would be discussed *ad infinitum* and *ad nauseam.*[62]

iv. BIBLICAL THEOLOGY

The third route was biblical theology. Rather than trying to define biblical theology as a discrete entity, it is more appropriate to examine the various meanings of the term, for it came to mean different things to different people. Originally, biblical theology simply described one part of the theological curriculum. If one looks at guides for theological students from the beginning of the century,[63] there is a progression as the student went from biblical theology, sometimes called exegetical theology, to dogmatic[64] or acromaic theology, to church history, and thence to other branches, until one got to polemic theology, the subject taught by the senior professor.[65] In other words, "biblical theology" as a technical term meant that part of the discipline of the theological curriculum that involved learning about the exegesis of the Bible. However, there was the sense that while not everyone in the pew would understand the subtleties of abstract theology, everyone could be expected to read the Bible and get out of it basic notions such as love, duty, and forgiveness.

---

[62] It is interesting that Paul Achtemeier, *The Inspiration of Scripture: Problems and Proposals* (Philadelphia: Westminster, 1980), deals with the question in much the same order as Töllner did. This is neither to suggest a direct dependence nor to deny the usefulness of Achtemeier's excellent book.

[63] See Loescher, Baumgarten, etc.

[64] Strictly speaking, dogmatic theology includes systematics and moral theology, but even in the eighteenth century the tendency to identify these two terms is often found.

[65] See Rudolf Mau, "Programme und Praxis der Theologiestudiums im 17. und 18. Jahrhundert," *Theologische Versuche* 11 (1979) 71–91.

This was a distinction that Spinoza himself would have approved of; it was also one that reemerged in Enlightenment theological discussions on the difference between theology and religion.

The relationship between the Bible and dogmatic theology and theology and the Bible had always been problematic. It was the Renaissance Humanists who showed that some biblical texts, properly understood, did not support the dogmatic system built upon them. While the Reformation churches did appeal to the Bible against the church system of their day, eventually they erected their own confessions, which often contained elements of, or references to, earlier theological statements. It was ironic that these confessions could themselves be charged with not being strictly biblical. This was the point made by the Socinians in the seventeenth century. Their reasons for denying the doctrine of the Trinity, namely, that it is not spelled out in its patristic form in the Bible, make them look to us more like Jehovah's Witnesses than modern Unitarians. However, the gap they noticed was real. Jean Le Clerc wrote a story in his youth about an experiment in which two children were isolated from each other and all theological teaching except for a knowledge of the Bible; as a result, one emerged as a Socinian in theology and the other as Trinitarian.

In the Lutheran church, the Pietists were a group that appealed to the Bible against the dogmatic formulations, and Philipp Spener, in his *Pia Desiderata*, recommended a return to a pure biblical theology. The contrast here was with the scholastic theology of Lutheran orthodoxy. There were two interesting attempts to take this route from the middle of the century, namely, Anton Friedrich Büsching's and Christian Albert Doederlein's.[66]

Büsching was not a Pietist and had been a pupil of Baumgarten's but unfortunately had no real ability for thinking about complicated matters. The title of Büsching's Latin work, translated into English, was "A Presentation of an abridgment of theology put together from Holy Scripture alone and purged from every scholastic word and notion."[67] In

---

[66] I cannot find any trace of any dependence between these two men, and in fact when a Swedish reviewer lumped them together, Doederlein made a point of rejecting the allegation. (He is not to be confused with Johann Doederlein, a far more significant theologian, who has a claim to being the first person to recognize Deutero-Isaiah as a separate book.)

[67] *Dissertatio theologica inauguralis exhibens epitomen theologiae e solis sacris litteris concinnatae et ab omnibus rebus et verbis scholasticis purgatae* (Göttingen: 1756).

fact, it was a collection of texts illustrating the basic tenets of traditional Lutheran theology.[68] His rather unimpressive work (one assumes that standards for doctoral dissertations have improved at Göttingen since his day) is notable for two features. The first is his fairly straightforward denunciation of the theological tradition in his dedicatory preface to von Münchhausen.[69] He claimed that his work was a dogmatic collection made up from purely divine sources and was purified from all human opinion, conjecture, argument, and tradition, things that are both absurd and pernicious in the interpretation of Scripture. The second feature was his rather simplistic standard for deciding what in Scripture is of divine origin. The divine origin of a saying is shown when it comes from an undoubtedly canonical book, when it is clear beyond dispute, and when it represents the words of God, Christ, or someone speaking from divine inspiration. Even in Büsching's time this was somewhat naïve, and one can only applaud the appropriateness of his decision to change his academic specialization.

Christian Doederlein's work is a German translation of a Latin inaugural lecture at the University of Rostock. Its title in English is "Formal Lecture setting out the great pre-eminence of biblical theology over the scholastic sort."[70] Doederlein gave us a little more to go on than Büsching did. Obviously a representative of an Enlightenment-tinged Pietism, Doederlein started from the effects of the Fall on all human attributes, including reason and the consequent necessity of the gift of the Spirit. It followed from this that the only secure source of knowledge is the Bible read under the guidance of the Spirit. Doederlein was well aware of the relationship between Christian theology and philosophy. He disapproved of the influence of Justin Martyr, Clement of Alexandria, and above all Origen in leading the church in the wrong direction, even as he saw certain contemporary philosophers having a similar effect. What he argued, then, is that the Bible should be studied entirely without presuppositions, by standard methods of interpretation; once its

---

[68] If one compares the table of contents of Büsching's work with that of Johannes Buddeus's *Institutiones theologae dogmaticae*, it is clear that both are following a traditional pattern. In the case of Büsching, one has to ask why this choice of subjects if he is trying to get away from tradition. The fact is that this is one of the recurring problems of biblical theology.

[69] This is, of course, the Hanoverian chancellor and not that teller of tall tales, Baron Münchausen, who was created by the eighteenth-century writer Rudolf Raspe.

[70] Christian Doederlein, *Feyerliche Rede von den hohen Vorzügen der biblischen Theologie vor der Scholastischen* (Halle: Johann Christian Grunerten, ca. 1758).

contents are mastered, one is then able to proceed to a true systematic theology, that is, one that is based on the sayings of the Bible alone.

That Büsching and Doederlein independently set out such similar views suggests that in the mid-eighteenth century, far from trying to control biblical theology, in fact it was dogmatic theology that was under pressure from the biblical side.[71] This is shown by a formal disputation preserved in a remote corner of the Yale Library on the subject "The pre-eminence of acromaic theology over that which is called biblical."[72] The author, Johannes Thomas Andreas Jockenack, was writing in response to Büsching, whom he cites by name.

Generally speaking, Jockenack was a much more subtle thinker than either Büsching or Doederlein, and some of the points he made are very good indeed. The line of argument he adopted was that within the Bible itself no method of coordinating its various doctrines is present; for this acromaic theology is necessary for putting things in order and making intelligent use of what is in Scripture. Furthermore, Jockenack could see that because the world of the eighteenth century was different from that of the first century, there was no obligation that all ideas should be expressed in first-century terms. In other words, he saw the necessity of constructive theology presenting biblical truths in terms of the historical period in which it finds itself. It is also important to take into account discoveries about the world that have been made since biblical times.[73] Jockenack, otherwise unknown to the history of scholarship, was a pupil of Semler's, under whose chairmanship the paper was given. It is not stretching matters too much to assume that while the hands were the hands of Jockenack, the voice was the voice of Semler, and this disputation is essentially the refutation of Büsching that Semler was rumored to be preparing.

---

[71] It appears to have been David Strauss's article on biblical theology that was the source of the idea that in the eighteenth century it was a case of biblical theology trying to escape from dogmatics. The situation was not the same in every case, but Strauss appears to be projecting nineteenth-century conservatism back onto the previous century.

[72] Johann Jockenack, *Dissertatio theologica de praestantia theologiciae acroamaticae prae sic dicta biblica* (Halle: 1757).

[73] Büsching, in fact, did this slightly in that in his discussion of the biblical texts describing the creation of the world, he slipped in the notion that creation was described as it appeared to someone on earth. This was a notion he borrowed from the physico-theology of his day, which had already found this ingenious way around the obvious problem produced by the Copernican worldview.

However well Jockenack and/or Semler may have defended dogmatic theology, the attempts to appeal to the Bible against so-called scholastic theology continued. But while Büsching and Doederlein had been relatively orthodox, two authors in the 1760s used the Bible as a means of setting forward a much more liberal view of theology, namely, Johann Bernhard Basedow, in his *Versuch einer freymuthigen Dogmatik*[74] ("Outline of a Frank System of Dogmatics"), and Carl Friedrich Bahrdt, in his *Versuch eines biblischen Systems der Dogmatik*[75] ("Outline of a Biblical System of Dogmatics.")

Basedow's theological education was rather limited, and in fact he was much more an educationalist than a thinker, but he set out to produce a modern dogmatic with the Bible as its basis. Bahrdt, at one time an associate of Basedow's and a notorious personage of his day, was a colorful character too complex to discuss fully here. Let it be said that he was a figure of Falstaffian proportions and inclinations, whose autobiography is well worth reading.[76] However, his *Versuch* echoed the same sort of intent that Basedow's book did; the difference was that Bahrdt had some claim to theological training and indeed had once held a university teaching position, during which time his father, also a professor, used to attend his lectures and give him a list of his grammatical mistakes at the end. Common to both Basedow and Bahrdt was the confusion of biblical and dogmatic theology with preference given to the biblical side of things—at least in theory.

Bahrdt said that the aim of a biblical system would be to leave to religion the natural simplicity that the word-fanciers had taken from it. Therefore, we look at the totality of the truths revealed by God in a natural and not an artificial order, under such means of expression that are taken from holy Scripture in a simple fashion. In fact, Bahrdt was putting biblical theology through the screen of a certain sort of Enlightenment religiosity, which was very far from being what the Bible actually contains. It dealt with problems by obscuring them and simply imposed on the Bible what a good eighteenth-century philosopher considered what the Bible might have said had he been asked to write it himself.

[74] Berlin: 1766.

[75] Two vols. (Gotha and Leipzig, 1769) 7.

[76] There is a good biography in English by Sten G. Flygt, *The Notorious Dr. Bahrdt* (Nashville: Vanderbilt, 1963).

Johannes Hofmann, a conservative theologian with Pietist leanings, attacked this notion of biblical theology in an inaugural address at Altdorf just seventeen years before Gabler's famous lecture. He also spoke on the preeminence of biblical theology, but biblical theology of a different sort.[77] Hofmann began with a critique of the contemporary situation, where the sacred name of biblical theology was being turned into sport by men who were unholy, impure, and ridiculous, who spoke idly of biblical theology, although they had never read with attentive, pious mind the oracles of the Spirit. I suspect that he had Bahrdt in mind when he added, "They expend only the hours left over from love and drink." Hofmann then went on to expound once again the distinction between biblical and acromaic theology, arguing that both were necessary.

What Hofmann objected to was the supposition that once you have dogmatic theology, the biblical sort is no longer required, and in this respect he quoted Melanchthon, who in the preface to his *Loci*, said that his aim was not to draw men into obscure and encumbered debates, but to draw them to Scripture. In particular, Hofmann singled out those who worked from theological theories alone without a solid knowledge of the Bible and who no longer wished to get a basic knowledge of their discipline but threw trendy words to their people. Hofmann's point, then, was simply the reiteration of what any competent theologian of his day would have accepted, namely, that the Bible is the foundation for Christian doctrine. His real concerns were either the rationalist thinkers like Bahrdt or the laziness of theological students, a point interestingly enough made by Zachariae.

It was Gotthelf Traugott Zachariae (1729–1777) who wrote the first biblical theology, in the modern sense of the word, that actually had this title.[78] In his introduction, Zachariae said that he set out to write a collection of proof texts, the so-called *dicta classica*, but he realized early on that this would no longer be enough and instead tried to distinguish what was of importance in the Bible only to the times in which it was written and what was of enduring value. This was one of the first at-

---

[77] Johannes Hofmann, *Oratio de theologiae biblicae praestantia* (Altdorf: 1770). (This date is written in hand in the copy of this address at the Bibliotheca. P. R. Stuttgart). I at one point expressed in print my doubts that any copies had survived. I would like to express my gratitude to the library of Memorial University of Newfoundland, which several years later located the copy in Stuttgart that I have used for my discussion.

[78] I have argued elsewhere that Spinoza's *Tractatus Theologico-Politicus*, to the extent that it was trying to explain what is important in the Bible, was in fact the earliest biblical theology, but Spinoza himself does not use this term.

tempts to face up to the fact that the Bible, too, has its history, and there is a yawning gulf between religion as it tended to be practiced in ancient Israel and what in that religion is of importance to us today.

The attempt to see the Old Testament not only against the background of its own age but also in relation to other religions was undertaken by Gottlieb Philipp Christian Kaiser. The first two volumes of his Old Testament theology were an attempt to fit the Old Testament into the current notion of comparative religion; in the third volume he lapsed back into a conventional orthodoxy.[79]

Finally, let us take another look at Gabler's address to see what he had in mind, given the sort of background we have discussed.[80] The title of his lecture ("On the Proper Distinction between Biblical and Dogmatic Theology and the Specific Objectives of each") suggests that it was concerned with the boundary between biblical and dogmatic theology and with the nature of biblical theology. If one looks closely, what he was trying to show in the first case was not the independence of biblical theology from dogmatics, but indeed the exact contrary. In the wake of attacks on dogmatic theology and the confusion between dogmatic and biblical theology that we find in Basedow and Bahrt, Gabler was trying to show the legitimate purpose and position of dogmatics. Then, in his discussion of biblical theology, he made a distinction between what was of temporal and what was of eternal importance in the Bible. While this was essentially the same distinction Zachariae was trying to make, Gabler, the pupil of Heyne and Eichhorn, showed a much more developed sense of the different sort of mentality behind the Bible. This he soon developed in his revised edition of Eichhorn's *Urgeschichte*, where he made extensive use of the new term "myth," which Eichhorn was very reluctant to use.

Gabler distinguished between a reconstruction of the religion of Israel as it existed in history and biblical theology, which he saw as an exercise in determining what from the Old Testament was of real importance to contemporary religion. Here one sees the division between works on biblical theology in the nineteenth and twentieth centuries:

[79] John Sandys-Wunsch, "P. C. Kaiser, La Théologie biblique et l'histoire des religions," *Revue d'histoire et de Philosophie Religieuse*, Festschrift for E. Jacob (1979) 391–96.

[80] A translation of the text can be found in John Sandys-Wunsch and Lawrence Eldredge, "J. P. Gabler and the Distinction between Biblical and Dogmatic Theology," *The Scottish Journal of Theology* 33 (1980) 133–58.

should biblical theology be the history of Israelite religion, or is it the description of the Bible's continuing importance?

10. *The curious history of the interpretation of the book of the*
   Revelation of St. John: a case study to illustrate how biblical exegesis
   changed in the development of the modern era

It has been argued that in the Enlightenment extraordinary changes took place in the nature of scholarly exegesis. To get some idea of the extent of these changes, it is useful to have a look at differing approaches to that most curious of all New Testament books, the Revelation of Saint John the Divine.

i. SOME BACKGROUND

The seventeenth century[81] had been a time of turbulent apocalyptic expectations[82] of many sorts, from the hopes of disorderly groups like the Levellers and Muggletonians in commonwealth England to the French nationalist variant in Isaac de La Peyrère. It should be borne in mind that not all these apocalyptic hopes were founded on the book of Revelation, for the Gospels themselves as well as the Pauline epistles have apocalyptic passages, and in fact La Peyrère based his apocalyptic expectations on the Epistle to the Romans, not the book of Revelation. Eschatological hopes were also nourished by the Old as well as the New Testament, and the book of Daniel had equal status with Revelation; hence the Fifth Monarchy Men in mid-seventeenth-century England based their hopes on the fifth kingdom in Daniel 12:.44 as the thousand-year reign of Christ.[83] In Isaac Newton's commentary on Daniel and Revelation, it is Daniel that got the major share of the discussion.[84]

---

[81] For a thorough treatment of hopes for the end in the seventeenth century, see Bryan W. Ball, *A Great Expectation: Eschatological Thought in English Protestantism to 1660* (Leiden: E. J. Brill, 1975). For a detailed look at many of the figures mentioned in this article, see Christopher Burdon, *The Apocalypse in England: Revelation Unravelling, 1700–1834* (New York: St. Martin's Press, 1997).

[82] I am using the word "apocalyptic" in a very general sense to describe hopes for some sort of dramatic divine intervention in human affairs that could be foretold from texts in the Bible.

[83] This group is the subject of the one humorous entry in *The Oxford Dictionary of the Christian Church* (1st ed., 504), which records the end of the sect by saying, "After an unsuccessful rising in Jan. 1661, its leaders were beheaded and the sect died out."

[84] *Observations upon the prophecies of Daniel, and the Apocalypse of St. John* (London: 1733). Reference in this article is to the edition prepared by Sir William Whitla, *Sir*

Two sorts of inheritance from the seventeenth-century interest in apocalyptic came down to the eighteenth century. One was a particular book entitled *Clavis Apocalypticum*[85] by Milton's Cambridge tutor Joseph Mede (1586–1638), which, as the most competent and well-known epitome of one sort of interpretation, exerted a dominant influence on many eighteenth-century works of a similar sort. In Germany the interpretation of the Apocalypse progressed more tentatively as a result of the condemnation of chiliasm in the Augsburg Confession, but the emergence of Pietism led to a renewed personal level in the interpretation of the Bible. In Pietist circles the emphasis on reading the Bible in general under the guidance of the Holy Spirit could cause problems, as Spener found out for himself; but in the interpretation of Revelation, exegesis that could claim the authority of the Holy Spirit was even more explosive, especially given Spener's own rather vague expression of a "hope for better times."[86]

There were at least seven different categories of interpretation in the study of the book of Revelation in the late seventeenth and eighteenth centuries: the prophetic, the Protestant mathematical, the Chamber of Commerce, the Roman Catholic, the antagonistic, the scholarly, and the aesthetic. Different as these might have been in their point of departure and final conclusions, all these approaches have in common that they led their adherents to write. But also to be reckoned with was an attitude of mind that served as a counterpoint to all the exegetical melodies. For in the background lurked the suspicion that Revelation was a dangerous enigma, a book that either appealed to unhinged minds or unhinged the minds that appealed to it. There have therefore always been those who have looked on the book of Revelation in much the same way as many

---

Isaac Newton's Daniel and the Apocalypse; with an introductory study of the nature and the cause of unbelief, of miracles and prophecy (London: J. Murray, 1922).

[85] English translation: *The Key of the Revelation searched and demonstrated out of the naturall and proper charecters* (sic) *of the visions with a comment thereupon, according to the rule of the same key,* trans. Richard More (London: 1643; Wing M. 1600). For a discussion of Mede, see Michael Murrin, "Revelation and two seventeenth century commentators," in C. A. Patrides and Joseph Wittreich, eds., *The Apocalypse in English Renaissance thought and literature* (Ithaca, N.Y.: Cornell University Press, 1984).

[86] Gerhard Maier, *Die Johannisoffenbarung und die Kirche* (Tübingen: Mohr, 1981) 353–66. It is a weakness of Maier's otherwise excellent work that he confines himself to German material. This means that he is not able to allow for the extent of English influence on early eighteenth-century German apocalyptic thought or for Swedenborg's on later developments.

British people view the House of Lords, that is, as an unavoidable embarrassment that will perhaps go away if ignored long enough.

This view of Revelation is found most notably in the younger Luther,[87] who admitted that he did not quite know what to make of the book, and was presupposed by Calvin, who, as Josephus Scaliger commented, showed his great intelligence in writing commentaries on every book of the Bible except the Apocalypse, and was also found in the guarded brevity of many theological compendia of the eighteenth century.[88] Interestingly enough, two very different men among those to be discussed below, Dom Augustin Calmet, the French Roman Catholic, and Johann Albrecht Bengel, the German Pietist, registered their own initial unease in writing about the Apocalypse, a task they only undertook at the outset because they had committed themselves to writing commentaries on all the books of the Bible.

ii. THE PROPHETIC APPROACH

The prophetic approach to the Apocalypse is represented by people who at another time might have been happy to have written the book. These were people who, finding echoes of their own psychology in the Apocalypse, claimed that they had received some sort of divine intervention or special message and who now came to give the true meaning of the book of Revelation on the basis of authority not vouchsafed to the rest of us. Thanks to Spener's emphasis on the inner testimony of the Holy Spirit as an exegetical approach, some of his followers were tempted to see the testimony of the Spirit within them as an independent source of authority. As a result, all Pietists found idiosyncrasy a great temptation, and every so often some of them succumbed. Of these, Joanna Eleonora Petersen (1644–1724), along with her husband Johann

---

[87] In his early preface to the book of Revelation, Luther expressed his opinion that the work was neither apostolic nor prophetic. He made the trenchant comment that "they are to be blessed who keep what is written therein; and yet no one knows what that is, to say nothing of keeping it." His summation was: "Finally, let everyone think of it as his own spirit gives him to think. My spirit cannot fit itself into this book." See W. G. Kümmel, *The New Testament: the History of the Investigation of Its Problems,* trans. S. McLean Gilmour and Howard C. Kee (London: SCM, 1973) 25–26.

[88] It is interesting to note the relatively little space given to discussing either Revelation or to the hopes of the end time in the dogmatics of two great eighteenth-century German theologians, Johannes Franciscus Buddeus and Siegmund Jacob Baumgarten. People tend not to write books on subjects that they feel are at best irrelevant.

Wilhelm Petersen (1649–1726), are excellent examples. In the Petersens' case, it led to a challenge to a particular tenet of orthodox doctrine along with other apocalyptic concerns. This is how Joanna described how she received her awareness of this idea:

> Towards the end of the year 1685, which year I had been told in a dream of heaven twenty years before, that in it I would have something revealed to me, I was prompted to go into my room and to read in the Bible. When I opened it, the words from Revelation 1:3 caught my eye: "Blessed is he who reads and they that hear the words of the prophecy and pay attention to what is written therein, for the time is nigh."[89]

A few lines later, after describing how she prayed for enlightenment, Joanna continues:

> When I began to read in all simplicity, my heart was filled with the light of God in such a way that all that I read in such a great revelation became clear and transparent and so many passages in Scripture that agreed with it which I looked up that I filled a complete sheaf of paper with these.

She then went in to show her work to her husband, who became very excited and showed her material that he had just himself finished writing, which was exactly the same. What is interesting is that this clear understanding of the book of Revelation was linked not so much to an expectation of the end, although that was obviously implied, but to the doctrine of the new creation of all things.[90] Essentially, this was a form of universalism that looked forward to the redemption of the whole of creation, and by implication a rejection of the Orthodox doctrines of eternal punishments for the damned,[91] an idea which Hirsch considers

---

[89] The quotations are taken from her Vorbericht to her *Einige Sendschrebien Betreffende die Nothwendigkeit Verschiedener bissher von den meisten Gelehrten in Verdacht gezogener Lehren, Sonderlich in diesen letzten Zeiten, da die Zuberetung zur Hochzeit des Lammes, mit Mit so grösserem Eyfer und Gleiss geschehen soll* (1714). Translations are mine.

[90] The urge to preach this doctrine of the *Wiederbringungen aller Dinge* was touched off by the Petersens' receipt of a tract by Jane Leade (1624–1704), an English woman who had a great influence on the development of non-establishment Pietism in Germany.

[91] Part and parcel of this vision was the overcoming of denominational and religious barriers among human beings, including the conversion of Jews and others, as well as the reuniting of all Christians, Lutheran, Reformed, and Roman Catholic.

to be the one original contribution of separatist Pietism to the development of Christian thought.[92]

This was not the first or last time that the Johannine Apocalypse would trigger a reaction in a person whom Jung would have categorized as a prophetic personality, but when one comes to Emanuel Swedenborg (1688–1772), one feels that he and the book of Revelation were made for each other.[93] Joanna and Johann Petersen's simultaneous inspiration, so reminiscent of one of the legends about the making of the Septuagint, pales into insignificance in comparison with Swedenborg's claim when he stated categorically:

> Every one can see that the Apocalypse can by no means be explained but by the Lord alone; for each word therein contains arcana which could never be known without a particular enlightenment, and thus revelation; wherefore it has pleased the Lord to open the sight of my spirit, and to teach me. Do not believe, therefore, that I have taken anything therein from myself, nor from any angel, but from the Lord alone.[94]

It follows logically from a claim to this sort of authority that Swedenborg did not need to argue whether his explanation was justified either by philological evidence or historical occurrences. The net effect was that Swedenborg reached a point where the biblical revelation was almost unnecessary. Kant, to put it mildly, was not impressed and wrote his *Träume eines Geistersehers* in response, but Swedenborg's ideas are still a living tradition in the Church of the New Jerusalem, of which William Blake was a member for a while and from which he derived the material for his own similar visions.

iii. THE PROTESTANT CALCULATORS

At the other end of the scale from the prophets are a group whom I have called the Protestant calculators, for this group of interpreters were nothing if not logical in their approach, not least of all in their use of

---

[92] Emanuel Hirsch, *Geschichte der neuern Evangelischen Theologie* (Gütersloh: Gerd Mohn, 1961) 2:232.

[93] Swedenborg wrote two large volumes about Revelation; *Apocalypsis revelata* ("The Apocalypse Revealed"), published during his lifetime, and the larger *Apocalypsis explicata secundum sensum spiritualem* ("The Apocalypse explained according to its spiritual sense"), published posthumously.

[94] *The Apocalypse Revealed* (New York: Swedenborg Foundation, 1950) 1:iv.

mathematics. They tended to see Revelation as essentially the mother of all quadratic equations, which, if solved for X, would explain either what had happened in the past or foretell what was to come in the future. If this seems to be taking things too far, consider the large number of distinguished mathematicians who applied their methods to the exegesis of this book, not least of all Sir Isaac Newton himself. One solid Schwabian, Philipp Matthäus Hahn, even invented a calculating machine to help him describe accurately the boundaries of the heavenly Jerusalem.[95]

Behind this approach was the fascination with world chronology, an interest of the Renaissance that carried into the seventeenth century when Archbishop James Ussher endorsed the date of the origin of the world as 4004 B.C. The logic appears to have been that if you can use biblical data to trace matters back to their origins, why not turn the process around and follow the trail to the end of the world? This involves treating prophecy as something to do with the future, not social criticism, and looking on works that we would call "apocalyptic" as prophecy at its best. The two prophets par excellence then become Daniel and St. John the Divine, who could be treated on the same level as parts of a larger whole. A second assumption that sounds rather strange to modern ears was that Revelation was put on the same footing as the Gospels, since it too professed to give the exact words of Christ. To be fair, even mathematicians could recognize differences of types of language. Newton said:

> For understanding the Prophecies, we are, in the first place, to acquaint ourselves with the figurative language of the Prophets. This language is taken from the analogy between the world natural, and an empire or kingdom considered as a world politic. Accordingly, the whole world natural consisting of heaven and earth, signifies the whole world politic, consisting of thrones and people, or so much of it as is considered in the Prophecy: and the things in that world signify the analogous things in this.[96]

Certain basic problems recur in this rational type of interpretation, namely, how various figures are to be identified with historical persons

---

[95] See Martin Brecht, "Philipp Mathäus Hahn," in Theo Sorg, ed., *Leben in Gang Halten, Pietismus und Kirche in Württemberg* (Metzingen: Franz, 1980) 92.

[96] *Sir Isaac Newton's Daniel and the Apocalypse,* 149.

and how one interprets one's position in the various seals that are broken or where the thousand-year kingdom fits in.[97]

Of the many eighteenth-century interpretations of the Apocalypse, the one that stands out from a scholarly point of view is that of Johann Albrecht Bengel (1687–1752), who in four major works set out his solution to the Johannine quadratic equation.[98] In the course of his textual, philological, and translation work mentioned earlier in this chapter, Bengel came up against the book of Revelation. He described his experience this way:

> After I had spent a considerable time on the criticism and exposition of the Greek New Testament, and, in the year 1724, was come as far as to the Revelation; I took in hand this part of Scripture very unwillingly, and my only motive for undertaking of it at all was, that the work might not come out deficient in a principal part, having no Design or expectation of making any extraordinary discovery. When I was come near the intended conclusion, there opened unexpectedly to my view a resolution of the prophetical numbers contained in the xiiith and xx1st chapters, and of the great things there spoken of. Now as I had not in the least before then been in search of this, so I had no reason to shut my eyes against the arising light; I went on therefore in this track, and frequently found that one thing after another laid itself open to me. The importance of the subject and regularity of the work, and my earnest desire to draw up a satisfactory plan of the agreement between the prophecies and the events (to the consideration of which I was awaken'd by the notorious tragical doings at Thorn,[99] which fell out even in our own time, by which the quantity of blood formerly spilt on the ground has been somewhat increased anew) induced me to communicate some part of my

[97] This aspect of apocalyptic hope is responsible for the words "chiliasm" or "millennialism," words for "a thousand" in Greek and Latin respectively.

[98] These were: *Erklärte Offenbarung Johannis* (Frankfort and Leipzig: 1740); *Ordo Temporum* (Stuttgart: 1741); *Gnomon Novi Testamenti* (1742; this actually treated the whole Bible as well as Revelation); and *Sechszig Erbauliche Reden* (1747). For details of his other writings on Revelation, see Maier, *Johannes Offenbarung*, 425–26. The English translations are from John Robertson's translation, *Bengelius's Introduction to his exposition of the Apocalypse with his preface to the work and the greatest part of the conclusion of it* (London: 1757).

[99] The massacre at Thorn happened in the year 1724, of which a short account may be seen in Salmon's modern History in the present state of Poland, Chap.v [Robertson's note].

thoughts to those who might in one way or other be assistant to me, or whom I might excite to a further pursuit after the truth.[100]

Bengel's approach, then, was completely rational; he made a point of stating to his anxious public:

> . . . but I assure them that I know nothing of any cabbala, of any divination, of any astral influence, or any ghost or apparition. The source of such and so very different opinions concerning a new discover of ancient truth is this,—that many do not understand, or do not consider, how rich a treasure the Holy Scriptures are. I am nothing; and if somewhat of the truth has fallen to my lot, I found it in the common way or high road to heaven, by searching the Word of God with simplicity, and without any option of mine.[101]

In other words, Bengel simply tried to interpret the text in an orderly, scientific manner, given, of course, his assumptions about how the text was to be seen. The exact results he got are too elaborate to discuss in detail, but certain features are worth noting.

Bengel set out his method of procedure in a systematic fashion. There were three stages: the literal or historical explanation; then the resolution of the proper length of the prophetical times; and finally the connecting of these times with particular parts of the history of past times and then to future occurrences. In calculating events to come, Bengel was honest enough to admit that he may have made mistakes. In the tables he prepared showing prophesied events and world history respectively, he saw 1836 as the decisive year when the era of *chronos* and the many kings will end and the thousand years of the binding of Satan begin. Whatever else he intended, he certainly was not encouraging people to get excited about an imminent eschatological happening.

Bengel deviated from some of the interpretations of the past, for example, the identity of the angel who brought the eternal gospel in Revelation 14:6ff. Usually this had been seen as Luther or Calvin, but Bengel's calculations around this passage made it refer to the early seventeenth rather than sixteenth century, so he identified this angel with Johan Arndt, often seen as a forerunner of Pietism. Then while Bengel agreed that the Reformers were correct to identify Rome and the

[100] Bengelius's Introduction, v–vii.
[101] Ibid., x.

papacy with many of the unpleasant creatures in Revelation, for him it was a mistake to interpret every frightful text as if it applied to Rome. Furthermore, the beast rising out of the sea is to be identified first with the Hildebrandine papacy; before that time one could still see the Roman church as a genuine part of the church universal.

Apart from fomenting occasional chiliastic expectations, Bengel's approach was to have a practical long-term effect, for he contended that knowing what would happen was not a reason for sitting back and doing nothing:

> Whatever God teacheth, that we ought to apply ourselves with diligence to learn; neither seeking for more, nor contenting ourselves with less: and we ought also to apply it all to his glory and our salvation, and to the exciting of our devotion; and not wast all our labour on meer knowledge. But many deal with the prophecies as they do with an enigma. Before it is solved, they have a tickling impatience, a longing expectation, and an agreeable solicitude about it: but as soon as it is solved, they are weary of this, and want a new one. And therefore we may fairly conclude that if any man could at once give full and satisfactory answers to all the questions among the learned, he would have little thanks from them; for he would but only spoil their play and their pastime. But those who receive the truth with due thankfulness and respect, as soon as they come to the knowledge of it apply it to use; and that particularly as well as in general.[102]

This was to mean that for those who followed Bengel in his interpretation, knowledge of the end times was that much more a summons to further efforts, not fatalistic resignation. In the nineteenth century this heritage was to lead into the activist tradition in Württemberg Pietism as represented by the Blumhardts.

iv. ROMAN CATHOLICS

The third group of interpreters is made up of Roman Catholics. From the time of the Reformation the book of Revelation presented difficulties for the Roman Catholic Church, because once you see the Apocalypse as a prophecy of what will happen to the church, the identification of the papacy with the beast or the whore of Babylon has an immediate appearance of plausibility. This step had already been taken by various

---

[102] Ibid, 323.

opponents of the papacy before the time of the Reformation,[103] but various reformers latched on to this identification with obvious relish. I think it is fair to say that Roman Catholic writers saw the interpretation of Revelation as a matter of damage control for several hundred years.

Cardinal Robert Bellarmine (1542–1621) mapped out two possible strategies: either Revelation referred only to the life of the church in the early centuries, or else it referred to happenings yet to come at the end of the world. In either case the papacy could not be a candidate for identification with any of the monsters described in the book. Jacques Bénigne Bossuet (1627–1704), a superb French stylist, adept ecclesiastical politician, and miserable personality that he was, wrote a commentary on the Apocalypse,[104] which, following Bellarmine, confined its historical references to the first centuries of the Christian church.[105] In all fairness to Bossuet, he did make some good objections to the polemical interpretations of the Protestants. His approach and conclusions were then adopted by the most influential biblical scholar of the eighteenth century, Augustin Calmet (1672–1757), the learned but disastrously conservative French commentator who was mercilessly attacked by Voltaire.[106]

There was, however, an English Roman Catholic bishop, Charles Walmesley (1722–1797), who achieved a certain amount of success by adopting a rather curious variation on the mathematical approach. In his *General History of the Christian Church,* published in 1771[107] under the pseudonym of Senior Pastorini, this Enlightenment calculator, who was influenced by Newton, argued that the modern age was the Fifth Age, which consisted of two parts. The first part was the time of the locusts,

---

[103] In fact, this identification predates the Reformation; in the conflict between the emperor and the pope in the thirteenth century, Pope Gregory IX called the emperor Frederick II "the beast," and the emperor replied by calling the Pope "the dragon." Frederick thereby set an example for other opponents of the medieval papacy.

[104] Jacques Bénigne Bossuet, *L'Apocalypse avec une explication* (Paris: 1856) 389–515.

[105] No historian of exegesis should allow Bossuet to escape his just condemnation before the bar of history for his singularly mean-minded treatment of Richard Simon.

[106] Calmet, who showed a surprisingly generous point of view for his times by getting permission to do his studies under a Protestant, unfortunately left himself open to Voltaire by defending even the most outrageous parts of the Old Testament. His twenty-three-volume *Commentaire litteral sur tous les livres de l'ancien et du nouveau Testament* (Paris: 1707–1716) was well reviewed, even in Germany.

[107] See Geoffrey Scott, "'The Times are Fast approaching': Bishop Charles Walmesley O.S.B. (1722–1797) as prophet," *Journal of Ecclesiastical History* 36 (1985) 590–604. Walmesley's work was reprinted many times. I am using the New York edition (D. & J. Sadler, 1860) as preserved in the ATLA microfiche format.

when the Protestants actively persecuted Roman Catholics, and the second part would be from 1675 until 1825, a time during which evil forces would produce a defection from all religion. In other words, Walmesley was using the weapons of the Protestants to carry the debate into what had been their own special preserve, while at the same time accounting for the growing tide of secularism and opposition to religion in general.

The subsequent influence of Walmesley's book was rather curious. On the Continent it was used by conservatives to defend the Roman Catholic church against the events and consequences of the French Revolution; on the other hand, in Ireland it functioned to help solidify Roman Catholic Irish opposition to England and became a staple of revolution.

v. The Chamber of Commerce Approach

I have called the fourth type of interpretation the Chamber of Commerce approach. This is found in *Phaenomena quaedam apocalyptica ad aspectum novi orbis configurata. or, Some few lines towards a description of the new heaven as it makes to those who stand upon the new earth*[108] by Samuel Sewall (1652–1730), a native of Boston, a former fellow of Harvard, who also took part in the Salem witchcraft trials. The closest literary type to this book is the sort of document drawn up by a city or country bidding for the site of the Olympics, though in this case Sewall was trying for bigger game by putting forward the New World's case for being the site of the New Jerusalem. He stated at the outset, "I have endeavored to prove that America's name is to have been fairly recorded in the Scriptures; particularly in the book of Psalms, in Daniel, and in the Revelation."[109] To make his case, Sewall argued, "So, many things alleged by Cardinal Bellarmine and others, about the descent into Hell are wonderfully suited to the going of Christ Jesus into America."[110] Lest one jump to the conclusion that he was reflecting negatively on his native land, elsewhere he rejects the notion that America is hell proper, though this was, of course, in the days before Texas joined the Union. However, since the original inhabitants of America were obviously descendants of the lost ten tribes of Israel, for "the West Indians seem to come of the East: as both speak some *Hebrew*," the choice of America for the site of

---

[108] Boston: B. Green and J. Allen, 1697.

[109] Samuel Sewall, *Phaenomena quaedam apocalyptica ad aspectum novi orbis configurata, or, Some few lines towards a description of the new heaven as it makes to those who stand upon the new earth* (Boston: B. Green and J. Allen, 1697) preface.

[110] Ibid., 40.

the New Jerusalem was appropriate and especially convenient to the English, who could then visit "the citizens of New Jerusalem, and their countrymen, all under one."[111]

Although nominally Sewall was following the arguments of the seventeenth-century interpreters of Revelation, such as Mede; in fact, the New World he is talking about has more in common with Dvořák than with Saint John. Here is the new self-consciousness of America coming to the fore, perhaps a great-grandfather of the notion of Manifest Destiny.

vi. THE ANTAGONISTIC APPROACH

The fifth type of interpretation is the out-and-out attack on the spirit and message of Revelation. The Enlightenment produced its share of criticisms of the content and nature of the Bible in the eighteenth century, but there was one attack on Revelation that is rather interesting. It was entitled *Horus oder Astrognostisches Endurtheil über Jesum und seine Jünger Mit einem Anhange von Europens neuern Aufklärung und von der Bestimmung des Menschen durch Gott: Ein Lesebuch zur Erholung für die Gelerten und ein Denkzeddel für Freimauerer.*[112] Published anonymously in 1783, its author is usually identified as the chemist Christian Ernest Wünsch (1744–1828). Curiously enough, this work, which reeks of the spirit of the later Enlightenment, began with a somewhat bitter attack on the followers of Voltaire. It then went on to give a general explanation of religion, namely, all *Volksreligionen* came from a single source—the ancient observation of the things of nature and the heavens. Therefore, the author calls his book an *Astrognostisches Endurtheil*, because *Astrognosis* describes the appearance of the heavens, whereas astronomy describes with mathematical measurements the real movement of bodies. In other words, he explained religion as a development of astrology.

This precursor of Cumont was in favor of the morality that true natural religion teaches but was against all the evils that positive religion has produced, such as prejudice against and hatred of those who think otherwise. Wünsch considered that Europe had made great progress in culture and civilization over the past two hundred years, but the general record of Christianity had been to forbid the use of reason. His exposition of Revelation, then, was to show both its astrological origins and the potential danger of its doctrines and of revealed religion in general.

[111] Ibid., 42.
[112] Halle-Leipzig: 1783.

vii. THE SCHOLARS AND THEIR OUTSIDER CRITIC

The modern scholarly approach to Revelation sees it as a human document written at a particular time and subject to the usual influences that history and culture have on writers. In fact, criteria from other religions had been applied to the Bible in general since the seventeenth century at least,[113] and there was at least one case in early eighteenth-century England of using a comparative approach to revelation—that of Charles Daubuz (1673–1713), *A Perpetual Commentary on the Revelation of St. John.*[114] Daubuz tended to give his comments a conservative twist, but there is no doubt that he saw the connections between Revelation and other ancient documents:

> Now if we find, that in the prophecies and visions of the Old Testament and of the new, and particularly in those of the *Revelation*, the Holy ghost has made use of such symbolic terms, images, or types, as were in use amongst the *Egyptians* and *Chaldeans*, or to other nations, which followed those studies and learning, and practis'd all those sorts of divination that are consequences of that learning; we have the reason in the world to think, that the Holy Ghost has therein adopted this symbolical language; whether they be visions and prophecies given to the *Israelites*, or afterwards to the Christian church. So that it must needs happen, that the symbolical language and character of the *Egyptians*, and other nations is like the symbolical language of the Holy Ghost; and consequently, that the *Revelation of St. John*, being written in that symbolical language, and giving an account of visions suitable to the symbolical character, may be illustrated thereby, and ought indeed to be explain'd accordingly: whether the symbolical characters be taken from the *Mosaïcal* books, and other subsequent prophecies, or even from the like analogical characters, not us'd in those ancient and divine prophecies; because the Christian dispensation, which that Revelation describes, may have some peculiar properties somewhat different from the Mosaïcal. And I cannot at present see, what any reasonable and unprejudiced man can object against it.[115]

Notwithstanding this tentative beginning, the development of the modern scholarly treatment of Revelation had to wait for the three great

---

[113] For example, John Spencer, *De legibus hebraeorum ritualibus et eorum rationibus* (Cambridge, 1685) Wing S. 4946.

[114] London: 1720.

[115] *A Perpetual Commentary on the Revelation of St. John* (London: 1720) 13.

scholars of the later eighteenth century: Johann David Michaelis (1717–1791), Johann Salomo Semler (1725–1791), and Johann Gottfried Eichhorn (1752–1827). It may be unkind to suggest that all three approached their subject with undue care, but there is no doubt that Michaelis both hid behind Luther and was rather coy in the way he put forward the excuse of his own ignorance, Semler's first official pronouncement on the subject was in a work ostensibly by someone else, and Eichhorn published his commentary in Latin, not something he was wont to do in his books on other subjects.

Michaelis is a fine example of the uneasy attitude toward Revelation described at the outset (see pp. 263–64). In his *Einleitung in die göttlichen Schriften des Neuen Bundes*,[116] he tackled the problems involved honestly but with a notable lack of relish:

> I come now to an important, but at the same time the most difficult and the most doubtful book in the whole New Testament. The various questions which here present themselves for examination, whether they related to the style of the Apocalypse, or the year in which it was published, or the qualifications, which every man must necessarily possess, who attempts to expound it, depend entirely on the main question, whether it is a genuine work of St. John the Evangelist, or not.[117]

Having confessed his inability to settle this main question with the certainty he attained in the study of other New Testament books, Michaelis went on:

> In the whole of this inquiry therefore I will accompany the reader as far as I think we can go with safety: I will point out to him likewise all the prospects, which lie before him: but when we are arrived at the place, where the path divides, I shall think proper to halt, and leave it to his own choice to take that road, which appears to him the best.[118]

While Michaelis did go through the evidence about possible interpretations, attestation of authorship in antiquity, and the problem of the language of the book, he hinted very gingerly at his own opinion by

[116] Two vols. (Göttingen: 1777).
[117] *Introduction to the New Testament*, trans. Herbert Marsh (London: 1823) 457.
[118] Ibid.

saying that if the Apocalypse were explained without presupposing it was a divine work,

> then we should have to inquire, not what events in history had resemblance to visions in the Apocalypse, but merely what the author of this work proposed to himself in the description of the visions, what events he himself supposed would happen, and what expectations the readers of this work, in the age when it was written, probably formed from it.[119]

His final conclusion was: "But this is an inquiry, which I have never instituted, and therefore I cannot say, what would be the result."[120] At this point I regret to say that one has no choice but to accuse Michaelis of utter cowardice.

Semler first indicated how he saw the Apocalypse when he published *Free Christian Inquiry into the So-called Revelation of John from the Posthumous Manuscript of a Frankish Scholar, edited with Various Annotations.*[121] This book was basically the work of Georg Ludwig Oeder, who had recently died, but Semler did not give the author's name, a procedure remarkably similar to Lessing's approach to the publication of Reimarus at about the same time. Oeder's work tended to concentrate on a criticism of Bengel; it is in Semler's incidental remarks that we can see the emergence of a purely historical approach to Revelation. For example, Semler argued:

> I hope to show that the whole image of 1000 years of a time of blessedness and peace on earth is a poem of Greek Jews based on the superstition of numbers, that one meets in many apocryphal books, especially 4 Esdras. From this a great part of the descriptions that read so wonderfully in the Apocalypse are directly borrowed and taken. Here I cannot see where the divine reputation of this piece can be derived, since we can plainly see the clear connection with the six so-called days of creation and the seventh day of rest.[122]

[119] Ibid., 518.

[120] Ibid.

[121] *Christliche freye Untersuchung über die so genannte Offenbarung Johannis aus der nachgelassenen Handschrift eines fränkishen Gelerhten herausgegeben mit eigenen Anmaerkungen* (Halle: 1769).

[122] *Christliche freye Untersuchung über die so genannte Offenbarung Johannis*, 102, note 78 [presumably by Semler]. Translation mine.

What Semler was doing was to start with the evidence relating to the Apocalypse in and for itself before going on to see connections between it and other books of the Bible. This fits in with the point he made in his early work, which was basically a guide for students:[123] "Holy Scripture consists of many books which were not written at the same time nor by a single author under the same circumstances and indeed which are not found at all times under the same circumstances."[124] The controversy that broke out over Semler's attitude toward the Apocalypse led him to write his *Abhandlung von freier Untersuchung des Canon; nebst Antwort auf die tübingische Vertheidigung des Apocalypsis*,[125] perhaps his best-known work.

The person who did undertake an inquiry of which Michaelis pretended he did not know the result was Eichhorn. But Eichhorn was even less fond of controversy than Michaelis, and I fear it is no accident that his work on the subject is one of the few books he wrote in Latin, namely, his *Commentarius in Apocalypsin Johannis* (Göttingen, 1791), though it must be admitted that in his *Einleitung in Das Neue Testament* (1804–1827), he expressed his views in German at his usual length.[126]

While much of what Eichhorn actually said about the Apocalypse looks rather strange now, his method was essentially that of modern scholarship. He saw the Apocalypse as the product of a Jewish-Christian writer who showed the inheritance of post-exilic Judaism.[127] On the one hand, the writer stood in that part of the prophet tradition where visions and symbols were used instead of coherent discourse.[128] On the other hand, the writer was influenced by the Greek dramatic tradition, and Revelation is best interpreted as a cosmic drama without any attempt at characterization. In effect, what Eichhorn was doing was grasping the nettle Michaelis shied away from; the Apocalypse is not to be seen as a

[123] *Versuch einer nähern Anleitung zu nützlichem Fleisse in der ganzen Gottesgelersamkeit für angehende studioso theologia* (Halle: 1757).

[124] Ibid., 175. Translation mine.

[125] Halle: 1776.

[126] Johann August Noesselt, *Anweisung zur Kenntnis der besten allgemeinern Bücher in allen Theilen der Theologie*, 4th ed. (Leipzig: 1800) 207, gives Eichhorn's commentary an especially high recommendation.

[127] It must be admitted that while Eichhorn combined lucky insights with great industry, systematic thought eluded him, and it is hard to decide whether he saw the postexilic period as the time of the loss of Hebrew originality or the time of Judaism's enlightenment.

[128] *Commentarius*, iii.

divinely inspired book containing useful knowledge about the future but is an example of a particular form of prophecy to be seen in terms of its own times. Its hopes were part of its background, but they are not necessarily of importance to us. Certainly they are not next year's history in symbolic form. The Apocalypse had been tamed, or at least it might have been had it not been for Herder's slightly earlier work.

viii. THE AESTHETIC APPROACH

Johann Gottfried Herder (1744–1803), very much the outsider of eighteenth-century theological thought, did not fit into the mold of academic biblical criticism as it was developing in Germany, to the point where it has been necessary to defend his contribution to posterity.[129] Herder was in many ways the German prototype of Coleridge. Blessed with a startlingly original mind, a strong aesthetic sensibility, and boundless enthusiasm, Herder was as willing as any radical critic to treat Revelation as a human book rather than as a cryptic revelation of extraordinary mysteries. The difference was that Herder saw Revelation as another example of the Hebrew poetic mind at work, and he was a person willing to suggest with a straight face that Hebrew poetry should be entered into with enthusiasm and delight by means of reciting it at dawn to the rising sun. In short, he liked and reveled in the book of Revelation, which was more than Semler, Michaelis, or Eichhorn would have been able to say. Furthermore, Herder felt that the book of Revelation was divinely inspired in the sense of being a human composition that makes its readers aware of the presence of God.

Depending on how you count documents, Herder wrote one or two books on Revelation. His first work *Johannes Offenbarung. Ein heiliges Gesicht. Ohn' einzelne Zeitendeutung verständlich,*[130] written about 1774 and circulated in manuscript form. The criticisms of this work led Herder to begin again with *Maran Atha: das Buch von der Zukunft des Herrn.*[131] Although the second work was rather less exuberant than the first, Herder's basic viewpoint remained unchanged. The book of Revelation is to be understood as poetry, that is, as a sort of discourse different from philosophy, which nonetheless deals with the important questions of life. It was written to be understood by its hearers without any special

---

[129] Klaus Scholder, "Herder und die Anfänge der historischen Theologie," *Evangelische Theologie* 22 (1962) 425–40.

[130] Bernhard Suphan, ed. *Sämtliche Werke* (Hildesheim: 1967) 9:1–100.

[131] Ibid., 101–86.

code or calculation, for Revelation is a combination of biblical images and John's description of events in Palestine of the first century A.D. that would have been familiar to the original readers of the book. The message John was trying to get across was that the hidden Christ reigns despite appearances to the contrary. "You live in a transitional time: the book of fate hangs hidden above you and your people: Weep not. The Lion of the tribe of Judah has triumphed; the Book is in his hand; he is bringing matters to a conclusion and will accomplish this task."[132]

Herder appealed to his reader to go beyond the dry cataloguing of the pedants to enter into the spirit of Revelation, to go beyond the discussion of the images and take them into his or her personal depths. This combination of the aesthetic sensitivity and the religious quest has little place in the rarified atmosphere of academic discourse, but during the horrors of the Second World War there were many who found their strength and their hope in Revelation's poetic vision of hope in the midst of horror. Perhaps of all the eighteenth-century interpreters, it was Herder, considered an idiosyncratic figure in the history of biblical exegesis, who finally was able to move from an explanation to an understanding of the book of Revelation.

10. *A concluding word*

So where is our conclusion? I would argue that in the eighteenth century the rising tide of historical studies affected all areas of theology, but especially biblical and dogmatic theology. It was dogmatics that was put on the defensive by the growing awareness of the role nonbiblical thinkers such as Aristotle and Plato had played in its development, and this meant that initially at least there was the temptation to seek unconditioned, direct-from-God advice in the Bible. In some more radical thinkers this could serve as a covert method of smuggling in their own all-too-modern thoughts. But eventually the rising historical-critical study of the Bible made this appeal less simple, and biblical theology itself had to deal with its own baggage of historic material that was out of keeping with the thought forms of the new age.

[132] Ibid., 241. My translation of "Du lebst in einer drückenden Zeit; das Buch des Schichsals hängt verschlossen über dir und deinem Volke; weine nicht! Es hat überwunden der Löwe vom Stamm Juda: das Buch ist in seiner Hand; er vollendet and wird vollenden."

Chapter 7

Aspects of Biblical Interpretation
in the Nineteenth Century

The effect of the eighteenth-century dethronement of the Bible on the nineteenth-century public was, strangely enough, best described by Charles Lamb in a memory of his childhood in part of his essay "Witches and Other Night-Fears":

> In my father's book-closet, the History of the Bible, by Stackhouse, occupied a distinguished station. The pictures with which it abounds —one of the ark, in particular, and another of Solomon's temple, delineated with all the fidelity of ocular admeasurement, as if the artist had been upon the spot—attracted my childish attention. . . . Stackhouse is in two huge tomes—and there was a pleasure in removing folios of that magnitude, which, with infinite straining, was as much as I could manage, from the situation which they occupied upon an upper shelf. I have not met with the work from that time to this, but I remember it consisted of Old Testament stories, orderly set down, with the *objection* appended to each story, and the *solution* of the *objection* regularly tacked to that. The *objection* was a summary of whatever difficulties had been opposed to the credibility of the history, by the shrewdness of ancient or modern infidelity, drawn up with an almost complimentary excess of candour. The *solution* was brief, modest, and satisfactory. The bane and antidote were both before you. To doubts so put, and so quashed, there seemed to be an end for ever. The dragon is dead, for the foot of the veriest babe to trample on. But—like as was rather feared than realised from that slain monster in Spenser—from the womb of those crushed errors young dragonets would creep, exceeding the prowess of so tender a Saint George as myself to vanquish. The habit of expecting objec-

tions to every passage, set me upon starting more objections, for the glory of finding a solution of my own for them. I became staggered and perplexed, a sceptic in long coats. The pretty Bible stories which I had read, or heard read in church, lost their purity and sincerity of impression, and were turned into so many historic or chronologic theses to be defended against whatever impugners. I was not to disbelieve them, but—the next thing to that—I was to be quite sure that some one or other would or had disbelieved them.

Lamb concluded from this experience that "credulity is the man's weakness but the child's strength." For better or worse, the nineteenth century was being pulled into adulthood and not everyone found the experience enjoyable.

It is the thesis of this book that the most important changes in biblical interpretation took place between 1700 and 1800, when even in many faculties of theology the Bible lost its cultural preeminence in Europe. In matters of science, chronology, ancient history, linguistics, geology, geography, and other disciplines, the Bible was no longer either the starting point or the final criterion. Not everyone was in agreement, but even among conservatives a new period had begun, for when conservatives argued that in fact science did support the biblical picture, the game was already up, for now it was the Bible that required the support of science and not vice versa. This is the modern world, when a lecture by a famous physicist on why he or she believes in God might well attract an audience, a lecture by a famous theologian on why she or he accepts the validity of modern physics would be looked upon as an exercise in eccentricity. By contrast, in du Bois's seventeenth-century monograph on cosmology, part of his argument for an earth-centered solar system is its basis in the Bible.[1]

The basic assumption behind modern biblical studies having been reached, the way was now open for investigating new sorts of questions. Having once decided that the Pentateuch was not an infallible heavenly document but rather a book from antiquity, scholars were free to discuss its relationship to the rest of the Old Testament. Why did parts of the Old Testament that were later than the time of Moses appear neither to know nor care about the regulations in the law given by him? If the Gospels were to be seen as historical documents, how were they related to each

---

[1] Jacob du Bois, *Dialogus Theologico-Astronomicuus. . . . Ex Sacris Litereis Terrae quietem, Soli vero motum competere probatur; adjuncta Refutatione Argumentorum Astronomicorum, quae in contrarium proferri solent* (Leiden: Petrus Leffen, 1653).

other, and how can the evidence be used to reconstruct the life of Jesus of Nazareth as a historical person?

Now the scholars of the nineteenth century were nothing if not industrious. It is hard not to feel a tinge of envy when one looks at the extended runs of the huge volumes they produced, though some consolation can be derived from the fact that very few bother to blow the dust off those volumes today.[2] It is beyond both the scope of this book and the competence of its author to discuss in detail all the major scholars of the nineteenth century.[3] The goal of this chapter, then, will be to point out the nontheological factors at work and then show the salient features of some important approaches to the study of the Old and New Testaments which were worked out then which are still with us today in slightly different formats.

I. Some External Factors [4]

1. *Printing with power*

Up to the beginning of the nineteenth century, printing presses were worked by human effort alone. When the steam engine could be hooked up to provide the compression required for an imprint, the process became both speedier and cheaper. Typesetting had been done by hand, letter by letter; in the nineteenth century, machines for setting type were developed that increased efficiency many times. Both newspapers and books profited.[5] Newspapers could now be inexpensive enough for most

---

[2] There are two further observations: the pleasant one is to discover how often such works were never read even in their own day, and having to cut the pages of a hundred-year-old book can be an occupation not exempt from glee. The less pleasant observation is how many modern books such as this one will suffer the same fate.

[3] To save reviewers trouble, let it be admitted outright that the author is not as familiar with the work of nineteenth-century scholars as with that of earlier authors. There are many more studies of biblical interpretation in this period than in the earlier ones.

[4] There is no lack of books about the nineteenth century. Two that are useful both for their observations and their indications of further reading are Peter Gay, *Schnitzler's Century: The Making of Middle-Class Culture 1815–1914* (New York: W. W. Norton, 2002), and J. W. Burrow, *The Crisis of Reason: European Thought, 1848–1914* (New Haven: Yale University Press, 2000). Gay is a very important antidote against many misconceptions about the era, and Burrow discusses intellectual and social currents in a remarkably clear fashion.

[5] P. M. Handover, "British Book Typography," in *Book Typography 1815–1965*, ed. Kenneth Davis (London: Ernest Benn, 1966) 139–54.

people to be able to afford them. Books could be provided to meet the needs of intelligent people in the working class who frequented working-men's associations. The Bohn Sixpenny Library of great classics was the symbol of the wider dispersal of knowledge and literature.

2. *Transportation and communications*

The railways meant wider contacts for a variety of purposes, from widening the mixture of the gene pool in the population to enabling more frequent personal contacts among scholars. Ruskin could be scornful of the cultural advantages of the railways, but when one thinks of Guillaume Postel making a two months' journey on foot at the age of seventy, one can see why contemporaries less vigorous than that remarkable eccentric never got to meet many of their colleagues throughout Europe. Similarly, shipping improved in reliability, regularity, frequency, and safety, especially with the development of marine steam engines. The Cunard Line could boast that it had never had a passenger fatality. American students could frequent European universities and take home new ideas and old books. [The library at Princeton Seminary owes many items in its special collections to the efforts of one of its earlier presidents, who bought quantities of books looted by French troops from Rhineland monasteries.]

Regular mail service began in England and spread to the rest of the world. Scholars could send and receive comments from colleagues around the world on a regular basis for a moderate charge. Telegraph lines linked countries and continents to produce a qualitative change in the speed of news and messages. The difference made by the transatlantic cable is illustrated by the fact that at the time of Lincoln's assassination, a permanent cable system had not been put in place, and it took ten days for the news of his death to travel from the United States to Europe.

3. *The drive to revive the past*

One common reaction to the disruptions, social or otherwise, of the French Revolution and the Napoleonic era was to retreat into some ideal era in the past. This had already begun in the latter part of the eighteenth century, but various streams of antiquarian enthusiasm, not to mention political reaction, became more visible. Appeals were made to the Reformation era or to the Middle Ages—anything that might bury the Enlightenment and all its enormities. This is why a sanitized version of medieval Catholicism and gothic architecture left an indelible mark on some churches, not least of all the Church of England, and why at the end of the century Joris Karl Huysmans, in his later Roman Catholic period, could refer approvingly of a character in his novel *La Cathédrale* as "un pélerin en plein moyen age"—"a pilgrim back to the fullness of the Middle Ages." The danger was that under the influence of a fascination with the past, the churches could be recruited as supports for political attempts to restore Europe to more or less its former condition, and in some countries church officials functioned as part of the machinery of reaction.

4. *Nationalism*

New notions were developed about what constituted human society and how it should be understood. Interest in the methods of government was nothing new; what was novel, was the emergence of different approaches to defining the nature of a nation and the emergence of debates about whether minorities—racial, religious, or however perceived—resident within a nation could be full citizens. This meant that nationality was no longer defined by dynastic loyalty; language became more important as one way of defining one's ideal citizenship, but to this the matter of race could be added. As racial myths about the superiority of Aryans and the dangers of racial impurity were added, it is possible to see the outlines of the coming horrors of the twentieth century.[6] Theologians themselves did not always remain aloof from the charms of worshiping at the shrines of other gods. Bruno Bauer, who began his career as a Hegelian theologian, was one of the first to raise the matter of the *Judenfrage* ("the Jewish question") in Germany. In biblical studies, the defining of the Israelites as Semites required the explanation of why they had had so much influence over Aryan culture.

An alternative to race and culture was the struggle between two classes of people within all nations. Revolutions and uprisings of workers against capitalists broke out sporadically in Europe, and in the United States the founding of the Knights of Labor by Samuel Gompers led to urban strife.

There was a general shift in the search for legitimacy. Is the state to be defined in terms of its national aspirations, often of a territorial sort, or is its essence to be found in its people as a whole or some definable group such as the proletariat? Furthermore, in earlier periods the state had been in theory under God's protection and indirect governance, so in

[6] Burrow, *The Crisis of Reason*, 92–108; 214–19.

theory, at least, there were some restraints on what a nation could do. But in a secular society the state might well assume God's role, and nationalism might well become the *de facto* state religion.

5. *The emergence of science*

Science came into its own as a discipline distinct from philosophy, yielding both generally accepted theories and practical guidance for more efficient ways of providing for human needs, both material and intellectual. While philosophy and biblical exegesis had had their spats over the years, science emerged as a far more formidable opponent for exegesis than philosophy. This concern about the possible implication of scientific discoveries for religion was already apparent in the early years of the nineteenth century, long before Darwin began to publish his theories.[7] In its success, science began to take on mythic proportions; it was seen not only as a way of finding out knowledge that might have practical applications, but the scientific method became a movement in itself, so that science could be billed as the wave of the future that could settle the whole gamut of humanity's problems.[8]

A word needs to be said about the impact of Darwin's ideas. It is necessary to distinguish between his theory of evolution as a scientific idea and its implication for religion and the Bible. There is no doubt that it was seen by some as the great comeuppance of both. An example of this attitude is found in the biography of Ernst Haeckel, the influential exponent of scientific atheism.

> On this theory the various species of animals had been developed from each other, without a new creative act. If man was an animal species in this sense, he also must have originated from other animals; and that would be bitter. The phrase shows that Darwin already saw clearly, and had abandoned his belief in a special creation of man. But this point was bound to make more bad blood than all the rest put together. God, now restricted to the direct production of the first living things, had lost man as well as the animals. Moreover, whatever interpretation was put upon the Mosaic narrative, the very source of theistic belief, the Bible, was called into question. How had we come to know of this story of divine creations? By the Bible, the

---

[7] See, for example, Baden Powell, "The Advance of Knowledge in the present times, considered especially in regard to Religion: A sermon. . . ." (London: C. and J. Rivington, 1826).

[8] Burrow, *The Crisis of Reason*, 31–67.

vehicle of revelation. But this Bible was the work of man, and man was now well within the bounds of nature, from which God had been excluded. How could he learn anything from revelation? The biblical writers had clearly only made conjectures. Some of them—with regard to Adam, for instance—were certainly incorrect. There was nothing in the Bible about evolution by means of selection. Indeed, was not the whole picture of a creating Deity an error? These thoughts were bound to press upon the religious mind with all their logical force. When they did so, the very foundations of theology became insecure, to a far more serious extent than Darwin's moderate conclusion suggested. When the book fell on this contentious ground, it was bound, even if it were only read in the last two pages, to provoke vast waves of hostility against its heretical zoology and botany, especially in England.[9]

Only defenders of biblical inerrancy would find the absence of any mention of evolution in the Bible a source of worry, but there was another issue at stake. It had been assumed in theories of the universe that one could find in the creation the marks of a benevolent creator. Wordsworth watching daffodils could enthuse about nature. The new biology changed the view from the beauty of the daffodils to the insidious work of the root weevils destroying the lovely flowers from below, or the poor industrious weevils being eaten from within by vicious bacteria, or the simple bacterium having its nucleus destroyed by a malevolent virus, and so on. All this is caught in Hardy's poem "In a Wood":

> Since then no grace I find
> Taught me of trees.
> Turn I back to my kind,
> Worthy as these.
> There at least smile abound,
> There discourse trills around,
> There now and then, are found
> Life-loyalties.

This is, of course, quite correct, but the existence of struggle, pain, and depredation in nature is a problem for theology rather than biblical studies.

One particular development that was to have an effect on biblical interpretation was the emergence of social science, ethnology, anthropology, and sociology. Out of various works in these fields emerged notions

---

[9] Wilhelm Bölsche, *Haeckel: His Life and Work,* trans. Joseph McCabe (London: T. Fisher Unwin, 1906) 126–27.

of social biology, race, and the degeneration of cultures that were applied backward onto the ancient past, so that peoples mentioned in the Bible were classified into categories they themselves showed no sign of being aware of.[10] In at least one case the work of a biblical scholar influenced developments in the social sciences, and that was the theory of the development of religion in William Robertson Smith.

6. *Industrialization and the resulting change in social conditions*

A hanger-on of science and technology was the new industrialism, with its rearrangement of urban life and the creation of ugly slum conditions, all in the name of industry and progress. To be fair, it is an arguable case that the factory workers were often better off than their cousins the agricultural laborers, but a new way of living had come into being. The growth of relatively large conglomerations of factory workers in the cities meant that the pattern of small communities based around agriculture disappeared for many people, and the problem of the alienation between people and their work, as described by the early Marx, emerged. For religious belief, this often led to a loosening of links with established churches and the development of other forms of cultural bonds.

The human imagination was both caught and crippled by this new development in the success of pragmatic technology and the consequent general increase in production and wealth. Jeremy Bentham achieved immortality by declaring that "shove ha'penny is as good as poetry," and along with Mr. Gradgrind of *Bleak House*, with his emphasis on facts, both were examples of attitudes easy to find. This attitude lingers on today in decisions in educational matters between basic subjects that can be applied to means of production and employment, and frills that only deal with the enrichment of human life and are easily dispensed with.

7. *The shape of education and the emergence of a wider reading public*

As part of the growing influence of science, universities began to change their format. Beginning in Germany,[11] research, especially scientific research, began to exercise a growing role, and even Oxford and

---

[10] If one examines the ancestors of various peoples as set out in parts of Genesis, it is hard to see any pattern corresponding to the groupings of nineteenth-century social science.

[11] See Nicholas Rupke, ed., *Göttingen and the Development of the Natural Sciences* (Göttingen: Wallstein Verlag).

Cambridge had to widen their traditional occupations as finishing schools for the gentry and as preserves for members of the Church of England. With the growth of a non-confessional environment, theology lost its central position and attraction, so that complaints about the mediocre abilities of many theological students began to be heard. Furthermore, new universities were founded, such as the universities of Berlin and London, where new ideals were espoused. In England and other parts of Europe, a larger part of the population was made up of well-educated and well-informed people able to make good use of the larger number of books that were being produced.

Two more factors that showed a growing sense of the desirability of spreading education to all sectors of society were the establishment of schools aimed at educating a far greater proportion of the young and the founding of public libraries and extensive museums. The net effect was to increase the educational level of the general population, which meant that what was happening to the study of religion in the groves of academe might well be shouted on the streets to the interest and/or the horror of listeners able to appreciate the implications of new ideas.

8. *Philosophical factors*

Those wanting a reasonable introduction to the general movement of thought in the nineteenth century could do worse than to begin with two books: J. W. Burrow, *The Crisis of Reason in the European Thought,* and Owen Chadwick, *The Secularisation of the European Mind in the Nineteenth Century.* While an overview of the whole situation cannot be undertaken, there are several parts of the larger picture that were important for the interpretation of the Bible.

The first was the influence of Hegelian thought. Hegelianism could be many things, from a bulwark of Christian orthodoxy to outright atheism, or even a means of social criticism in its Marxist format. What Hegelians tended to have in common was an interest in "Geist"—a word inadequately translated into English as "spirit"—and a more sophisticated explanation of causes in history. Geist takes a long time to explain even for those who feel they know what it means (which this present author does not), but it does tend to describe those things that cannot be discussed in science and which are nonetheless important to humanity. Somehow Geist managed to maintain some sort of religious overtones even in atheist discussions, leading to the resigned advice "Never trust a German who tells you he is an atheist."

290 What Have They Done to the Bible?

But for many it was Hegelian idealism that was the vehicle for bringing in a wider vision of human experience than the models that tended to reduce the qualitative experiences of human beings to personal or social forces quite unconnected to values. That is why Hegelianism in its old age managed to move across the Channel. After its comparative decline in Germany, it was picked up in Britain in the second half of the nineteenth century by thinkers such as Thomas Hill Green (1836–1882) and Edward Caird (1835–1908), for whom it fulfilled the function of keeping open the possibility of explanations of religion that were not simply scientific reductions.

Second, the sort of causal explanation preferred by Hegelians was dialectic; that is, instead of simply cause and effect, there was a threefold movement of thesis, antithesis, and synthesis. The best-known example of this was Marx's analysis of European history, in which the thesis— feudalism—came into conflict with the antithesis—the peasantry—and the synthesis was capitalism, which in turn led to the emergence of another antithesis—the proletariat—and the ensuing conflict will culminate in a classless society. This sort of explanation was not always appropriate in the areas where it was employed, but it did open the way to a more sophisticated picture of what actually happens in society.

One good example of a systematic application of Hegelianism to biblical exegesis was Johann Karl Wilhelm Vatke's *Die Religion des Alten Testamentes nach den kanonischen Büchern Entwickelt.*[12] It is an interesting case of, if not being right for the wrong reason, at least of arriving at a hypothesis by a different route. Vatke (1806–1886) wrote a biblical theology, in which genuine analysis of aspects of the documents was combined with the Hegelian dialectic of causation, producing a new view of Israelite religion, in which the synthesis was the emergence of law and ritual regulations as the final rather than the beginning stages of the history of the biblical documents. This happened to coincide with the results of the so-called Graf-Wellhausen theory, which was worked out on different grounds.[13]

---

[12] Berlin: 1835. This was to be a first part of a larger work entitled *Die Biblische Theologie wissenschaftliche Dargestellt*, but for various reasons Vatke was unable to complete his work.

[13] See L. Perlitt, *Vatke und Wellhausen: Geschichtsphilosophische Voraussetzungen und Historiographische Motive für die Darstellung der Religion und Geschichte Israels durch Wilhelm Vatke und Julius Wellhausen* (Berlin: Topelmann, 1965). Wellhausen himself is

Biblical studies and other humanities disciplines remained in Germany as part of Wissenschaft; in the English-speaking world they were not often included under the heading of science, however loosely defined. This left two basic problems. The first was how causation was to be described. If simple cause and effect was not always adequate, what might an alternative be? Second, if one begins from a belief in the reality of the material world, how can one allow for the importance of the human perception of qualities, since qualities such as the good and the beautiful escape measurement? Still, biblical studies and its cousin history tried to maintain some claims to scientific respectability by attention to the pragmatic.

The problem that was to emerge in the nineteenth century was, How can the facts of history be established, and what is the connection between such facts and one's beliefs and personal commitments?

9. Secularization

Of all the weasel words to be wary of in the study of religion, "secularization" is among the most skillful of the shape-shifters. It can stand for a decline in religious conviction, a decline in religious practice, a decline in the power and affluence of religious institutions, or a decline in the right of religious authorities to exercise office or voice in political matters. There is no doubt that secularization of some sort took place in Europe in the nineteenth century, but what sort and where is more difficult to be clear about. The most interesting, if perverse, attempt to measure the prevalence of religious belief was the method of the French *annales* scholars to measure the weight of candle wax burned as votive offerings in churches. Those who wish to make a solid beginning in this matter might want to read Owen Chadwick's *The Secularization of the European Mind in the Nineteenth Century*.[14]

---

sometimes criticized as having applied Hegelian categories to the biblical material. In fact, Wellhausen was not a Hegelian, and the charge against him appears to be a case of guilt by association with Vatke. However, Wellhausen was very generous to Vatke, and in the introduction to his *Prolegomena to a History of Israel* speaks very kindly of him. Vatke is a forgotten thinker in Germany, but in North America a Vatke Society carried on an active program under the auspices of the Society for Biblical Literature for many years.

[14] Owen Chadwick, *The Secularization of the European Mind in the Nineteenth Century* (Cambridge: Cambridge University Press, 1975) esp. 1–18.

II. Biblical Interpretation

A. OLD TESTAMENT

1. *The recovery of ancient languages, cultures and religions:*
   Egypt, Mesopotamia, and Palestine-Syria

It had always been apparent from the Bible itself and from classical sources that there were other civilizations in the Ancient Near East in biblical times. Unfortunately, knowledge of these other areas had only been available secondhand through Greek and Latin writings, often themselves not preserved in their entirety. Even as early as Herodotus (fifth century B.C.E.), people had marveled over Egyptian hieroglyphic writings and ascribed many mysteries to them, but apart from fantastic guesses, such as the work of Horapollo, there were no transcriptions of the characters or translations of the texts.[15] Mesopotamia was even less well-known. The Bible itself was the best source of knowledge of the non-Graeco-Roman world. In the nineteenth century all this changed.[16]

2. *Egypt*[17]

The fascination with Egypt had run high in France in the eighteenth century, thanks in part to the translation of part 3 of *Warburton's Divine*

---

[15] The work of Horapollo Niliacus is attributed to an Egyptian magus who claimed to have found the meanings of various hieroglyphic signs. A modern translation is *The Hieroglyphics of Horapollo*, trans. George Boas, Bollingen Series 23 (Princeton: Princeton University Press, 1993). What is missing in this latest translation compared with the sixteenth-century edition is the list of parallels between these signs and biblical sources that were in the latter, a feature that indicates something about the sixteenth century itself and may echo the notion of the *philosophia perennis.*

[16] A good example of the progress that had been made in the understanding of the background to the Old Testament is A. H. Sayce, *Early Israel and the Surrounding Nations* (London: Service & Paton, 1899). Sayce, who was professor of Assyriology at Oxford, pointed out in his introduction (xxvi): "Hebrew history is unintelligible as long as it stands alone, and the attempt to interpret it apart and by itself has led to little else than false and one-sided conclusions. . . ."

[17] On Egyptian language see Lesley and Roy Adkins, *The Keys of Egypt: The Obsession to Decipher Egyptian Hieroglyphs* (New York: HarperCollins, 2000); Erik Iversen, *The Myth of Egypt and Its Hieroglyphs in European Tradition* (Copenhagen, 1961; repr. Princeton: Princeton University Press, 1993); Richard Parkinson, *Cracking Codes: The Rosetta Stone and Decipherment* (Berkeley: University of California Press, 1999). On Egyptian culture see Rosalie David, *The Experience of Ancient Egypt* (London and New York: Routledge, 2000) esp. part 2, "The Development of Egyptology"; Leslie Greener, *The Discovery of Egypt* (New York: Viking, 1966); T.G.H. James, ed., *Excavating in*

Legation of Moses, which dealt with Egypt.[18] Interest in antiquities may have been part of the reason why the importance of the Rosetta Stone, discovered in 1799 during Napoleon's Egyptian campaign, was quickly recognized. This stone is an inscription of the same text in three writing systems: hieroglyphics proper, the demotic or cursive script developed from hieroglyphics, and Greek. Thanks to the work of Thomas Young, Jean François Champollion ("the younger") and Palmer, the Greek version was used as a means for deciphering the other two scripts, and the basis for the study of Egyptian inscriptions and documents was established.

3. *Mesopotamia*[19]

In Mesopotamia a less cumbersome script than hieroglyphics was developed. It was syllabic rather than pictographic, designed primarily to be written on clay tablets with a stylus and is named "cuneiform," from the Latin for "wedge," since the principal part of the script consists of triangular indentations.[20] In the eighteenth century Carsten Niebuhr,

---

Egypt: The Egypt Exploration Society 1882–1982 (Chicago and London: University of Chicago Press, 1982); John A. Wilson, *Signs and Wonders Upon Pharaoh* (Chicago: University of Chicago Press, 1964).

[18] The popularity of Egyptian themes was shown by the Empress Josephine, who, with her divorce money from Napoleon, ordered a dessert service from the Sèvres porcelain factory containing a long centerpiece comprising miniature replicas of some of the major monuments of Egypt; the plates were decorated with scenes of Egypt reproduced from drawings by Dominique Vivant-Denon, who had accompanied Napoleon on his Egyptian campaign in 1798. Eventually she declined it, after which it was bought by Louis XVIII, who gave it to the Duke of Wellington. It is now exhibited in Apseley House, his London residence. See Charles Truman, *The Sèvres Egyptian Service 1810–12* (London: Victoria and Albert Museum, 1982).

[19] On Mesopotamian scripts: Cyrus H. Gordon, *Forgotten Scripts: Their Ongoing Discovery and Decipherment,* rev. ed. (New York: Basic Books, 1982); Maurice Pope, *The Story of Decipherment: From Egyptian Hieroglyphs to Maya Script,* rev. ed. (London: Thames & Hudson, 1999), originally *The Story of Archaeological Decipherment: From Egyptian Hieroglyphs to Linear B,* 1975); Peter T. Daniels and William Bright, eds., *The World's Writing Systems* (New York and London: Oxford University Press, 1996); J. T. Hooker et al., *Reading the Past: Ancient Writing from Cuneiform to the Alphabet* (London: British Museum Publications, 1990). On Mesopotamian culture see Seton Lloyd, *Foundations in the Dust: The Story of Mesopotamian Exploration,* rev. ed. (London: Thames and Hudson, 1980); J. M. Sasson et al., eds. *Civilizations of the Ancient Near East,* 4 vols. (New York: Scribner's, 1995). This contains a great deal of material relating to various ancient cultures.

[20] The situation is a little more complicated than can be discussed in a general work, but while many of the cuneiform signs were originally pictographic, generally they

Michaelis's man in the Arab world, brought back very accurate drawings of cuneiform inscriptions. Georg Friedrich Grotefend (1775–1853) and others made some slight progress in their transcription, but it was not until Henry Rawlinson (1810–1895) found two multilingual transcriptions in 1835 that substantial accuracy was attained. As time went on, it was discovered that cuneiform had been invented by the Sumerians, a non-Semitic people, but it was eventually adopted for use in writing both Semitic languages such as Akkadian, the language of Assyria and Babylon, as well as non-Semitic tongues such as Hittite. Akkadian was used as a diplomatic language and pieces of correspondence between Egypt and various Canaanite cities in the fifteenth and fourteenth centuries B.C.E. were found in cuneiform tablets in excavations at Tel el-Amarna in Egypt.

The net effect of the decipherment of writings from ancient Israel's neighbors was to give a firsthand insight into the culture and religion of the ancient world in which the Old Testament was written. There were even some overlaps between the biblical historical accounts and ancient Near Eastern records, such as the Assyrian and Babylonian documents about campaigns in Palestine. There were also resemblances between the Near Eastern mythical texts and nonhistorical parts of the Old Testament, such as myths about creation. What became more and more clear was that the Hebrew Bible was produced by a small nation that derived much of its culture, its language, and its religious imagery and practices from the larger nations round about it.

This recognition led to a lively debate just after the end of the nineteenth century about whether the Old Testament was really as unique as had been assumed earlier. The debate took its name from the short work that triggered it, namely, *Bibel und Babel* ("Bible and Babel") by Friedrich Delitsch.[21] Delitsch, the son of a German scholar of the same name, reacted strongly against his father's very conservative position. He argued that discoveries from excavations, although relatively unknown to the public at that time, would lead to advances in the scholarly understanding of the nature of the Bible more radical than those already apparent in

---

function as syllables. It was in Syria that a cuneiform consonantal alphabet was developed, that is, signs indicated individual consonants. The Hebrew was essentially the same as this cuneiform alphabet, except that it was written in characters better adapted for writing with pen and ink. The Greeks were the first to have an alphabet that included the vowels as well as the consonants.

[21] Friedrich Delitsch, *Babel and Bible,* trans. C.H.W. Johns (London: Williams and Norgate, 1903).

the results of natural science. He also proposed that the Israelites would be shown to be the youngest among their neighbors, and many incidents recorded in the Old Testament were based on older Mesopotamian materials, such as the story of Moses in the bullrushes, which comes from a much older legend about Sargon I of Babylonia. Delitsch was not always tactful in his tone, but the fact remains that he was right in principle about many matters in the Old Testament, and this may well have contributed to the public's doubts about the infallibility of the Bible in an even more convincing manner than the more abstruse discussions about geology or evolution.

4. *Palestine–Syria*

In Palestine most documents were written on perishable materials rather than on clay tablets. This explains why apart from a few inscriptions and miscellaneous incidental texts, little written information has been discovered in Palestine itself. However, between 1890 and 1898 a large number of ancient manuscripts and fragments were discovered in the Geniza[22] of an old synagogue in Cairo, some of which were of Palestinian origin. That some of these Geniza documents were related to certain of the Dead Sea Scrolls discovered in the twentieth century has added piquancy to the work of interpreting both sets of documents.[23]

5. *The more accurate study of texts from other living religions: Hinduism, Zoroastrianism, Buddhism, and Chinese and Japanese religion*

Matteo Ricci (1552–1610) had attempted to mediate Chinese religion to the West in the sixteenth and seventeenth centuries, but the sympathetic interest of the Jesuit order, whether well-founded in fact or not,

[22] The Geniza was a room traditionally used for storing old manuscripts that were considered too holy to destroy. See Paul Kahle, *The Cairo Geniza* (Oxford: Blackwell, 1959).

[23] In the twentieth century two sources of written materials were discovered. The first source was the cuneiform texts discovered at Ras Shamra (ancient name Ugarit) in the 1920s on the Syrian coast; these gave us some insight into the mythology of the Canaanites. The second source was the Dead Sea Scrolls from the desert of Judah, discovered in the late 1940s; these have thrown light on the textual tradition of the Old Testament and the life of a sectarian community in the first century C.E. The Dead Sea Scrolls are important both for the textual traditions of the Old Testament and for supplementing our knowledge of life in Palestine between circa 150 B.C.E. and 70 C.E. Direct connections with the New Testament documents are somewhat more problematical.

was condemned by Pope Clement IX in 1704 and 1715. By the end of the eighteenth century, interest had been rekindled as the translations of Eastern texts such as the Zend Avesta became available and Christoph Meiners (1747–1810) wrote his history of religion, which enjoyed considerable influence.[24] Even biblical scholars took note. Gottlieb Philipp Christian Kaiser wrote the first two parts of his *Old Testament Theology* as a work of comparative religion.[25] In the nineteenth century the effort to understand other religions continued. Max Müller, a German who taught at Oxford, was responsible for a multivolume edition of the religions of the world, which was an attempt at an accurate and comprehensive translation of Eastern texts.[26] The net effect was that the more the Bible could be compared to other religious texts, the less it appeared to be incomparable in the second, more laudatory sense of the word.

But it was not just the "higher" religions that were compared with the Bible; scholars were looking at the religious systems of "primitives," that is, of nonliterate peoples located in Africa, Asia, and the South Pacific. Could these systems be evidence about how all religions arose and how they developed? Better still, given that the Old Testament could be seen as the work of an older culture, and if one then assumed that all religions developed along similar paths, might not the religions of modern primitives provide useful parallels to the older parts of Hebrew religion? The Old Testament was now seen by many scholars as the record of the religion of the Hebrews, so in addition to its dethronement as a universal standard of knowledge, might the Old Testament now be relegated to the rank of being one religious document among many?

6. *Further refinements in Hebrew and other grammars*

In the nineteenth century the less exciting but very valuable work on the grammar and vocabulary of the biblical languages continued. In the case of Old Testament languages, Akkadian, the language of the Babylonians and Assyrians, was discovered to be a Semitic tongue like Hebrew, and for the first time grammarians were able to compare Hebrew words with words from cognate languages contemporary with the Old Testament. Egyptian is not a Semitic language, but some Hebrew words were

---

[24] Christoph Meiners, *Grundriss der Geschichte aller Religionen* (Lemgo: Meyer, 1785).
[25] See J. Sandys-Wunsch, "P. C. Kaiser, La Théologie biblique et l'histoire des religions," *Revue d'histoire et de philosophie religieuse*, Festschrift for E. Jacob (1979) 391–96.
[26] Max Müller, *The Sacred Books of the East*, 51 vols.

discovered to be loan words from Egyptian, not least of all the name "Moses" itself. Wilhelm Gesenius produced both a dictionary of Hebrew and a Hebrew grammar, which has served as the basis of many dictionaries and grammars ever since.

7. The conservative reaction to historico-critical method and its consequences

Putting the clock back never succeeds completely, if for no other reason than that the memory of what one rejects is an active part of the reconstruction one attempts. In matters religious there were differences about what one wanted to return to. In 1817 Claus Harms (1778–1855), on the occasion of the three-hundredth anniversary of Luther's ninety-five theses, issued ninety-five theses of his own, in which he denounced the religion of reason, the unbelief of his times, and the attempt to unite the Lutheran Church with the Reformed. This set the tone for a new conservatism in some German universities, such as the work of Ernst Wilhelm Hengstenberg (1802–1869) and Friedrich August Tholuck (1799–1887). Having been tempted by more liberal positions themselves, their reaction against "liberal" theology was rather like the moral self-righteousness of the reformed rake. In Berlin, Hengstenberg's treatment of his colleague Vatke was ungenerous in the extreme, and Tholuck's history of rationalism[27] was very unfair in many of its judgments. In England, as mentioned above, the influence of the Romantic movement was to cause some people to return to a presumed medieval Catholicism, whether of doctrine, liturgy, or architecture.

In France the aristocracy as a group tended to reconcile itself with the Roman Catholic Church, and some scholars attempted a conservative revival in matters of exegesis. To be exact, there had been very few radical Roman Catholic scholars in France since Jean Hardouin (1646–1729), whose radical theories about the number of forgeries among ancient Christian writings were notorious throughout Europe. Jean Astruc (1684–1766), as discussed in the previous chapter (see pp. 239–40), was not a theologian but a physician by profession, and he was very careful to point out that his analysis of the documents in Genesis was meant to defend the Bible, not attack it.

Criticisms of the belief in the infallibility of the Bible came from self-styled enemies of the church like Voltaire, and this tended to have a

---

[27] *Geschichte des Rationalismus* (Berlin: Wigandt und Grieben, 1865).

negative effect on serious exegesis. For example, Joseph François du Clot (1745–1821), a Swiss Roman Catholic priest who had turned down a British invitation to go to Canada after the end of French rule in North America, saw his role as avenging the Bible from the attacks of its enemies.[28] Du Clot tended to confuse confutation with denunciation as he declared Buffon, Telliamed, Robinet, Diderot, and La Mettrie to be enemies of the Bible. Unfortunately, he spent a great deal of his time refuting Voltaire—unfortunate not in his attack on Voltaire, who was a relatively soft target for anyone who was a trained scholar, but unfortunate in that du Clot did not really come to terms with the sort of problems the Bible presents to any critical reader of whatever religious persuasion.

More constructive was a younger scholar, Marcel de Serres (1783–1862), who took a more reasonable tack.[29] Essentially, he played the Baconian card that the legislator of the Hebrews did not appear to have the intention of revealing the mysteries of the physical world; therefore the Bible is generally silent about natural phenomena. Moses only mentions them in order to establish a dogma or impose a duty, and he was careful to say no more than was necessary for this double purpose. Therefore, a defense of the accuracy of the Bible is no more than making sure that the general outline of the biblical report corresponds with the data of modern geology, which, says de Serres, it does. De Serres also put forward an argument that is still used, namely, that what science says about the world changes from century to century, and he cited as an example the progress made in chemistry in the previous hundred years, which would no doubt continue, so that by the end of the nineteenth century opinions current in his day would look very outmoded. This sense of a history to science is valid, and while it is not the answer to all negative opinions about the Bible, neither can it be ruled out completely. However, there was little sign of nineteenth-century French Roman Catholic biblical studies coming to terms with the problems of biblical interpretation, and a brilliant student like Loisy had to suffer the uncritical lectures of Vigoreux, for whom the Bible retained its historical infallibility.

In England there were people like Edward Pusey, who spent much of his life regretting the flirtation with Johann Friedrich Eichhorn's historical-

---

[28] Joseph-François du Clot, *La Sainte Bible vengée des attaques de l'incrédulité* (Paris: Gauthier Frères, 1834) 151. The first edition of this work was published in 1816.

[29] Marcel de Serres, *De La Cosmologie de Moïse comparée aus faits géologiques* (Paris: Lagny Frères, 1841).

critical approach, which he had had during his time at Göttingen.[30] But
the real problem was that a great deal of the history of exegesis had been
forgotten by both scholars and clergy. In the collections of small books
and pamphlets about the Colenso controversy in the Bodleian Library, it
is astonishing how ignorant the contributors were about not only the
earlier British contribution to modern biblical exegesis in the works of
Spencer, Burnet, and Middleton, but even of the sorts of works contained in Pearson's *Critici Sacri*. It was not as if the means were unavail-
able, for the two supplemental volumes of that collection were available
to the clergy from The Clerical Lending Library at 79 Pall Mall, and one
presumes that other important works were part of that collection. As a
result of this ignorance, the arguments against Colenso tended to be
either very naive or very bombastic. One of the lessons of church history
is that clergy ignorant of the basics of theology are more of a liability
than a help in a time of theological crisis.[31]

To be fair, there were conservatives who were aware of the past. One
of these was Edward Garbett (1817–1887), whose Boyle lectures in 1861
showed some familiarity with what had been said.[32] He was aware of the
Deist challenge to revelation and also of the work of recent critics, whom
he described as follows:

> The authority of the scriptural writers is attacked by charging them
> with mistakes in matters of fact and fallacies in matters of argument.
> Particular doctrines are singled out, and either dissolved into vague
> ambiguities, or openly discarded as obsolete. Separate passages and

---

[30] Pusey's attitude to the problem of religion and science was a rather smug description of theology: "On the solid foundation of the Rock, whereon it stands, it
looks out securely on the conflict of human opinions, as they toss to and fro on the
salt and bitter sea of this tempestuous word. It looks out securely, but with pity. . . ."
"Un-science, not Science, Adverse to Faith: a Sermon preached before the university
of Oxford on the twentieth Sunday after Trinity, 1878" (London: J. H. Parker & Co.,
1878) 8.

[31] By the end of the century some clergy were beginning to face up to the problem,
for example, the Rev. J. de Soyres, in an 1890 address to the St. John Clerical Association entitled "Christianity and Biblical Criticism" (Saint John, N.B.: J & A McMillan,
1890). At the end he quoted with approval a remark of a former teacher: "Remember
what Butler has so wisely taught us, that the only important question about Holy
Scripture is, whether it is what itself claims to be, not whether it is in all respects what
we may have imagined" (p. 20).

[32] Edward Garbett, *The Bible and its Critics: an Enquiry into the Objective Reality of
Revealed Truths*, Boyle lectures for 1861 (London: Seeley and Griffiths, 1861) 6.

isolated facts are submitted to a capricious criticism, which, discarding the impartiality of a judge, gloats over every imaginary difficulty, till the grain of sand swells to the fond eye of the critic into the dimension of a mountain. Such efforts singly may seem to be unimportant; but when we remember that they are made from a great variety of quarters, and urged assiduously by different schools of thought, which, differing fundamentally from each other in the very first principle of their schemes, are united in antagonism to the Christian Scriptures, the whole aggregate assumes formidable proportion.[33]

This, of course, is a fine example of both *argumentum ad hominem* and a failure to recognize problems honestly in the manner of the Renaissance critics. Garbett then gave an example of what is known in the sweet science as leading with your jaw:

I wish to shew that the contents of the Bible are revealed to us, not as temporary and occasional, true at one age, but admitting modification at another, but as certain facts, true once, and for ever, and for all men. To do this, I must either take each individual book, of which the Christian Scriptures are composed, and trace in each the character that it gives of itself, or, I must shew that the Bible is one complete book, of which all the parts are interchangeably bound together, and then the character which is asserted of one part will be applicable to all. Nay more, the very proof of this unity will go far to shew, that the doctrines of the Bible are not parts of a progressive human science, but of fixed and divine revelation.[34]

There were, then, two sorts of challenges to the authority of the Bible felt by the conservative-minded. The first was from science in its nineteenth-century cultural ascendancy, and the second from historico-critical studies on the composition of the Bible. The challenge of science was mainly from geology and cosmology in the first half of the century; in the second half it was the Darwinian firestorm that caused so much debate.

Nevertheless, as a supplement to the above remarks, it should be recorded that not everyone felt that the Bible was necessarily threatened by the demonstration of its cosmological weakness. Baden Powell in 1856 could say:

[33] Garbett, *The Bible and its Critics*, 3.
[34] Ibid., 40.

The disclosure of the true physical history of the origin of the existing state of the earth,—*entirely overthrows the supposed historical character of the narrative of the six days, and by consequence,—that respecting the consecration of the seventh day along with it,* and thus subverts entirely the whole foundation of the belief in an alleged primeval Sabbath, coeval with the world and with man, which has been so deeply mixed up with the prepossessions of a large class of religionists.[35]

Baden Powell's point was that modern science—in this case geology—shows that the first creation story in Genesis was not factually correct. This meant that it was no longer possible to argue that the seven-day week is part of the very structure of creation. But he was not upset by this; on the contrary; he was very content that the sort of arguments of some British sabbatarians were not supported by the physical evidence of creation.

8. *Essays and Reviews*

Darwin published his *Origin of Species* in 1859, but it was a book published a year later that caused a much greater sensation. Written by liberal Church of England clergymen, *Essays and Reviews* consisted of seven essays by a group under the leadership of Benjamin Jowett, the redoubtable head of Balliol College Oxford.[36] The reaction was extraordinary. Bishop Wilberforce, solidly in the tradition of bishops who itch to interfere in matters which they do not understand, raised the alarm. Two of the contributors were tried for heresy and sentenced to a year's deposition,[37] and over 11,000 clergymen of the Church of England signed a petition in favor of a biblical revelation and the doctrine of eternal punishments for the wicked. There have been better moments in Anglican history.

Three of the essays were principally concerned with matters of exegesis: Rowland Williams, "Bunsen's Biblical Researches"; C. W. Goodwin, "On the Mosaic Cosmogony"; and Jowett himself, "On the Interpretation of Scripture." H. B. Wilson, in "Séances Historiques de Genève. The National Church," included some observations on recent criticism of the New Testament, in which he pointed out that while Strauss had gone too

[35] Baden Powell, *Christianity without Judaism: Two sermons* (London: Spottiswoode & Co., 1856) 39.

[36] *Essays and Reviews* (London: John W. Parker and Son, 1860).

[37] But the decision was reversed by the Judicial Committee of the Privy council.

far in his Life of Jesus, nonetheless there were some parts of the accounts, such as the temptation of Jesus by the devil, that were better taken as images than facts.

On the whole, the degree of scholarship and cogency in these essays is very high, and some of the issues they raise are still with us. Williams aimed at introducing the general public to the moderate sort of German biblical exegesis represented by Baron Christian von Bunsen (1791–1860), and Goodman drove a few final nails into the coffin of the scientific validity of the Genesis story of the creation and form of the world. His judgment on the situation in the sixteenth and seventeenth centuries was an uncompromising "It would have been well if theologians had made up their minds to accept frankly the principle that those things for the discovery of which man has faculties specially provided are not fit objects of a divine revelation."[38] It is also worth noting that he gave a description of the gradual development of plant and animal life over large periods of years, showing that evolution as a theory was well-known before Darwin. Darwin's threat was that his form of the theory denied the existence of a benevolent creator whose handiwork betrayed his presence and his nature.

It was Jowett's essay that was the most important for its comprehension of the problems of biblical interpretation. In fact, despite certain assumptions about the history of civilization we might not want to be so sure about today, it is a superbly balanced discussion, which can still be read with profit. Jowett took into account the differences produced by the historical study both of the documents of the Bible itself and the manner in which these documents have been interpreted in Christian history. His recommendation of the value of the history of biblical interpretation was a fulsome tribute to an underrated discipline and concluded with a (to this reader at least) convincing conclusion that "It would be the history of the human mind in one of its most remarkable manifestations."[39]

Jowett's essay was divided into five sections: the causes of the extraordinary extent of the disagreement among Christians about how Scripture is to be interpreted and understood; the question of inspiration; the question of language; the differences between the exact interpretation of Scripture and how it is applied in religious life, education and literature; and a closer discussion of the application of Scripture to theology and

---

[38] *Essays and Reviews*, "Mosaic cosmogony," 209.
[39] Jowett, "On the Interpretation of Scripture," *Essays and Reviews*, 341.

life. While Jowett followed his outline reasonably well, the richness of observations he made defeats any attempt at a complete summary that is anything less than a transcription.[40]

In a nutshell, Jowett's position can be summarized as follows. One should not begin with a doctrine of inspiration that means that the Bible is to be treated in a different way than other books. There is only one meaning in a given text, and it is the meaning in the mind of the original writer of the passage. While discovering this original intention is difficult and inevitably hindered by the assumptions of the times of the interpreter, Jowett saw great strides being made in his own day in this undertaking. It is when this work of criticism is well-done that it will become clear how in some respects Scripture is indeed not like any other book, but only after the thoughts and language of the sacred writers have been explained in a careful and objective way.

Furthermore, in the matter of science and the Bible, an interpreter should admit that not everything in the Bible is consonant with modern science, and no attempt should be made to fight for a lost cause by trying to argue the factual accuracy of every statement in the Bible. One should not even expect that the Bible is an undifferentiated unity; rather, the unity is to be found in the progressive revelation of the will of God, culminating in the person of Jesus. It is an offense against truth to fudge the issue of the fallibility of various statements in the Bible, for while some people may be disturbed, the fact is that the situation is so well-known that pretending that it does not exist only puts the interpreter's integrity in doubt.

It has been argued that Jowett was not a completely modern exegete in that he considered the Bible to be the unchangeable word of God. In saying this, he has been accused of an unhistorical Platonist type of belief. I think a more reasonable interpretation of Jowett is that he believed that the Bible contained writings whose authors had important things to say about God. Interpretation goes wrong when the interpreters assume before starting that they know what sort of statements they will encounter and how they can get contemporary meanings out of them. Jowett's worry was that if the hard work of critical examination is bypassed, any sense of the actual meaning of the Bible would evaporate. This is how he described the problem:

---

[40] Anyone wishing to test the correctness of this statement could do worse than read Jowett's pungent observations on the importance and interpretation apportioned to some critical biblical texts. Ibid., 357–72.

> If words have more than one meaning, they may have any meaning. Instead of being a rule of life or faith, Scripture becomes the expression of the ever-changing aspect of religious opinions. The unchangeable word of God, in the name of which we repose is changed by each age and each generation in accordance with its passing fancy. The book in which we believe all religious truth to be contained is the most uncertain of all books, because interpreted by arbitrary and uncertain methods.[41]

The irony of this comment by Jowett is that it could be taken as a trenchant criticism of what sometimes is considered postmodernist interpretation, but what both this sort of postmodernism and the fanciful interpretation of older times do have in common is that their results are independent of the text and make the tradition of critical interpretation irrelevant. Where one might legitimately find Jowett's methods somewhat dated is his assumption that languages and cultures go through stages that are literally describable in terms of youth through to old age. A contemporary scholar would be likely to see this as a picture, helpful as a metaphor but illegitimate when pressed into service as the objective description of a demonstrable historical process.

9. John William Colenso (1814–1883)

In nineteenth-century Britain it was customary to storm on about "the Germans," who were seen as the source of sacrilegious criticism of the Bible. However, one of the more vigorous disputes of the century came indeed from abroad, but from a less expected quarter—the Zulus of South Africa. In order to understand how this ethnic group contributed to biblical scholarship, one has to take into account a particular feature of church hierarchy. Luminous intelligence has not always been seen as a quality requisite for bishops or indeed for administrators in analogous positions.[42] But if a bishop is both intelligent and afflicted with a conscience, his (and now her) episcopate is that much more likely to have a stormy course. Such a bishop was John William Colenso, who was sent to Natal to be bishop of a diocese whose principal inhabitants were Zulus and whose language he learned and for whom he wished to

---

[41] Jowett, "On the Interpretation of Scripture," *Essays and Reviews,* 172.
[42] Hence the American *bon mot* that the reason why angels find it hard to dance on the head of a pin is that so many pinheads one encounters are covered with miters.

translate the Bible. He was being helped by a Zulu, who, when translating the story of the Flood, asked:

> "Do you really believe all this happened thus,—that all the beasts, and birds, and creeping things upon the earth, large and small, from hot countries and cold, came thus by pairs, and entered into the ark with Noah? And did Noah gather good for them all, for the beasts and birds of prey, as well as the rest?" Colenso continued "Shall a man speak lies in the name of the Lord? Zech. xiii.3. I dared not do so."[43]

Things only got worse. Exodus 20:21-22 in the KJV reads: "And if a man smite his servant, or his maid, with a rod, and he die under his hand; he shall be surely punished. Notwithstanding, if he continue a day or two, he shall not be punished: for he is his money." Colenso's Zulu assistant was horrified.

> I shall never forget the revulsion of feeling, with which a very intelligent Christian native, with whose help I was translating these words into the Zulu tongue, first heard them as words said to be uttered by the same great and gracious Being, whom I was teaching him to trust in and adore. His whole soul revolted against the notion, that the Great and Blessed God, the Merciful Father of all mankind, would speak of a servant or maid as mere "money," and allow a horrible crime to go unpunished, because the victim of the brutal usage had survived a few hours.[44]

Had Colenso read La Peyrère or Voltaire, these observations would not have appeared so original. Jowett's point about the importance of the history of exegesis was demonstrated only two years after he had published it. Colenso was, in fact, not altogether ignorant of scholarship, but like many teachers before him, his student's questions forced him to rethink his position on the Bible and led to his publications on the Old Testament.

Archbishop Gray[45] of Capetown, not a bishop encumbered with a surfeit of intelligence, declared Colenso deposed for heresy in 1863, but

---

[43] John William Colenso, *The Pentateuch and Book of Joshua Critically Examined* (London: Longman, Green, Longman, Roberts, & Green, 1862) vii.

[44] Ibid., 9.

[45] In fairness to Gray, though he had only managed a fourth-class degree at Oxford, a tribute more to one's father's influence than one's academic attainments, he did exhibit qualities of courage and physical endurance.

the British legal system did not support him, and Colenso was able to continue in a sort of independent Church of England province that was finally in 1911 reunited with the rest of the South African dioceses. Thanks to his Zulu instructors, Colenso went on to write several works on the Old Testament that were appreciated in Europe in that, by raising questions of the physical impossibility of events covered in the Old Testament, he showed that some parts of it were not ancient records close in time to the events they nominally described. Colenso's somewhat massive work was neither an easy nor an attractive read, so his contribution to Old Testament studies has not left as vivid a memory as those of two other figures.

10. *William Robertson Smith (1846–1894) and* *Julius Wellhausen (1844–1918)*

In order to understand the development of Old Testament criticism in the nineteenth century, one must make a distinction between three separate subjects that in practice are inextricably intertwined: the history of Israel as a people/nation in the Ancient Near East; the history of Israel's religion and how its sacred sites, rituals, and requirements of its adherents changed through the centuries; the history of its sacred books and how they became combined to form the sacred Scriptures of the faith of Israel.

The traditional answer to the above questions was that Israel's history was recorded in the Pentateuch and the historical writings of the historical books (Joshua through 2 Kings and the two books of Chronicles). Thanks to Moses, Israel's religion, its nature, and its practices were defined by the Law given at Sinai and repeated in Deuteronomy before the entry into Canaan. Israel's religious history was a matter of recording how faithful Israel had remained to the laws given by Moses. The first and oldest sacred books, then, were the five books that comprised the Pentateuch, written almost entirely by Moses. Other books of the Old Testament were more recent, and the collection was put together by Ezra in the fifth century B.C.E.

We have seen how this picture began to fray around the edges as medieval Jewish rabbis and Christian scholars such as Masius, Pererius, and Richard Simon discussed possible pre-Mosaic and post-Mosaic items in the Pentateuch. Witter and especially Astruc began to investigate the possibility that the Pentateuch was made up of longer documents, each with its own characteristics. But for Astruc, these documents were themselves very ancient, older than Moses himself and used by him in the foundational document of Israel's religion. Thus the picture of the history of Israel, its religion, and its Scriptures remained much the same up to the end of the eighteenth century, however tattered the general outlines might have become. In the nineteenth century this picture was stood on its head, its elements disassembled, and the resulting fragments put into a new pattern.

The primary impulse for the reshaping of the picture came from Wilhelm Martin Leberecht De Wette (1780–1849), who in his *Religion des Alten Testaments* argued that Deuteronomy was the law book that was discovered in the temple in Josiah's day.[46] De Wette's argument was that if one considers the shape of the reformation of Israel's religion that Josiah introduced, it is not the law codes found in the second, third, and fourth books of the Pentateuch (Exodus, Numbers, and Leviticus), but rather the law of Deuteronomy that is the basis of the reforms that Josiah undertook in approximately 624 B.C.E. in the account in 2 Kings 22:1–23:24. That Deuteronomy's stipulation about the centralization of worship in one temple is not reflected in the historical books until the seventh century B.C.E., well on in Israel's history, is evidence that much of the legal material in the Old Testament represents not the oldest but rather the newest stage in Israel's religion and that some of the Pentateuch is newer than most other documents. This meant that a complete recasting of the history of Israel, its religion, and its Scriptures was required.

De Wette's work provided a good start, but it would take most of the century to work out how one could date other documents visible in the Pentateuch. By the end of the nineteenth century a consensus of sorts had been reached among many Old Testament scholars that there were four main documents underlying the Pentateuch; the documents were given letter names that corresponded to some extent with their contents:

"J" got its name from its use of the name "Jahweh" ["Jehovah"] from its outset; it was the oldest document, having been put together sometime after the time of David and was mostly narrative, though it also contained some laws.

---

[46] The omission of a more detailed discussion of de Wette's work preys on the conscience of the writer of this book. Fortunately, this has already been well done in John Rogerson, *W.M.L. de Wette, Founder of modern biblical Criticism: An intellectual Biography* (Sheffield: JSOT, 1992). Dr. Rogerson has written a series of books on the Bible and its interpretation, and while some of his arguments may be open to serious reservation, I myself have been unable to discover any.

"E" was named for "Elohim," the name it used for God before the revelation of God's proper name in Exodus 3:13-15. E was a later document, similar to J but not so well-preserved, and possibly of Israelite rather than Judean origin.[47]

"D" is named for Deuteronomy,[48] a law code surrounded with a series of warnings about falling short of one's duties that goes on interminably and is therefore easily identified as sermonic in style. The work of the Deuteronomic editor was thought to be detectable in small additions in the rest of the Pentateuch. De Wette had shown cause to date this work in the seventh or eighth century B.C.E.

"P" stands for "priestly" writer; this is the latest stratum in the Pentateuch and represents an interest in priestly matters, such as the temple and sacrifice, but it also includes some narrative, such as the first creation story in Genesis and a revelation of the divine name "Jahweh" in Exodus 6:2-3. P is the latest part of the Pentateuch, which acquired its present form some time during or after the exile of the Jews in Babylonia in the sixth century B.C.E.[49]

"JEDP" became the acronym of Pentateuchal criticism.

This revolution in the critical approach to the Pentateuch is associated with the name of Julius Wellhausen (1844–1918), but he was characteristically generous in acknowledging the work not only of de Wette but also of Vatke and George in Germany and of Reuss and Graf in France. It was Graf who communicated this solution to Wellhausen one day on a porch in Göttingen, a location that apparently still exists and is known to oral tradition in that city. Wellhausen, having grasped the force of

---

[47] In discussions of the history of Old Testament times, one should bear in mind that after Solomon the kingdom fell into two parts, Israel and Judah. This means that in the Old Testament, "Israel" can have two distinct meanings—either the whole of the Hebrew people or that part of it that made up the kingdom of Israel. Compare the use of "American," which is used both of citizens of the United States and citizens of other American countries of both continents.

[48] The name in Greek is from "deuteros" ("second") and "nomos" ("law"). In the Pentateuch, Deuteronomy is presented as a final sermon from Moses, which appears to be a second giving of the law.

[49] Any good Old Testament commentary will give the details of the presumed characteristics of these four sources, but in short the siglia were chosen for the following reasons. "J" used the name JHWH from the outset; "E" used the name "Elohim" until the revelation of the name JHWH to Moses in Exodus 3; "D" is for "Deuteronomic," which warns of falling away from the worship of JHWH or from having any sanctuary apart from Jerusalem; and "P" describes the priestly interests of the document it describes.

Graf's argument, went on to work out the theory in a much more detailed manner. For this reason the theory is sometimes referred to as the "Graf-Wellhausen theory."

According to Wellhausen's own account, his awareness of problems of consistency within the Old Testament was not due to the work of the great commentators of the sixteenth and seventeenth centuries or Astruc in the eighteenth.[50] In the introduction to his *Prolegomena to the History of Ancient Israel*,[51] he explains how it was ironically his fondness for other books in the Old Testament that forced him to examine the Pentateuch. In his early student days he was attracted to the stories of Saul and David, Ahab and Elijah, as well as the prophetic works of Amos and Isaiah. He paid little attention to the Pentateuch, but finally his conscience got the better of him and he tackled the legal sections of the Pentateuch. His reaction was:

> But it was in vain that I looked for the light which was to be shed from this source on the historical and prophetical books. On the contrary my enjoyment was marred by the Law . . . Dimly I began to perceive that throughout there was between them all the difference that separates two wholly distinct worlds.[52]

The aesthetic sense of the contrast between two different types of religious belief made it apparent that it was not the Pentateuch that was the basis for the religion of Israel in the time of the monarchy before Josiah. On the contrary, this was a later development, for "[T]o complete the marvel, in post-exile Judaism, the Mosaism which until then had been only latent suddenly emerges into prominence everywhere."[53]

As a result of his reorientation of the order of the documents, Wellhausen worked out a new picture of the history of Israel, the development of its religion, and the historical order of its Scriptures. which he laid out in the article "Israel," commissioned by Robertson Smith for the

---

[50] This is quite likely, for Wellhausen was not well-informed about the history of biblical interpretation. He mentions only Peyrerus [i.e., Isaac de La Peyrère] and Spinoza, but not the more substantial figures of Renaissance and Baroque scholarship. In this respect Robertson Smith was far more learned than Wellhausen.

[51] Julius Wellhausen, *Prolegomena to the History of Ancient Israel* (Gloucester, Mass., Peter Smith, 1973) 3–4. [This edition also includes a reprint of Wellhausen's article "Israel," written originally for the *Encyclopaedia Britannica*.]

[52] Ibid., 3.

[53] Ibid., 5.

Encyclopaedia Britannica.[54] Wellhausen argued that Israel the nation began not with the patriarchs of Genesis but with Moses. They managed to conquer some land in Palestine, but initially there was no state as such, but simply local groups that supported each other in times of war. They were not able to extirpate the Canaanite population, but they eventually managed to subdue and absorb them. Under the threat of new invaders, the Philistines,[55] prophets arose as troops of ecstatic enthusiasts who encouraged resistance, but it was by the eventual setting up of a regular kingdom to replace the tribal federation that Israel succeeded in repelling the threat under Saul and David.

What was constitutive of the unity of the Israelites was religion, the worship of Jehovah,[56] in whose name Israel fought its wars in the time of Moses and after. The important part of the religion of Jehovah was that it escaped from barren mythologizings[57] and concentrated on moral tasks, so that Jehovah became the Good of justice and right. The next stage in Israel's development after the founding of the monarchy came with the emergence of a new kind of prophecy—exceptional individuals very different from the prophetic groups from which they came.

Elijah was the forerunner of these true prophets. He objected to the intrusion of foreign cults because Jehovah was quite other than Baal. "To him first was it revealed that we have not in the various departments of nature a variety of forces worthy of our worship, but that there exists over all but one Holy One and one Mighty One, who reveals himself not in nature but in law and righteousness in the world of man." But it was Amos who was the founder and purest type of the new phase of prophecy. He emphasized that simply maintaining the cultus was not enough, for Jehovah was not capable of accepting a bribe; what Jehovah demanded was righteousness and what he hated was injustice. The natural

[54] Reprinted along with his *Prolegomena to the History of Ancient Israel* (see note 51 above).

[55] Philistines were also a non-Canaanite people who invaded the land at much the same time as the Israelites. Ironically, "Palestine," perhaps the name that best describes the area, is derived from the proper name "Philistine."

[56] Wellhausen used the divine name "Jehovah" in his discussion. This was due to the custom of his day; he was perfectly aware of the problematic nature of this pronunciation of the Tetragrammaton. The origins of the impossible name "Jehovah" have been discussed in an earlier chapter (see p. 48).

[57] By the term "mythologizing" Wellhausen meant myth in the sense of a story about goings-on among divine beings. Apart from a few isolated texts such as Psalm 80, the Old Testament is notably free of this sort of myth.

bond between Jehovah and the state was severed and made conditional on Israel's following the path of justice. Wellhausen saw the canonical prophets as the founders of ethical monotheism, but it was not a case of "the self-evolution of dogma,"[58] but an action by the providence of God. Here is the last holdout of the inspiration of the Bible in Wellhausen.

The next stage in the evolution of Israel's religion was the Deuteronomic legislation that was inspired by the prophets, in that it places the social interest above the cultus and that Jehovah requires of man to render to his fellow man his right. However, this change did not reflect prophecy entirely; "the prophetic ideas lost their purity when they became regulations."[59] The interests of the king and the priests, along with the incapacity of the masses, took away the spontaneity of the prophetic message and increased the power of the Jerusalem temple. This limitation of Deuteronomy was recognized by Jeremiah, for Amos and Hosea had hoped that their sense of the moral person based on an inner conviction could be made the basis of a national life. Jeremiah looked forward to a time when the law of God would be written on humanity's heart so that a new covenant could be established.

The final stage in the development of Judaism was the law of Ezra. "That externalisation towards which the prophetical movement, in order to become practical, had already been tending in Deuteronomy finally achieved its acme in the legislation of Ezra; a new artificial Israel was the result: but after all, the old would have pleased an Amos better."[60] At this point the history of Israel's religion and the history of its Scriptures intersect; the emergence of a collection of sacred books marks the triumph of the idea of law, for law leads to codification.

Wellhausen brought his history of Israel up to the medieval period, but it was his interpretation of the New Testament that showed his own position.[61] He considered that the Gospel develops the hidden impulses of the Old Testament. The importance of Jesus, then, was an idea of monotheism that did not consist of the happiness of Israel to be the chosen people of God, but rather of the claims of the Creator on the creature, of the reality of God dominating the whole of life. The Christian church was not the work of Jesus but a Jewish inheritance; like the Jews, the

---

[58] Wellhausen, "Israel," 474.

[59] Ibid., 483.

[60] Ibid., 497.

[61] In his latter years Wellhausen wrote several works on the Gospels, Acts, and Revelation. His works on the Gospels were reprinted as *Evangelien Kommentar*, 1982.

Christians, in reaction to the dominance of a state that was hostile, founded a religious community as their true fatherland.[62] But when the states became Christian, it was possible for Christians to have a natural fatherland in the state. "Now we must acknowledge that the nation is more certainly created by God than the Church and that God works more powerfully in the history of the nations than in Church history."[63]

On the whole, Wellhausen produced a coherently argued explanation for the development of Old Testament history and religion into the Judaism of the New Testament period and beyond. It had the attraction that it could both describe the history in a systematic manner and yet allow for the divine inspiration of God behind all the ups and downs of the development.

Wellhausen's interpretation of ancient Israel was very nineteenth century in some places, for example, his remark above about the centrality of the state. To what extent this may come from Hegel may be debated, but it is interesting to see how Wellhausen defined the state not as an institution that provides for religious conviction but as one that defines it. As a humane and decent man, Wellhausen would have been appalled at what totalitarian states of the twentieth century were to make of this idea. Obviously, Hitler did not derive his notions of the state from reading Wellhausen, but it is disconcerting to see a great scholar in an injudicious moment.

Another example of Wellhausen as a child of his times is the racial perception found in Wellhausen's article "Israel." On the emergence of Median power, he remarked: "The sovereignty of the world was beginning to pass out of the hands of the Semites into those of the Aryans."[64] Later Wellhausen quoted with approval Mommsen's remarks on the subject of the Jews in his *History of Rome:*

> But the Jew who has not, like the Occidental, received the Pandora's gift of political organisation, and stands substantially in a relation of indifference to the state, who, moreover, is as reluctant to give up the

---

[62] Ibid., 512.

[63] Ibid., 513. Here again, while Wellhausen was not a Hegelian in the strict sense of the word, one finds blocks of what appear to be Hegelian ideas cropping up in his work. Here the resemblance to Hegel's notions about the state is unmistakable. For those of us who remember the Nazi regime, this statement is also disquieting. That biblical interpretation is sometimes pressed into the service of eventually disastrous ideas is worth bearing in mind.

[64] Wellhausen, *Prolegomena*, 486.

essence of his national idiosyncrasy as he is ready to clothe it with any nationality at pleasure and to adapt himself up to a certain degree to foreign habits—the Jew was, for this very reason as it were, made for a state which was to be built on the ruins of a hundred living polities, and to be endowed with a somewhat abstract and, from the outset, weakened nationality. In the ancient world also Judaism was an effective leaven of cosmopolitanism and of national decomposition.[65]

In fairness to both Wellhausen and Mommsen, there is no clearly defined theory of race, but generalizations of this sort about nations being described in terms of their race or about the characteristics of Jews as a group induce a great sense of unease among those who have seen the horrors of Nazism.

William Robertson Smith (1846–1894) was a polymath who at one point in his career even applied for a university appointment in mathematics,[66] and whose critical views about the Old Testament got him expelled from his professorial chair by the Free Church of Scotland. He eventually wound up as editor of the ninth edition of the *Encyclopaedia Britannica,* known as "the scholars' edition" because of the number of articles commissioned from first-rate scholars, thanks to Robertson Smith's initiative. He was also university librarian at Cambridge and a fellow of Christ's College.

Robertson Smith's extraordinarily wide interests were to affect his approach to the Old Testament. He was aware of developments in biblical research in Germany, the Netherlands, and France and recognized their importance for understanding the history of the biblical documents. As noted above, his friendship with Wellhausen led him as editor of the *Encyclopaedia Britannica* to invite that *heros eponymous* of Pentateuchal criticism to contribute a long article on Israel.

At the same time, Robertson Smith, as well as being aware of what was happening in university faculties, was an excellent linguist, and he traveled far and often in the Near East, on one occasion with Sir Richard Burton, the translator of the *Arabian Nights.* He was fluent in Arabic; more important, he knew Arab culture firsthand, and most important of all, he liked it. Those who do not like a culture have little hope of understanding it.

---

[65] Ibid., 544.

[66] Another scholar who combined Oriental studies with mathematics was Reimarus.

Wellhausen, in his article "Israel," had mentioned the "individualisation of religion" as a result of the writing prophets. Robertson Smith would have agreed, but what for Wellhausen was only an incidental remark was for Robertson Smith a large part of his life's work. Whereas Wellhausen was working from within the German exegetical tradition with a little help from fragments of Hegelian philosophy, Robertson Smith put religion in the Old Testament into the larger context of ancient Semitic religion in general, investigating the questions of the reciprocal influence of society and the individual on the development of human consciousness. Although he was not the first to take these matters into account, his range of interests and actual knowledge were so great that his work was influential beyond the bounds of Old Testament studies. His pupil Sir James Frazer was the author of *The Golden Bough* and *Folkore of the Old Testament,* and both Emile Durkheim and Sigmund Freud owed a great deal to his work. With Robertson Smith the sociology and anthropology of religion got its start.[67]

Robertson Smith was interested in the religious context out of which the Old Testament grew. His great work on this subject was *Lectures on the Religion of the Semites.* From his work on pre-Islamic Arabs, he argued that ritual was the basic religious practice through which one could understand the stages of a religion's development, for ritual was earlier than and independent of mythology, and its original forms were discernible under the accretion of later explanations. Robertson Smith argued that the basic form of religion in kinship groups was sacrifice, and originally the function of sacrifice was communion with one another and with the group's god. Essentially, this was an act of the whole group; the development of individual consciousness was a later stage in the development of any religion. Should any breach of behavior have broken the unity that was created, sacrifice could also have the effect of atonement between the group and its god. Robertson Smith considered that ritual and the "holiness"[68] of sacred places existed in Israel from the

[67] Both anthropology and sociology are connected with Smith's name. I am not sure of what the difference between these two disciplines might be; it appears to be an item of arcane knowledge, like saw-filing in a lumber mill, whose niceties practitioners are reluctant to explain fully to someone not a member of the guild.

[68] It became apparent in the nineteenth century that holiness in the Old Testament was not necessarily moral in content; it simply described the sacred nature of a sanctuary or its objects. An obvious case is the story in 2 Samuel 6:7, where Uzzah was struck dead by the Lord simply for touching the ark in a misguided attempt to stop it from falling off the animals carrying it. I am not sure who first recognized the starting

very beginning. His view of the development of Israelite religion, then, saw the concern with ritual in the postexilic period as the result of a more general evolution than Wellhausen, who tended to see it in terms of a later development.

It is possible to criticize Robertson Smith for some of his assumptions, in particular that all religions develop along similar pathways and that totemism and mother-right are the earliest stages of all religions.[69] On the other hand, he went beyond the position of writers like Herder, whose awareness sprang from an armchair-based acquaintance with other cultures, in which the extraordinary differentness of other peoples was not fully appreciated.

Robertson Smith's approach to the prophets is a good example of one of the two directions the interpretation of the prophets had taken over the past two hundred years.[70] We have already seen that in the seventeenth century Grotius had argued that most Old Testament prophecies did not apply to times beyond those during which the prophets lived. Coccejus, on the other hand, had found in the prophets accurate predictions of many events over and beyond those in the New Testament. With the revival of a conservative interpretation of the Bible in the nineteenth century, the debate had to take place all over again. For some it was a matter of importance to distinguish between prophecies that had been fulfilled and those that were yet to be seen in events in the future. Indeed, this type of interpretation persists to this day; when the Chernobyl disaster took place, some found it natural to see the event foretold in the book of Revelation, not least of all from the fact that Chernobyl means "wormwood" in Russian, which leads easily to Revelation 8:11: "The name of the star is Wormwood. A third of the waters became wormwood, and many died from the water, because it was made bitter."

That prophets could be seen as other than foretellers of future events was already suggested by George Lorenz Bauer in his *Biblische Moral des Alten Testaments* (1803), which describes the view of the prophets

---

point of holiness, but Robertson Smith was certainly aware of its original nonmoral content.

[69] An excellent treatment of his methods is found in T. O. Beidelman, *W. Robertson Smith and the Sociological Study of Religion* (Chicago: University of Chicago Press, 1975). Beidelman's section on Robertson Smith's Lectures on the Religion of the Semites (28–67) is very helpful.

[70] W. Robertson Smith, *The Prophets of Israel and Their Place in History to the Close of the Eighth Century* B.C. (London: Adam and Charles Black, 1907).

directed not just on the future; rather, their speeches are for the most part concerned with morality and religion. It is true that Bauer still saw the prophets as upholders of the Mosaic legislation, but he recognized them as teachers rather than seers.[71]

Robertson Smith, in his *Prophets of Israel and Their Place in History*, agreed with Wellhausen that the prophets had indeed been a creative force in Israel's history. Smith tried to show how the prophets could be seen as the recipients of revelation, not as visionaries of the future, but as those who knew God and tried to express their awareness of his will in terms of the symbols and concepts of their own day. He tried to play down the ecstatic visions of the prophets and emphasized their shrewd common sense. For Smith, it was a fallacy to suppose that the seers of Israel looked into the future with the same perspicuity that they saw in events of their own day, for the business of the prophets was to signal the principle of divine grace, which rules the future, not to anticipate history. In effect, Smith was coming down hard on the side of Grotius, not Coccejus.

Robertson Smith's view of the prophets has its own nineteenth-century assumptions. His view of prophets publishing their sayings in small collections and then reediting them at a later date appears to have had more in common with contributors to the *Encyclopaedia Britannica* than with the situation in preexilic Israel. Similarly, he had the nineteenth-century worry about the inevitable decadence that follows a less strenuous way of living and for him Eastern history is full of the rapidity with which nations that have grown strong by temperance, discipline, and self-restraint pass from their highest glory into extreme corruption and social disintegration.[72] His praise of the frugal and hardworking free farmers of Israel suggested a hint of the British opinion in the time of the empire, that of all the Wogs that live east of Calais, only the Hill Tribes of India have preserved their dignity and trustworthiness.

In summary, Robertson Smith is an excellent example of how the currents of influence between biblical studies and other disciplines flowed in both directions. If studies of far-off people influenced the interpretation of the Old Testament, Robertson Smith's views on the religion of Israel in turn influenced scholars in the fields of sociology/anthropology, especially Emile Durkheim. One of Smith's pupils was Sir James Frazer,

---

[71] Georg Lorenz Bauer, *Biblische Moral des Alten Testaments* (Leipzig: Weygand, 1803) 42–43.

[72] Robertson Smith, *The Prophets of Israel*, 94.

who dedicated his *Golden Bough* to Robertson Smith and who went on to write a *Folklore of the Old Testament*. Robertson Smith's wider influence can be found even in the writings of Freud. But if Robertson Smith was a social scientist, he was also deeply committed to his religious faith, and often his remarks have as much to do with theology as with sociology. In the dichotomy we saw between Eichhorn and Gabler, Robertson Smith was on the side of Gabler.

11. A detached observation

We stand to learn as much about ourselves as about our subjects in the study of exegesis. For example, whereas Robertson Smith made it quite clear that there was and remains a difference between lower and higher stages in religious and moral development (and he had no doubts about what was higher), we at the present time prefer scare quotes around "higher forms of religion," and any sense of universal standards of morality is treated in much the same way that Victorians were reputed to have treated sex, namely, that in public we can only mention the topic under the disguise of euphemisms.[73]

B. NEW TESTAMENT

1. Work done on the text of the New Testament [74]

There were several hardworking New Testament textual scholars in the nineteenth century who collated manuscripts, refined the rules for judging among the texts, and published new editions of the New Testament. In England, Samuel Tregelles (1813–1875) devoted his life to preparing an edition of the New Testament to replace the *Textus Receptus,* and the team of Westcott and Hort published their edition of the Greek New Testament in 1881. However, no textual scholar was as lucky as the German

---

[73] It is beyond the scope of this work to discuss our current attitudes towards morality. The fact that it is considered reasonable to say "whatever you think is right, is right for you" is a symptom of the confusion in our culture; those who cannot see the ambiguity implicit in this statement are examples of the argument of Allan Bloom's *The Closing of the American Mind,* for however tendentious some of his positions may be, the fact is that the description he gives of some disquieting attitudes to morality among his students is quite accurate.

[74] For details see Bruce Metzger, *The Text of the New Testament,* 3rd ed. (Oxford: Oxford University Press, 1992) 119–46.

Constantine Tischendorf (1815–1874), who at the Monastery of Saint Catherine at Mount Sinai discovered a fourth-century C.E. codex of both Testaments in Greek that was on the point of being fed into a furnace.[75] Tischendorf produced several editions of the Greek New Testament. The 1877 edition I have access to has a format that has become standard, namely, the Greek text with the variants in a separate section below and marginal references to other New Testament passages. The number of variants listed is greater than in some more modern editions.[76]

2. *The problems of the value of the search for the historical Jesus*

In the late eighteenth century, when New Testament scholars had set out on a course of comparing the New Testament documents carefully with each other in the hopes of writing both a definite life of Jesus and a history of the early church, Reimarus and Lessing had each pointed out at least one enduring problem. Reimarus had asked on what grounds do you choose some New Testament reports as history and reject others as later accretions put in by those with a special interest in shifting the focus of the record? For Lessing, the question was how can one base the eternal truths of philosophy on the contingent events of history? David Strauss and Ernest Renan represent two different emphases in how they reconstructed the life of Jesus.[77]

3. *David Friedrich Strauss (1808–1874)*

Strauss was a German scholar whose *Leben Jesu* ("Life of Jesus") was translated into English by George Eliot and had a great influence on intellectual discussion in England. It was a huge work, covering every part of all four Gospels in detail, and was painstaking to the point of

---

[75] In fact, some of the Old Testament parts were lost, but the New Testament was saved entirely and is the only ancient uncial manuscript that is complete. For details of this matter see Metzger, *The Text of the New Testament*, 42–46.

[76] Novum Testamentum graece; ad antiquissimos testes denuo recensuit delectuque critico ac prolegomenis instruxit Constantinus de Tischendorf. Editio critica minor ex VIII. maiore desumpta (Leipzig: J. C. Hinrichs, 1877). I presume that this is a student edition derived from a larger work.

[77] A central work in recording the history of this undertaking is Albert Schweitzer, *Von Reimarus zu Wrede: Geschichte der Leben-Jesu-Forschung* (1906); English translation: *The Quest of the Historical Jesus: A Critical Study of Its Progress from Reimarus to Wrede*, various reprintings and editions.

paingiving. Strauss took eleven years to write the book, and George Eliot four years to translate it.[78]

Strauss made his basic assumptions clear in his discussion about what cannot be accepted as factual history:

> First. When the narration is irreconcilable with the known and universal laws which govern the course of events. Now according to these laws, agreeing with all just philosophical conceptions and all credible experience, the absolute cause never disturbs the chain of secondary causes by single arbitrary acts of interposition, but rather manifests itself in the production of the aggregate of finite causalities, and of their reciprocal action. When therefore we meet with an account of certain phenomena or events of which it is either expressly stated or implied that they were produced immediately by God himself (divine apparitions, voices from heaven and the like), or by human beings possessed of supernatural powers (miracles, prophecies), such an account is in so far to be considered as not historical. . . .[79]
>
> Secondly. An account which shall be regarded as historically valid, must neither be inconsistent with itself, nor in contradiction with other accounts. The most decided case falling under this rule, amounting to a positive contradiction, is when one account affirms what another denies. Thus, one gospel represents the first appearance of Jesus in Galilee as subsequent to the imprisonment of John the Baptist, whilst another Gospel remarks, long after Jesus had preached both in Galilee and in Judea, that "John was not yet cast into prison."[80]

Much of Strauss's discussion of the Gospels turns on the word "myth." Here again one must be on guard about any author's definition of this word. As seen in the previous chapter, "myth" as an early way of describing the world was used by both Eichhorn and Gabler, who got it from Heyne, yet while Gabler saw myth as a support for apologetics, Eichhorn used the term less and was not interested in apologetics. One way of making sense out of the various uses of the word "myth" is to

---

[78] For a more extensive discussion of Strauss, see Roy A. Harrisville and Walter Sundberg, *The Bible in Modern Culture* (Grand Rapids: Wm. B. Eerdmans, 2002) 83–103.

[79] David Friedrich Strauss, *The Life of Jesus Critically Examined*, trans. George Eliot (London: Swan Sonnenschein, 1898) 88.

[80] Ibid.

distinguish between those who see myth as a way of apprehending the world in symbolic terms and those who see myth as nonfactual, false, or even a deliberate falsification.[81] Strauss belonged to this second group.

Strauss began his work with an extended discussion of myth, providing an excellent summary of how the word had been used up to his time. He was aware that some had defined it as an earlier way of thinking about the world, but he was clear that myth is a history of events in which the divine enters, without intermediation, into the human, something that he sees as ipso facto impossible and the source of tensions between older myths[82] and the emerging awareness of the relation between cause and effect in higher civilizations.

The distinctions Strauss discussed among various types of myths are hard to summarize briefly, but the gist of his argument is that mythical elements in the Gospels have to be treated with great suspicion.[83] On this basis Strauss criticized the liberal scholar H.E.G. Paulus, who, although not a believer in miracles or direct divine intervention, nonetheless tried to extract a believable account out of an unbelievable one by explaining a miracle as an embroidered portrayal of a perfectly normal event whose factual basis could be recovered. The best known of these attempts was the explanation of the biblical story of the loaves and fishes in John 6:9-14. The explanation of the miracle was that the example of the boy prepared to share his meager meal so inspired the multitude that everybody brought out what they had hidden in their pockets and all were fed. For Strauss, this sort of attempt to find a historical kernel to a myth was comparable to trying to peel an onion to find its pit.

The effect of classifying many New Testament stories as myths was to eliminate any sense of historical happening of various accounts, thereby separating the Gospel narratives from any contact with actual events. Strauss himself was willing to admit some historical content in the Gospels, but the *reductio ad absurdum* of his method was taken by Bruno

---

[81] Langdon Gilkey, *Religion and the Scientific Future* (London: SCM, 1970), has a good discussion on the meaning of myth.

[82] It is a curiosity of George Eliot's translation that she renders the plural of "myth" as "mythi." It is possible that she was misled by the German "Mythus," interpreting it as a Latin word whose plural would indeed be "mythi," were it not that "Mythus" comes from the Greek word "mythos," which means "story" and whose plural is "mythoi."

[83] Strauss's discussion of the classification of myths is found in section 10 of his "Introduction," *The Life of Jesus*, 59–63.

Bauer,[84] who argued that everything in the New Testament is a myth and that Jesus never existed as a historical person.

Strauss's efforts were aimed at classifying accounts in the Gospels either as historical or mythical. His examination of passages was exhaustive, but in the long run he had two major faults. The first was that he did not pay enough attention to the Gospels as documents in their own right, with their own particular interests and methods. Logically, the determination of the sort of a document comes before the assessment of its historical accuracy. Second, while Strauss was willing to admit that somehow the historical Jesus of Nazareth inspired his followers, it is difficult to derive the reason for this influence from the relatively few dismembered details that Strauss considered historical.

Nonetheless, Strauss illustrated superbly Lessing's point about how contingent the facts of history are; the details of almost any event, and even the event itself, can be questioned. There is also something else worth remarking, namely, that Strauss's presuppositions about what can be true may be more crucial to his results than the actual evidence offered in an account. Essentially, he was working within the framework of the current debate of his day between naturalists and supernaturalists, in which he was siding with naturalists, for whom the test of reality consists in known and universal laws that govern the course of events. In other words, Strauss knew that some events in the New Testament were not historical before he even began to examine them, for he was assuming as a matter of dogma that it is impossible for God to have an immediate effect on the world.

The other point where Strauss's viewpoint is open to further discussion is the question asked by Leonard Hodgson about whether "it is necessary that a man should hold these beliefs about His [Jesus'] conception and resurrection in order to believe that He was God incarnate." To which Hodgson replied:

---

[84] Baur or Bauer is a common German name. In the late eighteenth and early nineteenth centuries, it is necessary to distinguish between Georg Lorenz Bauer (1755–1806), who, in dependence on Gabler, wrote on biblical theology and Hebrew mythology; Ferdinand Christian Baur (1792–1860), the radical church historian and founder of the second Tübingen School, who saw the early church in terms of the synthesis of the Petrine and Pauline traditions; and Bruno Bauer (1808–1882), whose Hegelianism assumed ever more radical proportions and who denied the existence of the historical Jesus and the early church.

The only possible answer to this question is "No." There are men who combine a genuine belief in Jesus Christ as God incarnate in the fullest sense of the words with a disbelief in the traditional account of the peculiar circumstances of His birth and resurrection. When men are actually doing a thing, it is no good saying that it cannot be done.[85]

4. *Ernest Renan (1823–1892)*

Renan was a French scholar who was a younger contemporary of Strauss's. In many ways he was a variant on Strauss, whose work he recommended in his preface to his *Vie de Jesus,* for like Strauss, he had no patience with any supernatural influences or explanations in a work of scientific history. Renan stated his position categorically in his introduction that history is scientific in method and precludes any appeal to miracles, whether in the explanations of incidents or the writings that record them. While Strauss would have accepted this initial position, Renan parted ways with him immediately after. The difference between the approaches of the two men is shown by the fact that while Strauss went on to write a dogmatics, Renan's life of Jesus was part of a five-volume work on the history of early Christianity. Strauss was in many ways more of a philosopher, in fact a Hegelian philosopher, and it is interesting that his account of Jesus' life finishes with a discussion of how a theologian who follows Strauss's conclusions reconciles the critical results with church dogma. Renan declined any relationship with theology as such; history was the antithesis of theology, and he saw himself as a historian.[86]

However, as a historian Renan set himself a formidable task: How did Christianity develop, and why did it inspire so many people? Reimarus's explanation of the post-crucifixion developments was simply that the apostles had gotten used to the good life of a disciple and were unwilling to go back to honest, hard work. Such a Jesus would have been far from an attractive figure for non-Jews, and indeed one gets the impres-

---

[85] Leonard Hodgson, *For Faith and Freedom: The Gifford Lectures 1955–1957* (Oxford: Basil Blackwell, 1956–1957) 2:91. [Hodgson was writing in the days before inclusive language was required.]

[86] Two of the great tribal differences within the humanities are between philosophers, who seek to bring the universe into a coherent whole, even if it means ignoring details, and historians, who so luxuriate in the abundance of details that they often have difficulty in integrating them into the pictures of larger entities.

sion that Reimarus himself found little in the figure of Jesus to add to the sublime religion of nature found in reason. Renan saw that this was simply not an adequate explanation.

Renan set out to re-create the Jesus of history. He was perfectly aware of what he was trying to do. He pointed out that if one confines oneself to what is absolutely certain, there is very little that one can say about Jesus. The indisputable details are that Jesus did exist and came from Nazareth. He preached in an attractive way and left aphorisms indelibly stamped on his disciples' minds. His two principal disciples were Cephas and John the son of Zebedee. He incurred the hatred of the orthodox Jews of his day, who succeeded in getting him put to death by Pontius Pilate, the then procurator of Judea. He was crucified outside the gate of the city; afterward some believed he had risen from the dead. Anything more than this, said Renan—Jesus' relationship to John, his messianic ideas, his belief he was the Messiah—is open to doubt. Renan pointed out that nonetheless the Gospels do contain much more than this summary, and while one cannot be absolutely certain of the details, one can make a conjectural reconstruction of what Jesus must have been like. One has to try to explain what is behind the Gospels without ever being sure of having found it.

Renan criticized liberal theology for its rejection of so many details of the Gospels, to the point where one would have a great deal of difficulty to explain what Jesus was like. He compared the liberals to the heretic Marcion, who on the basis of his Gnostic abhorrence of the physical world, tried to eliminate what he felt were material circumstances in the life of Jesus. In an analogous way, Ferdinand Christian Baur and David Strauss had eliminated material in the Gospels that did not fit in with their perceptions derived from philosophical necessity. They felt that the divine era that had developed within humanity is not to be made dependent on anecdotal incidents or with the particular life of an individual.

Renan, in his historical method, had an advantage over some of his German colleagues in that he had actually spent time in the Near East. He realized that in the Semitic world, people were not German philosophers, and that the surroundings were not the dank and cold world of northern Europe. Behind Renan's reconstructions one can feel the heat, the customs, and the psychological worldview of the East, to the point that one expects sand to fall off the pages of his work as one turns them. It is an easy comment to make that much of Renan's reconstruction was really Renan's imagination at work; however, it has to be admitted that the sort of Jesus Renan described, however inaccurate the picture may have been, nonetheless gave one a sense of why it was that some people loved the historical Jesus and others hated him to the point of wanting him executed. Renan closed his account of the death of Jesus with a passage which was written in prose so purple that it is hard to take it seriously unless written in French or sung, but which showed his own personal admiration for the Jesus he found in the Gospels:

> Rest now in thy glory, noble initiator. Thy work is completed; thy divinity is established. Fear no more to see the edifice of thy efforts crumble through a flaw. Henceforth, beyond the reach of frailty, thou shalt be present, from the height of the divine peace, in the infinite consequences of thy acts. At the price of a few hours of suffering, which have not even touched thy great soul, thou hast purchased the most complete immortality. For thousands of years the world will extol thee. Banner of our contradictions, thou wilt be the sign around which will be fought the fiercest battles. A thousand times more living, a thousand times more loved since thy death than during the days of thy pilgrimage here below, thou wilt become to such a degree the corner-stone of humanity that to tear thy name from this world would be to shake it to its foundations. Between thee and God men will no longer distinguish. Complete conqueror of death, take possession of thy kingdom, whither, by the royal road thou hast traced, ages of adorers will follow thee.[87]

5. *Problems with pure historicism*

By now it should be clear that the interpretation of the Bible is more than simply the examination of the text and grammatical structure of an ancient book. If we are to make sense of a work, we are caught up in both the problem of seeing what the ancient author was trying to say in his own time and what it might have of importance for us today. Now in this quest the historical method is applied to both the history of the text's origin and transmission and the historicity of the text's statements. By the middle of the nineteenth century, it became clear that the historical truth of almost every text in the Bible was open to challenge. The question was, What, then, if anything, can one believe? The answer to this question is found in a yet more difficult question: suppose that absolute certainty about an event could be established, would this either exhaust the mean-

[87] Renan, *Life of Jesus* (London: Watts, n.d.) 120. The translator's name is not given, but it may be Ames.

ing of the text or compel religious belief in the reader? The answer has to be no. This leads into our discussion of three men who pointed ways to possible alternatives to pure historicity: Søren Kierkegaard, Martin Kähler, and Alfred Loisy.

6. Søren Kierkegaard (1813–1855)

Only against the background of the new importance attributed to the historico-critical method of biblical interpretation can one begin to understand the philosophy of Kierkegaard. It is important to remember that in his work *Unscientific Postscript*, the word translated as "science" was the Danish equivalent of the German "Wissenschaft." Now, as discussed above, in English "science" is usually synonymous with "natural science," whereas in German Wissenschaft involves any scientific study, including the scientific investigation of the Bible.[88] Kierkegaard, then, in his *Unscientific Postscript*, was referring to the scholarly study of the Bible, and in it and his preceding work *Philosophical Fragments* he attacked the overreliance on fact as the source of truth, in the larger sense of the term, and at the same time showed the unsatisfactory nature of attempts by the idealist philosophers of his day to answer the questions of theology.

It was on this point of historical investigation that Kierkegaard challenged the philosophical theology of his day. If the aim of the historico-critical method was to get back to seeing Jesus as his contemporaries saw him, what difference would it make if this aim were achieved? Would it be an advantage to have been a contemporary of Jesus?

Kierkegaard based a large part of his argument in the *Philosophical Fragments* on Socrates. The point Socrates made in the *Meno* and elsewhere was that truth does not come from being informed by others; it is a process by which human beings remember the truth they have always had in them and with which they were born, although they had forgotten it. The work of Socrates, then, was to help people remember the truths they know. Strictly speaking, then, the ordinary teacher—or even Socrates—cannot communicate truth to the learner but can only help the learner recognize the truth that is within himself or herself.

But what if the truth within is eclipsed by error? If one is to get beyond the error that the Socratic teacher has shown the learner to be suffering

---

[88] For example, the title of an eminent German periodical is *Zeitschrift für die Alttestamentliche Wissenschaft*.

from, there must be a teacher who can give the learner the requisite condition to learn the truth. Only God can be this sort of teacher, for the learner is bound by error, which cannot be overcome simply by willing to be free from it. What is required is that God as the Teacher must give the learner a new being, so that the learner will owe everything to the Teacher. The thrust of Kierkegaard's argument here was that the Gospels involve not just useful information that can be applied simply by becoming aware of one's needs; rather, the problem is a fundamental flaw in human nature that needs divine intervention to redress it.

> What now shall we call such a Teacher, one who restores the lost condition and gives the learner the Truth? Let us call him *Saviour*, for he saves the learner from his bondage and from himself; let us call him *Redeemer*, for he redeems the learner from the captivity into which he had plunged himself, and no captivity is so terrible and so impossible to break, as that in which the individual keeps himself. And still we have not said all that is necessary; for by his self-imposed bondage the learner has brought upon himself a burden of guilt, and when the Teacher gives him the condition and the Truth he constitutes himself an *Atonement*, taking away the wrath impending upon that of which the learner has made himself guilty.[89]

Kierkegaard is not the easiest philosopher to read, and his interpreters make one think of Byron's quip about Coleridge: "I wish someone would explain his explanation." There is, I suggest, an easy way into Kierkegaard, and that is to think of him as a Lutheran. For Luther, sin was a primary part of the human experience. Sin was not just a mistake that knowledge would rectify, but a feature of humanity where only the grace of God could make a difference. If one accepts one's relationship with God as a free gift through the work of Christ, then one can both recognize the seriousness of the situation and get on with doing something about it.

Kierkegaard's first objection to Lessing, then, was that for Lessing Jesus was a teacher. Kierkegaard disputed the appropriateness of this category, and in order to explain why it did not describe Jesus, he took the example of Socrates, whom he saw as the ideal teacher. Socrates was a good teacher because he brought out what was already within a person. But suppose it is what is in a person, namely sin, that is the real problem? Socrates was of no help here; another sort of teacher was required.

[89] Søren Kierkegaard, *Philosophical Fragments,* trans. David Swenson (Princeton, N.J.: Princeton University Press, rev. edition, 1962) 21.

Another problem was the horrible ditch Lessing saw between the contingent nature of events and the truths of reason. But if reason is not so simple nor so virtuously inclined as Lessing thought, his point fails; the eternal truths of reason are simply not there. Kierkegaard also rejected the attempt to interpret the New Testament in terms of idealist philosophy, for it was an interpretation of the world as a process in which the unexpected, the unique, could not take place. In other words, for Kierkegaard it was the understanding of God that set the stage for the interpretation of Jesus, and for Kierkegaard God was not a cipher for an impersonal nexus of natural powers but the description of what Tillich would call "Being as gracious." Therefore the life of Jesus was much more than yet another exhortation to better behavior.

It goes without saying that the above is not an adequate discussion of Kierkegaard, but the point is that he recognized the basic presuppositions of the radical critics and found them out of keeping with a proper understanding of the Bible. That is why he seized the weakness of attempts to get back to the historical Jesus, making fun of how we will have to wait until Professor So-and-So finishes his latest book on Jesus before we can know how to be Christians. The attempt to get back to knowing as much about Jesus as his contemporaries did is doomed to irrelevance, for the person who lives as a Christian now knows as much about the faith as a Christian in the first century did.

7. *Martin Kähler (1835–1912)*

Although he had studied theology in Germany, Kierkegaard was neither primarily a biblical scholar nor a theologian. One person who was both who contributed to the discussion set off by the historical Jesus quest was Martin Kähler. Kähler wrote a work entitled *Der sogenannte historische Jesus and der geschictliche, biblische Christus*, translated as *The so-called historical Jesus and the historic, Biblical Christ*.[90] The title in German carries a meaning lost in the English translation; in German there are two words for "history"—"Historie" and "Geschichte." On occasion they can be synonyms, but they can also have different overtones. "Historie" can maintain the notion of what actually happened; "Geschichte" can have a wider sense of what is significant in what actually happened. For

---

[90] English translation of the 1896 German edition by Carl E. Bratten (Philadelphia: Fortress, 1966). The allusion to Strauss's work in the title is clear.

example, to say that the first atomic bomb was dropped in August 1945 is "Historie"; to go on to remark that this event marked the beginning of a qualitatively different threat in human relations is "Geschichte." Implied in Kähler's title from the outset, then, is the difference between Jesus as one person among many in first-century Palestine and Jesus as the Christ of Christian devotion.

Kähler opens his work with this summary of his thesis:

> . . . *the historical Jesus of modern authors conceals from us the living Christ.* The Jesus of the "Life-of-Jesus movement" is merely a modern example of human creativity, and not an iota better than the notorious dogmatic Christ of Byzantine Christology. One is as far removed from the real Christ as is the other. In this respect historicism is just as arbitrary, just as humanly arrogant, just as impertinently and "faithlessly Gnostic" as that dogmatic which in its day was also considered modern.[91]

Kähler argued that the New Testament evidence does not really support the weight of any historical constructions of what Jesus was like as a Galilean Jew living in the first century C.E. We are told little or nothing about his youth, his personal development, his appearance, his inner life, or even much about the course of his life. There are various fragments of traditions that can be put into no generalized picture that can be agreed upon by the scholars who attempt such a project.

Kähler pointed out that the motive for trying to write a life of Christ is to find a replacement for traditional Christology; the evidence of the New Testament does not support this effort. In short, we have no sources that measure up to the standards of historical science. We have to be content with a trustworthy picture of the Savior for believers, but this much can be found in the Gospels, for from the series of fragmentary traditions and portrayals colored by the writers' personalities "there gazes upon us a vivid and coherent image of a man, an image we never fail to recognize."

Kähler then went on to discuss the authority of the Bible, admitting the legitimacy of the methods employed in studying the Bible as any other book, but also rejecting the conclusion that it is no more important than any other book. Its authority is found in its testimony, albeit a less than perfect one, to the revelation of God to Israel and in Jesus.

---

[91] Ibid., 43.

8. *Alfred Loisy (1857–1940)*

> When Baron von Hügel
> Came to church with a bügel,
> The Abbé Loisy
> Asked him not to be so *noisy*.[92]

Loisy's *L'Evangile et l'église* ("The Gospel and the Church")[93] was written as a response to Harnack's *Das Wesen des Christentums* ("What Is Christianity?"). Of Harnack it is fair to say that his interpretation of Jesus tended to read liberal German Protestantism back into the first century C.E. What does not necessarily follow is that Harnack's version of the Christian faith was therefore discredited, but from the standpoint of the history of exegesis Loisy's criticism made some telling points against Harnack's method of biblical interpretation.

Loisy's exegetical method took into account the importance of tradition, both in the sense of how material came to be transmitted before it was written down and how it was subsequently interpreted by following generations. But there was also a metaphysical component to this emphasis on tradition. Influenced by Newman's idea of tradition as a legitimate and necessary development of the Christian faith, Loisy argued that the forms of faith were always dependent on tradition, even before the books of the New Testament were written. For Loisy it was as inappropriate to judge contemporary forms of the Christian faith from how it was in New Testament times as it would be to judge the ideal appearance of an adult dog from the shape of a puppy.

Essentially, the historical approach to the history of Christian doctrine had washed away the foundations of both Roman Catholic and Protestant theology. Careful studies had shown that both within the Bible and since its completion within the church, beliefs had changed their forms. Harnack had reconstructed the message of Jesus as a break from Judaism toward a noninstitutional faith in the goodness and love of God as Father. On the basis of this reconstruction, one could decide what was appropriate and what was not in the twentieth century. In some ways

---

[92] E. L. Mascall, *Pi in the High* (London: Faith Press, 1959) 61.
[93] Loisy's work came out in 1902. I am using Christopher Home's 1903 English translation as republished in Alfred Loisy, *The Gospel and the Church* (Philadelphia: Fortress, 1976). Harnack published his work in 1900. I am referring to the third edition of 1900: Adolph Harnack, *Das Wesen des Christentums* (Leipzig: J. C. Heinrichs'sche Buchhandlung, 1900).

it was an attempt to get back to an original deposit of faith by which subsequent beliefs could be judged. Loisy argued as a scholar against Harnack's reconstruction, but then as a theologian he went on to argue the legitimacy of what tradition had changed both in the biblical period and since then. Thus for Loisy it was clear that whereas Jesus and his disciples had expected the coming of the kingdom, what emerged instead was the church. What is interesting is that Harnack might have agreed with the historicity of this judgment at least for the disciples; the difference is that whereas Harnack saw the emergence of the institutional church as a mixed blessing at best, Loisy thought it was part of a legitimate process of development.

Loisy then went on to defend the history and the development of the church that was to excommunicate him a few years later in 1908. It is possible that for once the Vatican agreed with the cynic who prayed, "O Lord, defend me from my friends; I can defend myself from my enemies."[94] Even more ironically, Loisy has turned out to have more influence on current Roman Catholic thought than his pontifical adversaries. Pope Pius X's denunciation of modernism is not a document currently cherished, whereas a conference celebrating Loisy may well be sponsored by a Roman Catholic diocese.[95]

9. A sort of conclusion

The summing up of New Testament studies in the nineteenth century is that the historical approach to the documents worked out in the eighteenth century raised a series of questions.

What do we know for certain about the historical Jesus, the person who lived in Palestine in the first half century of the era that bears his name?[96] Did he see himself in any way as the Christ who figures in Christian theology and liturgy? This involves various questions, such as how are the Gospels connected, who wrote them and when? How does one explain the differences both of tone and of detail among the Gospels? How was the material they contained transmitted—orally or

---

[94] Attributed to Charles d'Hericault. I have not been able to trace this quotation to its source.

[95] This suggests a variation on a New Testament saying: "Your fathers excommunicated the prophets but you organize their conferences."

[96] The dating of the Christian era was done in the late classical period by the monk Dioysius Exiguus in the sixth century C.E. His calculations have not always been accepted and some would argue that in fact Jesus was born a few years B.C.E.

written? If Mark is the first Gospel, was there a document referred to as Q by the scholars?

Generally, there were two sorts of answers then as now. Should one revise one's version of the Christian faith in the light of a reconstruction of the historical Jesus, which you hope will not be disowned next year, or can one assume that while no particular detail of the New Testament is beyond doubt, nonetheless there is sufficient evidence to see what the early church saw in Jesus and to conclude that the faith he inspired meant that his picture was accurately transmitted at least for the demands of faith?

Hidden underneath this investigation are two different ideas of Jesus that one finds within the New Testament itself, namely, Jesus as pattern and Jesus as power. Jesus as pattern is the preaching of a radical love that stands on its own recommendation; Jesus as power is the Savior who makes the faith of sinful humanity possible. On one hand, one has the liberals, who took the view of Jesus as pattern; therefore one needs as much accurate information as possible so one can develop one's own views in a way commensurate with the pattern. This was the way of Strauss, Renan, and Harnack; on the other hand, a disparate group saw Jesus as power; in the case of Kierkegaard, Kähler, and Loisy, it was irrelevant if every detail about Jesus' life is accurately recorded; rather, it is his appeal to faith and to the consequences of this decision that Jesus' importance is found.

Epilogue

One of the readers of a first draft of this work suggested that I should finish with comments about the use/abuse of the Bible and how I would evaluate some of the ideas I have discussed. Speaking one's own opinions is always a temptation of a sort where I tend to give in with little fight.

I think that after five hundred years of work it is no longer possible to see the Bible as God's own words dictated to human scribes, who recorded them in a way that their only personal contribution was the style in which the message was written. I realize that there are those who disagree with me on this point, but while I respect their honesty and in many cases their ability, I can only see them as like those equally sincere and equally mistaken Japanese soldiers who despite all evidence to the contrary held out on remote Pacific islands for thirty years after the end of World War II. What is clear beyond reasonable doubt is that the Bible was written over a period of about a thousand years by people who had all the limitations of their own day and who, if you could gather them together in one room, would have had serious disagreements with each other.

Can one find any value in the Bible today? There are two distinct ways of approaching this question. The first is seeing the Bible as a part of ancient literature; the second is seeing the Bible as the foundation document of at least two and possibly three major religions.

1. *The Bible as ancient literature*

Of all the teachers I had at university, the most scathingly antireligious was a lecturer who was a perfect example of the French anticlerical tradition. It is no wonder, then, that I still remember vividly the day he remarked about his secularist education that his one great regret was that he had not been given any grounding in the Bible, for it was a great work of literature. The importance of literature is that it can provide us the means of interpreting ourselves, our world, and our place in this world. We find meaning for our lives in images even as our perceptions are sharpened by stories. Rollo May, at one time a well-known writer on psychology, once remarked that undergraduates learn more about human beings by reading novels than by taking psychology courses. Agatha Christie's Miss Marple solves crimes by relating the people she meets to types of people she has met before in her little village of St. Mary Meade. Literature or its oral/visual equivalent gives us not only entertainment but the means for measurement. Eventually intelligent people work these matters out for themselves, for from my own observations I find that among people under forty, it is possible to distinguish between those who have had a good liberal education from those who have not; after forty the distinction is blurred.

Unfortunately, the distinction between information and education has been blurred, even, or perhaps especially, in the universities. Information is something that comes from outside us about facts we ought to know: when does the next train leave; what are the effects of chemical waste; how does one build a better mousetrap, and so on. In contrast, education deals with values, and I am on the side of those who say that values cannot be taught in the same way that information can be imparted. The Platonic group of truth, beauty, and goodness can be discussed, debated, illustrated but never taught to those who do not find an inner echo of these matters. Psychopaths, sociopaths, and other dangerous deviants can often acquire information without great difficulty; they find it almost impossible to take morality seriously. Sometimes these people do acquire professional qualifications, but the result is to increase their capacity for doing damage, not their real humanity. Obviously, such abnormal individuals cannot be helped much in the usual educational systems; what is to be regretted is that students who could profit from the various ways in which beauty can be experienced, morality can be explored, and truth can be discussed do not have put before them these means for a richer life.

Great books, however described and listed, are one important means of eliciting from within ourselves the possibilities latent in our human inheritance. The Bible is one of these, even for those whose faith is very different from what is found in the Bible.

The Bible, at least in some of its parts, provides a series of magnificent images and observations, once one manages to put aside the problem of scientific truth. The story of Adam and Eve in the garden of Eden has nothing to do with how human beings descended from ape-like creatures (some further than others, one fears). Why are Adam and Eve tempted by what they do not have when they have everything they reasonably want, or how do they react to detection, where blame is shifted along from Adam to Eve to the snake? What does it mean to aspire to be like God (or gods)? In exploring the possible meanings of this myth, we are brought face-to-face with the recognition that Adam and Eve are not our ancestors but ourselves.

The authors of some of the stories in the Old Testament were very sophisticated observers who told things with a straight face. Does the writer of the story of Absalom's rebellion ever suggest that David has lost control? But can the reader miss the point behind so many of David's decisions and how he is only saved by the wisdom of his advisors? There may even be a certain coarse humor behind some incidents, such as the story about the concern among the administrators in the kingdom of Israel about whether David was getting a bit old for the job. To diagnose his general condition, the best-looking girl in the kingdom is popped into bed with him, and the statesmen, the generals, and the physicians peep from behind the curtains with bated breath. Then when nothing happens, they come to the regretful conclusion that there is no further doubt but that the old boy doesn't have it anymore.

The variety of the books within the Old Testament is very rich. Sometimes works stand in stark contrast to one another. The Song of Songs is a singularly sensual description of erotic love. This book is side by side with the other book in the Bible that requires no elaborate explanation, that is, Ecclesiastes, whose almost modern weary cynicism comes, I think, from both the author's and our culture's inability to love other people.

This rich variety within the Bible has been traditionally covered over by the need to turn everything in it into instant morality. If Samson is a model of virtue in his abstaining from alcohol, one is still left with a few questions about whether the example he set in his private life is one we would recommend, however many imitators he may have today. But once the pious or dogmatic overlay is put aside, the Bible is freed to talk to us on as deep a level as we are likely to find, and even those whose faith is not religious may find in it sources of amusement, enlightenment, and even, in their own way, inspiration.

2. *The Bible as a religious foundational document*

The other approach to the Bible is to find in it the basis of the religion one is trying to practice. Christians should never forget that Jews have at the very least an equal claim to the Hebrew Bible. Moslems see both testaments as books of God, though this perception is seen through the words of the Koran. As a Christian, I do not presume to speak on behalf of either of our cousins, but we should not lose sight of the fact that we have much in common with them and treat them as family.

I am a Christian of the Anglican persuasion, a presbyter, or priest, in good standing in my diocese. For what it may be worth, while I respect the integrity of those who disagree with me, I cannot see the Bible as an infallible book, but I do find in it the basis of my religion. Having said that, I limit the knowledge of God neither to the Bible nor even to one religion of a particular sort nor even to those who would deny the validity of any religion. If a world to come leaves us in any way as our recognizable selves, I would look forward, given the grace of God, to the company of many friends who may find themselves pleasantly surprised to be there, not to mention that of others who might at first be chagrined by my own presence.

I suggest that Jowett was correct in saying that the distinctiveness of the Bible comes not from a special method of interpreting it as a book different from other books, but only after we have applied to it the same criteria of text, translation, and proper grammatical interpretation we use for other books. It is simply nonsense to stick with the *Textus Receptus* of the Greek New Testament or the King James Version in English on the grounds that any subsequent attempts are ipso facto likely to be wrongheaded, if not outright sacrilegious. It is also important to recognize that the Bible is not always consistent within itself. A student once objected in a class I was teaching that Elijah's killing of the four hundred prophets of Baal seemed a little out of keeping with Jesus' injunction that we should love our enemies as ourselves. I pointed out that Elijah, unlike this student, had never heard the Sermon on the Mount. I was sure that had he done so, he would have been interested, but I was not willing to vouch for a positive response on his part.

If one is to use the Bible for guidance on how one should live one's own life, I think it is important that we do not fly in the face of what we know about it and its limitations, still less should we ask others to believe three impossible things before breakfast before they can be Christians. If someone is to reject the Christian faith, it should be on account of what the Bible points to, not the Bible itself. If the Genesis creation story is read for its statement that the world was created in six days (and it is pretty clear that it means six twenty-four-hour periods), being a Christian does not mean believing this in the face of common knowledge that it is incorrect, but rather the point of the second creation story is that the basic weakness of human nature is that we should try to be "like god or gods," that is, we want to act as if our wills and desires should be more important than those of other people. This is a very good explanation of what is meant by "sin"—it is selfishness, which means taking to myself the attributes of God, who alone can make this claim. If people reject Christianity because it means giving up their own wants and desires, resentments and hatreds, and so on, then they at least have the outline of the situation substantially correct.

To interpret the Bible in the context of faith means being honest about the Bible's own history and aware of our own traditions of interpreting it. This means two things:

i. We have to see the Bible as a book with a complex history of possibly a thousand years. It is made of different books, some of which contain different material within themselves. While there is a continuity among these works, we find qualitative leaps forward within the Bible; Jesus' teaching in the Sermon on the Mount is different from and infinitely superior to Elijah's notion that a good Baal prophet was a dead Baal prophet. It is less apparent that these leaps were either evolutionary or cumulative, for though I can sympathize with the anger and resentment exuded by Nahum and Obadiah, I find them less impressive than Isaiah's vision of the moral holiness of God, although Isaiah lived a century or more before Nahum and Obadiah.

Even within the New Testament we find very different interpretations of Jesus. For Matthew, he was a lawgiver, which is why Matthew's Gospel has the permission for divorce under certain circumstances. I suspect that this is an addition to the actual words of Jesus, but the reason is clear: almost any general law will have certain exceptions built into its wording to make it practicable in the messy world in which we live. Mark and Luke preserve the more accurate wording, but in this respect they are more removed from the exigencies of daily life. For Mark, Jesus was the divine interruption into the world who has broken down barriers. For Luke, Jesus was an infinitely kind and loving person who in the very moment of his worst agony could reach out to an absolutely undeserving individual and give him comfort and consolation. For John, Jesus was the incarnation of God's eternal wisdom and as much a fulfiller of Greek notions as Jewish ones. Paul preached God's acceptance of all on an "as is, where is" basis. James pointed out that while faith was fine, it had no importance unless it led to concrete virtuous acts.

ii. In the history of the Christian church's interpretation of the Bible, there is no doubt that the work of criticism and exact study undertaken by the church fathers began a process that made possible the developments of our understanding of the Bible as we have it now. The price that we have to pay is that it is now apparent that there are problems of the history and the interpretation of the Bible that we may never solve. It is also clear that the Bible cannot be seen as the source of simple, black-and-white answers to the questions that vex us, whether of how we define the Christian faith or how we see the Christian's duty in the world as it now exists. The world we live in today is radically different from the world in which the Bible was written both in its technology and its social structure. I see no reason to hold to the forms of first-century C.E. society any more than that we should live by its technology.[1]

There are at least three approaches to this unpleasant state of affairs in the interpretation of the Bible. The first is to deny that these differences exist. I sympathize, but then I also feel called to be as kind as possible to those who believe that the world is flat. The second is to appeal to some infallible authority on earth that interprets what the Bible says, whether it be a church or just the local minister. I find these appeals unconvincing. The third way was best described by a novelist rather than a biblical scholar. In *The Brothers Karamazov*, Dostoevsky created the figure of the Grand Inquisitor, a somewhat fallen cardinal who, faced with a highly unwelcome reappearance of Jesus, criticized him for offering freedom to human beings:

> Instead of taking men's freedom from them, Thou didst make it greater than ever! Didst Thou forget that man prefers peace, and even death, to freedom of choice in the knowledge of good and evil? Nothing is more seductive for man than his freedom of conscience, but nothing is a greater cause of suffering. And behold, instead of giving a firm foundation for setting the conscience of man at rest for

---

[1] The Amish are a religious group that is consistent in insisting that to live by the Bible means to live by its technology, and therefore they do not use cars and similar modern inventions. Those who wish to follow the Bible in everything might reflect on whether the Amish example should be followed.

ever, Thou didst choose all that is exceptional, vague and enigmatic;
Thou didst choose what was utterly beyond the strength of men. . . .
In place of the rigid ancient law, man must hereafter with free heart
decide for himself what is good and what is evil, having only Thy
image before him as his guide.[2]

A final observation

Throughout its history the church has been disfigured by its willingness to be more interested in orthodoxy than in the love of God and
neighbor. At one point orthodoxy was seen in terms of theological definitions; today it is more often ethical questions that cause dissent, especially the matter of homosexuality, though why this in particular I find
hard to understand. Now the dangers of orthodoxy as a sacred quest are
three: it is often a thinly disguised quest for power over others; it may be
a thin veneer over that oldest of temptations, the pride in one's own
righteousness; and it is often a championing of causes later seen to be
irrelevant. For a partial list of matters once considered nonnegotiable,
consider the questions of the lawfulness of interest on loans (usury),
marriage to a deceased wife's sister; and the Christian Lord's Day
(Sunday) interpreted as the Jewish Sabbath (Saturday). For items on a
similar list of matters not forbidden in the Bible but frowned upon since
then, consider slavery and polygamy.

Apart from the actual debate on the rights or wrongs of homosexuality, the real question is to what extent can we live with differences within
the Christian community? I would agree that there must be limits, but
on what grounds do we define them? Is it by appeals to legislation laid
down in the Bible, or is it by asking what are the basic forms of justice
and love? Sweatshops are a betrayal of justice just as adultery is a betrayal of love; one is explicitly mentioned in the Bible, the other is not.
Some forms of homosexuality are destructive and demeaning, but then
so are some expressions of heterosexuality. Is it possible to agree to disagree on whether all homosexuality is destructive or not? I would suggest that the Bible is not a list of established rules but an invitation to
reflection whose force is not necessarily weakened by people arriving at
different conclusions for the right reasons.

---

[2] Fyodor Dostoevsky, *The Brothers Karamazov*, trans. Constance Garnett (London:
Dent, 1927) 1:260–261.

Bibliography

When Dickens set out to write *A Tale of Two Cities*, he asked his friend Carlyle for a few books on the subject, since, after all, Carlyle had written a history of the French Revolution. Carlyle was only too happy to help and sent Dickens three cartloads of books. Some bibliographies can similarly be a bit overdone.

The purpose of this bibliography is not to list every work I have consulted or heard of, still less every work on the subject. For those who have a general interest in the subject and would like to read further, there is a list of general works, most of which have bibliographies that will point the enthusiast further. For specialists, there is a list of books referred to in each chapter to save a chase through the footnotes. Since specialists are by nature hunters of bibliography, I hope that the two sets will provide a sufficient guide to suggest where other quarry may be found.

I. General Reference

Especially recommended: It will be assumed that these works will be consulted as a matter of course, and specific references will not be included in the various chapters:

Baird, William. *History of New Testament Research*. 2 vols. Minneapolis: Fortress, 1992–2003. [Excellent; a third volume is planned.]

Cross, F. L., ed. *The Oxford Dictionary of the Christian Church*. London: Oxford University Press, 1957. [Indispensable for all aspects of theology. There have been two subsequent editions.]

Diestel, Ludwig. *Geschichte des Alten Testaments in der Christlichen Kirche*. 5 vols. Jena: 1869. [A standard reference work for over a hundred years.]

Harrisville, Roy A., and Walter Sundberg. *The Bible in Modern Culture*. 2nd ed. Grand Rapids, Mich.: Wm. B. Eerdmans, 2002. [Recommended. Covers the period from Spinoza; fewer authors treated in more detail than in this work.]

Hahn, Herbert F. *The Old Testament in Modern Research*. 2nd ed. Philadelphia: Fortress, 1966. [An older work but excellent for understanding Old Testament research in the nineteenth and twentieth centuries. As a student I was so absorbed by the first edition that I nearly missed dinner.]

Hayes, John H, ed. *Dictionary of Biblical Interpretation*. 2 vols. Nashville: Abingdon, 1999. [A standard work on the subject.]

McKim, Donald K., ed. *Historical Handbook of Major Biblical Interpreters*. Downers Grove, Ill.: InterVarsity Press, 1998. [Smaller in scope than the *Dictionary of Biblical Interpretation*, but contains some excellent articles.]

Meyer, Gottlob Wilhelm. *Geschichte der Schifterklärung seit der Wiederherstellung der Wissenschaften*. 5 vols. Göttingen: 1802–1809.

Saebø, Magne, ed. *Hebrew Bible/Old Testament*. Göttingen: Vandenhoeck und Ruprecht, 1996–. [Another volume to follow. Designed to be a successor to Ludwig Diestel. Thorough and accurate.]

Other resources often mentioned in the literature:

The Cambridge History of the Bible. 3 vols. Cambridge: Cambridge University Press, 1963–1970. [Sometimes disappointing, especially in the later periods.]

Kraus, H. J. *Die Biblische Theologie: Ihre Geschichte und Problematik*. Neukirchen-Vluyn: Neukirchener Verlag, 1970. [Accuracy has been challenged by some. To be used with caution.]

———. *Geschichte der historisch-kritischen erforschung des Alten Testaments*. 3rd ed. Neukirchen-Vluyn: Neukirchener Verlag, 1981. [Accuracy has been challenged by some.]

II. Microfilm and Microfiche

However well writers of second-source material (such as this book) try, there is nothing more enlightening than to read the original authors for themselves. Often even the shape and the size of the original publication can tell us a great deal about whom it was produced for. If you do not live around the corner from the Bodleian (and even if you do, even the Bodleian does not have everything) microform and microfilm are invaluable. It is true that the readers for these formats are hard on the eyes, but pages can be printed out if you wish to study them in some detail.

In my experience microforms are not always catalogued in detail. For example, a library may show that it has the Janz collection of German baroque literature, but it will not show the works individually. Even collections may not be described clearly. For example, I have known the Janz collection to be confused with the Yale collection of German baroque literature, which can be crucial, for the Yale collection includes the *Acta Eruditorum*, which was an important learned journal of its day.

The secret is to be open to unexpected surprises. For example, the University Microfilms Collection contains contemporary translations of La Peyrère's two most notorious works, as well as the Walton Polyglot and Pearson's *Critici Sacri*.

III. Digital Sources

Electronic resource information has a very short life. I will mention only five:

1. *American Theological Library Association.* The bibliographical resources offered are extraordinary; unfortunately the main database is rather expensive for individuals, but it is also indispensable. Most good libraries have a subscription accessible from within the library itself.

2. *Religious and Theological Abstracts* is a much smaller production available in digital format, but its reviews of items are informative, and sometimes it finds articles not mentioned elsewhere. Its price is low enough for individuals to be able to afford it.

3. *Index Theologicus: Zeitschriften-Inhaltsdienst Theologie.* University of Tübingen Library. Another excellent database, which often contains European articles not listed in the American Theological Library Association sources. Its price is also within the reach of individuals.

4. *www.bautz.de* is a website whose modest ambition is to give information about every important Christian theologian (and some not so important). As a result, this is a necessary first stop for serious scholarship. (This work also exists in a printed version in thirteen volumes.)

5. *Gallica at the Bibliothèque Nationale in Paris.* This website has an extraordinary selection of books in French that are available in their entirety without cost for the trouble of downloading.

Bibliographical references from chapters of this work.

Chapter 1

Reference List

Hill, Christopher. *The English Bible and the Seventeenth-Century Revolution*. London: Allen Lane/Penguin, 1993.

Jeremias, Joachim. *The Eucharistic Words of Jesus*. Trans. Norman Perrin. London: SCM, 1966.

Metzger, Bruce. *The Text of the New Testament: Its Transmission, Corruption, and Restoration*. 3rd ed. New York: Oxford University Press, 1992.

Saenger, Paul. "Silent Reading: Its Impact on Late Medieval Script and Society." *Viator* 13 (1982) 367–414.

Sandys-Wunsch, John. "A Few Kind Words About the Enlightenment." *Theology* (May/June 1998) 196–202.

Shils, Edward. *Tradition*. Chicago: University of Chicago Press, 1981.

Sparks, H.F.D. "Jerome as Biblical Scholar." In *Cambridge History of the Bible*, 1:510–541. Cambridge: Cambridge University Press, 1970.

Thiselton, Anthony C. *The Two Horizons: New Testament Hermeneutics and Philosophical Description*. Grand Rapids, Mich.: Wm. B. Eerdmans, 1980.

Chapter 2

Reference List

Bodensten von Carolstadt, Andres. *De Cononicis Scripturis Libellus*. Wittenberg: Apud Johannem Vkidi Montanum, 1520.

Bouwsma, William J. *Concordia Mundi: The Career and Thought of Guillaume Postel (1510–1581)*. Cambridge, Mass.: New York: Harvard University Press, 1957.

Bruce, F. F. *The Epistle to the Hebrews*. Grand Rapids, Mich.: Wm. B. Eerdmans, 1964.

The Canons and Decrees of the Sacred and Oecumenical Council of Trent. Trans. J. Waterworth. London: Burns and Oates, n.d.

Carpzov, Johann Gottlob. *Introductio in libros canonicos bibliorum Veteris Testamenti*. Leipzig: Lanckii, 1721.

Castellio, Sebastian. Concerning Heretics: *Whether They Are to Be Persecuted and How They Are to Be Treated*. Ed. and trans. Roland H. Bainton. New York: Octagon Books, 1965.

Celenza, Christopher S. "Renaissance Humanism and the New Testament: Lorenzo Valla's Annotations to the Vulgate." *Journal of Medieval and Renaissance Studies* 24 (1994) 33–52.

Combe, Edward. *An Argument for the Authority of Scripture from the Latin of Socinius after the Steinfurt Copy. To Which Is Prefix'd a Short Account of His Life.* London: 1731.

de Jonge, H. J. "Joseph Scaliger's Historical Criticism of the New Testament." *Novum Testamentum* 38 (1996) 176–93.

Diestel, Ludwig. *"Geschichte Des Alten Testaments in der Christlichen Kirche.* 5 vols. Jena: 1869.

Feld, Helmut. "Der Humanisten Streit um Hebräer 2,7 (Psalm 8,6)." *Archiv für Reformrationsgeschichte* 61 (1970) 5–35.

Grafton, Anthony. *Forgers and Critics: Creativity and Duplicity in Western Scholarship.* Princeton: Princeton University Press, 1990.

———. "Joseph Scaliger and Historical Chronology: The Rise and Fall of a Discipline." *History and Theory* 14 (1975) 156–85.

Hamilton, Alistair. "Eastern Churches and Western Scholarship." In *Rome Reborn: The Vatican Library and Western Culture.* Ed. Anthony Grafton. Washington: Library of Congress; New Haven: Yale University Press in association with the Biblioteca Apostolica Vaticana, Vatican City, 1993.

Jardine, Lisa. "Lorenzo Valla: Academic Skepticism and the New Humanist Dialectic." In *The Skeptical Tradition.* Ed. Miles Bunyeat, 253–86. Berkeley: University of California, 1983.

Kelley, Donald R. *Foundations of Modern Historical Scholarship.* New York: Columbia University Press, 1970.

Meyer, Gottlob Wilhelm. *Geschichte Der Schrifterklärung* (1802). Göttingen: Rouers, 1802.

More, Henry. *Conjectura Cabbalistica or, A Conjectural Essay of Interpreting the Mind of Moses, in the Three First Chapters of Genesis, According to a Threefold Cabbala.* London: William Morden, 1662.

Pearson, John, et al., eds. *Critici Sacri sive Doctissimorum Virorum in Ss. Biblia Annonationes & Tractus.* 9 vols. London: Jacob Flesher, 1660.

Peden, Allison. "The Medieval Antipodes." *History Today* (1995) 27–33.

Pererius, Benedictus Valentinus. *Commentariorum et Disputationem in Genesim* (1594). Lyon: ex officina Iuntarum, 1594.

Pintus, Hector. *In Esaiam Prophetam Commentaria.* Louvain: Paanum, 1567.

Reland, (H)Adrian. *Decas Exercitationum Philologicarum de Vera Prounanciatione Nominis JEHOVAH.* Utrecht: 1709.

Rummel, Erika. *The Humanist-Scholastic Debate in the Reformation.* Cambridge, Mass.: Harvard University Press, 1995.

Saenger, Paul. "Silent Reading: Its Impact on Late Medieval Script and Society." *Viator* 13 (1982) 367–414.

Sandius, Christophorus. *Nucleus Historiae Ecclesiasticae Exhibitus in Historia Arianorum . . . Quibus Praefixus Est Tractatus de Veteribus Scriptoribus Ecclesiasticis.* 2nd rev. ed. Cologne: Apud Johannem Nicolai, 1676.

Semler, Johann Salomo, ed. *De Forma Orationis Scriptorum Evangelicorum, Et Aliis Quibusdam Consideratione Non Indignis.* Halle: 1776.

Simon, Richard. *Histoire critique des principaux commentateurs du Nouveau Testament depuis le commencement du Christianisme jusques à nôtre temps.* Rotterdam: 1693.

Sparks, H.F.D. "Jerome as Biblical Scholar." In *Cambridge History of the Bible,* 1:510–541. Cambridge: Cambridge University Press, 1970.

Williams, Arnold. *The Common Expositor: An Account of the Commentaries on Genesis 1527–1633.* Chapel Hill: University of North Carolina Press, 1948.

Chapter 3

Reference List

Belaval, Yvon, and Dominique Bourel. *Le Siècle des Lumières et la Bible.* Paris: Beauchesne, 1986.

Bentley, Jerry H. *Humanists and Holy Writ: New Testament Scholarship in the Renaissance.* Princeton: Princeton University Press, 1983.

Bertramus, Bonaventura Cornelius. *De Republica Ebraeorum.* In Constantine l'Empereur, *Critici Sacri,* VI (1695).

Blackwell, Richard J. *Galileo, Bellarmine, and the Bible.* Notre Dame: University of Notre Dame, 1991.

Bochart, Samuel. *Geographia Sacra seu Phaleg e Canaan.* Ed. Petrus de Villemandy. 4th ed. Louvain: Cornelium Boutestyn et Jordanum Luchtmans, 1707.

Bots, Hans. "Hugo Grotius et André Rivet: Deux Lumières Opposées, Deux Vocations Contradictoires." In *Hugo Grotius Theologian: Essays in Honour of G.H.M. Posthumus Meyjes.* Ed. Henk J. M. Nellen and Edwin Rabbie. Leiden: E. J. Brill, 1994.

Buddeus, Johannes Franciscus. *Isagoge Historico-Theologica ad Theologiam Universam Singulasque Ejus Partes, Novis Supplementis Auctorior.* Leipzig: Fritsche, 1729.

Burnett, Stephen G. *From Christian Hebraism to Jewish Studies Johannes Buxtorf (1564–1629) and Hebrew Learning in the Seventeenth Century.* Leiden: E. J. Brill, 1996.

Butlin, Robin A. "A Sacred and Contested Place: English and French Representations of Palestine in the Seventeenth Century." In *Place, Culture and Identity: Essays in Historical Geography in Honour of Alan R. H. Baker*. Ed. Robin A. Butlin and Iain S. Black, 91–131. Quebec: Les Presses de l'Université Laval, 2001.

Buxtorf, Johannis Fil. *Anticritica seu Vindiciae Veritatis Hebraicae Adversus Ludovici Cappelli Criticam Vocat Sacram, Ejusque Defensionem*. Basel: Sumptibus Haeredum Ludovici Regis, 1653.

Calov, Abraham. *Commentarius in Genesin*. Wittemberg: Michaelis Meyeri, 1671.

Castellion, Sébastien. *De L'art de Douter et de croire, d'ignorer et de savoir*. Geneva: Jeheber, 1953.

Combe, Edward. *An Argument for the Authority of Scripture, from the Latin of Socinius After the Steinfurt Copy. To Which Is Prefix'd a Short Account of His Life*. London, 1731.

de Jonge, H. J. "Grotius' View of the Gospels and the Evangelists." In *Hugo Grotius Theologian: Essays in Honour of G.H.M. Posthumus Meyjes*. Ed. Henk J. M. Nellen and Edwin Rabbie, 65–74. Leiden: E. J. Brill, 1994.

———. "The Study of the New Testament in the Dutch Universities 1575–1700." *History of Universities* 1 (1981) 113–29.

Derham, William. *Astro-Theology: or, A Demonstration of the Being and Attributes of God, From a Survey of the Heavens*. London: 1715.

———. *Physico-Theology* (1714). London: W. Innys, 1714.

Dibon, Paul. *Regards sur la Hollande du siècle d'or*. Naples: Vivarium, 1990.

Diestel, Ludwig. "*Geschichte des Alten Testaments in der Christlichen Kirche*. 5 vols. Jena: 1869.

du Bois, Jacobus. *Dialogus Theologico-Astronomicus . . . Ex Sacris Litereis Terrae Quietem, Soli Vero Motum Competere Probatur; Adjuncta Refutatione Argumentorum Astronomicorum, Quae in Contrarium Proferri Solent*. Leiden: Petrus Leffen, 1653.

Estius, Guilielmus, *Annotationes in Praecipua ac Difficiliora Sacrae Scripturae Loca* (1629). Douai: Patté, 1629.

Fantoli, Annibale *Galileo: For Copernicanism and for the Church*. Trans. George V. Coyne, S.J. 2nd ed. Rome: Vatican Observatory Publications, 1996.

Grafton, Anthony. "Isaac La Peyrère and the Old Testament." 204–13. Cambridge, Mass.: Harvard University Press, 1991.

———. "Joseph Scaliger and Historical Chronology: The Rise and Fall of a Discipline." *History and Theory* (1975) 14:156–185.

Hill, Christopher. *The English Bible and the Seventeenth-Century Revolution*. London: Allen Lane/Penguin, 1993.

————. "Till the Conversion of the Jews." In R. H. Popkin, ed. *Millenarianism and Messianism in English literature and Thought 1650–1800*, 12–36. Leiden: E. J. Brill, 1988.

Israel, Jonathan. *Radical Enlightenment: Philosophy and the Making of Modernity 1650–1750*. Oxford: Oxford University Press, 2001.

Kraus, H. J. *Die Biblische Theologie: Ihre Geschichte und Problematik*. Neukirchen/Vluyn: Neukirchener, 1970.

Laplanche, François. *L'Ecriture, le Sacré et l'Histoire*. Amsterdam and Maarssen: APA–Holland University Press, 1986.

Lindberg, David C., and Ronald L. Numbers., eds. *God and Nature: Historical Essays on the Encounter Between Christianity and Science*. Berkeley: University of California Press, 1986.

Morin, Jean. *Exercitationes Biblicae de Hebraei Graecique Textus Sinceritate de Germana LXX Interpretum Translatione Dignoscenda, Illiusque cum Vulgata Conciliatione*. Paris: A. Vitray, 1633.

Nicolson, Adam. *God's Secretaries: The Making of the King James Bible*. New York: HarperCollins, 2003.

Pettegree, Andrew. "The Politics of Toleration in the Free Netherlands, 1572–1620." In *Tolerance and Intolerance in the European Reformation*. Ed. Ole Peter Grell and Bob Scribner, 182–98. Cambridge: Cambridge University Press, 1996.

Pintard, René. *Le Libertinage érudit dans la première moitié du XVIIᵉ siècle*. Geneva: Slatkine, 1983.

Popkin, Richard H. *Isaac La Peyrère (1596–1676): His Life, Work and Influence* (1986). Leiden: E. J. Brill, 1986.

————. *The Third Force in Seventeenth Century Thought*. Leiden: E. J. Brill, 1992.

———— and Charles B. Schmitt. *Scepticism from the Renaissance to the Enlightenment*. Wiesbaden: Otto Harassowitz, 1987.

———— and Arjo Vanderjagt. *Scepticism and Irreligion in the Seventeenth and Eighteenth Centuries*. Leiden: E. J. Brill, 1993.

Reimmann, Jacob Friedrich. *Historia Universalis Atheismi et Atheorum*. Hildesheim: Ludwig Schroeder, 1725.

Reventlow, Henning Graf. "L'Exegèse Humaniste de Hugo Grotius." In *Le Grand Siècle et la Bible*. Ed. Jean-Robert Armogathe. Paris: Beauchesne, 1989.

Robertson, James. *Clavis Pentateuchi*. Edinburgh: Fleming and Neill, 1770.

Rosse, Alexander. *The New Planet No Planet or, The Earth Non Wandring Star Except in the Wandring Heads of Galileans*. London: T. Young, 1646.

Sandys, George. *Sandys Travailes: Containing a History of the Original and Present State of the Turkish Empire*. London: Richard Cotes/John Sweeting, 1652.

Sandys-Wunsch, John. "The Influence of Jewish Mysticism on Renaissance Biblical Interpretation." In *Mysticism: Select Essays: Essays in Honour of John Sahadat*. Ed. Melchior Mbonipa, Guy Bonneau, and Kenneth-Roy Bonin, 47–69. Sudbury, Ontario: Editions Glopro, 2002.

——. "Spinoza the First Biblical Theologian," *Zeitschrift für alttestamentliche Wissenschaft* 93 (1981) 327–42.

Schoeps, Hans Joachim. *Philosemitismus im Barock*, 2:135–139. Tübingen: J.C.B. Mohr, 1952.

Scholder, Klaus. *Ursprünge und Probleme der Bibelkritik im 17. Jahrhundert*. Munich: Chr. Kaiser, 1966.

Simon, Richard. *Histoire critique des principaux commentateurs du Nouveau Testament depuis le commencement du Christianisme jusques à nôtre temps*. Rotterdam: 1693.

à Lapide, Cornelius. *Commentaria in Scripturam Sacram*. Vol. 1: *In Pentateuchum Moisis*. Paris: Vives, 1859.

Chapter 4

Reference List

Allen, Don Cameron. "The Renaissance Looks at Comets." (Racine, Wis.: Johnson Foundation, 1966).

Bochart, Samuel. *Geographia. Sacra seu Phaleg e Canaan*. Ed. Petrus de Villemandy. 4th ed. Louvain: Cornelium Boutestyn and Jordanum Luchtmans, 1707.

Burnet, Thomas. *Archaeologiae Philosophicae*. London: Walter Kettilby, 1692.

——. *Doctrina Antiqua de Rerum Originibus: or, an Inquiry into the Doctrine of the Philosophers of All Nations, Concerning the Original of the World*. London: E. Curll, 1736. [English translation of *Archaeologiae Philosophicae*].

——. *The Theory of the Earth* (1684). London: Walter Kettilby, 1684.

Comes, Natalis [Conti, Natale]. *Mythologiae sive Explicationis Fabularum*. Geneva: Samuel Crispinus, 1620.

Doederlein, Johann Christoph. *Christliche Religionsunterricht nach den Burdürfnissen Unserer Zeit*. Nuremberg: Nowrath, 1787.

Edelmann, Johann Christian. *Moses mit Aufgedeckten Angesichte*. N.p.: 1740.

Fischer, G. N. "Was Ist Aufklärung?" *Berlinisches Journal für Aufklärung* 1 (1788) 12–46.

Fisher, Samuel. *Rusticus ad Academicos*. London: Robert Wilson, 1660.

Gould, Stephen J. "The Reverend Thomas' Dirty Little Planet" In *Ever Since Darwin*, 141–46. New York: W. W. Norton, 1977.

Grafton, Anthony. "Joseph Scaliger and Historical Chronology: The Rise and Fall of a Discipline." *History and Theory* 14 (1975) 156–85.

Grotius, Hugo. *Traité du Pouvoir du Magistrat Politique sur les Choses Sacrées*. London: 1751.

Hill, Christopher. *The English Bible and the Seventeenth-Century Revolution*. London: Allen Lane/Penguin, 1993.

De Iside et Osiri de Plutarch. Trans. J. Gwyn Griffiths. Cambridge: University of Wales Press, 1970.

Israel, Jonathan. *Radical Enlightenment: Philosophy and the Making of Modernity 1650–1750*. Oxford: Oxford University Press, 2001.

Kirchner, Joachim. *Das Deutsche Zeitschriftenwesen: Sein Geschichte und Seine Probleme*. 2nd ed. 2 vols. Wiesbaden: Otto Harassowitz, 1958–1962.

———. *Die Grundlagen des Deutschen Zeitschriftenwesens*. Leipzig: Karl W. Hiersmann, 1928.

Klauber, Martin I. "The Formula Consensus Helvetica." *Trinity Journal* 11 (1990) 103–23.

L. P. *Two Essays Sent in a Letter from Oxford, to a Nobleman in London*. London: n.p., 1695.

Le Clerc, Jean. *Concerning the Inspiration of the Holy Sciptures: Translated out of French*. London: 1690.

———. *Ars Critica* (1698). London: Apud Rob. Clavel, 1698.

———. *Bibliotheque Universelle et Historique* (1686–1694).

———. *De L'Incredulité*. Paris: Migne, 1865.

———. *Supplement to Dr. Hammond's Paraphrase and Annotations on the New Testament* (1699). London: Sam. Buckley, 1699.

———. *Twelve Dissertations Out of Monsieur Le Clerk's Genesis*. London: R. Baldwin, 1696.

——— (anon). *Sentimens de Quelques Theologiens de Hollande sur l'histoire Critique du Vieux Testament* (1685). Amsterdam: 1685.

Mau, Rudolf. "Programme und Praxis der Theologiestudiums im 17. und 18. Jahrhundert." *Theologische Versuche* 11 (1979) 71–91.

Meyer, Ludwig. *La Philosophie interprète de l'Écriture Sainte* (1988). Paris: Intertextes éditeur, 1988.

———. *Philosophia Scripturae Interpres: Exercitatio Paradoxa*. Halle: Jo. Christ. Hendel, 1776.

Nicholson, Marjorie Hope. *Mountain Gloom and Mountain Glory: The Development of the Aesthetics of the Infinite.* Ithaca: Cornell University Press, 1959.

The Oxford Companion to Classical Literature. Ed. Sir Paul Harvey. Oxford: Clarendon Press, 1937.

Pearson, John, and others, eds. *Critici Sacri sive Doctissimorum Virorum in Ss. Biblia Annonationes & Tractus.* 9 vols. London: Jacob Flesher, 1660.

Pitassi, Maria Cristina. *De L'Orthodoxie aux lumières: Genève 1670–1737.* Geneva: Labor et Fides, 1992.

———. *Entre Croire et Savoir: Le problème de la méthode critique chez Jean Le Clerc.* Leiden: E. J. Brill, 1987.

Poole, Matthew. *Annotations upon the Holy Bible.* London: Thomas Parkhurst et al., 1683.

———. *Synopsis Criticorum Aliorumque S. Scripturae Interpretum.* London: Cornelius Bee, 1669.

Popkin, Richard H. "Some New Light on the Roots of Spinoza's Science of Bible Study." In *Spinoza and the Sciences.* Ed. Marjorie Grene and Debra Nails, 171–88. Dordrecht: D. Reidel, 1986.

———. "Spinoza and Biblical Scholarship." In *The Books of Nature and Scripture: Recent Essays on Natural Philosophy, Theology and Biblical Criticism in the Netherlands of Spinoza's Time.* Ed. James E. Force and Richard H. Popkin, 1–20. Dordrecht: Kluwer, 1994.

———. "Spinoza and Samuel Fisher." *Philosophia* 15, no. 3 (1985) 219–36.

Preus, J. Samuel. "The Bible and Religion in the Century of Genius." *Religion* 28 (1998) 3–14.

———. "A Hidden Opponent in Spinoza's Tractatus." *Harvard Theological Review* 88 (1995) 361–88.

Ranson, Patric. *Richard Simon: Ou du caractère illegitime de l'Augustinisme en théologie.* Lausanne: L'Âge d'Homme, 1990.

Rappaport, Rhoda. *When Geologists Were Historians, 1650–1750.* Ithaca: Cornell University Press, 1997.

Reventlow, Henning Graf. *The Authority of the Bible and the Rise of the Modern World.* Trans. John Bowden. Philadelphia: Fortress Press, 1985.

Rée, Jonathan. "The Brothers Koerbagh." *London Review of Books* 24, no. 2 (2002) 21–24.

Selden, John. *De Diis Syris.* Leiden: Elzevir, 1629.

[Simon, Richard]. *Apologie pour l'Auteur de l'Histoire Critique du Vieux Testament.* Rotterdam: Reinier Leers, 1689.

Simon, Richard. *Critical History of the Old Testament.* London: Walter Davies, 1682.

———. *Histoire critique des principaux commentateurs du Nouveau Testament depuis le commencement du Christianisme jusques à nôtre temps.* Rotterdam: 1693.

———. *Histoire critique du Vieux Testament.* Rotterdam: Reinier Leers, 1685.

———. *Lettres choisies de M. Simon.* 2nd ed. Rotterdam: 1702. [Rprt. Frankfort-am-Main, 1967.]

———. *Critical Enquiries into the Various Editions of the Bible . . . Together with Animadversions upon a Small Treatise of Dr. Isaac Vossius Concerning the Oracles of the Sibylls and an Answer to the Objections of the Late Critica Sacra.* London: Tho. Braddyll, 1684.

Spencer, John. *De Legibus Hebraeorum Ritualium et Earum Rationibus.* Cambridge: John Hayes, 1685.

———. *Dissertatio de Urim et Thummim.* London: Timothy Garthwait, 1669.

———. *A Dissertation Concerning Prodigies, To Which Is Added a Short Treatise Concerning Vulgar Prophecies.* London: 1665.

Sprat, Thomas. *The History of the Royal-Society for the Improving of Natural Knowledge.* London: J. Martyn, 1667.

Stanley, Thomas. *The History of Philosophy.* London: Humphrey Moseley and Thomas Dring, 1656.

Stillingfleet, Edward. *Origines Sacrae, or a Rational Account of the Grounds of Christian Faith as to the Truth and Divine Authority of the Scriptures.* London: Henry Mortlock, 1675.

Stölle, Gottlieb. *Anleitung zur Historie der Gelahrtheit.* 4th ed. Jena: Johann Meyers sel. Erben, 1736.

———. *Anleitung zur Historie der theologischen Gelahrheit.* Jena: Johann Meyers sel. Erben, 1739.

van Dale, Antonius. *De Oraculis Ethnicorum Dissertationes Duae.* Amsterdam: Boom, 1683.

[Ward, Seth]. *Vindiciae Academiarum.* Oxford: Thomas Robinson, 1654.

Webster, Jo. *Academiarum Examen, or the Examination of Academies.* London: Giles Culvert, 1654.

Wilson, John. *The Scriptures Genuine Interpretation Asserted or, a Discourse Concerning the Right Interpretation of Scripture Wherein a Late Excertation, Intitled, Philosophia S. Scripturae Interpres, is Examin'd, and the Protestant Doctrine in that Point vindicated.* London: Boulter, 1678.

Chapter 5

Reference List

Aland, Kurt. "Bibel und Bibeltext bei August Hermann Francke und Johann Albrecht Bengel." In *Pietismus und Bibel.* Ed. K. Aland, 89–147. Witten: Luther Verlag, 1970.

———. "The Text of the Church." *Trinity Journal,* n.s. 8 (1987) 131–44.

Bengel, Johann Albrecht. *Hē Kaivē Diēthēkē, Novum Testamentum Graecum, Ita Adornatum ut Textus Probatarum Editionum Medullam Margo Variantium Lectionum. . . . Apparatu Subiunctvs Criseos Sacrae Millianae Praesertim Compendium, Limam, Supplementum ac Fructum Exhibeat.* Tübingen: J. G. Cotta, 1734.

Bentham, Edward. *Reflexions upon the Study of Divinity.* Oxford: Clarendon, 1771.

Biblia Hebraica/Cum Notis Hebraicis et Lemmatibus Latinis. Ed. Danielis Ernesti Jablonski. Berlin: Knebel, 1699.

Buddeus, Johannes Franciscus. *Isagoge Historico-Theologica ad Theologiam Universam Singulasque ejus Partes, Novis Supplementis Auctorior.* Leipzig: Fritsche, 1729.

Burke, Peter. *Vico.* Oxford: Oxford University Press, 1985.

Chladenius, Johann Martin. *Einleitung zur Richtigen Auslegung Vernünftige Reden und Schriften.* Düsseldorf: Stern Verlag Janssen & Co., 1969. [Rprt. of original 1742 edition.]

Collins, Anthony. *A Discourse of Free-Thinking.* London: n.p., 1713.

Cotoni, Marie-Helene. *L'Exégèse du Nouveau Testament dans la Philosophie Française du dix-huitième siècle.* Oxford: The Voltaire Foundation, 1984.

de Malesherbes, Lamoignon. *Mémoires sur la librairie et sur la liberté de la presse.* Paris: Slatkine, 1969. [Rprt. of 1809 edition.]

Edelmann, Johann Christian. *Selbstbiographie: Geschrieben 1752.* Berlin: Wiegand, 1849.

Force, James E. *William Whiston: Honest Newtonian.* Cambridge: Cambridge University Press, 1985.

Francke, August Hermann. *A Guide to the Reading and the Study of Holy Scripture.* Trans. William Jacques. London: 1815.

Franz, Gunther. "Bücherzensur und Irenik." In *Theologie und Theologen an der Universität Tübingen.* Ed. M. Brecht. Tübingen: Mohr, 1977.

Grafton, Anthony. *Forgers and Critics: Creativity and Duplicity in Western Scholarship.* Princeton: Princeton University Press, 1990.

Grossmann, Walter. *Johann Christian Edelmann: From Orthodoxy to Enlightenment.* The Hague: Mouton, 1976.

Hirsch, Emanuel. *Geschichte der Neuern Evangelischen Theologie.* 5 vols. 3rd ed. Gütersloh: C. Bertelsmann, 1964.

Kierkegaard, Søren. *Concluding Unscientific Postscript.* Trans. David Swenson and Walter Lowrie. Princeton: Princeton University Press, 1968.

Krentz, Edgar M. *Essays on Theological Librarianship.* Philadelphia: American Theological Library Association, 1980.

Lods, Adolphe. "Un Précurseur Allemand de Jean Astruc: Henning Bernard Witter." *Zeitschrift fur alttestamentliche Wissenschaft* 43 (1925) 134–35.

Loescher, Valentin Ernst. *Breviarium Theologicae Exegeticae, Regulas de Legitima Scripturae Sacrae Interpretatione.* Frankfort: Gaarmann, 1715.

Marsauche, Patrick. "Présentation de Dom Augustin Calmet (1672–1757)." In *Le Grand Siècle et la Bible.* Ed. Jean-Robert Armogathe, 233–53. Paris: Beauchesne, 1989.

Mau, Rudolf. "Programme und Praxis der Theologiestudiums im 17. und 18. Jahrhundert." *Theologische Versuche* 11 (1979) 71–91.

Michaelis, Johann David. *Lebensbeschreibung von ihm Selbst Abgefasst.* Rinteln and Leipzig: 1793.

The Moral Philosopher: In a Dialogue Between Philalethes a Christian Deist, and Theophanes a Christian Jew . . ., Thomas Morgan. London: n.p., 1737.

Noesselt, Johann August. *Anweisungen zur Kenntnis der Besten Allgemeinern Bücher in Aller Theilen der Theologie.* 1st ed. Leipzig: Weygand, 1779.

Paulsen, Friedrich. *Geschichte des Gelehrten Unterrichts auf den Schulen und Universitäten.* addt. R. Lehmann. Berlin: de Gruyter, 1965.

Rambach, Johann Jakob. "Hessiches Heb-Opfer Theolgischer und Philologischer Anmerkungen." Giessen: Johann Philip Krieger, 1735.

Randolph, John. *Enchiridion Theologicum or a Manual for the Use of Students in Divinity.* Oxford: J. Fletcher, 1792.

Reventlow, Henning Graf. *The Authority of the Bible and the Rise of the Modern World.* Trans. John Bowden. Philadelphia: Fortress Press, 1985.

Schloemann, Martin. *Siegmund Jacob Baumgarten.* Göttingen: Vandenhoeck und Ruprecht.

[Schmidt, Johann Lorenz]. *Die Göttliche Schriften von der Zeiten des Messie Jesus der erste Theil . . . Nach einer Freyen Übersetzung welche durch und durch mit Anmerkungen Erläutert und Bestätigt Wird.* Wertheim: Nehr, 1735.

Schwarzbach, Bertram Eugen. "Dom Augustin Calmet: Homme des Lumières Malgré Lui." *Dix-Huitième Siècle* 34 (2002) 451–63.

Semler, Johann Salomo. *Lebensbeschreibung von ihm selbst Abgefasst.* Halle: 1782.

Sinnhold, Johann Nicolaus, ed. *Ausführliche Historie der Verruffenene Sogennanten Wertheimischen Bibel*. Erfuhrt: Johann Heinrich Nonne, 1739.

Spencer, John. *De Legibus Hebraeorum Ritualium et Earum Rationibus*. Cambridge: John Hayes, 1685.

Sprat, Thomas. *History of the Royal-Society of London*. London: J. Martin, 1667.

Stolzenburg, Arnold F. *Die Theologie des Jo. Franc. Buddeus und des Chr. Matt. Pfaff*. Berlin: Towitzsche und Sohn, 1926.

Tindal, Matthew. *Christianity as Old as the Creation: or, the Gospel, a Republication of the Religion of Nature*. London: 1730.

Toland, John. *Christianity not Mysterious: or a Treatise Shewing that there is Nothing in the Gospel Contrary Reason, nor above It . . .* London: Sam. Buckley, 1696.

van den Berg, J. "The Leiden Professors of the Schultens Family and their Contacts with British Scholars." *Durham University Journal* 75 (1982) 1–14.

Vitringa, Campegius. *Commentarius in Librum Prophetiarum Jesaiae*. Herborn: Johann Nicolai Andreae, 1722.

Novum Testamentum Graecum, Opera et Studio Joannis Jacobi Wetsetenii. Amsterdam: Officina Dommeriana, 1751–1752.

White, Samuel. *A Commentary on the Prophet Isaiah wherein the Literal Sense of His Prophecy's [sic] is briefly Explained*. London: Arthur Collins, 1709.

Witter, Henning Bernhard. *Iura Israelitarum in Palaestinam Terram Channanaeam Commentatione in Genesin Perpetua Sic Demonstrata*. Hildesheim: Schröder, [1711].

Wolff, Christian. *Anmerckungen über Die Vernünftige Gedanken* (1736) 612–23. 1736.

———. "Von dem Gebrauche der Demonstrativischen Lehrart in Erklärung der Heiligen Schrift." *Kleine Schriften*, 234–61. Halle: Renger, 1755.

Chapter 6

Reference List

Achtemeier, Paul. *The Inspiration of Scripture: Problems and Proposal*. Philadelphia: Westminster, 1980.

Aner, Karl. *Die Theologie der Lessingzeit*. Halle/Salle: Max Niemeyer, 1929.

Bahrt, C(K)arl Friedrich. *Versuch Eines Biblischen Systems Der Dogmatik*. 2 vols. Gotha and Leipzig, n.p., 1769.

Ball, Bryan W. *A Great Expectation: Eschatological Thought in English Protestantism to 1660*. Leiden: E. J. Brill, 1975.

Basedow, Johann Bernhard. *Versuch Einer Freymuthigen Dogmatik*. Berlin: 1766.

Bengel, Johann Albrecht. *Bengelius's Introduction to His Exposition of the Apocalypse with His Preface to the Work and the Greatest Part of the Conclusion of It*. Trans. John Robertson. London: 1747.

———. *Erklärte Offenbarung Johannis und Vielmehr Jesu Christi aus dem Revidirten Grund-Text Übersetzte*. Frankfort and Leipzig: Erhardt, 1740.

———. *Gnomon Novi Testamenti*. Tubingen: Schramm, 1742.

———. *Ordo Temporum*. Stuttgart: Erhard, 1741.

Bossuet, Jacques-Benigne. *L'Apocalypse avec une Explication*. Paris: 1856.

Brecht, Martin. "Philipp Matthäus Hahn." In *Leben in Gang Halten, Pietismus und Kirche in Württemberg*. Ed. Theo Sorg, 89–104. Metzingen: Franz, 1980.

Buddeus, Johannes Franciscus. *Institutiones Theologiae Dogmaticae*. Leipzig: Fritsch, 1724.

Burdon, Christopher. *The Apocalypse in England: Revelation Unravelling, 1700–1834*. New York: St. Martin's Press, 1997.

Büsching, Anton Friedrich. *Epitome Theologiae e Solis Sacris Litteris Concinnatae*. Göttingen: Eilias Luzac, 1756.

Comes, Natalis [Conti, Natale]. *Mytshologiae sive Explicationis Fabularum*. Geneva: Samuel Crispinus, 1620.

Eichhorn, Johann Gottfried. Einleitung ins Alte Testament. 2nd ed. Leipzig: Weidmans, 1787.

———. *Urgeschichte*. Ed. J. P. Gabler. Altdorf and Nürnberg: Monat und Kussler, 1790.

Ernesti, Johann August. "De Vanitate Philosophantium in Interpretatione Librorum Sacrorum." *Opuscula Philologica et Critica*, 233–51. Leiden: Luchtmans, 1764.

Flygt, Sten Gunnar. *The Notorious Dr. Bahrdt*. Nashville: Vanderbilt, 1963.

Formey, Johann Heinrich. *Abhandlung über dem Ursprung der Gesellschaft und der Sprache*. Berlin: Joachim Pauli, 1763.

Heinrich, Christian Gottfried. *Versuch einer Geschichte der verschiedener Lehrarten der Christlichen Galubenswahrheiten*. Leipzig: Weidmann, 1790.

Herder, Johann Gottfried. *Johannes Offenbarung. Ein Heiliges Gesicht. ohn' Einzelne Zeitendeutung Verständlich*. Ed. Bernhard Suphan, 1–100. *Sämtliche Werke*, vol. 9. Hildesheim, 1967.

Heussi, Karl. *Kompendium der Kirchengeschichte*. Tübingen: Mohr, 1960.

Hirsch, Emanuel. *Geschichte der Neuern Evangelischen Theologie.* Gütersloh: C. Bertelsmann, 1949.

Hofmann, Johannes George. *Oratio de Theologliae Biblicae Praestantia.* Altdorf: Johannis Paulus Meyer, 1770.

Hornig, Gottfried. *Die Anfänge der Historische-Kritischen Theologie: Johann Salomo Semlers Schriftverständnis und seine Stellung zu Luther.* Göttingen: Vandenhoeck und Ruprecht, 1961.

Jockenack, Johannes Thomas Andreas. *Dissertatio Theologica de Praestantia Theologicae Acroamaticae prae sic dicta Biblica.* Halle: 1757.

Le Clerc, Jean. *Harmonia Evangelia.* Amsterdam: Sumptibus Huguetanorum, 1699.

Lessing, Gotthold Ephraim. *Lessing's Theological Writings* (1956). London: Adam & Charles Black, 1956.

Lowth, Robert. *Lectures on the Sacred Poetry of the Hebrews; Translated from the Latin of the Right Rev. Robert Lowth.* Trans. G. Gregory. London: J. Johnson, 1787.

Lowth, William. *A Vindication of the Divine Authority and Inspiration of the Writings of the Old and New Testament.* Oxford: 1692.

Maier, Gerhard. *Die Johannesoffenbarung und die Kirche.* Tübingen: Mohr, 1981.

Mede, Joseph. *The Key of the Revelation Searched and Demonstrated out of the Naturall and Proper Charecters (sic) of the Visions with a Comment Therepon, According to the Rule of the Same Key.* Trans. Richard More. London: 1643.

Michaelis, Johann David. *Einleitung in die Göttlichen Schriften des Neuen Bundes.* Göttingen: 1777.

―――. *Fragen an Eine Gesellschaft Gelehrter Männer, die auf Befehl des Königes von Dänemark nach Arabien reisen.* Frankfurt am Main, 1762.

―――. *Introduction to the New Testament.* Trans. Herbert Marsh. Cambridge: Archdacon, 1793.

―――. *Mosaisches Recht.* 2nd ed. Frankfurt am Main: Johann Gottlied Garbe, 1775.

Murrin, Michael. "Revelation and Two Seventeenth Century Commentators. In C. A. Patrides and Joseph Wittreich, eds. *The Apocalypse in English Renaissance Thought and Literature.* Manchester: University of Manchester Press, 1984.

Noesselt, Johann August. *Anweisung zur Kenntnis der Besten Allgemeinern Bücher in Aller Theilen der Theologie.* 4th ed. Leipzig: Weygand, 1800.

Petersen, Johanna Eleonora. *Einige Sendschrebien Betreffende die Nothwendigkeit Verschiedener Bissher von den Meisten Gelehrten in Verdacht Gezogener Lehren, Sonderlich in Diesen Letzten Zeiten . . .* n.p.: n.p., 1714.

Reimarus, Herbert Samuel. *The Goal of Jesus and His Disciples.* Trans. George Wesley Buchanan. Leiden: E. J. Brill, 1970.

————. *Apologie oder Schutzschrift für die Vernünftigen Verehrer Gottes.* Ed. Gerhard Alexander. [Frankfurt am Main]: Insel Verlag, [1972].

————. *Die Vornehmste Wahrheiten der Natürlichen Religion.* Göttingen: Vandenhoeck und Ruprecht, 1985.

Sandius, Christophorus. *Nucleus Historiae Ecclesiasticae Exhibitus in Historia Arianorum . . . Quibus Praefixus Est Tractatus de Veteribus Scriptoribus Ecclesiasticis,* 2nd rev. ed. Cologne: Apud Johannem Nicolai, 1676.

Sandys-Wunsch, John. "J. P. Gabler and the Distinction Between Biblical and Dogmatic Theology." *The Scottish Journal of Theology* 33:133–158.

Scholder, Klaus. "Herder und die Anfänge der Historischen Theologie." *Evangelische Theologie* 22 (1962) 425–40.

Schweitzer, Albert. *The Quest of the Historical Jesus (Von Reimarus zu Wrede).* Trans. W. Montgomery, 1906. [Frequently reprinted.]

Scott, Geoffrey. "'The Times Are Fast Approaching': Bishop Charles Walmesley O.S.B. (1722–1797) as Prophet." *Journal of Ecclesiastical History* 36 (1985) 590–604.

Semler, Johann Salomo. *Abhandlung von Freier Untersuchung des Canon: Nebst Antwort auf die Tübingische Vertheidigung des Apocalypsis.* Halle: Hemmerde, 1776.

————. *Antwort auf das Bahrdische Glaubensbekenntnis.* Halle: 1779.

————. *Apparatus ad liberalem Veteris Testament interpretationem.* Halle: Hemmerde, 1773.

————. *Christliche freye Untersuchung über die so genannte Offenbarung Johannis, aus der nachgelassenen Handschrift eines fränkischen Gelehrten herausgegeben. Mit einigen Anmerkungen von D. Joh. Salomo Semler.* Halle: 1769.

————. *Historische und kritische Sammlung über die so genannten Beweisstellen in der Dogmatik.* Halle und Helmstedt: Hemmerde, 1764.

————. *Versuch einer freiern theologischen Lehrart zur Bestätigung und Erläuterung seines Lateinischen Buchs.* Halle: Hemmerde, 1777.

————. *Versuch einer nähern Anleitung zu nützlichem Fleisse in der ganzen Gottesgelersamkeit für angehende Studiosus Theologiae.* Halle: Justinus Gebauer, 1757.

————. *Vorbereitung zur theologischen Hermaneutik.* 2 vols. Halle: Carl Hermann Hemmerde, 1760.

Smend, Rudolph. "Johann Philipp Gablers Begründung der biblischen Theologie." *Evangelische Theologie* 22 (1962) 345–57.

————. "Johann David Michaelis und Johann Gottfried Eichhorn—Zwei Orientalisten am Rande der Theologie." In *Theologie in Göttingen: Eine Vorlesungsreihe.* Ed. Rudolph Smend, 58–81. Göttingen: Vandenhoeck und Ruprecht, 1987.

Stäudlein, Carl Friedrich. *Geschichte der Theologischen Wissenschaften.* Göttingen: 1810–1811.

Swedenborg, Emanuel. *The Apocalypse Explained.* New York: Swedenborg Foundation, 1956–1961.

————. *The Apocalypse Revealed.* Trans. John Whitehead. New York: Swedenborg Foundation, 1954.

Töllner, Johann Gottlieb. *Die Göttliche Eingebung der Heiligen Schrift.* Metau and Leipzig: Hinz, 1772.

von Goethe, Johann Wolfgang. *The Autobiography (Dichtung und Wahrheit).* Trans. John Oxenford. New York: Horizon, 1969.

Whitla, Sir William. *Sir Isaac Newton's Daniel and the Apocalypse; With an Introductory Study of the Nature and the Cause of Unbelief, of Miracles and Prophecy.* London: J. Murray, 1922.

Witter, Henning Bernhard. *Iura Israelitarum in Palaestinam Terram Channanaeam Commentatione in Genesin Perpetua Sic Demonstrata.* Hildesheim: Schröder, [1711].

Chapter 7

Reference List

Bauer, Georg Lorenz. *Biblische Moral des Alten Testaments.* Leipzig: Weygand, 1803.

Beidelman, Thomas O. *W. Robertson Smith and the Sociological Study of Religion.* Chicago: University of Chicago Press, 1975.

Bölsche, Wilhelm. *Haeckel: His Life and Work.* Trans. Joseph McCabe. London: T. Fisher Unwin, 1906.

Burrow, John Wyon. *The Crisis of Reason: European Thought, 1848–1914.* New Haven: Yale University Press, 2000.

Chadwick, Owen. *The Secularization of the European Mind in the Nineteenth Century.* Cambridge: Cambridge University Press, 1975.

Colenso, John William. *The Pentateuch and Book of Joshua Critically Examined.* London: Longman, Green, Longman, Roberts, & Green, 1862. [Other volumes followed.]

Delitsch, Friedrich. *Babel and Bible.* Trans. C.H.W. Johns. London: Williams and Norgate, 1903.

de Serres, Marcel. *De la Cosmologie de Moïse comparée aus faits géologiques.* Paris: Lagny Frères, 1841.

de Soyres, John. *Christianity and Biblical Criticism.* Saint John, N. B.: J & A McMillan, 1890.

du Bois, Jacobus. *Dialogus Theologico-Astronomicuus. . . . Et Ex Sacris Litereis Terrae Quietem, Soli Vero Motum Competere Probatur; Adjuncta Refutatione Argujmentorum Astronomicorum, Quae in Contrarium Proferri Solent.* Leiden: Petrus Leffen, 1653.

du Clot, Joseph-François. *La Sainte Bible vengée des attaques de l'incrédulité.* Paris: Gauthier Frères, 1834.

Essays and Reviews. London: John W. Parker and Son, 1860.

Garbett, Edward. *The Bible and Its Critics: An Enquiry into the Objective Reality of Revealed Truths.* Boyle Lectures for 1861. London: Seeley and Griffiths, 1861.

Gay, Peter. *Schnitzler's Century: The Making of Middle-Class Culture 1815–1914.* New York: W. W. Norton, 2002.

Gilkey, Langdon. *Religion and the Scientific Future.* London: SCM, 1970.

Göttingen and the Development of the Natural Sciences. Ed. Nicholas Rupke. Forthcoming from Wallstein Verlag.

Handover, P. M. "British Book Typography." In *Book Typography 1815–1965.* Ed. Kenneth Davis, 139–54. London: Ernest Benn, 1966.

Harrisville, Roy A., and Walter Sundberg. *The Bible in Modern Culture.* 2nd ed. Grand Rapids: Mich.: Wm. B. Eerdmans, 2002.

Hodgson, Leonard. *For Faith and Freedom: The Gifford Lectures 1955–1957.* Oxford: Basil Blackwell, 1956–1957.

Kahle, Paul. *The Cairo Geniza.* Oxford: Blackwell, 1959.

Kierkegaard, Søren. *Concluding Unscientific Postscript.* Trans. David Swenson and Walter Lowrie. 2nd ed. Princeton: Princeton University Press, 1968.

———. *Philosophical Fragments.* Trans. David Swenson. Rev. ed. Princeton: Princeton University Press, 1962.

Kähler, Martin. *The So-Called Historical Jesus and the Historic Biblical Christ.* Trans. Carl E. Bratten. Philadelphia: Fortress Press, n.d.

Loisy, Alfred. *The Gospel and the Church,* Trans. Christopher Home (1903). Philadelphia: Fortress Press, 1976.

Mascall, Eric Lionel. *Pi in the High.* London: Faith Press, 1959.

Meiners, Christoph. *Grundriss der Geschichte aller Religionen.* Lemgo: Meyer, 1785.

Müller, Max. *The Sacred Books of the East.* Oxford: 1879–1910 [A series of 50 volumes.]

Perlitt, Lothar. *Vatke und Wellhausen: Geschichtsphilosophische Voraussetzungen und historiographische Motive für die Darstellung der Religion und Geschichte Israels durch Wilhelm Vatke und Julius Wellhausen.* Berlin: Topelmann, 1965.

Powell, Baden. *The Advance of Knowledge in the Present Times, Considered Especially in Regard to Religion: A Sermon. . . .* London: C. and J. Rivington, 1826.

———. *Christianity Without Judaism: Two Sermons.* London: Spottiswoode & Co., 1856.

Pusey, Edward Bouverie. *Un-Science, Not Science, Adverse to Faith: A Sermon Preached Before the University of Oxford on the Twentieth Sunday After Trinity, 1878.* London: J. H. Parker & Co., 1878.

Renan, Ernest. *Vie de Jésus.* Paris: Michel Lévy Frères, 1863.

Rogerson, John William. *The Bible and Criticism in Victorian Britain: Profiles of F. D. Maurice and William Robertson Smith.* Journal for the Study of the Old Testament Supplement 201. Sheffield: Sheffield Academic Press, 1995.

———. *W.M.L. De Wette, Founder of Modern Biblical Criticism: An Intellectual Biography.* Journal for the Study of the Old Testament. Sheffield: 1992.

Sandys-Wunsch, John. "A Few Kind Words About the Enlightenment." *Theology* (May/June 1998) 196–202.

———. "P. C. Kaiser, La Théologie biblique et l'histoire des religions." *Revue d'Histoire et de Philosophie Religieuse.* Festschrift for E. Jacob (1979) 391–96.

Sayce, Archibald Henry. *Early Israel and the Surrounding Nations.* London: Service & Paton, 1899.

Smith, W. Robertson. *The Prophets of Israel and Their Place in History to the Close of the Eighth Century B.C.* London: Adam and Charles Black, 1907.

Strauss, David Friedrich. *The Life of Jesus Critically Examined,* Trans. George Eliot: London: Swan, Sonnenschein, 1898.

Tholuck, Friedrich A. G. *Abriss einer Geschichte der Umwälzung welche seit 1750 auf dem Gebiete der Theologie in Deutschland statt gefunden.* Hamburg: Perthes.

———. *Geschichte des Rationalismus.* Berlin: Wigandt und Grieben, 1865.

Tischendorf, Constantin von. *Testamentum Graece / Ad Antiquissimos Testes Denuo Recensuit Delectuque Critico an Prolegomnis Instruxit Constantinus de Tischendorf, Editio Critica Minor Ex VIII. Maiore Desumpta.* Leipzig: J. C. Hinrichs, 1877.

Truman, Charles. *The Sèvres Egyptian Service 1810–1812.* London: Victoria and Albert Museum, 1982.

Vatke, Johann Karl Wilhelm. *Die Religion des Alten Testamentes nach den Kanonischen Büchern Entwickelt.* Th.1. Berlin, 1835.

von Harnack, Adolph. *Das Wesen des Christentums.* 3rd ed. Leipzig: J. C. Heinrichs'sche Buchhandlung, 1900.

Wellhausen, Julius. *Prolegomena to the History of Ancient Israel and Israel.* Gloucester, Mass.: Peter Smith, 1973.

Index of Subjects

Index of Names—before 1900

Index of Names—after 1900

Index of Scriptural References

John 1:1	10–11	Rom 5:12-14	52
John 2:13	65	Rom 9	62
John 5:11	65		
John 6:4	65	1 Cor 11:5	252
John 6:9-14	320	1 Cor 11:10	16
John 7:53–8:11	3, 63-64		
John 11:55	65	Heb 2:6	67
John 12:45	59	Heb 8:1-7	69
John 19:14	65		
		1 John 5:7	53, 68
Acts 15:20	138	Rev 8:11	315